Access Your Free Subscription to *N.C. Crimes Online*

The purchase of this supplement includes FREE access to the ⟨ ⟩ugh **May 1, 2021**. The online version offers the following features:

- Updated content through December 2019
- Keyword searching
- Linking to cross-references
- Printable pages
- Accessibility anywhere your electronic device can connect to the Internet
- Collapsible and expandable statutes

First-Time Registrants

Follow the instructions below to begin using the online version of *N.C. Crimes:*

- Visit **bit.ly/nccrimesonline2020**
- Use the registration code **nccrimesonline2020-h18129**
- Enter your information to complete your account profile
- You will receive a confirmation email ensuring your access has been properly authenticated

Returning Users*

Follow the instructions below to update and renew your access to the online version:

- Log into your *N.C. Crimes Online* account
- Go to the "Account Updates" box on the right-hand side of the page
- Click the link at "Start Here" to update your information
- Click "Edit" **above** your profile information
- Replace your current registration code with **nccrimesonline2020-h18129**
- Click "Save" at the bottom of the page

* Users who have not created or renewed an account after March 2018 may need to follow the "First-Time Registrants" steps.

For questions about your online subscription,
contact **sales@sog.unc.edu** or call **919.962.2761**.

For information about other publications and resources
from the School of Government, visit **sog.unc.edu**.

2019 Cumulative Supplement to NORTH CAROLINA

CRIMES

A Guidebook on the Elements of Crime

Seventh Edition

Jessica Smith
James M. Markham

The School of Government at the University of North Carolina at Chapel Hill works to improve the lives of North Carolinians by engaging in practical scholarship that helps public officials and citizens understand and improve state and local government. Established in 1931 as the Institute of Government, the School provides educational, advisory, and research services for state and local governments. The School of Government is also home to a nationally ranked Master of Public Administration program, the North Carolina Judicial College, and specialized centers focused on community and economic development, information technology, and environmental finance.

As the largest university-based local government training, advisory, and research organization in the United States, the School of Government offers up to 200 courses, webinars, and specialized conferences for more than 12,000 public officials each year. In addition, faculty members annually publish approximately 50 books, manuals, reports, articles, bulletins, and other print and online content related to state and local government. The School also produces the *Daily Bulletin Online* each day the General Assembly is in session, reporting on activities for members of the legislature and others who need to follow the course of legislation.

Operating support for the School of Government's programs and activities comes from many sources, including state appropriations, local government membership dues, private contributions, publication sales, course fees, and service contracts.

Visit sog.unc.edu or call 919.966.5381 for more information on the School's courses, publications, programs, and services.

Michael R. Smith, DEAN
Thomas H. Thornburg, SENIOR ASSOCIATE DEAN
Jen Willis, ASSOCIATE DEAN FOR DEVELOPMENT
Michael Vollmer, ASSOCIATE DEAN FOR ADMINISTRATION

FACULTY

Whitney Afonso
Trey Allen
Gregory S. Allison
Lydian Altman
David N. Ammons
Ann M. Anderson
Maureen Berner
Frayda S. Bluestein
Kirk Boone
Mark F. Botts
Anita R. Brown-Graham
Peg Carlson
Connor Crews
Leisha DeHart-Davis
Shea Riggsbee Denning
Sara DePasquale
Jacquelyn Greene
Margaret F. Henderson
Norma Houston
Cheryl Daniels Howell
Willow S. Jacobson
Robert P. Joyce
Diane M. Juffras

Dona G. Lewandowski
Adam Lovelady
James M. Markham
Christopher B. McLaughlin
Kara A. Millonzi
Jill D. Moore
Jonathan Q. Morgan
Ricardo S. Morse
C. Tyler Mulligan
Kimberly L. Nelson
David W. Owens
William C. Rivenbark
Dale J. Roenigk
John Rubin
Jessica Smith
Meredith Smith
Carl W. Stenberg III
John B. Stephens
Charles Szypszak
Shannon H. Tufts
Aimee N. Wall
Jeffrey B. Welty (on leave)
Richard B. Whisnant

Printed in the United States of America

24 23 22 21   2 3 4 5

ISBN 978-1-56011-977-7

Contents

8
Threats, Harassment, Stalking, and Violation of Domestic Protective Orders   55

11

Crime against Nature, Incest, Indecent Exposure, and Related Offenses   103

12

Kidnapping and Related Offenses   107

13

Larceny, Possession of Stolen Goods, Embezzlement, and Related Offenses   115

14

Robbery, Extortion, and Blackmail   133

15

Burglary, Breaking or Entering, and Related Offenses   137

16

Fraud, Forgery, False Pretenses, and Related Offenses   143

17

Arson and Burning Offenses   155

18

Trespass, Property Damage, and Littering   159

19

Disorderly Conduct, Riot, and Gang Offenses   165

28

Motor Vehicle Offenses   257

Introduction

This book supplements NORTH CAROLINA CRIMES: A GUIDEBOOK ON THE ELEMENTS OF CRIME (UNC School of Government, 7th ed. 2012). It includes cases decided and legislation enacted through December 31, 2019. Chapter and page numbers used throughout this supplement refer to chapters and pages in the main edition.

Due to the very large body of case law regarding charging language that threatened to overwhelm the book, all notes on that topic have been deleted from this supplement. Please consult the following resources for more information. For a detailed paper on point, see, Jessica Smith *The Criminal Indictment: Fatal Defect, Fatal Variance, and Amendment,* ADMINISTRATION OF JUSTICE BULLETIN No. 2008/03, www.sog.unc.edu/publications/ bulletins/criminal-indictment-fatal-defect-fatal-variance-and-amendment. For all relevant cases decided since 2008, see JESSICA SMITH, SMITH'S CRIMINAL CASE COMPENDIUM (under heading "Criminal Procedure," subheading "Indictment & Pleading Issues").

1
States of Mind

General Intent and Specific Intent (page 4)

Delete the second sentence of the first paragraph of this section and replace it with the following:

Examples of general intent crimes include assault on a law enforcement officer in violation of G.S. 14-33(c)(4), State v. Mylett, 253 N.C. App. 198, 209 (2017); assault with a firearm on a law enforcement officer, State v. Childers, 154 N.C. App. 375, 382 (2002); and shooting into occupied property, State v. Byrd, 132 N.C. App. 220, 222 (1999); State v. Maldonado, 241 N.C. App. 370, 374 (2015); State v. Bryant, 244 N.C. App. 102, 109 (2015).

Add the following at the end of the third paragraph:

; *Maldonado*, 241 N.C. App. at 373–74 (same; shooting into occupied property).

Wantonly (page 7)

For another case supporting the statement in this section that this mental state is essentially the same as willfully, see *State v. Hunt*, 250 N.C. App. 238, 243 (2016).

Criminal Negligence (page 7)

Add the following at the end of this section:

In assault cases, the State is required to allege a theory of criminal negligence. State v. Stevens, 228 N.C. App. 352, 357 (2013) (error in an assault on a child under 12 case where criminal negligence was not alleged in the indictment).

Strict Liability (page 9)

As a result of 2015 legislation, S.L. 2015-181, the first three bullets in this section should read as follows:

- G.S. 14-27.24 (first-degree statutory rape). State v. Anthony, 351 N.C. 611, 616 (2000) (noting that first-degree statutory rape is a strict liability crime); State v. Rose, 312 N.C. 441, 445 (1984) (noting that for first-degree statutory rape, mistake regarding the victim's age is no defense); State v. Ainsworth, 109 N.C. App. 136, 145 (1993) ("Criminal mens rea is not an element of statutory rape.").
- G.S. 14-27.29 (first-degree statutory sexual offense). *Anthony*, 351 N.C. at 616–18 (construing former G.S. 14-27.4 and noting that consent is not a defense to statutory sexual offense).
- G.S. 14-27.25, -27.30 (respectively, statutory rape and sexual offense of a person 15 years old or younger). *Anthony*, 351 N.C. at 616–18 (construing former G.S. 14-27.7A (statutory rape or sexual offense of a person who is 13, 14, or 15 years old) and holding that consent is not a defense under that statute); State v. Browning, 177 N.C. App. 487, 491 (2006) ("Statutory rape under [former G.S.] 14-27.7A is a strict liability crime."); State v. Sines, 158 N.C. App. 79, 84 (2003) ("Statutory sexual offense and statutory rape are categorized as strict liability crimes.").

Delete the fourth bullet in this section.

Add the following paragraph to the bulleted list in this section:

- G.S. 90-95(d1)(1)c. (possession of pseudoephedrine after methamphetamine conviction). State v. Miller, 246 N.C. App. 330, 335 (2016), *rev'd on other grounds*, 369 N.C. 658 (2017).

In the sixth paragraph of this section, delete the citation to *State v. Haskins*.

2
Bars and Defenses

Bars to Prosecution (page 13)

Double Jeopardy (page 13)

The sixth paragraph of this section states that even when offenses are not the same, legislative intent controls whether multiple punishments may be imposed at the same trial. It goes on to indicate that some decisions analyze this issue as one of double jeopardy. For another such case, see *State v. Baldwin*, 240 N.C. App. 413, 425 (2015) (because the assault inflicting serious bodily injury statute begins with the language "[u]nless the conduct is covered under some other provision of law providing greater punishment," the trial court erred by sentencing the defendant to this Class F felony when it also sentenced the defendant for assault with a deadly weapon with intent to kill inflicting serious injury, a Class C felony).

Add the following to this section:

> For a case where the trial court's erroneous entry of judgment of not guilty by reason of insanity did not create a jeopardy bar to further proceedings, see *State v. Payne*, 256 N.C. App. 572, 589–90 (2017) (the trial court's order dismissing the charges with leave did not constitute an acquittal to which jeopardy attached; the order was more akin to a procedural dismissal than a substantive ruling).
>
> For additional support for the statement in this section that double jeopardy does not prevent a retrial when the first trial ended in a hung jury, see *State v. Allbrooks*, 256 N.C. App. 505, 510 (2017). Jeopardy continues after a hung-jury mistrial such that a voluntary dismissal entered after the mistrial terminates jeopardy in the defendant's favor, and thus bars retrial. State v. Courtney, 372 N.C. 458 (2019).

Delete the last paragraph of this section and replace it with the following:

> For a more detailed discussion of double jeopardy, see Robert Farb, *Double Jeopardy and Related Issues, in* NORTH CAROLINA SUPERIOR COURT JUDGES' BENCHBOOK (Oct. 2013), http://benchbook.sog.unc.edu/criminal/double-jeopardy.

Lack of Jurisdiction (page 16)

As a result of 2014 legislation, S.L. 2014-100, sec. 34.30.(b), add the following to the list of statutes in this section:

> **§ 14-7.45. Crimes committed by use of unmanned aircraft systems.**
> All crimes committed by use of an unmanned aircraft system, as defined in G.S. 15A-300.1, while in flight over this State shall be governed by the laws of this State, and the question of whether the conduct by an unmanned aircraft system while in flight over this State constitutes a crime by the owner of the unmanned aircraft system shall be determined by the laws of this State.

Expiration of Statute of Limitations (page 17)

The text discusses G.S. 15-1, which contains the two-year statute of limitations for misdemeanors. Effective for offenses committed on or after December 1, 2017, S.L. 2017-212, sec. 5.3 amends G.S. 15-1 to provide that all misdemeanors except malicious misdemeanors must be charged within two years after commission. The statute had provided that the misdemeanor had to "be presented or found by the grand jury" within two years. The amended statute also provides that if any pleading is defective (it had been limited to indictments), another prosecution may be instituted for the same offense within one year after the State abandoned the first prosecution. This legislation was in response to *State v. Turner*, 250 N.C. App. 776 (2016), which held that the statute of limitations barred prosecution in that case, but which later was reversed per curiam by the North Carolina Supreme Court. State v. Turner, 371 N.C. 427 (2018) (reversing for the reasons stated in State v. Curtis, 371 N.C. 355 (2018)). The statute of limitations remains tolled by the filing of a citation, magistrate's order, or misdemeanor statement of charges in district court when a defendant is subsequently charged in superior court by presentment and indictment. State v. Stevens, ___ N.C. App. ___, 831 S.E.2d 364, *temp. stay allowed*, ___ N.C. ___, 829 S.E.2d 907 (2019) (mem.).

2019 legislation, S.L. 2019-245, effective for offenses committed on or after December 1, 2019, lengthens the statute of limitations applicable to five misdemeanor offenses as follows:

Under G.S. 15-1, the following misdemeanors have a ten-year statute of limitations:
- G.S. 7B-301(b) ("Duty to Report Abuse, Neglect, Dependency, or Death")
- G.S. 14-27.33 ("Sexual Battery")
- G.S. 14-202.2 ("Indecent Liberties Between Children")
- G.S. 14-318.2 ("Child Abuse")
- G.S. 14-318.6 ("Failure to Report Crimes against Juveniles")

Defenses That Justify (page 18)

Self-Defense, Defense of Others, and Defense of Property (page 18)

Add the following at the end of the first paragraph of this section:

A defendant is not entitled to a self-defense instruction when he or she claims the killing was accidental. State v. Harvey, 372 N.C. 304 (2019).

Add the following at the end of the third paragraph of this section:

; John Rubin, *The Statutory Law of Self-Defense in North Carolina*, N.C. CRIM. L.: A UNC SCH. OF GOV'T BLOG (June 4, 2019), https://nccriminallaw.sog.unc.edu/the-statutory-law-of-self-defense-in-north-carolina (discussing, among other cases, State v. Copley, ___ N.C. App. ___, 828 S.E.2d 35, *temp. stay allowed*, ___ N.C. ___, 827 S.E.2d 307 (2019) (noting that the new defensive force statute, G.S. 14-52.2, includes the curtilage of the home)).

Add the following at the end of the last paragraph of this section:

A person has the right to resist an unlawful arrest with the use of force reasonably necessary to prevent an unlawful restraint of the person's liberty. State v. Burwell, 256 N.C. App. 722, 730–31 (2017) (the trial court did not err by failing to instruct the jury on the right to resist an unlawful arrest where the arrest was lawful). If an officer uses excessive force to execute a lawful arrest, the person arrested may defend against the excessive force. *Id.* at 736 (the trial court did not err by failing to instruct the jury on the right to defend oneself from excessive force by an officer where the officer's use of force was not excessive).

Necessity and Duress (page 18)

For another case discussing the elements of the defense of necessity and holding that it is a defense to impaired driving, see *State v. Miller*, 258 N.C. App. 325, 327 (2018) (the trial court erred by failing to give a jury instruction on necessity).

For another case supporting the statement in this section that duress is not a defense to any charge of intentional homicide, see *State v. Faulk*, 256 N.C. App. 255, 258–59 (2017) (citing *Cheek* and other precedent to hold that the trial court did not err by failing to instruct the jury on duress as a defense to premeditated and deliberate first-degree murder).

For a case where the defendant was not entitled to a jury instruction on duress, see *State v. Burrow*, 248 N.C. App. 663, 666–67 (2016) (attempted felony breaking or entering case; among other things, the defendant failed to show that his actions were caused by a reasonable fear that he would suffer immediate death or serious bodily injury if he did not act). For a contrasting case holding that the evidence supported an instruction on duress, see *Miller*, 258 N.C. App. at 327 (impaired driving case).

Public Authority (page 19)

The G.S. 20-145 exemption from speed limits does not apply to bail bondsmen. State v. McGee, 234 N.C. App. 285, 288 (2014).

Defenses Showing Lack of Blameworthiness (page 20)

Entrapment (page 21)

State v. Keller, ___ N.C. App. ___, 828 S.E.2d 578, *temp. stay allowed*, ___ N.C. ___, 827 S.E.2d 529 (2019) (mem.) (no error to decline to instruct on entrapment where the defendant had a predisposition and willingness to solicit a minor by computer, and a detective merely afforded him an opportunity to do so by impersonating a child online).

The trial court erred by refusing to instruct on entrapment in a drug delivery case where an undercover officer tricked the defendant into believing that the officer was romantically interested in the defendant to persuade him to obtain cocaine, the defendant had no predisposition to commit the offense, and the criminal design originated solely with the officer. State v. Foster, 235 N.C. App. 365, 374–76 (2014).

Failure of Proof or "Negating" Defenses (page 22)

Accident (page 22)

The trial court did not err by refusing to instruct the jury on the defense of accident in a child sexual offense case where no evidence indicated that the defendant digitally penetrated the victim accidentally. State v. Clapp, 235 N.C. App. 351, 361 (2014).

For another case supporting the statement in this section that the defense of accident is not available if the defendant was engaged in misconduct at the time of the killing, see *State v. Robinson*, 251 N.C. App. 326, 327 (2016) ("A person who, while carrying a loaded firearm, starts a physical fight and discharges the firearm injuring another person, is not entitled to a jury instruction on the defense of accident.").

For a case where the trial court erred by failing to instruct the jury on the defense of accident, see *State v. Bediz*, ___ N.C. App. ___, 837 S.E.2d 188 (2019) (the defendant's testimony in his assault trial that he was trying park his car and did not realize he had hit the victim with his side-view mirror was sufficient evidence from which a jury could have found that he hit the victim unintentionally).

3
Participants in Crimes

Principals—Acting in Concert (page 29)
Notes (page 29)
Generally (page 29)
The acting in concert theory generally does not apply to possession offenses, as it tends to become confused with other theories of guilt, State v. Diaz, 155 N.C. App. 307 (2002), but there are times when it is appropriate, *see, e.g.*, State v. Glover, ___ N.C. App. ___, 833 S.E.2d 203 (2019) (acting in concert instruction appropriate when the defendant allowed his friend to keep her drugs in his metal tin, where they would be safe from others).

Element (1) (page 29)
The fact that a person helped plan a crime, was available to an accomplice by telephone when it was committed, or was present at the crime scene after the offense occurred does not establish constructive presence. State v. Hardison, 243 N.C. App. 723, 725–26 (2015).

For cases holding that the evidence was insufficient to establish that the defendant was actually or constructively present, see *State v. Greenlee*, 227 N.C. App. 133, 138 (2013) (obtaining property by false pretenses case arising out of sales of stolen goods to a pawn shop), and *Hardison*, 243 N.C. App. at 725–26 (contaminating a public water system case where the defendant was never present when the accomplice broke the water lines in question).

For cases holding that the evidence was sufficient to establish that the defendant was actually or constructively present when a crime occurred, see *State v. Guy*, ___ N.C. App. ___, 822 S.E.2d 66 (2018) (although the defendant was not identified as being at the scene of a robbery, a witness saw a fleeing car blow a tire and, less than one minute later and within a quarter-mile of the scene, an officer found the defendant changing a tire on his car; the victim's stolen debit card and a gun matching one described by the victim as having been used during the robbery were found in close proximity to the car); *State v. Johnson*, 251 N.C. App. 260, 272–73 (2016) (among other things, the victim's blood was found on the defendant's pants and after the shooting the defendant aided the shooter in a fight with the victim to gain control of the gun).

Element (2) (page 29)
For a larceny case where the evidence was sufficient as to this Element, see *State v. Glidewell*, 255 N.C. App. 110, 117–18 (2017) (the defendant rode with his accomplice to the store in question and together they entered the store, looked at merchandise, and were seen on surveillance video concealing merchandise; the two left the store within seconds of each other and departed the premises in the same vehicle).

Element (3) (page 30)

The defendant need not expressly vocalize his or her assent to the criminal conduct; all that is required is an implied mutual understanding or agreement. State v. Marion, 233 N.C. App. 195, 204–05 (2014) (evidence was sufficient to support convictions for murder, burglary, and armed robbery on theories of acting in concert and aiding and abetting where, among other things, the defendant was present for discussions and aware of the group's plan to commit a robbery and remained in the vicinity of the crime scene where she helped by telling her accomplices that two of them had fled and encouraging the others to hurry up and leave).

For a larceny case where the evidence was sufficient as to this Element, see *Glidewell*, 255 N.C. App. at 117–18 (the defendant rode with his accomplice to the store in question and together they entered the store, looked at merchandise, and were seen on surveillance video concealing merchandise; the two left the store within seconds of each other and departed the premises in the same vehicle).

For a case where the evidence was insufficient with respect to this Element, see *State v. Holloway*, 250 N.C. App. 674, 684–85 (2016) (the State presented no evidence that the defendant had a common plan or purpose to possess drugs or paraphernalia with his alleged accomplice, McEntire; at most, the evidence showed that the two were acquainted and that the defendant was present when drugs were found at McEntire's home; mere presence at the scene of a crime is insufficient where the State presented no evidence that the two shared any criminal intent).

Extent of criminal liability (page 30)

Although a group initially planned to rob just one person at a residence, their attempted robbery of a second person found there was in pursuit of the group's common purpose. State v. Jastrow, 237 N.C. App. 325, 330 (2014).

Aiding and Abetting (page 31)

Notes (page 31)

Generally (page 31)

For another case supporting the statement in this note that actual or constructive presence is not required to prove a crime under the theory of aiding and abetting, see *State v. Dick*, 370 N.C. 305, 310–11 (2017).

Element (2) (page 32)

For cases where the evidence was sufficient to support convictions on a theory of aiding and abetting, see *State v. Bauguss*, ___ N.C. App. ___, 827 S.E.2d 127 (2019) (sufficient evidence to convict the defendant of statutory sexual offense of a child by an adult on an aiding and abetting theory when he encouraged the victim's mother to perform sex acts on the victim and asked for photos and videos of specific sex acts); *State v. Cannon*, 254 N.C. App. 794, 797 (2017) (the evidence was sufficient as to aiding and abetting a larceny where, among other things, Amanda Eversole was seen trying to leave a Denver, NC, Walmart store without paying for items and her companion William Black was caught on surveillance video taking items from the store; Black was found sitting in a vehicle owned by the defendant, parked in the lot, filled with store goods, and positioned for easy escape; and the defendant, who was at the scene, claimed that he just met Eversole and Black and was paid $50 to drive to the Denver Walmart from Gastonia), *aff'd per curiam*, 370 N.C. 487 (2018); and *State v. Marion*, 233 N.C. App. 195, 204–05 (2014) (the evidence was sufficient to support convictions for murder, burglary, and armed robbery on theories of acting in concert and aiding and abetting where, among other things, the defendant was present for discussions about and aware of the group's plan to commit a robbery and remained in the vicinity of the crime scene where she helped by telling her accomplices that two of them had fled and encouraging the others to hurry up and leave).

Related Offenses Not in This Chapter (page 34)

Add the following offense to this list:

Bank examiner aiding and abetting by making false or fraudulent report. G.S. 53C-8-7.

Accessory before the Fact to a Felony (page 34)

Punishment (page 34)

Replace the citation at the end of this section with the following:

G.S. 14-5.2; *see* State v. Larrimore, 340 N.C. 119 (1995); State v. Grainger, 367 N.C. 696, 699 (2014) (because the defendant's conviction for first-degree felony murder was not based solely on the uncorroborated testimony of a principal, the exception in G.S. 14-5.2 did not apply). A defendant is convicted of a capital felony when he or she is convicted of first-degree murder, even if the case was tried non-capitally. State v. Grainger, 224 N.C. App. 623, 630–31 (2012), *rev'd on other grounds*, 367 N.C. 696 (2014) (noting that this conclusion was central to the decision of the North Carolina Court of Appeals holding that the G.S. 14-5.2 exception applied; the state supreme court held that the exception did not apply for a separate reason: because the conviction did not rest on uncorroborated testimony of a principal).

4

Punishment under Structured Sentencing

Felonies (page 39)

Prior Record Level (page 40)

Delete the last paragraph of this section.

Aggravating and Mitigating Factors (page 41)

As a result of 2013 legislation, S.L. 2013-284, sec. 2(b); S.L. 2013-368, sec. 14, the first sentence of the fourth paragraph in this section should read as follows:

> G.S. 15A-1340.16(d) sets out more than twenty statutory aggravating factors, including, among others, that the crime was especially heinous, atrocious, or cruel, *id.* § -1340.16(d)(7); that the victim was very young, very old, or mentally or physically infirm or handicapped, *id.* § -1340.16(d)(11); and that the defendant involved a person under the age of 16 in the commission of the crime, *id.* § -1340.16(d)(13).

Sentence Disposition (page 43)

Active Punishment (page 43)

As a result of 2017 legislation, S.L. 2017-186, sec. 2(qqq), replace the references to the "Department of Correction" in this section with: Division of Adult Correction and Juvenile Justice.

Intermediate punishment (page 44)

2012 legislation, S.L. 2012-146, amended G.S. 15A-1343(a1), adding the following condition to those listed on page 45:

- Abstain from alcohol consumption and submit to continuous alcohol monitoring when alcohol dependency or chronic abuse has been identified by a substance abuse assessment.

Community punishment (page 45)

2012 legislation, S.L. 2012-39, repealed G.S. 15A-1382.1(b). Thus, the last paragraph of this section (page 46) should be deleted.

Restitution (page 46)

Delete the second sentence of the third paragraph in this section.

2019 legislation, S.L. 2019-216, passed in response to a 2018 constitutional amendment on victims' rights, N.C. Const. art. I, § 37, makes changes to the offenses covered by the CVRA. Delete the bulleted list in this same paragraph and replace it with the following:

- Any offense against the person, defined as a felony violation of Subchapters III and VII of G.S. Chapter 14; Article 39 of Chapter 14; any offense in Chapter 20 with an element that involves impairment of the defendant or injury or death to the victim; a violation of a valid protective order under G.S. 50B-4.1, including but not limited to G.S. 14-134.3 and -269.8; Article 35 of Chapter 14 if the elements of the offense involve communicating a threat or stalking; any other offense that triggers the enumerated victims' rights, as required by the North Carolina Constitution. G.S. 15A-830(6a).
- Any felony property crime, defined as a felony violation of Subchapter IV or V of G.S. Chapter 14. G.S. 15A-830(3b).

Special Provisions (page 47)

Class A felonies (page 47)

Delete the last sentence of this section and replace it with the following:

For a discussion of capital sentencing issues, see Jeffrey B. Welty, North Carolina Capital Case Law Handbook (UNC School of Government, 3d ed. 2013).

Armed habitual felon (new note)

2013 legislation, S.L. 2013-369, sec. 26, created a new armed habitual felon status. Put simply, when a person who has been convicted of one firearm-related felony commits a second such offense, the defendant may, in the discretion of the district attorney, be charged as an armed habitual felon. If convicted, the defendant must be sentenced as a Class C felon with a minimum 120-month prison term. *See generally* G.S. 14-7.35 through -7.41 (enacted by S.L. 2013-369, sec. 26).

Habitual breaking and entering status offender (page 48)

2017 legislation, S.L. 2017-176, sec. 3(a), amended G.S. 14-7.25, adding the following offense to the covered felony breaking and entering offenses included in this section's bulleted list:

- Breaking or entering with intent to terrorize or injure an occupant of the building under G.S. 14-54(a1) (covered in this supplement under "Felony Breaking or Entering of a Building").

Firearm or deadly weapon enhancement (page 48)

2013 legislation, S.L. 2013-369, sec. 5, amended the enhancement described in this section so that punishment applies as follows:

- If the felony is a Class A through E felony, the minimum term of imprisonment is increased by 72 months; the applicable maximum is the maximum that corresponds to the enhanced minimum.
- If the felony is a Class F or G felony, the minimum term of imprisonment is increased by 36 months; the applicable maximum is the maximum that corresponds to the enhanced minimum.
- If the felony is a Class H or I felony, the minimum term of imprisonment is increased by 12 months; the applicable maximum is the maximum that corresponds to the enhanced minimum.

G.S. 15A-1340.16A(c) (as amended by S.L. 2013-369, sec. 5).

Conditional discharge for certain drug offenders (page 49)

Replace this section with the following text:

> G.S. 90-96, as amended by S.L. 2017-102, sec. 38, allows for conditional discharge of certain drug convictions in specified circumstances.

Methamphetamine enhancement (page 49)

As a result of 2013 legislation, S.L. 2013-124, sec. 2, the following should be added at the end of this section:

> If a defendant is convicted of manufacturing of methamphetamine and a person under 18 years old or a disabled or elder adult
>
> - resided on the property used for the manufacture of methamphetamine or
> - was present where methamphetamine was being manufactured,
>
> the defendant's minimum sentence must be increased by 24 months. G.S. 15A-1340.16D(a1). If both a minor and a disabled or elder adult resided on the property or were present, the minimum sentence must be increased by 48 months. *Id.* The maximum sentence is the maximum that corresponds to the enhanced minimum. The terms "disabled adult" and "elder adult" are defined by cross-reference to G.S. 14-32.3(d). *Id.* § (a2). The facts supporting the enhancement must be alleged in an indictment or information and proved to a jury beyond a reasonable doubt, unless the defendant pleads guilty or no contest to the issue. *Id.* §§ (b), (c).

Domestic violence protective order enhancement (page 50)

The G.S. 50B-4.1(d) enhancement does not apply to felony convictions when the defendant also is charged with a Class A or B1 felony or charged under G.S. 50B-4.1(f) or (g). State v. Jacobs, 239 N.C. App. 425, 427 (2015) (trial court erred by enhancing the defendant's conviction for assault with a deadly weapon with intent to kill inflicting serious injury and attempted second-degree kidnapping where the defendant also was charged with a violation of G.S. 50B-4.1(g)).

Criminal gang activity enhancement (new note)

G.S. 15A-1340.16E, enacted by S.L. 2017-194, sec. 5, creates certain sentencing enhancements that apply when the offense is committed as part of criminal gang activity and when the defendant is a criminal gang leader or organizer. The enhancements do not apply to any gang offense included in Article 13A of G.S. Chapter 14 (the North Carolina Criminal Gang Suppression Act). The statute specifies the procedural requirements for application of the enhancements.

Misdemeanors (page 50)

Sentence Disposition (page 52)

Active punishment (page 52)

2014 legislation, S.L. 2014-100, sec. 16C.1, made changes to the place of confinement for misdemeanants.

Special Provisions (page 53)

Infamous or related misdemeanor enhancement (page 53)

The evidence was sufficient to establish that the defendant obstructed justice with deceit and intent to defraud where he gave eight different statements to authorities, providing an array of scenarios surrounding the victim's death and identifying four different individuals as the perpetrator, and admitted that he had been untruthful to investigators. State v. Cousin, 233 N.C. App. 523, 530–31 (2014).

Enhancement for criminal gang activity (page 54)

As a result of 2017 legislation, S.L. 2017-194, sec. 11, the enhancement under G.S. 14-50.22 applies to any misdemeanor committed for the benefit of, at the direction of, or in association with, any "criminal gang." The term "criminal gang" is defined in the statute accompanying "Soliciting Participation in Criminal Gang Activity" in this supplement.

Conditional discharge for certain drug offenders (page 54)

Replace this section with the following text:

G.S. 90-96, as amended by S.L. 2017-102, sec. 38, allows for conditional discharge of certain drug convictions in specified circumstances.

Tables

Table 1 (page 55)

2013 legislation, S.L. 2013-410, sec. 3(a), amended the punishment for a Class A felony from "Life Imprisonment Without Parole or Death" to "Life Imprisonment With Parole or Without Parole, or Death."

Table 2A (page 58)

2013 legislation, S.L. 2013-101, sec. 6, made three changes to the maximum sentences grid, effective October 1, 2013, and applicable to offenses committed on or after that date:

The maximum sentence for a 66-month minimum is 92 months.

The maximum sentence for an 86-month minimum is 116 months.

The maximum sentence for a 216-month minimum is 272 months.

Tables 3 and 3A (pages 60, 62)

These forms have been updated. Revised N.C. AOC forms are available here: www.nccourts.org/Forms/FormSearch.asp.

Table 4 (page 63)

2013 legislation, S.L. 2013-360, sec. 18B.13, amended the misdemeanor sentencing grid shown in this table. Specifically, for misdemeanor offense Class 3 at prior conviction level II, the punishment should read:

1–15 days C if one to three prior convictions

1–15 days C/I if four prior convictions

That same legislation also enacted G.S. 15A-1340.23(d), providing that "[u]nless otherwise provided for a specific offense, the judgment for a person convicted of a Class 3 misdemeanor who has no more than three prior convictions shall consist only of a fine."

5
General Crimes

Attempt (page 67)

Notes (page 67)

Generally (page 67)

For another case on the elements of attempt, see *State v. Floyd*, 369 N.C. 329 (2016).

Evidence that the defendant committed a completed crime is sufficient to support a conviction of an attempt to commit that crime. State v. Baker, 369 N.C. 586, 598 (2017) (evidence that a completed rape occurred was sufficient to support a conviction for attempted rape); State v. Primus, 227 N.C. App. 428, 431–32 (2013) (evidence that a completed larceny occurred was sufficient to support a conviction for attempted larceny).

Element (1) (page 68)

In attempted rape cases, the State need not show that the defendant made an actual physical attempt to have intercourse. State v. Baker, 245 N.C. App. 94, 98–99 (2016), *rev'd on other grounds*, 369 N.C. 586 (2017). Intent is established "if the evidence shows that defendant, at any time during the incident, had an intent to gratify his passion upon the victim, notwithstanding any resistance on her part." *Id.* (internal quotation marks, citations omitted).

For cases where the evidence was sufficient to show an intent to engage in a sexual assault, see *State v. Marshall*, 246 N.C. App. 149, 157 (2016) (the evidence was sufficient to establish attempted sex offense and attempted rape; after isolating the victim from her husband, one of the perpetrators said, "Maybe we should," to which the other responded, "Yeah"; an accomplice then forced the victim to perform fellatio on him; after the defendant touched the victim, saying, "Nice," the victim's husband tried to protect her and was shot; a reasonable jury could infer that the defendant intended to engage in a continuous sexual assault involving both fellatio (like his accomplice) and rape and was thwarted only because of the husband's intervention); *State v. Minyard*, 231 N.C. App. 605, 616–17 (2014) ("The act of placing one's penis on a child's buttocks provides substantive evidence of intent to commit a first degree sexual offense, specifically anal intercourse."); *State v. Miles*, 237 N.C. App. 170, 173–74 (2014) (the defendant's conduct before and after his request that the victim perform fellatio on him sufficiently established that he intended to commit a sexual offense by force and against her will).

For a case where the evidence was insufficient to show an intent to engage in a sexual assault, see *Baker*, 245 N.C. App. at 100 (the defendant sat next to the victim, touched her shoulder and chest, and tried to get her to lie down).

Element (2) (page 68)

Delete the citation to *State v. Lawrence* in this note and replace it with the following:

State v. Bauguss, ___ N.C. App. ___, 827 S.E.2d 127 (2019) (an attempted sexual offense charge was proper based on the defendant's instruction to the victim's mother to dress the victim without panties and other overt actions that were part of the defendant's scheme to groom the victim for sexual activity);

Attempted homicide (page 68)

The crime of attempted first-degree felony murder does not exist under North Carolina law. State v. Marion, 233 N.C. App. 195, 202 (2014).

For another case holding that assault with a deadly weapon with intent to kill inflicting serious injury is not a lesser-included offense of attempted first-degree murder and that a defendant may be convicted of and punished for both offenses, see *State v. Rogers*, 219 N.C. App. 296, 307–08 (2012).

Conspiracy to commit attempted murder is a cognizable offense in North Carolina. State v. Lyons, ___ N.C. App. ___, 836 S.E.2d 917 (2019).

Attempted assault (page 69)

Delete the text of this note and replace it with the following:

In *State v. Floyd*, 369 N.C. 329 (2016), the supreme court held that attempted assault is a crime in North Carolina; it reversed the court of appeals, which had held that attempted assault with a deadly weapon inflicting serious injury is not a recognized crime because it constituted an attempt of an attempt. *Id.* The *Floyd* court concluded that "[a]ttempted assault is not an attempt of an attempt because assault may be defined by the show-of-violence rule," a form of assault that "does not involve an attempt to cause injury to another person, but is based upon a violent act or threat that causes fear in another person." *Id.* at 336.

Conspiracy (page 72)

Notes (page 72)

Element (1) (page 72)

Circumstantial evidence can establish the scope of the agreement. State v. Fish, 229 N.C. App. 584, 591–92 (2013) (evidence that the defendant and an accomplice stole property valued at more than $1,000 established that they had an agreement to do so).

For a case where there was sufficient evidence of a conspiracy to possess a stolen pistol, see *State v. Greene*, 251 N.C. App. 627, 635 (2017) (after the defendant made a phone call from jail to his alleged co-conspirator, the co-conspirator showed up at the residence near where the pistol was found and admitted to "working with" the defendant).

For other cases where there was sufficient evidence of an agreement to commit robbery, see *State v. Stroud*, 259 N.C. App. 411, 419 (2018) (the evidence was sufficient to establish an agreement to commit robbery where the victim identified the defendant, Raborn, and Bowen as the perpetrators and the defendant confirmed to a detective the accuracy of Bowen's statement that the robbery was in retaliation for the victim's robbery of Bowen's cousin); *State v. Young*, 248 N.C. App. 815, 822 (2016) (circumstantial evidence established that the defendant and his accomplices agreed to rob a second victim; the accomplices agreed to take the first victim's car and then commit other unlawful acts, with the defendant wielding a shotgun and another person driving the vehicle; the acts against the second victim occurred within minutes of and very near the acts against the first); *State v. Oliphant*, 228 N.C. App. 692, 704 (2013) (implied agreement to commit armed robbery where the defendants approached the victim from behind and one held a gun while the other reached for the victim's cell phone); and *State v. Rogers*, 227 N.C. App. 617, 623–24 (2013) (conspiracy to commit armed robbery; implied understanding to use a dangerous weapon).

For a case where there was insufficient evidence of an agreement to commit robbery, see *State v. Fleming*, 247 N.C. App. 812, 819 (2016) (the "mere fact that the crime the defendant allegedly conspired with others to commit took place does not, without more, prove the existence of a conspiracy").

For other cases where the evidence was insufficient to establish an agreement to engage in drug offenses, see *State v. Velazquez-Perez*, 233 N.C. App. 585, 593 (2014) (among other things, there was no evidence that the driver of a vehicle owned by an alleged co-conspirator knew about drugs hidden in the vehicle), and *State v. McClaude*, 237 N.C. App. 350, 353–54 (2014) (following *State v. Euceda-Valle*, 182 N.C. App. 268 (2007), where the evidence showed only that drugs were found in a car driven by another person in which the defendant was a passenger).

For cases where the evidence was sufficient to show an agreement to engage in drug offenses, see *State v. Winkler*, 368 N.C. 572, 581–83 (2015) (rejecting the defendant's argument that the evidence showed only "the mere existence of a relationship between the two individuals"); *State v. Glisson*, 251 N.C. App. 844, 848–49 (2017) (sufficient evidence to establish that the defendant conspired with an accomplice to traffic in opium where, among other things, the defendant brought the accomplice to all three controlled buys, the drugs were maintained in the same vehicle as the accomplice, and the defendant exchanged the drugs and counted the money in front of the accomplice); *State v. Garrett*, 246 N.C. App. 651, 656–57 (2016) (sufficient evidence of conspiracy to sell methamphetamine where the incident arose out of a controlled buy involving the defendant and two accomplices); *State v. Torres-Gonzalez*, 227 N.C. App. 188, 195 (2013) (conspiracy to traffic in cocaine by possession where the defendant and an accomplice worked together to complete a drug sale); and *State v. Davis*, 236 N.C. App. 376, 385 (2014) (implied agreement to engage in drug trafficking by manufacture where the defendant was present at the scene and aware that his accomplice was involved in producing methamphetamine and the defendant was involved in the manufacturing process; "Where two subjects are involved together in the manufacture of methamphetamine and the methamphetamine recovered is enough to sustain trafficking charges, we hold the evidence sufficient to infer an implied agreement between the subjects to traffic in methamphetamine by manufacture and withstand a motion to dismiss.").

Multiple convictions and punishments (page 74)
For cases where the evidence supported the existence of multiple conspiracies, see *State v. Stimpson*, 256 N.C. App. 364, 371, 807 S.E.2d 603, 608 (2017) (holding that the evidence supported five separate offenses of conspiracy to commit armed robbery arising from five separate incidents; concluding, in part, that the random nature and happenstance of the robberies did not indicate a single conspiracy and that the victims selected and crimes committed arose at random and by pure opportunity), *aff'd per curiam*, 371 N.C. 470 (2018); *Glisson*, 251 N.C. App. at 849–50 (the evidence supported the existence of multiple separate conspiracies to traffic in controlled substances; noting the time between the transactions and that each was initiated by an informant or a detective).

Relation to other offenses (page 75)
Conspiracy to commit attempted murder is a cognizable offense in North Carolina. State v. Lyons, ___ N.C. App. ___, 836 S.E.2d 917 (2019).

Withdrawal (new note)
Due process is not violated when the trial court puts the burden on the defendant to prove withdrawal from the conspiracy. Smith v. United States, 568 U.S. 106, 110 (2013).

Related Offenses Not in This Chapter (page 75)

As a result of 2015 legislation, S.L. 2015-47, delete the last offense in this list and replace it with the following:

Furnishing poison, controlled substances, deadly weapons, cartridges, ammunition, or alcoholic beverages to inmates; furnishing tobacco products or mobile phones to inmates; furnishing mobile phones to delinquent juveniles. G.S. 14-258.1.

Continuing Criminal Enterprise—Non-Drug Offenses (page 75)

Statute (page 75)

2012 legislation, S.L. 2012-38, amended G.S. 14-7.20, making three changes. First, subsection (a) was amended to read:

> (a) Except as otherwise provided in subsection (a1) of this section, any person who engages in a continuing criminal enterprise shall be punished as a Class H felon and in addition shall be subject to the forfeiture prescribed in subsection (b) of this section.

Second, a new subsection, (a1), was enacted as follows:

> (a1) Any person who engages in a continuing criminal enterprise where the felony violation required by subdivision (c)(1) of this section is a violation of G.S. 14-10.1 shall be punished as a Class D felon and, in addition, shall be subject to the forfeiture prescribed in subsection (b) of this section.

Third, the first sentence of subsection (b) was amended to read:

> (b) Any person who is convicted under subsection (a) or (a1) of this section of engaging in a continuing criminal enterprise shall forfeit to the State of North Carolina:

Punishment (page 76)

Delete the first sentence of this section and replace it with the following:

> Class H felony, G.S. 14-7.20(a), except that if the offense constitutes the crime of terrorism under G.S. 14-10.1, it is punished as a Class D felony. G.S. 14-7.20(a1); *see generally* "Terrorism" in Chapter 20 (Bombing, Terrorism, and Related Offenses) in this supplement.

Accessory after the Fact to a Felony (page 76)

Notes (page 77)

Element (2) (page 77)

For an additional case supporting the statement in this note that a person does not become an accessory after the fact simply because he or she knew that a crime was committed and failed to provide information about it, see *State v. Ditenhafer*, 258 N.C. App. 537, 551–52 (2018) (the evidence was insufficient to support a charge of accessory after the fact to sexual activity by a substitute parent based on the allegation that the defendant failed to report her husband's sexual abuse of her daughter; merely failing to report a crime is insufficient evidence of this Element), *aff'd in part*, ___ N.C. ___, 834 S.E.2d 392 (2019).

For a case where the evidence was sufficient as to this Element, see *State v. Cousin*, 233 N.C. App. 523, 532–33 (2014) (there was sufficient evidence of accessory after the fact to murder where the defendant made false statements to the police to shield the perpetrator's identity; the defendant gave eight different written statements to authorities, providing an array of scenarios surrounding the victim's death and identifying four different individuals as the perpetrator; he also admitted that he had been untruthful to investigators).

Element (3) (page 78)

For a case where the evidence was sufficient to show that the defendant knew the identity of the murderer and was protecting that person from apprehension, see *Cousin*, 233 N.C. App. at 532.

For a case where the evidence was sufficient to establish that the defendant knew that a gun he hid previously was used to commit a murder, see *State v. Schiro*, 219 N.C. App. 105, 113–14 (2012).

Multiple convictions and punishments (page 78)

No double jeopardy violation occurred when the trial court sentenced the defendant for felony obstruction of justice and accessory after the fact to murder arising out of the same conduct. *Cousin*, 233 N.C. App. at 537 (reasoning that each offense contains an element not in the other).

6
Homicide

Murder (page 83)

First-Degree Murder (page 83)

Statute (page 83)

Several pieces of legislation, S.L. 2017-94; S.L. 2017-115, sec. 9; S.L. 2013-47; S.L. 2013-410, sec. 3(a); and S.L. 2012-165, amended G.S. 14-17. The amended statute reads:

> **§ 14-17. Murder in the first and second degree defined; punishment.**
>
> (a) A murder which shall be perpetrated by means of a nuclear, biological, or chemical weapon of mass destruction as defined in G.S. 14-288.21, poison, lying in wait, imprisonment, starving, torture, or by any other kind of willful, deliberate, and premeditated killing, or which shall be committed in the perpetration or attempted perpetration of any arson, rape or a sex offense, robbery, kidnapping, burglary, or other felony committed or attempted with the use of a deadly weapon shall be deemed to be murder in the first degree, a Class A felony, and any person who commits such murder shall be punished with death or imprisonment in the State's prison for life without parole as the court shall determine pursuant to G.S. 15A-2000, except that any such person who was under 18 years of age at the time of the murder shall be punished in accordance with Part 2A of Article 81B of Chapter 15A of the General Statutes.
>
> (a1) If a murder was perpetrated with malice as described in subdivision (1) of subsection (b) of this section, and committed against a spouse, former spouse, a person with whom the defendant lives or has lived as if married, a person with whom the defendant is or has been in a dating relationship as defined in G.S. 50B-1(b)(6), or a person with whom the defendant shares a child in common, there shall be a rebuttable presumption that the murder is a "willful, deliberate, and premeditated killing" under subsection (a) of this section and shall be deemed to be murder in the first degree, a Class A felony, if the perpetrator has previously been convicted of one of the following offenses involving the same victim:
>> (1) An act of domestic violence as defined in G.S. 50B-1(a).
>> (2) A violation of a domestic violence protective order under G.S. 50B-4.1(a), (f), (g), or (g1) or G.S. 14-269.8 when the same victim is the subject of the domestic violence protective order.
>> (3) Communicating a threat under G.S. 14-277.1.
>> (4) Stalking as defined in G.S. 14-277.3A.
>> (5) Cyberstalking as defined in G.S. 14-196.3.
>> (6) Domestic criminal trespass as defined in G.S. 14-134.3.

(b) A murder other than described in subsection (a) or (a1) of this section or in G.S. 14-23.2 shall be deemed second degree murder. Any person who commits second degree murder shall be punished as a Class B1 felon, except that a person who commits second degree murder shall be punished as a Class B2 felon in either of the following circumstances:

(1)   The malice necessary to prove second degree murder is based on an inherently dangerous act or omission, done in such a reckless and wanton manner as to manifest a mind utterly without regard for human life and social duty and deliberately bent on mischief.

(2)   The murder is one that was proximately caused by the unlawful distribution of any opium, opiate, or opioid; any synthetic or natural salt, compound, derivative, or preparation of opium, or opiate, or opioid; cocaine or other substance described in G.S. 90-90(1)d.; methamphetamine; or a depressant described in G.S. 90-92(a)(1), and the ingestion of such substance caused the death of the user.

(c) For the purposes of this section, it shall constitute murder where a child is born alive but dies as a result of injuries inflicted prior to the child being born alive. The degree of murder shall be determined as described in subsections (a) and (b) of this section.

Punishment (page 84)

Replace the last sentence of the second paragraph in this section with the following:

For a discussion of capital law, see JEFFREY B. WELTY, NORTH CAROLINA CAPITAL CASE LAW HANDBOOK (UNC School of Government, 3d ed. 2013).

Add the following to the end of the third paragraph in this section:

In *Miller v. Alabama*, 567 U.S. 460, 479 (2012), the U.S. Supreme Court held that an automatic sentence of life imprisonment without the possibility of parole for a person under 18 years old who is convicted of murder violates the Eighth Amendment. Because North Carolina law had required such a sentence for a juvenile's conviction for first-degree murder, the General Assembly enacted legislation to bring the state's law in compliance with *Miller*. S.L. 2012-148. That legislation authorizes a sentence of life imprisonment with the possibility of parole after 25 years for defendants convicted of first-degree murder who were under 18 years old at the time of the offense. G.S. 15A-1340.19A. If a conviction is based solely on the felony murder rule, the court must impose this sentence. G.S. 15A-1340.19B(a)(1). In other first-degree murder cases, the court must conduct a hearing to determine whether the defendant should be sentenced to life imprisonment with or without the possibility of parole. *Id.* § (a)(2).

The last paragraph of this section cites G.S. 15A-2005(b). 2015 legislation, S.L. 2015-247, sec. 5, amended that statute to, among other things, replace the term "mentally retarded" with "intellectual disability."

Notes (page 84)

Elements (1) and (2) (page 84)

G.S. 14-17(c) provides that it is murder when a child is born alive but dies as a result of injuries inflicted prior to the child being born alive. *See* State v. Broom, 225 N.C. App. 137, 143–44 (2013) (the trial court did not err by denying the defendant's motion to dismiss first-degree murder charges where the victim was in utero at the time of the incident but was born alive and lived for one month before dying).

Element (3)(a)(i) (page 84)

This note describes three forms of malice. Delete (1) and replace it with the following:

(1)   express malice, in the form of hatred, ill will, or spite, State v. Reynolds, 307 N.C. 184, 191 (1982);

Replace the paragraph after the numbered list in this note with the following:

The second form of malice—commission of an inherently dangerous act—sometimes is called "depraved heart malice." State v. Lail, 251 N.C. App. 463, 468 (2016). Although depraved heart malice is frequently used to support second-degree murder convictions based on impaired driving, it is not limited to cases involving impaired driving. *Id.* at 469–70 (citing cases). The second form of malice was found when the defendant, knowing that two people became violently ill after using certain drugs, supplied the same drugs to the victim, who later died. *Liner*, 98 N.C. App. 600.

Element (3)(a)(ii) (page 85)

For additional cases where the evidence was sufficient to establish premeditation and deliberation, see *State v. Madonna*, 256 N.C. App. 112, 115–16 (2017) (among other things, the defendant-wife and victim-husband had been arguing about financial matters; the defendant was having a romantic relationship with her therapist and planned to ask the victim for a divorce; Internet searches were done on the home computer for "upon death of a veteran," "can tasers kill people," "can tasers kill people with a heart condition," "what is the best handgun for under $200," "death in absentia USA," and "declare someone dead if missing 3 years"; on the date of death the defendant got a gun and knife from her nephew, telling him that she was concerned about her safety due to break-ins in her neighborhood; she then went on a drive with the victim and used the gun to shoot him and the knife to stab him twelve times; she later messaged her therapist "it's almost done" and "it got ugly"; and after the incident, the defendant disposed of her bloodstained clothing, threw away the victim's medications and identification, and said that he had either gone to Florida or was at a rehabilitation center); *State v. Hicks*, 241 N.C. App. 345, 355–56 (2015) (among other things, there was no provocation by the unarmed victim; the defendant shot the victim at least four times; and after the shooting, the defendant immediately left the scene without aiding the victim); *State v. Mitchell*, 240 N.C. App. 246, 256 (2015) (among other things, there was no provocation by the victim; just before the shooting, the defendant said he was going to shoot a man over a trivial matter; the defendant shot the victim three times; and the victim may have been turning away or trying to escape at the time); *State v. Horskins*, 228 N.C. App. 217, 225–26 (2013) (after exchanging words in a nightclub parking lot, the defendant shot the unarmed victim, who had not reached for a weapon, had not engaged the defendant in a fight, and did not provoke the defendant's violent response; after the victim fell from the defendant's first shot, the defendant shot the victim six more times; and the defendant left the scene and attempted to hide evidence); *State v. Rogers*, 227 N.C. App. 617, 621–22 (2013) (the victim begged for his life and was shot eight times, primarily in the head and chest, and there was a lack of provocation); and *State v. Broom*, 225 N.C. App. 137, 144 (2013) (the defendant was having an affair with another woman and wanted his wife to terminate her pregnancy; he became angry when his wife said that if they divorced she might move out of the state with their children; and before he shot her, the defendant placed his wife's cell phone out of her reach).

2017 legislation added a new subsection, (a1), to the statute, creating a rebuttable presumption that certain domestic violence murders are "willful, deliberate and premeditated" under certain circumstances. G.S. 14-17(a1), *as amended by* S.L. 2017-94. *See* Jeff Welty, *Many Questions and a Few Answers about Britny's Law*, N.C. Crim. L.: A UNC Sch. of Gov't Blog (Aug. 28, 2017), https://nccriminallaw.sog.unc.edu/many-questions-answers-britnys-law/.

Element (3)(b) (page 86)

Add the following at the end of the first paragraph of this note:

; State v. Grullon, 240 N.C. App. 55, 60–61 (2015) (neither specific intent to kill nor deadly purpose to kill is required; the evidence was sufficient where the defendant ambushed the victim for the purpose of committing a robbery).

Add the following at the end of the second paragraph of this note:

> For recent cases where the evidence was sufficient to establish lying in wait, see *State v. Cox*, 256 N.C. App. 511 (2017) (rejecting the defendant's argument that the evidence was insufficient because he announced his presence; the evidence showed that the victim exited his residence to speak with the defendant, that the defendant did not threaten or harm the victim during their conversation, and that after waiting for the victim to return inside, the defendant fired into the residence, killing the victim; the victim was taken by surprise and had no opportunity to defend himself); *State v. Gosnell*, 231 N.C. App. 106, 113 (2013); and *Grullon*, 240 N.C. App. at 61–62 (the defendant hid under a darkened staircase for the purpose of robbing the victim).
>
> To starve a victim is to willfully deprive him or her of the food or liquids necessary in the nourishment of the human body to sustain life. The deprivation need not be absolute, but if it is so severe as to cause death, it may be the basis for murder by starving. State v. Cheeks, ___ N.C. App. ___, 833 S.E.2d 660 (2019) (adopting a definition previously set out by the North Carolina Supreme Court in dicta in *State v. Evangelista*, 319 N.C. 152 (1987)). Murder by starving does not require as an element that the defendant have a legal duty (as a parent or formal caregiver, for example) to feed the victim; the victim's situational dependence on the defendant for food or water can suffice. *Id.* at ___, 833 S.E.2d at 677. Just as with murder by poisoning or torture, murder by starving implies the requisite malice, and a separate showing of malice is not necessary. *Id.* at ___, 833 S.E.2d at 678.

Element (3)(c) (page 86)

Add the following to the fourth paragraph of this note:

> For another case supporting the statement in this note that felonious child abuse can support a felony murder charge, see *State v. Perry*, 229 N.C. App. 304, 318 (2013). For another case supporting the statement in this note that discharging a firearm into occupied property can support a felony murder charge, see *State v. Juarez*, 243 N.C. App. 466, 469 (2015), *rev'd on other grounds*, 369 N.C. 351 (2016).

The sixth paragraph of this note discusses the continuous transaction doctrine. Add the following to that discussion:

> There need not be a causal relationship between the underlying felony and the homicide; all that is required is that the felony and the killing occur in a single transaction. State v. Maldonado, 241 N.C. App. 370, 376 (2015). However, the felony murder rule will not apply where there is a break in the chain of events between the felony and the act causing death. *Id.* For a case where the court rejected the defendant's argument that such a break occurred, see *id.* (in a case where the felony murder charge was based on shooting into occupied property, the court rejected the defendant's argument that the victim's attempt to take his gun after he entered the house constituted a break in the chain of events that led to her later shooting death at the defendant's hand inside the property).

Replace the last sentence of the sixth paragraph of this note with the following:

> For a fuller discussion of the continuous transaction doctrine, see Jeffrey B. Welty, North Carolina Capital Case Law Handbook 22–23 (UNC School of Government, 3d ed. 2013).

Delete the seventh paragraph and replace it with the following:

> Although the felony and the homicide must be part of a continuous transaction, *State v. Jones*, 353 N.C. 159 (2000), suggests that when the underlying offense is an assault on a single victim who dies from injuries inflicted during the assault, the assault cannot be used as an underlying felony for purposes of the felony murder rule. *Id.* at 170 n.3 (reasoning that "[o]therwise, virtually all felonious assaults on a single victim that result in his or her death would be first-degree murders via felony murder, thereby negating lesser homicide charges such as second-degree murder and manslaughter"). However, if the transaction involves multiple assaults, only one of which caused death, the *Jones* rule does not apply. For example, in *State v. Carroll*, 356 N.C. 526 (2002), the defendant committed a nonfatal assault on the victim

with a machete and then killed her by strangulation. The state supreme court held that the felony assault with a machete was a separate offense from the strangulation and properly was used as a felony to support felony murder. *Id.* at 535. Additionally, the *Jones* rule applies only when a single victim is involved; cases involving multiple victims fall outside of this rule. *Jones*, 353 N.C. at 170 n.3 (distinguishing the single-victim scenario from one involving a felonious assault on one victim that results in the death of another victim); State v. Jackson, 189 N.C. App. 747, 752 n.3 (2008). The court of appeals has interpreted these cases as "stand[ing] for the limited proposition that a single assault on one victim that leads to that person's death cannot serve as the underlying felony for purposes of the felony murder rule." State v. Spruiell, 252 N.C. App. 486, 496 (2017) (footnote omitted). It has, however, rejected the "far broader proposition that *no* offense—regardless of whether the offense is classified as an assault or as some other crime—can serve as the basis for a felony murder conviction where the crime results from a 'single assaultive act' against one victim." *Id.* at 494–99. And it has held—in the context of an ineffective assistance of counsel claim—that notwithstanding *Jones*, a felony murder conviction can be based on the predicate felony of discharging a weapon into occupied property where a single shot was fired at a single victim. *Id.* at 499–500. *Spruiell* is consistent with pre-*Jones* cases that upheld felony murder convictions based on non-assault offenses that caused death. *See, e.g.*, State v. King, 316 N.C. 78 (1986) (felony murder based on discharging a firearm into occupied property); State v. Pierce, 346 N.C. 471, 493 (1997) (same based on felonious child abuse).

Replace the last sentence of the eleventh paragraph with the following:

> For a fuller discussion of the merger rule, see Jeffrey B. Welty, North Carolina Capital Case Law Handbook 113–14 (UNC School of Government, 3d ed. 2013).

Proximate cause (page 88)

The defendant's shooting of the victim's mother while the victim was in utero was a proximate cause of the victim's death after being born alive, where the gunshot wound required the child's early delivery, which in turn caused a complicating condition that resulted in death. State v. Broom, 225 N.C. App. 137, 143 (2013).

Greater and lesser-included offenses (page 90)

Replace the first sentence of this note with the following:

> Second-degree murder is a lesser-included offense of premeditated and deliberate first-degree murder, State v. Stevenson, 327 N.C. 259, 263 (1990), but not of first-degree felony murder, State v. Frazier, 248 N.C. App. 252, 258 (2016).

Delete the last sentence of this note.

Attempted first-degree murder (page 90)

The crime of attempted first-degree felony murder does not exist under North Carolina law. State v. Marion, 233 N.C. App. 195, 202 (2014).

Related Offenses Not in This Chapter (page 90)

Add the following offenses to this list:

> Interfering with gas, water, or electric meters and causing death. G.S. 14-151.
> Violation of Chapter 95, Article 15 (Passenger Tramway Safety) causing death.
> G.S. 95-125.3(g), *as enacted by* S.L. 2017-211, sec. 14(c).

The last listed offense should read:

> "Concealing a Death" (Chapter 21).

Second-Degree Murder (page 90)

Punishment (page 91)

As a result of 2012 and 2017 legislation, S.L. 2012-165; S.L. 2017-115, sec. 9, delete the text of this section and replace it with the following:

> Class B1 felony, except that punishment is as a Class B2 felony when (1) the malice necessary to prove second-degree murder is based on an inherently dangerous act or omission, done in such a reckless and wanton manner as to manifest a mind utterly without regard for human life and social duty and deliberately bent on mischief (this is the second form of malice discussed in the note on Element (3)(a)(i) to "First-Degree Murder" (page 84)); or (2) the murder was proximately caused by the unlawful distribution of any opium, opiate, or opioid; any synthetic or natural salt, compound, derivative, or preparation of opium, or opiate, or opioid; cocaine or other substance described in G.S. 90-90(1)d.; methamphetamine; or a depressant described in G.S. 90-92(a)(1), and the ingestion of such substance caused the death of the user. G.S. 14-17(b).

Notes (page 91)

Element (3) (page 91)

For another second-degree murder case involving impaired driving, see *State v. Grooms*, 230 N.C. App. 56, 68–69 (2013) (there was sufficient evidence of malice where the defendant drove impaired and killed two bicyclists; the defendant was warned of the dangers of drinking and driving and his prior incident of doing so on the same road led a passenger to fear for her life; his blood alcohol level was 0.16; the defendant knowingly consumed an illegal controlled substance that caused impairment; the defendant swerved off the road three times before the collision, giving him notice that he was driving dangerously; the defendant failed to watch the road and made a phone call right before the collision; and the defendant failed to apply his brakes before or after the collision, to call 911, or to aid the victims).

Insert the following after the first sentence of the first full paragraph on page 92:

> State v. Schmieder, ___ N.C. App. ___, 827 S.E.2d 322 (2019) (defendant's two-decade-long history of prior driving convictions, including speeding, reckless driving, illegal passing, and failure to reduce speed, coupled with witness testimony about his speeding, close following, and improper passing, was sufficient for a reasonable jury to infer that he acted with malice); State v. Rollins, 220 N.C. App. 443, 453–55 (2012) (the defendant drove without a license after being cited twice for that offense; the defendant took control of the vehicle from another driver by climbing over the back seat while the vehicle was moving; the defendant was evading the police because he had shoplifted items in the vehicle; the defendant drove well in excess of the speed limit, crossed a yellow line to pass, passed vehicles using a turn lane, drove through a corn field and ditch, and again crossed the center line, colliding with another vehicle while traveling 66 mph and without applying his brakes; and to avoid arrest, the defendant repeatedly struck an injured passenger as he tried to exit the vehicle and escape);

Insert the following paragraph at the end of this note:

> For a case where the evidence showed that the death resulted from a mishap with a gun and that there was insufficient evidence of malice, see *State v. Hatcher*, 231 N.C. App. 114, 118–20 (2013).

Death resulting from distribution and ingestion of a controlled substance (page 92)

This note states that if a defendant unlawfully distributes opium, cocaine, or a derivative of either substance, or methamphetamine, and ingestion of that substance causes the user's death, the defendant is guilty of second-degree murder. The statute, however, has been amended; it now applies to any opium, opiate, or opioid; any synthetic or natural salt, compound, derivative, or preparation of opium, opiate, or opioid; cocaine or other substance described in G.S. 90-90(1)d.; methamphetamine; or a depressant described in G.S. 90-92(a)(1). G.S. 14-17(b)(2), *as amended by* S.L. 2017-115, sec. 9.

Add the following to this note:

> Where there was no evidence that the defendant intended to kill the victim by selling him methadone, the trial court did not err by instructing the jury on second-degree murder and involuntary manslaughter. State v. Barnes, 226 N.C. App. 318, 329–30 (2013) (rejecting the defendant's argument that under G.S. 14-17 he could have been convicted only of second-degree murder).

Murder of an Unborn Child (page 94)
Related Offenses Not in This Chapter (page 96)

Add the following offense to this list:

> Sale of remains of an unborn child. G.S. 14-46.1.

Manslaughter (page 96)

Voluntary Manslaughter (page 96)
Notes (page 96)
Elements (1) and (2) (page 96)
Although no intent to kill is required for this crime, the act that causes death must be intentional. State v. English, 241 N.C. App. 98, 107 (2015) (the evidence was sufficient to show that the defendant intentionally hit the victim with her car).

Element (3) generally (page 96)
No legally adequate provocation existed when the victim insisted, shortly after having sex with the defendant, that he allow her to use his cell phone to text another man saying that she and the defendant were no longer in a relationship, and when the defendant refused, the victim taunted him. State v. Chaves, 246 N.C. App. 100, 105 (2016) (internal quotation marks, citations omitted) (noting that "[m]ere words, however abusive or insulting are not sufficient provocation" and that "this level of provocation must ordinarily amount to an assault or threatened assault by the victim against the perpetrator").

Although evidence that a defendant acted in the heat of passion can negate the malice required for the greater offenses of first- and second-degree murder, the State need not prove that the defendant acted in the heat of passion in order to obtain a conviction for voluntary manslaughter. State v. Coleman, 254 N.C. App. 497 (2017) (rejecting the defendant's argument that the trial court should have granted his motion for a directed verdict on voluntary manslaughter because the State presented no evidence that he acted in the heat of passion).

Multiple convictions and punishments (page 98)
G.S. 20-141.4(c) does not bar simultaneous prosecutions for involuntary manslaughter and death by vehicle; it only bars punishment for both offenses when they arise out of the same death. State v. Elmore, 224 N.C. App. 331, 336 (2012).

Involuntary Manslaughter (page 99)

Notes (page 99)

Element (3)(a) (page 100)

Other acts that fall within this Element include

- misdemeanor improper storage of a firearm, State v. Lewis, 222 N.C. App. 747, 752 (2012);
- supplying alcohol to a person under 21, State v. Noble, 226 N.C. App. 531, 536–37 (2013) (person under 21 died from alcohol poisoning; the defendant aided and abetted the victim in the possession or consumption of alcohol in violation of G.S. 18B-302); and
- affray, State v. Gomola, 257 N.C. App. 816, 818–19 (2018) (also holding that the trial court committed prejudicial error by not giving a jury instruction on defense of others as a defense to affray, the unlawful act underlying the involuntary manslaughter charge; if the jury had been given the instruction, it may have determined that the defendant's involvement in the affray was not unlawful).

Element (3)(b) (page 100)

For another case where the defendant's culpably negligent act was sufficient to support a conviction of this offense, see *State v. Fisher*, 228 N.C. App. 463, 473–75 (2013) (the defendant attacked the victim, leaving him semiconscious; instead of taking the victim to be picked up by his parents as arranged, the defendant drove him to an isolated area and again beat him; the defendant abandoned the victim outside knowing that the temperature was in the 20s and that the victim was injured, intoxicated, and not wearing a shirt; the defendant realized that his actions put the victim in jeopardy; and after being told that the victim was missing and that officers were concerned about him, the defendant lied about the victim's whereabouts, hindering efforts to find and help the victim).

Proximate cause (page 100)

For a case where improper storage of a firearm was the proximate cause of a child's death, see *Lewis*, 222 N.C. App. at 752.

Submitting involuntary manslaughter to the jury as a lesser-included offense of first-degree murder (page 101)

Add the following citation to the first paragraph of this note:

State v. Coleman, 254 N.C. App. 497, 505–06 (2017) (holding that the defendant was not entitled to a jury instruction on involuntary manslaughter; reasoning that in the context of a shooting, for a defendant to be entitled to such an instruction there must be evidence of "the absence of intent to discharge the weapon"; and explaining: "This distinguishes involuntary manslaughter from its voluntary counterpart, which requires proof of intent.").

As a result of 2019 legislation, S.L. 2019-83, add the following new offense, effective for offenses committed on or after December 1, 2019, to this chapter:

Death by Distribution of Certain Controlled Substances (new crime)

Statute

> **§ 14-18.4. Death by distribution of certain controlled substances; aggravated death by distribution of certain controlled substances; penalties.**
>
> (a) Legislative Intent. – The General Assembly recognizes that deaths due to the opioid epidemic are devastating families and communities across North Carolina. The General Assembly finds that the opioid crisis is overwhelming medical providers engaged in the

lawful distribution of controlled substances and is straining prevention and treatment efforts. Therefore, the General Assembly enacts this law to encourage effective intervention by the criminal justice system to hold illegal drug dealers accountable for criminal conduct that results in death.

(b) Death by Distribution of Certain Controlled Substances. – A person is guilty of death by distribution of certain controlled substances if all of the following requirements are met:

    (1)   The person unlawfully sells at least one certain controlled substance.

    (2   The ingestion of the certain controlled substance or substances causes the death of the user.

    (3)   The commission of the offense in subdivision (1) of this subsection was the proximate cause of the victim's death.

    (4)   The person did not act with malice.

(c) Aggravated Death by Distribution of Certain Controlled Substances. – A person is guilty of aggravated death by distribution of certain controlled substances if all of the following requirements are met:

    (1)   The person unlawfully sells at least one certain controlled substance.

    (2)   The ingestion of the certain controlled substance or substances causes the death of the user.

    (3)   The commission of the offense in subdivision (1) of this subsection was the proximate cause of the victim's death.

    (4)   The person did not act with malice.

    (5)   The person has a previous conviction under this section, G.S. 90-95(a)(1), 90-95.1, 90-95.4, 90-95.6, or trafficking in violation of G.S. 90-95(h), or a prior conviction in any federal or state court in the United States that is substantially similar to an offense listed, within seven years of the date of the offense. In calculating the seven-year period under this subdivision, any period of time during which the person was incarcerated in a local, state, or federal detention center, jail, or prison shall be excluded.

(d) Certain Controlled Substance. – For the purposes of this section, the term "certain controlled substance" includes any opium, opiate, or opioid; any synthetic or natural salt, compound, derivative, or preparation of opium, opiate, or opioid; cocaine or any other substance described in G.S. 90-90(1)(d); methamphetamine; a depressant described in G.S. 90-92(a)(1); or a mixture of one or more of these substances.

(e) Lesser Included Offense. – Death by distribution of certain controlled substances constitutes a lesser included offense of aggravated death by distribution of certain controlled substances in violation of this section.

(f) Samaritan Protection. – Nothing in this section shall be construed to restrict or interfere with the rights and immunities provided under G.S. 90-96.2.

(g) Lawful Distribution. – This section shall not apply to any of the following:

    (1)   Issuing a valid prescription for a controlled substance for a legitimate medical purpose by an individual practitioner acting in the usual course of professional practice.

    (2)   Dispensing, delivering, or administering a controlled substance pursuant to a prescription, by a pharmacy permitted under G.S. 90-85.21, a pharmacist, or an individual practitioner.

(h) Penalties. – Unless the conduct is covered under some other provision of law providing greater punishment, the following classifications apply to the offenses set forth in this section: (1) Death by distribution of certain controlled substances is a Class C felony. (2) Aggravated death by distribution of certain controlled substances is a Class B2 felony.

Elements

A person guilty of this offense

    (1) unlawfully

    (2) and without malice

(3) sells at least one certain controlled substance, *and*

(4) ingestion of the certain controlled substance or substances causes the user's death, *and*

(5) sale of the certain controlled substance is the proximate cause of the death.

Punishment

Class C felony.

Notes

Element (1)

This offense does not apply to controlled substances issued by prescription for a legitimate medical purpose by a practitioner acting in the usual course of professional practice or to a controlled substance dispensed, delivered, or administered by a pharmacy, pharmacist, or individual practitioner. G.S. 14-18.4(g).

Element (2)

See the discussion of this Element (designated as Element 3) of "Voluntary Manslaughter," above.

Element (3)

For the purposes of this offense, "certain controlled substance" means any opium, opiate, or opioid; any synthetic or natural salt, compound, derivative, or preparation of opium, opiate, or opioid; cocaine or any other substance described in G.S. 90-90(1)d.; methamphetamine; a depressant described in G.S. 90-92(a)(1); or a mixture of one or more of these substances. G.S. 14-18.4(d).

Element (5)

See the note "Proximate cause" under "First-Degree Murder," above.

Multiple convictions and punishments

This offense is a lesser-included offense of "Aggravated Death by Distribution of Certain Controlled Substances." G.S. 14-18.4(e).

Samaritan protection

This offense does not restrict or interfere with the limited immunity from prosecution under G.S. 90-96.2 for persons seeking medical assistance for themselves or others in the event of a drug-related overdose.

As a result of 2019 legislation, S.L. 2019-83, add the following new offense, effective for offenses committed on or after December 1, 2019, to this chapter:

Aggravated Death by Distribution of Certain Controlled Substances (new crime)

Statute

See G.S. 14-18.4(c), reproduced above.

Elements

A person guilty of this offense

(1) unlawfully

(2) and without malice

(3) sells at least one certain controlled substance, *and*

(4) ingestion of the certain controlled substance or substances causes the user's death, *and*

    (5) sale of the certain controlled substance is the proximate cause of the death, *and*

    (6) the person has a previous conviction within seven years of the date of the offense under G.S. 14-18.4, 90-95(a)(1), 90-95.1, 90-95.4, 90-95.6, 90-95(h), or any state or federal offense that is substantially similar to an offense listed.

Punishment

Class B2 felony.

Notes

Element (1)

See the discussion of this Element of "Death by Distribution of Certain Controlled Substances," above.

Element (2)

See the discussion of this Element (designated as Element 3) of "Voluntary Manslaughter," above.

Element (3)

See the discussion of this Element of "Death by Distribution of Certain Controlled Substances," above.

Element (5)

See the note "Proximate cause" under "First-Degree Murder," above.

Element (6)

In calculating the seven-year lookback period for the prior offenses described in this Element, any period of time during which the person was incarcerated in a local, state, or federal detention center, jail, or prison shall be excluded. G.S. 14-18.4(c)(5).

Samaritan protection

This offense does not restrict or interfere with the limited immunity from prosecution under G.S. 90-96.2 for persons seeking medical assistance for themselves or others in the event of a drug-related overdose.

Death by Vehicle (page 103)

Statute (page 103)

2012 legislation, S.L. 2012-165, amended subsection (a6) of G.S. 20-141.4 by deleting the last sentence of that subsection. That same legislation also amended subsection (b), the punishment provision, to provide:

    (b) Punishments.—Unless the conduct is covered under some other provision of law providing greater punishment, the following classifications apply to the offenses set forth in this section:

        (1) Repeat felony death by vehicle is a Class B2 felony.

        (1a) Aggravated felony death by vehicle is a Class D felony. Notwithstanding the provisions of G.S. 15A-1340.17, the court shall sentence the defendant in the aggravated range of the appropriate Prior Record Level.

        (2) Felony death by vehicle is a Class D felony. Notwithstanding the provisions of G.S. 15A-1340.17, intermediate punishment is authorized for a defendant who is a Prior Record Level I offender.

        (3) Aggravated felony serious injury by vehicle is a Class E felony.

        (4) Felony serious injury by vehicle is a Class F felony.

        (5) Misdemeanor death by vehicle is a Class A1 misdemeanor.

Felony Death by Vehicle (page 104)

Punishment (page 104)

As a result of the 2012 legislation noted above, delete the text of this section and replace it with the following:

> Class D felony. G.S. 20-141.4(b)(2). Notwithstanding G.S. 15A-1340.17, intermediate punishment is authorized for a defendant who is a Prior Record Level I offender. *Id.*

Notes (page 104)

Element (4) (page 104)

Impairment can be shown by a combination of evidence that a defendant has both ingested an impairing substance and operated a vehicle in a manner showing that he or she was oblivious to a visible risk of harm. State v. Shelton, ___ N.C. App. ___, 824 S.E.2d 136 (2019) (sufficient evidence of impairment where, in addition to blood tests revealing Oxycodone and Tramadol in the defendant's blood in amounts greater than 25 nanograms per milliliter, the defendant did not see the victim standing on the side of the road while other witnesses did, was not aware that he had struck the victim, and drove away from the scene despite knowing that his brakes were inoperable).

Element (5) (page 104)

Impairment can be the proximate cause of death despite the existence of other contributing factors. *Shelton*, ___ N.C. App. at ___, 824 S.E.2d at 142 ("[T]he fact that [the defendant's] brakes were in poor condition is not incompatible with the proposition that he was driving while impaired and that his impairment constituted a proximate cause of the death . . . .").

Multiple convictions and punishments (page 104)

Delete the first paragraph of this note and replace it with the following:

> G.S. 20-141.4(b), the punishment provision for all death by vehicle offenses, provides, in part, that unless the conduct is covered under some other provision of law providing greater punishment, repeat felony death by vehicle is a Class B2 felony, aggravated felony death by vehicle is a Class D felony, felony death by vehicle is a Class D felony, and misdemeanor death by vehicle is a Class A1 misdemeanor. Thus, a defendant may not be punished for a death by vehicle offense when the defendant is convicted also for an offense carrying a greater punishment and both offenses are based on the same conduct. State v. Davis, 364 N.C. 297, 303 (2010) (the trial court erred by imposing punishment for felony death by vehicle (then a Class E felony) and second-degree murder (Class B2 felony)).

Insert the following at the end of the second paragraph of this note:

> G.S. 20-141.4(c) does not bar simultaneous prosecutions for involuntary manslaughter and death by vehicle; it only bars punishment for both offenses when they arise out of the same death. State v. Elmore, 224 N.C. App. 331, 334–36 (2012).

Related Offenses Not in This Chapter (page 105)

Add the following offense to this list:

> Death by impaired boating offenses. G.S. 75A-10.3.

Aggravated Felony Death by Vehicle (page 105)

Punishment (page 105)

As a result of the 2012 legislation noted above, delete the text of this section and replace it with the following:

> Class D felony. G.S. 20-141.4(b)(1a). Notwithstanding G.S. 15A-1340.17, the defendant must be sentenced in the aggravated range. *Id.*

Repeat Felony Death by Vehicle (page 106)

Punishment (page 106)

As a result of the 2012 legislation noted above, delete the text of this section and replace it with the following:

> Class B2 felony. G.S. 20-141.4(b)(1).

Notes (page 106)

Multiple convictions and punishments (page 107)

Delete the text of this note and replace it with the following:

> See this note to "Felony Death by Vehicle," as amended by this supplement.

7
Assaults

Simple Assault (page 111)

Statute (page 111)

2012 legislation, S.L. 2012-149, enacted a new subsection, (c1), to G.S. 14-33 as follows:

> (c1) No school personnel as defined in G.S. 14-33(c)(6) who takes reasonable actions in good faith to end a fight or altercation between students shall incur any civil or criminal liability as the result of those actions.

2015 legislation, S.L. 2015-62, sec. 4(b), amended the definition of "in the presence of a minor" in G.S. 14-33(d)(2) to read as follows:

> (2) "In the presence of a minor" means that the minor was in a position to see or hear the assault.

2019 legislation, S.L. 2019-194, effective for offenses committed on or after December 1, 2019, enacted a new subdivision, (c)(9), to G.S. 14-33 as follows, creating a new Class A1 misdemeanor:

> (9) Assaults a transportation network company (TNC) driver providing a transportation network company (TNC) service. For the purposes of this subdivision, the definitions for "TNC driver" and "TNC service" as defined in G.S. 20-280.1 shall apply.

Notes (page 113)

Element (1) (page 113)

Add the following citation after the first sentence of this note:

> State v. Floyd, 369 N.C. 329 (2016);

Add the following to this note:

> For another case defining and explaining the two forms of assault discussed in this note, see *State v. Floyd*, 369 N.C. 329 (2016). In *Floyd* the North Carolina Supreme Court explained that its case law regarding the second form of assault—assault by show of violence—"appears to have evolved from early cases in which a person caused another to flee, leave a place sooner than desired, or otherwise alter course through the threatened use of a weapon." *Id.* at 336 (going on to discuss one of the court's earliest assault by show of violence cases, *State v. Shipman*, 81 N.C. 513 (1879)). Importantly, in *Floyd* the court held that assault by show of violence "does not involve an attempt to cause injury to another person, but is based upon a violent act or threat that causes fear in another person." *Id.* It continued: "Accordingly, although North Carolina law provides one definition of assault that describes the offense in terms of 'an overt act or an attempt, or the unequivocal appearance of an attempt,' our common law also provides a second definition that does not include any reference to attempt." *Id.* The court went on to hold that "[a]ttempted assault is not an attempt of an attempt because assault may be

defined by the show-of-violence rule." *Id.* It explained that "there is substantial overlap between the two definitions of assault because an overt act or attempt to do immediate physical injury to another person is likely to constitute a show of violence that causes fear and a change of behavior." *Id.* at 337. "As a result," it concluded, "relying upon the show-of-violence rule to define attempted assault does not create a significant limitation on the conduct covered by this offense." *Id.* Ultimately, the *Floyd* court reversed the court of appeals, which had held that the offense of attempted assault with a deadly weapon inflicting serious injury is not a recognized crime in North Carolina because it constituted an attempt of an attempt. *Id.*

2012 legislation, S.L. 2012-149, enacted G.S. 14-33(c1), providing that no school personnel defined in G.S. 14-33(c)(6) who take reasonable actions in good faith to end a fight or altercation between students shall incur any civil or criminal liability as the result of those actions.

Attempted assault (page 114)
Delete the text of this note and replace it with the following:

In *State v. Floyd*, 369 N.C. 329 (2016), the state supreme court held that attempted assault is a crime in North Carolina; it reversed the court of appeals, which had held that attempted assault with a deadly weapon inflicting serious injury is not a recognized crime because it constituted an attempt of an attempt. *Id.* The *Floyd* court concluded that "[a]ttempted assault is not an attempt of an attempt because assault may be defined by the show-of-violence rule," a form of assault that "does not involve an attempt to cause injury to another person, but is based upon a violent act or threat that causes fear in another person." *Id.* at 336.

District attorney approval required for charging (new note)
As a result of 2012 legislation, S.L. 2012-149, G.S. 15A-301(b1) requires district attorney approval before a magistrate may charge a school employee defined in G.S. 14-33(c)(6) with an offense that occurred while the school employee was in the process of discharging his or her duties of employment. The new statute does not apply to traffic offenses or to offenses that occur in the presence of an officer. Additional procedures are specified if the district attorney declines to accept this authority to approve charges. Although not specifically targeted to assaults, the new statute is most likely to apply with respect to these crimes.

Greater and lesser-included offenses (page 114)
Simple assault is a lesser-included offense of common law robbery. State v. Cromartie, 257 N.C. App. 790, 796 (2018).

Multiple convictions and punishments (page 114)
The State presented substantial evidence supporting two separate assaults where the defendant attacked his wife with his hands and, when his child intervened with a baseball bat to protect his mother, the defendant grabbed the bat and used it to beat his wife; the assaults involved separate thought processes, they were distinct in time, and the victim sustained injuries on different parts of her body as a result of each assault. State v. Wilkes, 367 N.C. 116 (2013) (affirming per curiam 225 N.C. App. 233 (2013)). For a case where the State sufficiently proved two distinct incidents of assault with a deadly weapon inflicting serious injury supporting two convictions, see *State v. Lanford*, 225 N.C. App. 189, 204 (2013) (rejecting the argument that only one offense occurred because the assaults were part of chronic and continual abuse).

A defendant's raising a gun and firing it—two acts that occurred in rapid succession without interruption—cannot support two separate counts of assault (one for assault by pointing a gun and one for assault with a deadly weapon). State v. Jones, ___ N.C. App. ___, 829 S.E.2d 507 (2019).

Assaults Inflicting a Particular Type of Injury (page 115)

Assault Inflicting Serious Injury (page 115)
Notes (page 115)

Element (3) (page 115)

Insert the following after the first sentence of the last paragraph of this note:

> State v. Anderson, 222 N.C. App. 138, 145 (2012) (the trial court did not err by instructing the jury that three gunshot wounds to the leg constituted serious injury where the victim was hospitalized for two days, had surgery to remove a bone fragment, and experienced pain at the time of trial);

Multiple convictions and punishments (page 116)

Add the following to the string cite following the fourth sentence of this note:

> State v. Fields, ___ N.C. App. ___, 827 S.E.2d 120, *discretionary review allowed,* ___ N.C. ___, 830 S.E.2d 816 (2019) (mem.) (based on the "unless covered" language in G.S. 14-33, a defendant may not be convicted and sentenced for both assault inflicting serious bodily injury (Class F felony) and habitual misdemeanor assault (Class H felony)); State v. Perry, ___ N.C. App. ___, 818 S.E.2d 699 (2018) (based on the "unless covered" language in G.S. 14-33, a defendant may not be convicted of assault on a child under G.S. 14-33 (Class A1 misdemeanor) and assault under G.S. 14-32 (felonious assault with a deadly weapon with intent to kill inflicting serious injury (Class C felony)) based on the same conduct); State v. McPhaul, 256 N.C. App. 303, 306 (2017) (based on the "unless covered" language in G.S. 14-32.4 (assault inflicting serious bodily injury, a Class F felony), the defendant could not be convicted of both that offense and assault with a deadly weapon with intent to kill inflicting serious injury, a Class C felony); State v. Baldwin, 240 N.C. App. 413, 425–26 (2015) (same); State v. Coakley, 238 N.C. App. 480, 491–92 (2014) (based on the "unless covered" language in G.S. 14-32.4(a) (assault inflicting serious bodily injury, a Class F felony), the defendant could not be convicted for both that offense and the more serious offense of assault with a deadly weapon inflicting serious injury under G.S. 14-32(b), a Class E felony); State v. Jones, 237 N.C. App. 526, 532–33 (2014) (because of the "unless the conduct is covered" language in the assault on a female statute, the trial court erred by sentencing the defendant to that offense (Class A1 misdemeanor) and habitual misdemeanor assault (Class H felony) when both convictions were based on the same conduct); State v. Jamison, 234 N.C. App. 231, 238–39 (2014) (the defendant could not be convicted and sentenced for both assault inflicting serious bodily injury (Class F felony) and assault on a female (Class A1 misdemeanor) when based on the same conduct; the "unless covered" language in the assault on a female statute reflects a legislative intent to limit a trial court's authority to impose punishment for that offense when punishment also is imposed for higher-class offenses that apply to the same conduct).

The courts have noted that *Hines,* discussed in this note, is distinguishable from this line of cases because the offenses at issue there (aggravated assault on a handicapped person and armed robbery) were based on distinct conduct, not the same act. *Jones,* 237 N.C. App. at 531–32. And the court of appeals has held that the "unless covered" language does not preclude multiple assault convictions when the assault convictions are based on separate and distinct conduct. State v. Harding, 258 N.C. App. 306, 318 (2018) (notwithstanding the "unless covered" language in G.S. 14-33(c) with respect to assault on a female, the defendant was properly convicted of that offense (a Class A1 misdemeanor) and the more serious offense of assault by strangulation (a Class H felony) where the convictions were based on separate conduct; the defendant's act of pinning down the victim and choking her to stop her from screaming supported the assault by strangulation conviction and his separate and distinct acts of grabbing her hair, tossing her down a rocky embankment, and punching her face and head multiple times supported the assault on a female conviction).

Delete the second to last sentence of this note.

Related Offenses Not in This Chapter (page 117)

Add the following offense to this list:

Violation of Chapter 95, Article 15 (Passenger Tramway Safety) causing serious injury. G.S. 95-125.3(g), *as enacted by* S.L. 2017-211, sec. 14(c).

Assault Inflicting Serious Bodily Injury (page 117)

Notes (page 118)

Element (3) (page 118)

Add the following after the last bullet in this note:

- the victim had broken bones in her face, a broken hand, and a cracked knee; she could not see properly out of her eye at the time of trial and she testified that her hand and eye "hurt all of the time," State v. Jamison, 234 N.C. App. 231, 235–36 (2014);
- the defendant's bites to the victim's body caused extreme pain, skin removal, hospitalization, and permanent scarring, State v. Burwell, 256 N.C. App. 722, 727–28 (2017);
- the victim, a transgender woman, suffered a long rip in her genitals that required stitches and pain medication, resulted in time off from work, and caused significant pain for six months, in addition to a jagged scar that the court deemed a serious permanent disfigurement, State v. Fields, ___ N.C. App. ___, 827 S.E.2d 120, *discretionary review allowed*, ___ N.C. ___, 830 S.E.2d 816 (2019) (mem.);
- the victim had a concussion and severe headaches that continued four years after the attack, State v. Griffin, ___ N.C. App. ___, 826 S.E.2d 253 (2019); and
- the victim's fractured eye socket resulted in the "protracted loss or impairment of the function of a bodily member or organ" when it left her completely blind in one eye for one week and her vision was not fully restored for two full weeks after the assault; she could not drive for one week and was not able to return to work until her vision was completely restored, State v. Rushing, ___ N.C. App. ___, 836 S.E.2d 262 (2019).

Add the following at the end of this note:

For a case where the evidence was insufficient to establish that an officer sustained serious bodily injury from the defendant's bites, see *State v. Williams*, 255 N.C. App. 168, 181–83 (2017) (the injury did not rise to the level of a permanent or protracted condition causing extreme pain where, among other things, upon leaving the hospital the officer returned to the police station to complete paperwork and went to work the following day; also rejecting the argument that the officer suffered serious, permanent disfigurement because a bite mark–shaped discoloration remained on his forearm for approximately two years after the incident, concluding that the presence of a minor scar or other mild disfigurement alone does not constitute serious bodily injury).

For a case involving a charge of child abuse inflicting serious bodily injury under G.S. 14-318.4(a3) where the evidence was insufficient to establish serious bodily injury, see *State v. Dixon*, 258 N.C. App. 78, 85–86 (2018) (scars from surgery to address an injury to the victim's leg did not by themselves constitute serious bodily injury where, by the time of trial, the victim was engaged in unrestricted physical activities and an expert testified that she would have no permanent disfiguration or loss or impairment of function due to the scars; the evidence did not establish that the victim experienced a permanent or protracted condition causing extreme pain where she testified that her leg stopped hurting long before trial and the evidence showed that she was cleared to engage in normal activities within nine months of surgery; no evidence showed that the victim was ever at risk of death due to the injury).

Assault Inflicting Physical Injury by Strangulation (page 119)

Notes (page 119)

Element (3) (page 119)

The evidence was sufficient to establish assault by strangulation where the defendant strangled the victim twice; a medical expert testified that the victim's injuries were consistent with strangulation; and photographic evidence showed bruising, abrasions, and a bite mark on and around the victim's neck. State v. Lowery, 228 N.C. App. 229, 232–33 (2013) (rejecting the defendant's arguments that the statute required "proof of physical injury beyond what is inherently caused by every act of strangulation" or extensive physical injury).

Element (4) (page 119)

The statute does not require a particular method of restricting the victim's airway, such as direct application of force to the trachea. State v. Lanford, 225 N.C. App. 189, 197 (2013). Thus, the evidence is sufficient when it shows that the defendant obstructed the victim's airway by putting his hand over her nose and mouth. *Id.*

Deadly Weapon Assaults (page 120)

Assault with a Deadly Weapon (page 120)

Notes (page 120)

Element (3) (page 120)

For a case where the trial court properly concluded that a knife was not a deadly weapon per se and left that determination to the jury, see *State v. Edgerton*, 234 N.C. App. 412, 419 (2014) (there was conflicting evidence regarding whether or not the knife was capable of producing death or great bodily harm; among other things, a witness testified that the knife was so dull that even though the defendant was "sawing" the victim's neck with it, the knife left only nicks on her neck), *rev'd on other grounds*, 368 N.C. 32 (2015).

Insert the following after the citation to *State v. Ferguson* in the fourth bullet on page 121:

> State v. Spencer, 218 N.C. App. 267, 274–75 (2012) (based on a vehicle's high rate of speed and the fact that the victim had to take affirmative action to avoid harm, a car was a deadly weapon as a matter of law);

Insert the following after the eighth bullet on page 121:

> • a kitchen table chair, State v. James, 224 N.C. App. 164, 170 (2012);

Insert the following at the end of this note:

> Because there was evidence that the defendant assaulted the victim with a lawn chair and not with his fists alone, the State was not required to present evidence as to the defendant's and the victim's size or condition. State v. Mills, 221 N.C. App. 409, 413 (2012).

Greater and lesser-included offenses (page 122)

Assault with a deadly weapon is a lesser-included offense of armed robbery. State v. Hinton, 361 N.C. 207, 210 (2007); State v. Richardson, 279 N.C. 621, 628 (1971).

Multiple convictions and punishments (page 122)

A defendant's raising a gun and firing it—two acts that occurred in rapid succession without interruption—cannot support two separate counts of assault (one for assault by pointing a gun and one for assault with a deadly weapon). State v. Jones, ___ N.C. App. ___, 829 S.E.2d 507 (2019).

Related Offenses Not in This Chapter (page 123)

Remove the following offense from this list:

Transporting dangerous weapon or substance during emergency; possessing off premises; exceptions. G.S. 14-288.7.

Assault with a Deadly Weapon with Intent to Kill (page 123)

Notes (page 124)

Element (1) (page 124)

A concurring opinion in *State v. Floyd*, 369 N.C. 329, 342 (2016), states that the court's decision in *State v. Birchfield*, 235 N.C. 410, 413 (1952), "recognized that the statutory definition of 'assault' under [G.S. 14-32] requires a completed battery."

Element (4) (page 124)

For additional assault cases where the evidence was sufficient to show an intent to kill, see *State v. Cox*, 256 N.C. App. 511, 524–25 (2017) (rejecting the defendant's argument that the State was required to prove that the defendant specifically intended to kill victim Stokes when he fired into a trailer while Stokes and others were inside; the court reasoned that "[i]t is not determinative . . . whether or not Defendant knew Stokes was in the trailer," concluding that there was sufficient evidence that the defendant "intended to kill whoever was inside the trailer" where, among other things, he fired numerous shots into the trailer knowing it was occupied); *State v. Stewart*, 231 N.C. App. 134, 145–46 (2013) (after shooting and killing eight people, the defendant ignored an officer's instruction to drop his shotgun, reloaded it, and fired at the officer); *State v. Stokes*, 225 N.C. App. 483, 485 (2013) (during a robbery the defendant fired a gun beside the victim's head, and the victim thought the defendant was going to kill him); and *State v. Wilkes*, 225 N.C. App. 233, 237 (the defendant hit the victim with a bat and, after she fell to her knees, he repeatedly struck her head until she lost consciousness, she never fought back, and the wounds could have been fatal; the circumstances of the attack, including the parties' conduct, provided additional evidence of intent to kill, including that the two had a volatile relationship and the victim had recently filed for divorce), *aff'd per curiam*, 367 N.C. 116 (2013).

Assault with a Deadly Weapon Inflicting Serious Injury (page 124)

Notes (page 125)

Element (1) (page 125)

A concurring opinion in *State v. Floyd*, 369 N.C. 329, 342 (2016), states that the court's decision in *State v. Birchfield*, 235 N.C. 410, 413 (1952), "recognized that the statutory definition of 'assault' under [G.S. 14-32] requires a completed battery."

Multiple convictions and punishments (page 125)

This offense is not a lesser-included offense of assault by a prisoner with a deadly weapon inflicting bodily injury, and thus a defendant may be convicted of and sentenced for both crimes. State v. Smith, ___ N.C. App. ___, 832 S.E.2d 921 (2019).

Assault with a Deadly Weapon with Intent to Kill Inflicting Serious Injury (page 125)

Notes (page 126)

Element (1) (page 126)

A concurring opinion in *State v. Floyd*, 369 N.C. 329, 342 (2016), states that the court's decision in *State v. Birchfield*, 235 N.C. 410, 413 (1952), "recognized that the statutory definition of 'assault' under [G.S. 14-32] requires a completed battery."

Greater and lesser-included offenses (page 126)

Replace the first sentence of this note with the following:

Because all of the elements of (1) simple assault, (2) assault with a deadly weapon, (3) assault with a deadly weapon with intent to kill, (4) assault inflicting serious injury, and (5) assault with a deadly weapon inflicting serious injury are included in assault with a deadly weapon with intent to kill inflicting serious injury, all of those offenses are lesser-included offenses of this offense.

Multiple convictions and punishments (page 126)

Assault with a deadly weapon with intent to kill inflicting serious injury is not a lesser-included offense of attempted first-degree murder; a defendant may be convicted of and punished for both offenses. State v. Rogers, 219 N.C. App. 296, 307–09 (2012).

Assault by Pointing a Gun (page 126)

Notes (page 127)

Element (2) (page 127)

For a case with multiple victims where the court rejected the defendant's argument that the State's evidence was too vague for the jury to infer that he pointed the gun at any particular person, see *State v. Pender*, 243 N.C. App. 142, 153 (2015) (witnesses testified that the defendant waved the gun "at us" and pointed the gun "toward everybody in one room").

Related Offenses Not in This Chapter (page 127)

Remove the following offense from this list:

Transporting dangerous weapon or substance during emergency. G.S. 14-288.7.

Discharging Barreled Weapons and Firearms (page 128)

Discharging a Barreled Weapon or Firearm into Occupied Property (page 128)

Notes (page 128)

Element (1) (page 128)

Insert the following after the first sentence of this note:

State v. Bryant, 244 N.C. App. 102, 109–10 (2015).

Element (3) (page 128)

Add the following at the end of the second paragraph of this note:

; State v. Hicks, 241 N.C. App. 345, 353 (2015) (same); State v. Mitchell, 240 N.C. App. 246, 257–58 (2015) (same; the evidence was sufficient where the defendant's hips, chest, and head were outside the vehicle and part of his leg and arm were inside it).

Element (4) (page 129)

Replace the second paragraph of this note with the following:

To be guilty of this offense, a defendant must discharge the weapon "with knowledge that the building is then occupied . . . or when he has reasonable grounds to believe that the building might be occupied." State v. James, 342 N.C. 589, 596 (1996) (quoting *State v. Williams,* 284 N.C. 67, 73 (1973), and emphasizing the word "might" in this standard); *see also* State v. Everette, 361 N.C. 646, 650 (2007). For cases where there was sufficient evidence that the defendant had reasonable grounds to believe that property might be occupied, see *State v. Jones,* ___ N.C. App. ___, 829 S.E.2d 507 (2019) (defendant slowly drove by the house a few minutes before shooting into it, and then stepped out of his car and loudly called to people in the house, challenging them to come outside); *Everette,* 361 N.C. at 651 (lights were on in a restaurant in an area known to be crowded in the early morning hours, the surrounding streets were crowded, and nearby establishments remained open until the early morning); *James,* 342 N.C. at 597 (reasonable grounds to believe that cars were occupied when the defendant fired a semiautomatic weapon in a club's parking lot knowing that vehicles were parked there and that people who had left the club were in the parking lot); and *State v. Charleston,* 248 N.C. App. 671, 676 (2016) (a shooting into the victim's residence occurred in a residential neighborhood in the evening while the victim's car was parked outside her home).

Add the following text to this note:

A residence was occupied when the family was on the front porch. State v. Miles, 223 N.C. App. 160, 163–64 (2012).

Multiple convictions and punishments (page 129)

Add the following text to the first paragraph of this note:

Multiple convictions are also proper when a single shot enters multiple dwellings. State v. Ray, 97 N.C. App. 621 (1990) (two convictions under G.S. 14-34.1 did not violate double jeopardy where the defendant fired a single bullet that entered two apartments). Multiple charges are not proper, however, when a single shot injures multiple occupants of the same dwelling. State v. Miller, ___ N.C. App. ___, 833 S.E.2d 644 (2019) (requiring the court to arrest judgment on one of two convictions under G.S. 14-34.1 resulting from a single shot into a single occupied vehicle).

Discharging a Barreled Weapon or Firearm into an Occupied Dwelling or Occupied Conveyance in Operation (page 130)

Notes (page 130)

Multiple convictions and punishments (page 130)

No violation of double jeopardy occurred when the defendant was sentenced for three counts of discharging a firearm into occupied property where each shot was "distinct in time, and each bullet hit the [house] in a different place." State v. Kirkwood, 229 N.C. App. 656, 667–68 (2013) (internal quotation marks, citations omitted).

Discharging Firearm within Occupied Building, etc. to Incite Fear (new crime)

This offense was enacted by 2013 legislation, S.L. 2013-144.

Statute

§ 14-34.10. Discharge firearm within enclosure to incite fear.
Unless covered under some other provision of law providing greater punishment, any person who willfully or wantonly discharges or attempts to discharge a firearm within any occupied building, structure, motor vehicle, or other conveyance, erection, or enclosure with the intent to incite fear in another shall be punished as a Class F felon.

Elements

A person guilty of this offense

(1) willfully or wantonly
(2) discharges or attempts to discharge a firearm
(3) within any occupied building, structure, motor vehicle, or other conveyance, erection, or enclosure
(4) with the intent to incite fear in another.

Punishment

Class F felony. G.S. 14-34.10.

Notes

Element (1). See this note to "Discharging a Barreled Weapon or Firearm into Occupied Property" in the main volume.

Element (2). See this note to "Discharging a Barreled Weapon or Firearm into Occupied Property" in the main volume. Note that unlike the other "Discharging Barreled Weapons and Firearms" offenses, this one only covers discharge of a firearm, not a barreled weapon.

Element (3). For the meaning of the term "occupied," see the note on Element (4) to "Discharging a Barreled Weapon or Firearm into Occupied Property" in the main volume. Note that this offense covers discharge of a firearm "within" the building, etc. The other "Discharging Barreled Weapons and Firearms" offenses cover discharging "into" the specified location.

Attempt. See this note to "Discharging a Barreled Weapon or Firearm into Occupied Property" in the main volume.

Multiple convictions and punishments. See this note to "Discharging a Barreled Weapon or Firearm into Occupied Property" in the main volume. This statute begins with the language, "Unless covered under some other provision of law providing greater punishment." For a discussion of the meaning of this phrase, see this note on "Assault Inflicting Serious Injury" in the main volume.

Related Offenses Not in This Chapter

See the offenses listed under "Discharging a Barreled Weapon or Firearm into Occupied Property" in the main volume.

Assault on a Female (page 133)

Notes (page 133)

Greater and lesser-included offenses (page 133)
Assault on a female is not a lesser-included offense of first-degree sexual offense. State v. Martin, 222 N.C. App. 213, 221–22 (2012).

Assaults Involving Children (page 133)

Assault in the Presence of a Minor (page 134)

Statute (page 134)

2015 legislation, S.L. 2015-62, sec. 4(b), amended G.S. 14-33(d)(2) as noted under "Simple Assault," above in this supplement.

Notes (page 135)

Element (4) (page 135)
Delete the first sentence of this note and replace it with the following:

"In the presence of a minor" means that the minor was in a position to see or hear the assault. G.S. 14-33(d)(2).

Female Genital Mutilation of a Child (new crime)

This offense was enacted by 2019 legislation, S.L. 2019-183, effective for offenses committed on or after October 1, 2019.

Statute

§ 14-28.1. Female genital mutilation of a child.
(a) Legislative Intent. – The General Assembly finds that female genital mutilation is a crime that causes a long-lasting impact on the victim's quality of life and has been recognized internationally as a violation of the human rights of girls and women. The practice is mostly carried out on girls under the age of 15 years old. The General Assembly also recognizes that the practice includes any procedure that intentionally alters or injures the female genital organs for nonmedical reasons. These procedures can cause severe pain, excessive bleeding, urinary problems, and death. Therefore, the General Assembly enacts this law to protect these vulnerable victims.
(b) Mutilation. – A person who knowingly and unlawfully circumcises, excises, or infibulates the whole or any part of the labia majora, labia minora, or clitoris of a child less than 18 years of age is guilty of a Class C felony.
(c) Consent to Mutilation. – A parent, or a person providing care to or supervision of a child less than 18 years of age, who consents to or permits the unlawful circumcision, excision, or infibulation, in whole or in any part, of the labia majora, labia minora, or clitoris of the child, is guilty of a Class C felony.
(d) Removal for Mutilation. – A parent, or a person providing care to or supervision of a child less than 18 years of age, who knowingly removes or permits the removal of the child from the State for the purpose of having the child's labia majora, labia minora, or clitoris circumcised, excised, or infibulated, is guilty of a Class C felony.
(e) Exceptions. – A surgical operation is not a violation of this section if the operation meets either of the following requirements: (1) The operation is necessary to the health of

the person on whom it is performed and is performed by a person licensed in the State as a medical practitioner. (2) The operation is performed on a person in labor who has just given birth and is performed for medical purposes connected with that labor or birth by a person licensed in this State as a medical practitioner or certified nurse midwife, or a person in training to become licensed as a medical practitioner or certified nurse midwife.

(f) No Defense. – It is not a defense to prosecution under this section that the person on whom the circumcision, excision, or infibulation is performed, or any other person, believes that the circumcision, excision, or infibulation is required as a matter of custom or ritual, or that the person on whom the circumcision, excision, or infibulation is performed consented to the circumcision, excision, or infibulation.

Elements

A person guilty of this offense

(1) knowingly and unlawfully
(2) (a) circumcises,
    (b) excises, *or*
    (c) infibulates
(3) the whole or part of the labia majora, labia minora, or clitoris
(4) of a child less than 18 years of age.

Punishment

Class C felony. G.S. 14-28.1(b).

Notes

Element (2). Circumcision, excision, and infibulation describe different procedures falling under the umbrella term of female genital mutilation. The term "circumcision"—though rejected by medical practitioners because it suggests a fallacious analogy to male circumcision—generally refers to a partial removal of the clitoris. In "excision," both the clitoris and labia minora are typically removed. In "infibulation," the clitoris and some or all of the labia minora are removed and the labia majora are cut and stitched, often to cover part of the vaginal opening. Martha C. Nussbaum, Sex and Social Justice 119–20 (1999).

Exceptions. Surgical operations are not a violation of this offense when performed (1) by a licensed medical practitioner for the health of the person on whom the procedure is performed or (2) by a licensed medical practitioner, certified midwife, or person in training to become licensed or certified on a person in labor or a person who has just given birth. G.S. 14-28.1(e). That the procedure is conducted as a matter of custom, ritual, or by consent is no defense to this offense. *Id.* § (f).

Related Offenses Not in This Chapter

Consenting to Genital Mutilation. G.S. 14-28.1(c).
Removal for Genital Mutilation. G.S. 14-28.1(d).
See "Child Abuse" offenses in Chapter 9 (Abuse and Neglect) of the main volume.

Assaults on Persons with Disabilities (page 139) (revised title)

Simple Assault on a Person with a Disability (page 139) (revised title)
Statute

2018 legislation, S.L. 2018-47, sec. 4(m), amended the statute to read as follows:

> **§ 14-32.1. Assaults on individuals with a disability; punishments.**
>
> (a) For purposes of this section, an "individual with a disability" is an individual who has one or more of the following that would substantially impair the ability to defend oneself:
>
> (1) A physical or mental disability, such as a decreased use of arms or legs, blindness, deafness, intellectual disability, or mental illness.
> (2) An infirmity.
>
> (b) through (d) Repealed by Session Laws 1993 (Reg. Sess., 1994), c. 767, s. 31, effective October 1, 1994.
>
> (e) Unless the conduct is covered under some other provision of law providing greater punishment, any person who commits any aggravated assault or assault and battery on an individual with a disability is guilty of a Class F felony. A person commits an aggravated assault or assault and battery upon an individual with a disability if, in the course of the assault or assault and battery, that person does any of the following:
>
> (1) Uses a deadly weapon or other means of force likely to inflict serious injury or serious damage to an individual with a disability.
> (2) Inflicts serious injury or serious damage to an individual with a disability.
> (3) Intends to kill an individual with a disability.
>
> (f) Any person who commits a simple assault or battery upon an individual with a disability is guilty of a Class A1 misdemeanor.

Elements (page 139)

As a result of the 2018 legislation noted above, the elements to this offense should now read:

A person guilty of this offense

(1) commits an assault or battery
(2) on an individual with a disability
(3) knowing or having reason to know that the individual has a disability.

Notes (page 139)

Terminology change (new note)

The 2018 legislation noted above replaced the statutory term "handicapped" with the term "individual with a disability." Except as updated here, the notes in the main volume continue to reference the old statutory term "handicapped" that was interpreted by the relevant case law.

Element (2) (page 139)

As a result of the 2018 legislation noted above, delete the first paragraph of this note and replace it with the following:

The statute defines an "individual with a disability" as a person who has one or both of the following conditions, substantially impairing the ability to defend: (1) a physical or mental disability, such as a decreased use of arms or legs, blindness, deafness, intellectual disability, or mental illness; or (2) an infirmity. G.S. 14-32.1(a).

Add the following to this note:

There was a sufficient factual basis to support a plea where the victim was 80 years old, crippled by arthritis in her knees, and walked with a crutch. State v. Collins, 221 N.C. App. 604, 607–08 (2012).

Aggravated Assault on a Person with a Disability (page 140) (revised title)

Elements (page 140)

As a result of the 2018 legislation noted above, the elements to this offense should now read:

A person guilty of this offense

    (1) commits an assault or battery

    (2) on an individual with a disability

    (3) knowing or having reason to know that the individual has a disability *and*

    (4) (a) uses a deadly weapon or other means of force likely to cause serious injury or serious damage to a person with a disability,

         (b) inflicts serious injury on a person with a disability, *or*

         (c) intends to kill a person with a disability.

Notes (page 140)

Terminology change (new note)

The 2018 legislation noted above replaced the statutory term "handicapped" with the term "individual with a disability." Except as updated here, the notes in the main volume continue to reference the old statutory term "handicapped" that was interpreted by the relevant case law and to reference the old name of the related offense "Simple Assault on a Handicapped Person."

Assaults on Government Officers, Employees, and Similar Persons (page 141)

Assault on a Governmental Officer or Employee (page 141)

Notes (page 141)

Element (2) (page 141)

Add the following to the second paragraph of this note:

For a case supporting the statement in this paragraph, see *State v. Mylett*, 253 N.C. App. 198, 209 (2017) (holding that the mens rea element of this offense "is satisfied whenever a defendant while in the course of assaulting another individual instead assaults an individual he knows, or reasonably should know, is a government officer"). *See also* State v. Burwell, 256 N.C. App. 722, 727 (2017) (proving assault inflicting serious bodily injury on an officer under G.S. 14-34.7(a) requires proof that the defendant knew or had reasonable grounds to know that the victim was a law enforcement officer).

The evidence was sufficient to show that the defendant knew or had reasonable grounds to know that the victim was a law enforcement officer where the officer arrived in a marked patrol vehicle, was uniformed, and told the defendant that he was a law enforcement officer. *Burwell*, 256 N.C. App. at 728.

Element (3) (page 141)

Add the following to the first paragraph of this note:

An officer was discharging the duties of his office when (1) after transporting the defendant to the jail and escorting him to a holding cell, the officer remained at the jail, State v. Friend, 237 N.C. App. 490, 495 (2014) (reasoning that by remaining at the jail, the officer was ensuring the safety of other officers), and (2) responding to a report about a trespasser, the officer was conducting investigative work and acting on the results of his investigation. *Burwell*, 256 N.C. App. at 728.

Delete the third paragraph of this note and replace it with the following:

> In *Friend*, the court stated that "unlike the offense of resisting, delaying, or obstructing an officer, criminal liability for the offense of assaulting an officer is not limited to situations where an officer is engaging in lawful conduct in the performance or attempted performance of his or her official duties." *Friend*, 237 N.C. App. at 495 (citation omitted). *See also Burwell*, 256 N.C. App. at 728 (citing *Friend* for this proposition).

Assault with a Firearm on a Law Enforcement Officer, Probation or Parole Officer, Member of the National Guard, or Detention Facility Employee (page 145) (revised title)

Statute (page 145)

2015 legislation, S.L. 2015-74, sec. 2, changed the title of the statute and added a new subsection, (a1), to the statute to read as follows:

> **§ 14-34.5. Assault with a firearm on a law enforcement, probation, or parole officer, or on a member of the North Carolina National Guard, or on a person employed at a State or local detention facility.**
> (a1) Any person who commits an assault with a firearm upon a member of the North Carolina National Guard while the member is in the performance of his or her duties is guilty of a Class E felony.

Elements (page 145)

As a result of the 2015 legislation noted immediately above, Element (3) should read as follows:

> (3) on a
> (a) law enforcement officer,
> (b) probation officer,
> (c) parole officer,
> (d) member of the North Carolina National Guard, *or*
> (e) state or local government detention facility employee

Punishment (page 145)

2019 legislation, S.L. 2019-116, increases the punishment for this offense for offenses committed on or after December 1, 2019, when committed against certain victims as follows:

> Class E felony if committed against a member of the North Carolina National Guard. G.S. 14-34.5(a1). Class D felony if committed against a law enforcement officer, probation officer, parole officer, or state or local government detention facility employee. *Id.* §§ (a), (b).

Assault Inflicting Physical Injury on a Law Enforcement Officer, Probation or Parole Officer, Member of the National Guard, or Detention Facility Employee (page 146) (revised title)

Statute (page 146)

2015 legislation, S.L. 2015-74, sec. 1, amended the statute to read as follows:

> **§ 14-34.7. Certain assaults on a law enforcement, probation, or parole officer, or on a member of the North Carolina National Guard, or on a person employed at a State or local detention facility; penalty.**
> (a) Unless covered under some other provision of law providing greater punishment, a person is guilty of a Class F felony if the person assaults a law enforcement officer, probation officer, or parole officer while the officer is discharging or attempting to discharge his or her official duties and inflicts serious bodily injury on the officer.

(a1) Unless covered under some other provision of law providing greater punishment, a person is guilty of a Class F felony if the person assaults a member of the North Carolina National Guard while he or she is discharging or attempting to discharge his or her official duties and inflicts serious bodily injury on the member.

(b) Unless covered under some other provision of law providing greater punishment, a person is guilty of a Class F felony if the person assaults a person who is employed at a detention facility operated under the jurisdiction of the State or a local government while the employee is in the performance of the employee's duties and inflicts serious bodily injury on the employee.

(c) Unless covered under some other provision of law providing greater punishment, a person is guilty of a Class I felony if the person does any of the following:

(1) Assaults a law enforcement officer, probation officer, or parole officer while the officer is discharging or attempting to discharge his or her official duties and inflicts physical injury on the officer.

(2) Assaults a person who is employed at a detention facility operated under the jurisdiction of the State or a local government while the employee is in the performance of the employee's duties and inflicts physical injury on the employee.

(3) Assaults a member of the North Carolina National Guard while he or she is discharging or attempting to discharge his or her official duties and inflicts physical injury on the member.

For the purposes of this subsection, "physical injury" includes cuts, scrapes, bruises, or other physical injury which does not constitute serious injury.

Elements (page 147)

As a result of the 2015 legislation noted immediately above, Element (2) should read as follows:

(2) on a
   (a) law enforcement officer,
   (b) probation officer,
   (c) parole officer,
   (d) member of the North Carolina National Guard, *or*
   (e) state or local government detention facility employee

Assault Inflicting Serious Injury or Serious Bodily Injury on a Law Enforcement Officer, Probation or Parole Officer, Member of the National Guard, or Detention Facility

Employee (page 147) (revised title)

Statute (page 147)

As a result of the 2015 legislation noted above, the statutory citation in this section should read as follows:

See G.S. 14-34.7(a), (a1), and (b).

Elements (page 147)

As a result of the 2015 legislation noted above, Element (2) should read as follows:

(2) on a
   (a) law enforcement officer,
   (b) probation officer,
   (c) parole officer,
   (d) member of the North Carolina National Guard, *or*
   (e) state or local government detention facility employee.

Punishment (page 148)

Delete the citation in this section and replace it with the following:

G.S. 14-34.7.

Notes (page 148)

Element (4) (page 148)

2015 legislation, S.L. 2015-74, sec. 1, revised the title of this offense, deleting the words "serious injury" and thus calling into question the reasoning of the *Crawford* case cited in this note. If this statutory change was meant to abrogate *Crawford*, only proof of serious bodily injury would satisfy the statute.

In *State v. Williams*, 255 N.C. App. 168 (2017), the court had to determine whether the evidence was sufficient to show serious bodily injury. The trial court had instructed the jury that "[s]erious bodily injury is an injury that creates or causes serious permanent disfigurement, a permanent or protracted condition that causes extreme pain, or permanent or protracted loss or impairment of the function of any bodily member or organ." *Id.* at 179. The *Williams* court determined that "[b]ecause the trial court limited its instruction concerning serious bodily injury to the above, we do not consider any other potential definitions of 'serious bodily injury.'" *Id.*

Malicious Conduct by a Prisoner (page 148)

Statute (page 148)

2017 legislation, S.L. 2017-186, sec. 2(gg), amended the statute, and 2018 legislation, S.L. 2018-67, sec. 2, substantially rewrote it to read as follows:

> **§ 14-258.4. Malicious conduct by prisoner.**
> (a) Any prisoner who knowingly and willfully throws, emits, or causes to be used as a projectile, any bodily fluids, excrement, or unknown substance at an employee, while the employee is in the performance of the employee's duties, is guilty of a Class F felony.
> (b) Any prisoner who knowingly and willfully exposes genitalia to an employee while the employee is in the performance of the employee's duties is guilty of a Class I felony.
> (c) The provisions of this section apply to violations committed inside or outside of the prison, jail, detention center, or other confinement facility.
> (d) Sentences imposed under this Article shall run consecutively to and shall commence at the expiration of any sentence being served by the person sentenced under this section.

Elements (page 148)

As a result of the legislation noted above, the elements of this offense should read as follows:

A person guilty of this offense

(1) while a prisoner
(2) knowingly and willfully
(3) throws, emits, or causes to be used as a projectile, any bodily fluids, excrement, or unknown substance
(4) at an employee, while the employee is in the performance of the employee's duties.

Punishment (page 149)

As a result of the 2018 legislation noted above, add the following to this section:

This offense is in G.S. Chapter 14, Article 33 (Prison Breach and Prisoners). The statute provides that "[s]entences imposed under this Article shall run consecutively to and shall commence at the expiration of any sentence being served by the person sentenced under this section." G.S. 14-258.4(d). This appears to mean that any sentence imposed for an Article 33 offense must run consecutively to a sentence being served for this offense.

Notes (page 149)

Generally (new note)

The 2018 legislation noted above substantially rewrote the statute. The notes in the main volume continue to apply to prosecutions initiated under the old statute and to the new statute to the extent there is overlap.

Element (1) (under amended version of the statute)

Prior to the 2018 amendments, the statute applied to certain persons in the "custody" of specified entities. As amended in 2018, it now applies to any "prisoner," but the definition of that term tracks the old statutory language. Specifically, the term "prisoner" includes any person in the custody of the Division of Adult Correction and Juvenile Justice of the Department of Public Safety, any law enforcement officer, or any local confinement facility as defined in G.S. 153A-217 or -230.1, including persons pending trial, appellate review, or presentence diagnostic evaluation. G.S. 14-254.5(2).

The offense need not occur at a custodial facility; the statute specifies that the offense applies to conduct "committed inside or outside of the prison, jail, detention center, or other confinement facility." G.S. 14-258.4(c).

Element (4) (under amended version of the statute)

An employee is defined to mean any person hired or contracted to work for the State or for a local government. G.S. 14-254.5(1).

Multiple convictions and punishments (page 149)

A defendant may be convicted of two counts of this offense for two acts that occurred during one incident. State v. Heavner, 227 N.C. App. 139, 146 (2013) (the defendant spit on an officer's forehead while the defendant was in a house; five minutes later he spit on the officer's arm after being taken out of the house).

Related Offenses Not in This Chapter (page 149)

Prisoner exposing genitalia to employee. G.S. 14-258.4(b) (enacted by S.L. 2018-67, sec. 2).

Assault on an Executive, Legislative, or Court Officer (page 150)

Statute (page 150)

2014 legislation, S.L. 2014-119, sec. 6(a), amended G.S. 14-16.6(a) to read as follows:

> (a) Any person who assaults any legislative officer, executive officer, or court officer, or assaults another person as retaliation against any legislative officer, executive officer, or court officer because of the exercise of that officer's duties, or any person who makes a violent attack upon the residence, office, temporary accommodation or means of transport of any one of those officers or persons in a manner likely to endanger the officer or person, shall be guilty of a felony and shall be punished as a Class I felon.

2014 legislation, S.L. 2014-100, sec. 17.1(v), amended G.S. 14-19.9 to read as follows:

> Any person who has been elected to any office covered by this Article but has not yet taken the oath of office shall be considered to hold the office for the purpose of this Article and G.S. 143B-919.

Elements (page 150)

As a result of the legislative changes noted above, Element (2) should read as follows:

(2) any
   (a) executive officer,
   (b) legislative officer,
   (c) court officer, *or*
   (d) other person as retaliation against any executive officer, legislative officer, or court officer because of the exercise of that officer's duties.

Notes (page 150)

Additional conduct included within statute (page 151)

As a result of the first legislative change noted above, replace the text of this note with the following:

The statute also prohibits a violent attack on the residence, office, temporary accommodation, or means of transport of any covered officer in a manner likely to endanger the officer, as well as a similar attack on the residence, office, temporary accommodation, or means of transport of any person as retaliation against any executive officer, legislative officer, or court officer because of the exercise of that officer's duties. G.S. 14-16.6(a).

Assaults on Firefighters and Emergency and Medical Personnel (page 155)

Assault on a Firefighter or Medical Personnel Inflicting Physical Injury (page 155)
(revised title)

Statute (page 155)

2015 legislation, S.L. 2015-97, amended both the title of the statute and subsection (a)(3), as further amended by 2019 legislation, S.L. 2019-228, to read as follows:

§ 14-34.6. Assault or affray on a firefighter, an emergency medical technician, medical responder, and hospital personnel.
   (a)(3) Hospital personnel and licensed healthcare providers who are providing or attempting to provide health care services to a patient.

2017 legislation, S.L. 2017-57, sec. 16B.3(a), added a new subsection, (a)(6), as follows:

   (6) Hospital security personnel.

Elements (page 156)

As a result of the 2015, 2017, and 2019 legislation noted above, Elements (2)(d) through new Element (2)(f) should read as follows:

   (d) a medical responder,
   (e) hospital personnel and licensed healthcare providers who are providing or attempting to provide healthcare services to a patient, *or*
   (f) hospital security personnel.

Assault on a Firefighter or Medical Personnel Inflicting Serious Injury or Inflicting Physical Injury and Using a Deadly Weapon Other Than a Firearm (page 157) (revised title)

Elements (page 157)

As a result of the 2015, 2017, and 2019 legislation noted above, Elements (2)(d) through new Element (2)(f) should read as follows:

> (d) a medical responder,
> (e) hospital personnel and licensed healthcare providers who are providing or attempting to provide healthcare services to a patient, *or*
> (f) hospital security personnel.

Element (4)(b) of this offense should read:

> causes physical injury and uses a deadly weapon other than a firearm.

Punishment (page 157)

As a result of the 2019 legislation noted above, the punishment for this offense is amended as follows, effective for offenses committed on or after December 1, 2019:

> Class G felony. G.S. 14-34.6(b).

Assault on a Firefighter or Medical Personnel Causing Physical Injury and with a Firearm (page 158) (revised title)

Elements (page 158)

As a result of the 2015, 2017, and 2019 legislation noted above, Elements (2)(d) through new Element (2)(f) should read as follows:

> (d) a medical responder,
> (e) hospital personnel and licensed healthcare providers who are providing or attempting to provide healthcare services to a patient, *or*
> (f) hospital security personnel.

Revise Element (4) and add Element (5) as follows:

> (4) causes physical injury *and*
> (5) uses a firearm.

Punishment (page 158)

As a result of the 2019 legislation noted above, the punishment for this offense is amended as follows, effective for offenses committed on or after December 1, 2019:

> Class E felony. G.S. 14-34.6(c).

Habitual Misdemeanor Assault (page 161)

Notes (page 161)

Element (1)(a)(ii) (page 161)

Add the following citations after the first sentence of this note:

> G.S. 14-33.2; State v. Garrison, 225 N.C. App. 170, 174 (2013) (trial court erred by failing to instruct the jury that the assault under G.S. 14-33 must have inflicted physical injury).

Malicious Injury by Use of an Explosive or Incendiary (page 164)

Related Offenses Not in This Chapter (page 164)

Remove the following offense from this list:

> Transporting dangerous weapon or substance during emergency; possessing off premises; exceptions. G.S. 14-288.7.

8
Threats, Harassment, Stalking, and Violation of Domestic Protective Orders

Communicating Threats (page 167)

Notes (page 167)

Element (4) (page 168)

For a case where the State presented sufficient evidence that a detention officer believed that the defendant—an inmate—would carry out his threats against her, see *State v. Hill*, 227 N.C. App. 371, 378–80 (2013).

Related Offenses Not in This Chapter (page 168)

Add the following offenses to this list:

Cyberbullying of school employee by student. G.S. 14-458.2.

Threat of Mass Violence on Educational Property or Place of Worship. G.S. 14-277.6; -277.7, *as enacted by* S.L. 2018-72, secs. 1–2.

Threat to Kill or Inflict Serious Injury on Executive, Legislative, or Court Officers (page 168)

Statute (page 168)

2014 legislation, S.L. 2014-119, sec. 6(b), amended G.S. 14-16.7 to read as follows:

(a) Any person who knowingly and willfully makes any threat to inflict serious bodily injury upon or to kill any legislative officer, executive officer, or court officer, or who knowingly and willfully makes any threat to inflict serious bodily injury upon or kill any other person as retaliation against any legislative officer, executive officer, or court officer because of the exercise of that officer's duties, shall be guilty of a felony and shall be punished as a Class I felon.

(b) Any person who knowingly and willfully deposits for conveyance in the mail any letter, writing, or other document containing a threat to commit an offense described in subsection (a) of this section shall be guilty of a felony and shall be punished as a Class I felon.

Elements (page 169)

As a result of the legislative change noted above, Element (5) should read as follows:

(5) any
    (a) executive officer,
    (b) legislative officer,
    (c) court officer, *or*
    (d) any person as retaliation against any executive officer, legislative officer, or court officer because of the exercise of that officer's duties.

Harassing Telephone Calls (page 169)

Using Threatening Language on the Telephone (page 170)
Related Offenses Not in This Chapter (page 171)

Remove the following offense from this list:

False report of emergency. G.S. 14-401.8.

Cyberstalking (page 174)
Statute (page 174)

2015 legislation, S.L. 2015-282, added new subsections (a)(3) and (4) as follows:

(3) Electronic tracking device.—An electronic or mechanical device that permits a person to remotely determine or track the position and movement of another person.

(4) Fleet vehicle.—Any of the following: (i) one or more motor vehicles owned by a single entity and operated by employees or agents of the entity for business or government purposes, (ii) motor vehicles held for lease or rental to the general public, or (iii) motor vehicles held for sale, or used as demonstrators, test vehicles, or loaner vehicles, by motor vehicle dealers.

That same legislation added a new subsection, (b)(5), as follows:

(5) Knowingly install, place, or use an electronic tracking device without consent, or cause an electronic tracking device to be installed, placed, or used without consent, to track the location of any person. The provisions of this subdivision do not apply to the installation, placement, or use of an electronic tracking device by any of the following:

    a. A law enforcement officer, judicial officer, probation or parole officer, or employee of the Division of Corrections, Department of Public Safety, when any such person is engaged in the lawful performance of official duties and in accordance with State or federal law.

    b. The owner or lessee of any vehicle on which the owner or lessee installs, places, or uses an electronic tracking device, unless the owner or lessee is subject to (i) a domestic violence protective order under Chapter 50B of the General Statutes or (ii) any court order that orders the owner or lessee not to assault, threaten, harass, follow, or contact a driver or occupant of the vehicle.

c. A legal guardian for a disabled adult, as defined in G.S. 108A-101(d), or a legally authorized individual or organization designated to provide protective services to a disabled adult pursuant to G.S. 108A-105(c), when the electronic tracking device is installed, placed, or used to track the location of the disabled adult for which the person is a legal guardian or the individual or organization is designated to provide protective services.

d. The owner of fleet vehicles, when tracking such vehicles.

e. A creditor or other secured party under a retail installment agreement involving the sale of a motor vehicle or the lessor under a retail lease of a motor vehicle, and any assignee or successor in interest to that creditor, secured party, or lessor, when tracking a motor vehicle identified as security under the retail installment sales agreement or leased pursuant to a retail lease agreement, including the installation, placement, or use of an electronic tracking device to locate and remotely disable the motor vehicle, with the express written consent of the purchaser, borrower, or lessee of the motor vehicle.

f. The installation, placement, or use of an electronic tracking device authorized by an order of a State or federal court.

g. A motor vehicle manufacturer, its subsidiary, or its affiliate that installs or uses an electronic tracking device in conjunction with providing a vehicle subscription telematics service, provided that the customer subscribes or consents to that service.

h. A parent or legal guardian of a minor when the electronic tracking device is installed, placed, or used to track the location of that minor unless the parent or legal guardian is subject to a domestic violence protective order under Chapter 50B of the General Statutes or any court order that orders the parent or legal guardian not to assault, threaten, harass, follow, or contact that minor or that minor's parent, legal guardian, custodian, or caretaker as defined in G.S. 7B-101.

i. An employer, when providing a communication device to an employee or contractor for use in connection with his or her work for the employer.

j. A business, if the tracking is incident to the provision of a product or service requested by the person, except as limited in sub-subdivision k. of this subdivision.

k. A private detective or private investigator licensed under Chapter 74C of the General Statutes, provided that (i) the tracking is pursuant to authority under G.S. 74C-3(a)(8), (ii) the tracking is not otherwise contrary to law, and (iii) the person being tracked is not under the protection of a domestic violence protective order under Chapter 50B of the General Statutes or any other court order that protects against assault, threat, harassment, following, or contact.

Unauthorized Use of Electronic Tracking Device (new crime)

This offense was created by the 2015 legislation noted immediately above.

Statute

See G.S. 14-196.3(b)(5), reproduced above in this supplement.

Elements

A person guilty of this offense

    (1) knowingly *and*

    (2) without consent

    (3) (a) installs, places, or uses an electronic tracking device *or*

        (b) causes an electronic tracking device to be installed, placed, or used

    (4) to track the location of any person.

Punishment

Class 2 misdemeanor. G.S. 14-196.3(d).

Notes

Element (1). See "Knowingly" in Chapter 1 (States of Mind).

Element (3). An "electronic tracking device" refers to an electronic or mechanical device that permits a person to remotely determine or track the position and movement of another. G.S. 14-196.3(a)(3).

Exceptions. See this note to "Using Electronic Mail or Communication to Threaten or Extort" in the main volume.

G.S. 14-196.3(b)(5), reproduced above, sets out eleven exceptions to this offense, including, among others, exceptions for law enforcement officers engaged in their duties, owners of fleet vehicles, certain creditors, and private detectives and private investigators in certain circumstances.

Related Offenses Not in This Chapter

None.

Cyberbullying (page 179)

Statute (page 179)

2012 legislation, S.L. 2012-149, sec. 3, amended G.S. 14-458.1(a)(3) to read as follows:

    (3) Make any statement, whether true or false, intending to immediately provoke, and that is likely to provoke, any third party to stalk or harass a minor.

That same legislation amended G.S. 14-458.1(a)(5) and (6) to read as follows:

    (5) Sign up a minor for a pornographic Internet site with the intent to intimidate or torment the minor.

    (6) Without authorization of the minor or the minor's parent or guardian, sign up a minor for electronic mailing lists or to receive junk electronic messages and instant messages, with the intent to intimidate or torment the minor.

Elements (page 180)

Elements (2)(c), (e), and (f) should be revised to conform to the legislative changes noted above. Element 2(c) should be revised to read:

(c) to make any statement intending to immediately provoke, and that is likely to provoke, any third party to stalk or harass a minor,

Elements (2)(e) and (f) should be revised to read:

(e) sign up a minor for a pornographic Internet site with the intent to intimidate or torment the minor, *or*

(f) without authorization of the minor or the minor's parent or guardian, sign up a minor for electronic mailing lists or to receive junk electronic messages and instant messages, with the intent to intimidate or torment the minor.

Notes (page 181)

Element (2)(a) (page 181)

2012 legislation, S.L. 2012-149, sec. 2, amended G.S. 14-453(7c) to include within the meaning of the term "profile" "a Web site user's personal page or section of a page made up of data, in text or graphical form, which displays significant, unique, or identifying information, including, but not limited to, listing acquaintances, interests, associations, activities, or personal statements."

Constitutionality (new note)

In *State v. Bishop*, 368 N.C. 869 (2016), the state supreme court held that G.S. 14-458.1(a)(1)d. is unconstitutional; that portion of the cyberbullying statute criminalizes use of a computer or computer network, with the intent to intimidate or torment a minor, to post or encourage others to post on the Internet private, personal, or sexual information pertaining to a minor and is listed as Element (2)(a)(iv) in the main volume of this book. The court found that the provision restricts speech; the restriction is content based; and the statute is not narrowly tailored to the State's asserted interest in protecting children from the harms of online bullying; it thus concluded that the provision violates the First Amendment to the U.S. Constitution. *Id.* at 872–80.

Related Offenses Not in This Chapter (page 181)

Add the following offense to this list:

Cyberbullying of school employee by student. G.S. 14-458.2.

Stalking (page 182)

Misdemeanor Stalking (page 183)

Notes (page 183)

Constitutionality (page 184)

As applied to a defendant who posted unwelcome comments about a victim on social media, the court of appeals deemed North Carolina's stalking statute a content-based restriction on speech that violates the First Amendment to the U.S. Constitution. Other non-expressive conduct by the defendant, including delivering gifts to the victim's workplace or emailing the victim's friend, were not constitutionally protected. State v. Shackelford, ___ N.C. App. ___, 825 S.E.2d 689 (2019). A prior version of the stalking statute was upheld in the face of a challenge that it was unconstitutionally vague. State v. Watson, 169 N.C. App. 331 (2005).

Jury instructions (new note)

When the charged conduct encompasses conduct occurring both before and after statutory amendments that changed the elements of this offense, the trial court must submit a special verdict form to the jury. State v. Williams, 226 N.C. App. 393, 401 (2013) (plain error to fail to do so).

Stalking When a Court Order Is in Place (page 186)

Notes (page 186)

Element (5) (page 186)

This Element is satisfied when the order is a pretrial release order specifying that the defendant have no contact with the victim. State v. Mitchell, 259 N.C. App. 866, ___, 817 S.E.2d 455, 458 (2018) (rejecting the defendant's argument that he was not subject to pretrial release orders because he never posted bond and remained in jail when he contacted the victim).

Violation of a Domestic Violence Protective Order (page 186)

Misdemeanor Violation of a Domestic Violence Protective Order (page 187)

Notes (page 187)

Element (1) (page 187)

For a case where the evidence was insufficient to establish that the defendant knowingly violated a domestic violence protective order (DVPO), see State v. Williams, 226 N.C. App. 393, 406 (2013) (DVPO required the defendant to "stay away from" the victim's place of work without identifying her workplace; there was no evidence that the defendant was aware that the victim worked at the location he visited).

Element (2) (new note)

The evidence was insufficient to establish that the defendant violated a DVPO provision that he "stay away from" the victim's workplace when he was seen at a mall parking lot when the victim was working at a salon in the mall. Williams, 226 N.C. App. at 410 (the defendant was not in a location that would permit him to harass, communicate with, follow, or even observe the victim).

Element (2)(a) (page 187)

Add the following citation at the end of the last paragraph of this note:

State v. Poole, 228 N.C. App. 248, 259 (2013) (pursuant to legislative amendments to the statute, an ex parte DVPO is valid).

Add the following text to the end of this note:

Although a 2012 case held that a consent DVPO that lacks a finding that the defendant committed an act of domestic violence is void ab initio, Kenton v. Kenton, 218 N.C. App. 603 (2012), and cannot support a charge under this statute, 2013 legislation changed that rule. Specifically, S.L. 2013-237 amended G.S. 50B-3 to provide that a consent protective order may be entered without findings of fact and conclusions of law if the parties agree in writing. The statute further provides that such a consent protective order is valid and enforceable.

Repeat Violation of a Domestic Violence Protective Order (page 188)

Notes (page 189)

Multiple convictions and punishments (page 189)

Delete all text after the first sentence of this note and replace it with the following:

Thus, a defendant may not be convicted of this offense and another that is sentenced more severely when the convictions are based on the same conduct. State v. Jones, 237 N.C. App. 526, 530–32 (2014) (trial court erred by sentencing the defendant for felony violation of a domestic violence protective order (Class H felony) and interfering with a witness (Class G felony) based on the same conduct). For a discussion of this issue in the assault context, see this note under "Assault Inflicting Serious Injury" in Chapter 7 (Assaults).

Violation of a Domestic Violence Protective Order with a Deadly Weapon (page 189)

Related Offenses Not in This Chapter (page 190)

Add the following offense to this list:

Purchase or possession of firearms by person subject to domestic violence order prohibited. G.S. 14-269.8; 50B-3.1(j).

Entering Domestic Violence Safe House or Haven (page 190)

Notes (page 190)

Element (3) (page 190)

For a defendant to be guilty of this offense, the State need not show that the defendant actually entered the building housing the safe house or haven; it need only prove that the defendant entered the real property on which the building was located. State v. Williams, 247 N.C. App. 239, 242 (2016).

9

Abuse and Neglect

Child Abuse (page 193)

Misdemeanor Child Abuse (page 193)

Notes (page 193)

Element (2) (page 194)

For cases where the evidence was sufficient as to this Element, see *State v. Reed*, 371 N.C. App. 106 (2018) (per curiam) (the state supreme court reversed the court of appeals for the reasons stated in the dissent; the evidence showed that while the defendant used the bathroom in her home for a few minutes, her toddler fell into an outdoor pool and drowned; in the opinion below, the dissenting judge concluded that the State presented sufficient evidence of the defendant's failure to supervise the child); *State v. Osborne*, ___ N.C. App. ___, 821 S.E.2d 268 (2018) (officers found the defendant unconscious from an apparent drug overdose in a hotel room, where they also found the defendant's two young children and drug paraphernalia; after the defendant was revived she admitting having used heroin), *rev'd on other grounds*, 372 N.C. 619 (2019); *State v. Watkins*, 247 N.C. App. 391, 395–96 (2016) (the defendant left a 2-year-old alone in a vehicle and out of her sight line for more than six minutes; one of the vehicle's windows was open, the outside temperature was 18 degrees, and weather included sleet, snow, and wind; the court relied on the harsh weather conditions, the child's young age, and the danger of him being abducted or subjected to physical harm).

Child abuse reporting (page 194)

As a result of 2013 legislation, S.L. 2013-52, sec. 7, delete the text of this note and replace it with the following:

G.S. 7B-301(a) requires any person or institution suspecting that a child has been abused to report the incident to the local director of the local social services department. Any person or institution that knowingly or wantonly fails to make the required report or that knowingly or wantonly prevents another person from making a report is guilty of a Class 1 misdemeanor. G.S. 7B-301(b). Additionally, any director of social services who receives a report of a juvenile's sexual abuse in a child care facility and who knowingly fails to notify the State Bureau of Investigation is guilty of a Class 1 misdemeanor. *Id.* § (c).

Multiple convictions and punishments (page 195)

For a case where the State sufficiently proved three instances of felony child abuse, see *State v. Lanford*, 225 N.C. App. 189, 204 (2013) (rejecting the argument that the fact that the assaults were part of chronic and continual abuse precluded such a holding).

Related Offenses Not in This Chapter (page 195)

Add the following offenses to this list:

> "Sale, Surrender, or Purchase of a Minor," in Chapter 12 (Kidnapping and Related Offenses) of this supplement.
>
> Unlawful transfer of custody of minor child. G.S. 14-321.2.

Replace the last offense in this list with the following:

> Unlawful payments related to adoption. G.S. 48-10-102.

Child Abuse—Inflicting Serious Mental or Physical Injury (page 195)

Statute (page 195)

2013 legislation, S.L. 2013-35, modified the punishments set out in G.S. 14-318.4 for felony child abuse as described below.

Another piece of 2013 legislation, S.L. 2013-52, sec. 3, added a new subsection, (a6), as follows:

> (a6) For purposes of this section, a "grossly negligent omission" in providing care to or supervision of a child includes the failure to report a child as missing to law enforcement as provided in G.S. 14-318.5(b).

Punishment (page 196)

2013 legislation, S.L. 2013-35, increased the punishment for this offense from a Class E to a Class D felony.

Notes (page 196)

Element (2) (page 196)

For another case holding that when the State proceeds under Element (2)(b), it need not prove that the defendant intended to inflict serious injury, see *State v. Frazier*, 248 N.C. App. 252, 260–61 (2016) (the State need only prove that the assault was intentional and that it resulted in serious injury).

Child Abuse—Willful Act or Omission Causing Serious Mental or Physical Injury (page 197)

Punishment (page 198)

2013 legislation, S.L. 2013-35, increased the punishment for this offense from a Class H to a Class G felony.

Notes (page 198)

Element (2)(b) (new note)

Failing to report the disappearance of a child as required by G.S. 14-318.5(b) constitutes a grossly negligent omission. G.S. 14-318.4(a6); see "Failure to Report the Disappearance of a Child" (new crime), below in this supplement.

Child Abuse—Inflicting Serious Bodily Injury or Mental or Emotional Injury (page 198)

Punishment (page 199)

The 2013 legislation cited immediately above increased the punishment for this offense from a Class C to a Class B2 felony.

Notes (page 199)

Element (3)(a) (page 199)

There was sufficient evidence of serious bodily injury where the victim experienced subarachnoid hemorrhaging. State v. Bohannon, 247 N.C. App. 756, 763 (2016).

Child Abuse—Willful Act or Omission Causing Serious Bodily Injury (page 200)

Notes (page 200)

Element (2)(b) (new note)

Failing to report the disappearance of a child as required by G.S. 14-318.5(b) constitutes a grossly negligent omission. G.S. 14-318.4(a6); see "Failure to Report the Disappearance of a Child" (new crime), below in this supplement.

Child Abuse—Prostitution (page 201)

Punishment (page 201)

The 2013 legislation cited above increased the punishment for this offense from a Class E to a Class D felony.

Related Offenses Not in This Chapter (page 201)

Add the following offense to this list:

> "Sale, Surrender, or Purchase of a Minor," in Chapter 12 (Kidnapping and Related Offenses) of this supplement.

Replace the last offense in this list with the following:

> Unlawful payments related to adoption. G.S. 48-10-102.

Child Abuse—Sexual Act (page 202)

Punishment (page 202)

The 2013 legislation cited above increased the punishment for this offense from a Class E to a Class D felony.

Notes (page 202)

Element (2)(a) (page 202)

The text of this note discusses whether the definition of "sexual act" in G.S. 14-27.1(4), recodified by 2015 legislation, S.L. 2015-181, sec. 2, as G.S. 14-27.20(4), applies to this offense. Delete the text of this note and replace it with the following:

> The term "sexual act" is undefined for this offense, and recent case law interpreting its meaning is conflicting. In *State v. Alonzo*, ___ N.C. App. ___, 819 S.E.2d 584, *discretionary review allowed in part*, 371 N.C. 778 (2018) (mem.), the court of appeals concluded that the definition in G.S. 14-27.20(4) applies. That statute defines sexual act to include cunnilingus, fellatio, analingus, anal intercourse, or the penetration by any object into the genital or anal opening of another person's body, but not vaginal intercourse. In *State v. Gonzales*, ___ N.C. App. ___, 823 S.E.2d 886 (2019), however, the court deemed its prior precedent in *State v. McClamb*, 234 N.C. App. 753 (2014), controlling and held that vaginal intercourse is included within the definition of sexual act as it is used in G.S. 14-318.4(a2).

Failure to Report Crimes Against Juveniles (new crime)

Statute

§ 14-318.6. Failure to report crimes against juveniles; penalty.

(a) Definitions. – As used in this section, the following definitions apply:

(1) Juvenile. – As defined in G.S. 7B-101. For the purposes of this section, the age of the juvenile at the time of the abuse or offense governs.

(2) Serious bodily injury. – As defined in G.S. 14-318.4(d).

(3) Serious physical injury. – As defined in G.S. 14-318.4(d).

(4) Sexually violent offense. – An offense committed against a juvenile that is a sexually violent offense as defined in G.S. 14-208.6(5). This term also includes the following: an attempt, solicitation, or conspiracy to commit any of these offenses; aiding and abetting any of these offenses.

(5) Violent offense. – Any offense that inflicts upon the juvenile serious bodily injury or serious physical injury by other than accidental means. This term also includes the following: an attempt, solicitation, or conspiracy to commit any of these offenses; aiding and abetting any of these offenses.

(b) Requirement. – Any person 18 years of age or older who knows or should have reasonably known that a juvenile has been or is the victim of a violent offense, sexual offense, or misdemeanor child abuse under G.S. 14-318.2 shall immediately report the case of that juvenile to the appropriate local law enforcement agency in the county where the juvenile resides or is found. The report may be made orally or by telephone. The report shall include information as is known to the person making it, including the name, address, and age of the juvenile; the name and address of the juvenile's parent, guardian, custodian, or caretaker; the name, address, and age of the person who committed the offense against the juvenile; the location where the offense was committed; the names and ages of other juveniles present or in danger; the present whereabouts of the juvenile, if not at the home address; the nature and extent of any injury or condition resulting from the offense or abuse; and any other information which the person making the report believes might be helpful in establishing the need for law enforcement involvement. The person making the report shall give his or her name, address, and telephone number.

(c) Penalty. – Any person 18 years of age or older, who knows or should have reasonably known that a juvenile was the victim of a violent offense, sexual offense, or misdemeanor child abuse under G.S. 14-318.2, and knowingly or willfully fails to report as required by subsection (b) of this section, or who knowingly or willfully prevents another person from reporting as required by subsection (b) of this section, is guilty of a Class 1 misdemeanor.

(d) Construction. – Nothing in this section shall be construed as relieving a person subject to the requirement set forth in subsection (b) of this section from any other duty to report required by law.

(e) Protection. – The identity of a person making a report pursuant to this section must be protected and only revealed as provided in G.S. 132-1.4(c)(4).

(f) Good-Faith Immunity. – A person who makes a report in good faith under this Article, cooperates with law enforcement in an investigation, or testifies in any judicial proceeding resulting from a law enforcement report or investigation is immune from any civil or criminal liability that might otherwise be incurred or imposed for that action, provided that person was acting in good faith.

(g) Law Enforcement Duty to Report Evidence to the Department of Social Services. – If any law enforcement officer, as the result of a report, finds evidence that a juvenile may be abused, neglected, or dependent as defined in G.S. 7B-101, the law enforcement officer shall make an oral report as soon as practicable and make a subsequent written report of the findings to the director of the department of social services within 48 hours after discovery of the evidence. When a report of abuse, neglect, or dependency is received, the director of the department of social services shall make a prompt and thorough assessment, in accordance with G.S. 7B-302, to determine whether protective services should be provided or the complaint filed as a petition.

(h) Nothing in this section shall be construed as to require a person with a privilege under G.S. 8-53.3, 8-53.7, 8-53.8, or 8-53.12 or with attorney-client privilege to report pursuant to this section if that privilege would prevent them from doing so.

Elements

A person guilty of this offense

    (1) is any person

    (2) 18 years of age or older

    (3) who

        (a) knows *or*

        (b) should have reasonably known

    (4) that a juvenile has been or is the victim of

        (a) a violent offense,

        (b) a sexual offense, *or*

        (c) misdemeanor child abuse under G.S. 14-318.2, *and*

    (5) knowingly or willfully

    (6) (a) fails to report as required by G.S. 14-318.6(b) *or*

        (b) prevents another person from reporting as required by G.S. 14-318.6(b).

Punishment

Class 1 misdemeanor. G.S. 14-318.6(c).

Notes

Element (1). This offense can apply to any person over the age of 18; no special relationship with the victim is required.

Element (4). "Juvenile" is a person who is younger than 18 years of age and is not married, emancipated, or a member of the United States Armed Forces. G.S. 7B-101(14). The person's age at the time of the enumerated offenses applies. *Id.* § 14-318.6(a)(1).

Element (4)(a). "Violent offense" is defined in G.S. 14-318.6(a)(5) as "[a]ny offense that inflicts upon the juvenile serious bodily injury or serious physical injury by other than accidental means," and an attempt, solicitation, or conspiracy to commit any such offense or aiding and abetting such an offense. "Serious physical injury" and "serious bodily injury" are defined in G.S. 14-318.4(d). See the notes on Element (3) to "Child Abuse—Inflicting Serious Mental or Physical Injury" and on Element (3)(a) to "Child Abuse—Inflicting Serious Bodily Injury or Mental or Emotional Injury," above.

Element 4(b). "Sexual offense" is not a defined term for this crime. It may have been intended to refer to "sexually violent offense," as defined in G.S. 14-318.6(a)(4) by reference to G.S. 14-208.6(5), or to sexual offense crimes, such as "First-Degree Forcible Sexual Offense" under G.S. 14-27.4.

Element 4(c). Only "Misdemeanor Child Abuse" (Chapter 9) is covered under this Element. Other child abuse crimes may be covered under Element (4)(a) to the extent they meet the definition of a violent offense.

Element (6). Under G.S. 14-318.6(b), a person who knows or should have reasonably known about covered offenses against a juvenile must immediately report the case, orally or by telephone, to the appropriate local law enforcement agency in the county where the juvenile resides or is found. The report shall include information as is known to the person making it, including listed information about the victim; the victim's parent, guardian, custodian, or caretaker; the person who allegedly committed the offense; and other listed information. The person making the report must give his or her name, address, and telephone number; however, his or her identity must be protected and only revealed as provided in G.S. 132-1.4(c)(4).

Good-faith immunity. A person who, in good faith, makes a report under this law, cooperates with law enforcement in an investigation, or testifies in any judicial proceeding resulting from a law enforcement report or investigation is immune from any civil or criminal liability that might otherwise be incurred or imposed for that action. G.S. 14-318.6(f).

Exceptions. A person with a privilege under G.S. 8-53.3 (psychologist-patient), 8-53.7 (social worker), 8-53.8 (counselor), 8-53.12 (agents of rape crisis centers and domestic violence programs), or an attorney-client privilege is not required to report if that privilege would prevent him or her from doing so. G.S. 14-318.6(h).

Related Offenses Not in This Chapter

"Concealing a Death" (Chapter 21)

Failure to report abuse, neglect, dependency, or death of a juvenile. G.S. 7B-301(b).

Misdemeanor failure to report the disappearance of a child who might be in danger. G.S. 14-318.5(c).

Failure to Report the Disappearance of a Child (new crime)

Statute

§ 14-318.5. Failure to report the disappearance of a child to law enforcement; immunity of person reporting in good faith.

(a) The following definitions apply in this section:

(1) Child.—Any person who is less than 16 years of age.

(2) Disappearance of a child.—When the parent or other person providing supervision of a child does not know the location of the child and has not had contact with the child for a 24-hour period.

(b) A parent or any other person providing care to or supervision of a child who knowingly or wantonly fails to report the disappearance of a child to law enforcement is in violation of this subsection. Unless the conduct is covered under some other provision of law providing greater punishment, a violation of this subsection is punishable as a Class I felony.

(c) Any person who reasonably suspects the disappearance of a child and who reasonably suspects that the child may be in danger shall report those suspicions to law enforcement within a reasonable time. Unless the conduct is covered under some other provision of law providing greater punishment, a violation of this subsection is punishable as a Class 1 misdemeanor.

(d) This section does not apply if G.S. 110-102.1 is applicable.

(e) Notwithstanding subsection (b) or (c) of this section, if a child is absent from school, a teacher is not required to report the child's absence to law enforcement officers under this section, provided the teacher reports the child's absence from school pursuant to Article 26 of Chapter 115C of the General Statutes.

(f) The felony of failure to report the disappearance of a child as required by subsection (b) of this section is an offense additional to other civil and criminal provisions and is not intended to repeal or preclude any other sanctions or remedies.

(g) Any person who reports the disappearance of a child as required by this section is immune from any civil or criminal liability that might otherwise be incurred or imposed for that action, provided that the person was acting in good faith. In any proceeding involving liability, good faith is presumed.

Elements

A person guilty of this offense

    (1) is a parent or any other person providing care to or supervision of a child *and*

    (2) knowingly or wantonly

    (3) fails to report

    (4) the disappearance of a child

    (5) to law enforcement.

Punishment

Class I felony. G.S. 14-318.5(b).

Notes

Element (1). A child is a person less than 16 years of age. G.S. 14-318.5(a)(1).

Element (4). The disappearance of a child occurs "[w]hen the parent or other person providing supervision of a child does not know the location of the child and has not had contact with the child for a 24-hour period." G.S. 14-318.5(a)(2).

Exceptions and immunity. This offense "does not apply if G.S. 110-102.1 is applicable." G.S. 14-318.5(d). G.S. 110-102.1 pertains to reports of missing or deceased children by child care providers.

If a child is absent from school, a teacher is not required to report the absence to law enforcement officers, provided the teacher reports the child's absence from school pursuant to Article 26 of G.S. Chapter 115C. G.S. 14-318.5(e).

Any person who reports the disappearance of a child as required is immune from any civil or criminal liability that might result from that action, so long as the person acted in good faith, which is presumed. G.S. 14-318.5(g).

Multiple convictions and punishments. The statute provides that "[u]nless the conduct is covered under some other provision of law providing greater punishment," a violation is a Class I felony. G.S. 14-318.5(b). This may suggest that a defendant cannot be convicted of this offense and another offense providing greater punishment. See the note on this Element to "Assault Inflicting Serious Injury" in the main volume. However, this conclusion is unclear given that the statute also provides that the crime "is an offense additional to other civil and criminal provisions and is not intended to repeal or preclude any other sanctions or remedies." G.S. 14-318.5(f).

Related Offenses Not in This Chapter

"Concealing a Death" (Chapter 21)

Misdemeanor failure to report the disappearance of a child who might be in danger.
    G.S. 14-318.5(c).

Contributing to a Juvenile's Being Delinquent, Undisciplined, Abused, or Neglected (page 203)

Statute (page 203)

Effective December 1, 2019, the 2017 Juvenile Justice Reinvestment Act, S.L. 2017-57, sec. 16D.4, amends the statute to make it apply to persons who are at least 18 years old. *Id*. sec. 16D.4(p). After that Act takes effect, the first sentence of the statute should read as follows:

> Any person who is at least 18 years old who knowingly or willfully causes, encourages, or aids any juvenile within the jurisdiction of the court to be in a place or condition, or to commit an act whereby the juvenile could be adjudicated delinquent, undisciplined, abused, or neglected as defined by G.S. 7B-101 and G.S. 7B-1501 shall be guilty of a Class 1 misdemeanor.

As a result of 2017 legislation, S.L. 2017-186, sec. 2(ii), replace the reference to the Department of Juvenile Justice with the Juvenile Justice Section of the Division of Adult Correction and Juvenile Justice of the Department of Public Safety.

Elements (page 203)

As a result of the 2017 legislation noted above, effective December 1, 2019, Element (1) should read as follows:

> (1) is at least 18 years old *and*

The statutory reference in Element (6)(d) should read:

> G.S. 7B-101(15).

Notes (page 203)

Generally (new note)

This offense does not require the defendant to be the juvenile's parent, guardian, custodian, or caretaker. State v. Stevens, 228 N.C. App. 352, 355 (2013); State v. Harris, 236 N.C. App. 388, 394 (2014) (following *Stevens*).

Element (4) (page 203)

Effective December 1, 2019, the 2017 Juvenile Justice Reinvestment Act, S.L. 2017-57, sec. 16D.4, raises the age of juvenile jurisdiction to 18 and extends the court's jurisdiction over juveniles. As a result, when that Act takes effect, the second sentence of this note should read as follows:

> Although a delinquent juvenile is within the court's jurisdiction when the juvenile is at least 6 years old and less than 20 years old, G.S. 7B-1501(7) (defining a delinquent juvenile), *as amended by* S.L. 2017-57, sec. 16D.4(a); *id.* § -1601 (specifying the court's jurisdiction over delinquent juveniles), *as amended by* S.L. 2017-57, sec. 16D.4(b), because only a juvenile under 18 can be adjudicated delinquent, see the note on Element (6)(a), immediately below, for purposes of this Element, 18 rather than 20 years old constitutes the upper age limit for delinquent juveniles to be within the jurisdiction of the court.

Element (6)(a) (page 204)

Effective December 1, 2019, the 2017 Juvenile Justice Reinvestment Act, S.L. 2017-57, sec. 16D.4, amends the definition of delinquent juvenile. *Id*. sec. 16D.4(a). After that Act becomes effective, this note should read as follows:

> A delinquent juvenile is
>
> - any juvenile who, while less than 16 years old but at least 6 years old, commits a crime or infraction under state law or under a local government ordinance, including violation of the motor vehicle laws, or who commits indirect contempt by a juvenile as defined in G.S. 5A-31 and

- any juvenile who, while less than 18 years old but at least 16 years old, commits a crime or an infraction under state law or under a local government ordinance, excluding violation of the motor vehicle laws, or who commits indirect contempt by a juvenile as defined in G.S. 5A-31.

G.S. 7B-1501(7), *as amended by* S.L. 2017-57, sec. 16D.4(a).

Element (6)(c) (page 204)

2018 legislation, S.L. 2018-68, amended the definition of "abused juvenile" to include juveniles less than 18 years old who are victims of human trafficking, involuntary servitude, or sexual servitude.

Element (6)(d) (page 204)

2018 legislation, S.L. 2018-68, sec. 8.1(b), amended the definition of "neglected juvenile" to include juveniles less than 18 years old who are victims of human trafficking, involuntary servitude, or sexual servitude.

Add the following to this note:

The State presented sufficient evidence of this Element where (1) the defendant failed to supervise her child, who fell into an outdoor pool and drowned while the defendant was in the bathroom, State v. Reed, 371 N.C. 106 (2018), (2) the defendant took the juvenile away from the area near the juvenile's home, ignored the juvenile after he was injured, and abandoned the sleeping juvenile in a parking lot, State v. Stevens, 228 N.C. App. 352, 357 (2013), and (3) the defendant entered the child's bedroom, tried to get her to drink liquor, squeezed her buttocks, and asked to suck on her chest, State v. Harris, 236 N.C. App. 388, 395 (2014) (the child "was clearly placed in a location in which and subject to conditions under which she could not and did not receive proper care from her caretakers").

Jury instructions (new note)

The jury instructions should define the statutory terms "delinquent," "undisciplined," "abused," and "neglected." *Harris*, 236 N.C. App. at 397 n.4.

Related Offenses Not in This Chapter (page 204)

Add the following offenses to this list:

"Sale, Surrender, or Purchase of a Minor," in Chapter 12 (Kidnapping and Related Offenses) of this supplement.

Unlawful transfer of custody of minor child. G.S. 14-321.2.

The offense listed as "Selling cigarettes to minors. G.S. 14-313" should read as follows:

Youth access to tobacco products, tobacco-derived products, vapor products, and cigarette wrapping papers. G.S. 14-313.

Replace the second to last offense in this list with the following:

Unlawful payments related to adoption. G.S. 48-10-102.

10
Sexual Assaults

2012 legislation, S.L. 2012-40, amended G.S. 7B-1111(a) to provide that a court may terminate parental rights upon a finding that the parent "has been convicted of a sexually related offense under Chapter 14 of the General Statutes that resulted in the conception of the juvenile." All of the offenses covered in this chapter fall within Chapter 14 of the General Statutes.

2014 legislation, S.L. 2014-100, sec. 17.1(r), amended various sex offender statutes, substituting the words "Department of Public Safety" for the term "Division" in all instances except where the relevant statute refers to the Division of Adult Correction.

2015 legislation substantially reorganized and revised the rape and sex offense statutes. S.L. 2015-181. Specific changes are noted in the sections that follow.

Rape (page 217)

First-Degree Forcible Rape (page 217)

Statute (page 217)

2015 legislation, S.L. 2015-181, secs. 3(a) and (b), recodified and amended the statute. 2017 legislation, S.L. 2017-30, sec. 1, further amended the statute. The amended statute provides:

> **§ 14-27.21. First-degree forcible rape.**
> (a) A person is guilty of first-degree forcible rape if the person engages in vaginal intercourse with another person by force and against the will of the other person, and does any of the following:
> (1) Uses, threatens to use, or displays a dangerous or deadly weapon or an article which the other person reasonably believes to be a dangerous or deadly weapon.
> (2) Inflicts serious personal injury upon the victim or another person.
> (3) The person commits the offense aided and abetted by one or more other persons.
> (b) Any person who commits an offense defined in this section is guilty of a Class B1 felony.
> (c) Upon conviction, a person convicted under this section has no rights to custody of or rights of inheritance from any child born as a result of the commission of the rape, nor shall the person have any rights related to the child under Chapter 48 or Subchapter 1 of Chapter 7B of the General Statutes.

2019 legislation, S.L. 2019-245, effective for offenses committed on or after December 1, 2019, adds new G.S. 14-27.20(1a).

> **§ 14-27.20. Definitions.**
> (1a) Against the will of the other person. – Either of the following:
> a. Without consent of the other person.
> b. After consent is revoked by the other person, in a manner that would cause a reasonable person to believe consent is revoked.

Elements (page 217)

As a result of the 2017 legislation noted above, Element (5)(a) should read as follows:

> (a) uses, threatens to use, or displays a dangerous or deadly weapon (or what reasonably appears to be a dangerous or deadly weapon),

Punishment (page 218)

As a result of the 2015 legislative change noted above, the statutory citation in this section should be to G.S. 14-27.21(b).

Notes (page 218)

Element (1) (page 218)

As a result of 2015 legislation, S.L. 2015-181, sec. 15, the statutory citation included in the first paragraph of this note should be to G.S. 14-27.36.

Add the following to this note:

> For a case where there was sufficient evidence of vaginal intercourse notwithstanding the child victim's use of ambiguous terms, see *State v. Combs*, 226 N.C. App. 87, 90–91 (2013) (the child used terms such as "manhood" and "middle hole" but went on to explain what these terms meant).
>
> For a case where there was sufficient evidence of penetration even though the victim did not remember the incident, see *State v. White*, ___ N.C. App. ___, ___, 820 S.E.2d 116, 121 (2018) (bystanders responding to the victim's screams found the defendant straddling her in an alley in a "missionary position"; when the defendant was pushed away, his pants were down and he had an erection and the victim's underwear and pants were at her ankles; and a nurse found debris and a small black hair most consistent with a pubic hair inside the victim's vagina, the victim did not have pubic hair, and the nurse testified that debris cannot enter the vaginal walls in their normal collapsed state and that "they only open up if something is introduced inside of them").

Element (2) (page 218)

As a result of 2015 legislation, S.L. 2015-181, sec. 15, the statutory citation included in this note should be to G.S. 14-27.34.

Element (3) (page 218)

The evidence sufficiently established use of force when, after the victim repeatedly declined the defendant's advances, the defendant pushed her to the ground and got on top of her. State v. Norman, 227 N.C. App. 162, 167–68 (2013) (rape and sexual offense case).

In a second-degree sexual offense case, the court held that the touching was by force and against the victim's will when the defendant surprised a store shopper by putting his hand up her skirt and penetrating her vagina; the court rejected the defendant's argument that because his action surprised the victim, she did not have the opportunity to consent or resist and that therefore he did not act by force and against the victim's will. State v. Henderson, 233 N.C. App. 538, 540–41 (2014).

Evidence (1) that a juvenile threatened the minor victims he had met at a school for special needs with exposing their secrets and their participation with him in sexual activities and (2) of a power differential between the juvenile and the victims was insufficient to establish constructive force; for constructive force to apply, threats resulting in fear, fright, or coercion must be threats of physical harm. *In re* T.W., 221 N.C. App. 193, 199 (2012).

Although constructive force can be inferred from a special relationship, such as between a parent and a child, such an inference is inappropriate where the relationship between a juvenile defendant and the victims was one of "leader to . . . follower[s] among children in school" and did "not involve the same wielding of authority, disparity of power, and degree of fear that occurs between an abusive parent and a child." *Id.* at 200.

Element (4) (page 218)

As a result of 2019 legislation, S.L. 2019-245, delete the note to Element (4) and replace it with the following text:

> Under G.S. 14-27.20(1a), an offense is against the will of the other person if it is either without the consent of the other person or after consent is revoked by the other person in a manner that would cause a reasonable person to believe that consent is revoked. That statutory provision was intended to supersede *State v. Way*, 297 N.C. 293 (1979), in which the state supreme court held under a prior North Carolina rape statute that if penetration initially occurred with a victim's consent, no rape occurs despite the victim's withdrawal of consent during the same act of intercourse. Evidence of physical resistance is not necessary to prove a lack of consent. State v. Hall, 293 N.C. 559 (1977).

Element (5)(a) (page 218)

As a result of the 2015 legislation noted above, the statutory citation in the first paragraph of this note should be to G.S. 14-27.21(a)(1).

Element (5)(b) (page 219)

There was sufficient evidence that the victim suffered serious personal injury where the victim had blood on her lip and bruises on her ribs, arms, and face and was in pain for four or five days after the incident; because she felt unsafe, the victim left her boyfriend, terminated her lease, and moved in with her family; and at the time of trial, roughly a year later, the victim still felt unsafe being alone, State v. Gates, 245 N.C. App. 525, 528 (2016); the victim, who was seven months pregnant, struggled to protect her stomach while the defendant dragged her down thirty-three concrete stairs and into nearby woods; a nurse compared the victim's injuries to "road rash" that one might suffer after falling off a motorcycle traveling at 55 mph; and the victim testified that her injuries were painful and that at the time of trial she still had extensive scars, State v. Gentle, 260 N.C. App. 269, ___, 817 S.E.2d 833, 838 (2018); and the defendant was a 43-year-old male approximately 5'10" tall with a medium build and the victim was a 22-year-old female, approximately 5'1" tall and weighing 96 pounds; the defendant unexpectedly grabbed the victim and threw her down a steep, rocky embankment, punched her face and head, straddled her, pinned her down, and strangled her; the victim suffered a head injury; experienced pain for days; had two black eyes, body bruises, and hoarseness in her voice; had difficulty concentrating and remembering; experienced short-term memory loss from the attacks; and testified that she continued to have trouble trusting people, opening up to others, and maintaining friendships, State v. Harding, 258 N.C. App. 306, 319–20 (2018).

Element (5)(d) (page 220)

For a case applying the general rule that actual or constructive presence is not required for aiding and abetting to this Element in a first-degree sexual offense case and finding that the evidence was sufficient, see *State v. Dick*, 370 N.C. 305, 312 (2017) (although the defendant was alone in a room with the victim when the sexual offense occurred, the defendant, together with his accomplices, taped the victim's mouth and taped her hands behind her back, moved her into the bedroom where the sexual offense occurred, removed her clothes, and touched her inappropriately).

Jury instructions (new note)

When the evidence of penetration is clear and positive, the trial court does not err by failing to instruct the jury on attempt. State v. Matsoake, 243 N.C. App. 651, 658–59 (2015) (rape case); State v. Norman, 227 N.C. App. 162, 168 (2013) (same). However, when the evidence of penetration is conflicting, the trial court should instruct on attempt, though it may not be plain error to fail to do so. State v. Carter, 366 N.C. 496, 500–01 (2013) (no plain error; sex offense); State v. Boyett, 229 N.C. App. 576, 578, 741 (2013) (no plain error; rape and incest case).

Defendant under 14 (page 221)

As a result of 2015 legislation, S.L. 2015-181, sec. 15, the statutory citation included in this note should be to G.S. 14-27.35.

Greater and lesser-included offenses (page 221)

For another case holding that assault on a female is not a lesser-included offense of first-degree sexual offense, see *State v. Martin*, 222 N.C. App. 213, 221–22 (2012).

In a 2012 case, the state court of appeals held that a defendant cannot be convicted of second-degree sexual offense (mentally disabled victim) and crime against nature (where lack of consent was based on the fact that the victim was mentally disabled, incapacitated, or physically helpless) based on the same conduct (fellatio). State v. Hunt, 221 N.C. App. 489, 495–97 (2012), *aff'd on other grounds*, 367 N.C. 700 (2014) (per curiam). The court found that "on the . . . facts of [the] case," crime against nature was a lesser-included offense of second-degree sexual offense and that conviction of both offenses violated double jeopardy. *Id.* However, the North Carolina Supreme Court previously held that crime against nature is not a lesser-included offense of forcible sexual offense, State v. Etheridge, 319 N.C. 34, 50–51 (1987); State v. Warren, 309 N.C. 224, 230–31 (1983), and that a definitional test—not a factual test—applies when determining whether offenses are lesser-included offenses. State v. Nickerson, 365 N.C. 279, 280 (2011); *Warren*, 309 N.C. at 230–31; *see also* State v. Robinson, 368 N.C. 402, 407–08 (2015) (applying a definitional test to the analysis).

As a result of the 2015 legislation noted above, (1) the penultimate sentence of the fifth paragraph in this note should read as follows:

But when a short-form rape indictment is not used and the indictment charges the crime using the language in the rape statute, assault on a female may not be submitted to the jury unless it has been separately charged. *State v. Hedgepeth*, 165 N.C. App. 321 (2004) (decided under former G.S. 14-27.2).

As a result of that same legislation, the citations in the last paragraph of this note should read as follows:

G.S. 14-27.23(e); -27.28(d).

Multiple convictions and punishments (page 222)

A defendant may be sentenced for statutory rape and incest arising out of the same transaction. State v. Marlow, 229 N.C. App. 593, 599–600 (2013) (reasoning that the offenses are not the same under the *Blockburger* test (referencing Blockburger v. United States, 284 U.S. 299 (1932)).

A defendant may be convicted and sentenced for both statutory rape of a 13-, 14-, or 15-year-old and second-degree rape of a mentally disabled person when the convictions are based on a single act of sexual intercourse. State v. Banks, 367 N.C. 652, 658–59 (2014).

Convicted defendant has no rights to custody or inheritance (page 223)

As a result of the 2015 legislation noted above, the text of this note should begin as follows: "G.S. 14-27.21(c) provides."

Related Offenses Not in This Chapter (page 223)

Add the following offense to this list:

Committing or attempting to commit sexual penetration on human remains. G.S. 14-401.22(c). Sexual contact or penetration under pretext of medical treatment. G.S. 14-27.33A.

Second-Degree Forcible Rape (page 223)

Statute (page 223)

As a result of 2015 legislation, S.L. 2015-181, secs. 4(a) and (b), recodifying and amending the statute, and 2018 legislation, S.L. 2018-47, sec. 4(b), further amending it, the statute now reads as follows:

> **§ 14-27.22. Second-degree forcible rape.**
>
> (a) A person is guilty of second-degree forcible rape if the person engages in vaginal intercourse with another person:
>
> (1) By force and against the will of the other person; or
>
> (2) Who has a mental disability or who is mentally incapacitated or physically helpless, and the person performing the act knows or should reasonably know the other person has a mental disability or is mentally incapacitated or physically helpless.
>
> (b) Any person who commits the offense defined in this section is guilty of a Class C felony.
>
> (c) Upon conviction, a person convicted under this section has no rights to custody of or rights of inheritance from any child conceived during the commission of the rape, nor does the person have any rights related to the child under Chapter 48 of the General Statutes or Subchapter 1 of Chapter 7B of the General Statutes.

Elements (page 223)

As a result of 2018 legislation, S.L. 2018-47, sec. 4(a), and to correct a typographical error in the main volume, the elements of this offense should read as follows:

A person guilty of this offense

(1) has vaginal intercourse

(2) with a person

(3) and the intercourse is

    (a) by force and against the person's will *or*

    (b) with a person

        (i) who has a mental disability,

        (ii) is mentally incapacitated, *or*

        (iii) is physically helpless *and*

the defendant knew or should have known that the victim has a mental disability, is mentally incapacitated, or is physically helpless.

Punishment (page 224)

As a result of the 2015 legislation noted above, the statutory citation in this note should be to G.S. 14-27.22(b).

Notes (page 224)

Elements (3)(b)(i), (ii), and (iii) (page 224)

These notes cite G.S. 14-27.1. That statute was recodified as G.S. 14-27.20 by 2015 legislation. S.L. 2015-181, sec. 2.

Element (3)(b)(i) (page 224)

As a result of 2018 legislation, S.L. 2018-47, sec. 4(a), delete the first paragraph of this note and replace it with the following:

> A person who has a mental disability is one "who has an intellectual disability or a mental disorder that temporarily or permanently renders the victim substantially incapable of appraising the nature of his or her conduct, or of resisting the act of vaginal intercourse or a sexual act, or of communicating unwillingness to submit to the act of vaginal intercourse or a sexual act." G.S. 14-27.20(2a).

As a result of that same legislation, replace the term "mentally disabled" as used in the second paragraph of this note with "mentally disabled, as that term was used in a prior version of the statute."

Reversing a case cited in this note, *State v. Hunt*, 211 N.C. App. 452 (2011), the North Carolina Supreme Court held that expert testimony is not required for the State to establish that the victim had a mental disability, as that term was used in a prior version of the statute, for purposes of second-degree sexual offense. State v. Hunt, 365 N.C. 432, 441 (2012).

Element (3)(b)(ii) (page 224)

As a result of 2018 legislation, S.L. 2018-47, sec. 4(a), further amended by 2019 legislation, S.L. 2019-245, sec. 6.(c), delete the first sentence of this note and replace it with the following:

> "Mentally incapacitated" means that any act has rendered the victim substantially incapable of either appraising the nature of his or her conduct or resisting the act. G.S. 14-27.20(2).

Element (3)(b)(iii) (page 224)

Add the following citation at the end of the first paragraph of this note:

> State v. Lopez, ___ N.C. App. ___, 826 S.E.2d 498 (2019) (a victim, who had no prior sexual relationship with the defendant and who consumed sizable portions of alcohol, was physically ill at a club, was unable to remember anything after leaving the club, was physically unable to resist the defendant, and was, therefore, physically helpless).

Convicted defendant has no rights to custody or inheritance (page 225)

As a result of the 2015 legislation noted above, the statutory citation in this note should be to G.S. 14-27.22(c).

First-Degree Statutory Rape (page 225)

Statute (page 225)

2015 legislation, S.L. 2015-181, secs. 3(b) and 6, removed first-degree statutory rape from old G.S. 14-27.2 (recodified by the same legislation as G.S. 14-27.21), recodifying it as follows:

> **§ 14-27.24. First-degree statutory rape.**
> (a) A person is guilty of first-degree statutory rape if the person engages in vaginal intercourse with a victim who is a child under the age of 13 years and the defendant is at least 12 years old and is at least four years older than the victim.
> (b) Any person who commits an offense defined in this section is guilty of a Class B1 felony.
> (c) Upon conviction, a person convicted under this section has no rights to custody of or rights of inheritance from any child born as a result of the commission of the rape, nor shall the person have any rights related to the child under Chapter 48 or Subchapter 1 of Chapter 7B of the General Statutes.

No substantive changes were made to the elements of the offense.

Punishment (page 226)

As a result of the 2015 legislation noted above, the statutory citation in this section should read: G.S. 14-27.24(b).

Notes (page 226)

Element (2) (page 226)

For another case supporting the statement in this note that mistake of age is no defense to this crime, see *State v. Ward*, 250 N.C. App. 254, 263 (2016).

Add the following citation to the third sentence of the first paragraph of this note regarding the lack of a requirement for certified copies of birth records:

> ; State v. DeJesus, ___ N.C. App. ___, 827 S.E.2d 744 (2019) (a non-original copy of the victim's Honduran birth certificate, obtained through her school records, properly established her age).

Consent (page 226)

For another case supporting the statement in this note that consent is no defense to this crime, see *Ward*, 250 N.C. App. at 263.

Sex offender registration (page 227)

Add the following citation at the end of this note:

, as amended by S.L. 2017-102, sec. 5.

Statutory Rape by an Adult (page 227)

Statute (page 227)

2015 legislation, S.L. 2015-181, secs. 5(a) and (b), recodified and amended the statute. The new title of the statute is:

§ 14-27.23. Statutory rape of a child by an adult.

A conforming change was made to subsection (a) so that it reads:

(a) A person is guilty of statutory rape of a child by an adult if the person is at least 18 years of age and engages in vaginal intercourse with a victim who is a child under the age of 13 years.

Due to other recodifications made in that same legislation, conforming changes were made to subsection (e) so that it reads:

(e) The offense under G.S. 14-27.24 is a lesser included offense of the offense in this section.

Punishment (page 228)

As a result of the 2015 legislation noted above, the statutes referenced in this section should be to the same subsections in new G.S. 14-27.23.

Add the following to this section:

The trial court has no discretion to sentence the defendant to less than 300 months for this offense. State v. Agustin, 229 N.C. App. 240, 246 (2013).

This section indicates that the statutory provision providing that a defendant may be sentenced to an active term above that normally provided for a Class B1 felony if the judge finds egregious aggravation appears to run afoul of the United States Supreme Court decision in *Blakely v. Washington*, 542 U.S. 296 (2004) (holding that any factor, other than a prior conviction, that increases punishment beyond the prescribed statutory maximum must be submitted to the jury and proved beyond a reasonable doubt). In *State v. Singletary*, 247 N.C. App. 368, 384–85 (2016), the North Carolina Court of Appeals so held as to the parallel punishment provision for Statutory Sexual Offense by an Adult; that holding almost certainly applies to this offense as well.

Notes (page 228)

Lifetime satellite-based monitoring (page 228)

As a result of the 2015 legislation noted above, the statutory citation in this note should be to G.S. 14-27.23(b).

Convicted defendant has no rights of custody or inheritance (page 228)

As a result of the 2015 legislation noted above, the statutory citation in this note should be to G.S. 14-27.23(d).

Statutory Rape of a Person 15 or Younger by a Defendant Who Is at Least 12 Years Old and at Least Six Years Older Than the Victim (page 229) (revised title)

Statute (page 229)

2015 legislation both amended and recodified the statute. S.L. 2015-62, sec. 1(a); S.L. 2015-181, secs. 7(a) and (b). As amended, the statute reads as follows:

§ 14-27.25. Statutory rape of person who is 15 years of age or younger.

(a) A defendant is guilty of a Class B1 felony if the defendant engages in vaginal intercourse with another person who is 15 years of age or younger and the defendant is at least 12 years old and at least six years older than the person, except when the defendant is lawfully married to the person.

(b) Unless the conduct is covered under some other provision of law providing greater punishment, a defendant is guilty of a Class C felony if the defendant engages in vaginal intercourse with another person who is 15 years of age or younger and the defendant is at least 12 years old and more than four but less than six years older than the person, except when the defendant is lawfully married to the person.

Elements (page 229)

As a result of the statutory changes noted above, elements (2) and (3) should read as follows:

(2) with a child who is 15 years old or younger *and*
(3) the defendant is
    (a) at least 12 years old *and*
    (b) at least six years older than the child.

Punishment (page 229)

As a result of the 2015 legislative changes noted above, the statutory citation in this section should be to G.S. 14-27.25(a).

Notes (page 229)

Element (2) (page 229)

As a result of the statutory changes noted above, the crime now applies whenever the victim is 15 years of age or younger.

Exceptions (page 230)

As a result of the 2015 legislation noted above, the statutory citation in this note should be to G.S. 14-27.25(a).

Statutory Rape of a Person 15 or Younger by a Defendant Who Is at Least 12 Years Old and Is More Than Four but Less Than Six Years Older Than the Victim (page 231) (revised title)

Statute (page 231)

2015 legislation both amended and recodified the statute. S.L. 2015-62, sec. 1(a); S.L. 2015-181, secs. 7(a) and (b). The amended statute is reproduced in this supplement under "Statutory Rape of a Person 15 or Younger by a Defendant Who Is at Least 12 Years Old and at Least Six Years Older Than the Victim."

Elements (page 231)

As a result of the statutory changes noted above, elements (2) and (3) should read as follows:

(2) with a child who is 15 years old or younger *and*
(3) the defendant is
    (a) at least 12 years old *and*
    (b) more than four but less than six years older than the child.

Punishment (page 231)

As a result of the 2015 legislation noted above, the statutory citation in this section should be to G.S. 14-27.25(b).

Notes (page 231)

Multiple convictions and punishments (new note)

2015 legislation amended the statute to provide that punishment is as a Class C felony "[u]nless the conduct is covered under some other provision of law providing greater punishment." G.S. 14-27.25(b), *as amended by* S.L. 2015-62, sec. 1(a); S.L. 2015-181, secs. 7(a) and (b). This means that a defendant cannot be punished for this offense and one that provides for harsher punishment.

Sexual Offenses (page 231)

First-Degree Forcible Sexual Offense (page 231)

Statute (page 231)

2015 legislation, S.L. 2015-181, secs. 8(a) and (b), recodified and amended the statute. 2017 legislation, S.L. 2017-30, sec. 2, further amended the statute. The amended statute reads as follows:

> **§ 14-27.26. First-degree forcible sexual offense.**
> (a) A person is guilty of a first degree forcible sexual offense if the person engages in a sexual act with another person by force and against the will of the other person, and does any of the following:
> > (1) Uses, threatens to use, or displays a dangerous or deadly weapon or an article which the other person reasonably believes to be a dangerous or deadly weapon.
> > (2) Inflicts serious personal injury upon the victim or another person.
> > (3) The person commits the offense aided and abetted by one or more other persons.
> > (b) Any person who commits an offense defined in this section is guilty of a Class B1 felony.

Elements (page 232)

As a result of the 2017 legislation noted above, Element (5)(a) should read as follows:

> (a) uses, threatens to use, or displays a dangerous or deadly weapon (or what reasonably appears to be a dangerous or deadly weapon),

Punishment (page 232)

As a result of the 2015 legislation noted above, the statutory citation in this section should be to G.S. 14-27.26(b).

Notes (page 232)

Element (1) (page 232)

This note cites G.S. 14-27.1 and -27.10. Those statutes were recodified as G.S. 14-27.20 and -27.36, respectively, by 2015 legislation. S.L. 2015-181, secs. 2, 15.

Add the following to this note:

> The defendant's act of forcing the victim at gunpoint to penetrate her vagina with her own fingers constitutes a sexual act. State v. Green, 229 N.C. App. 121, 128 (2013).

Proof of vaginal penetration cannot support a sexual offense conviction; a sexual act other than vaginal intercourse is required. State v. Spence, 237 N.C. App. 367, 378–79 (2014).

When the sex act is fellatio, proof of penetration is not required. *In re* J.F., 237 N.C. App. 218, 225–26 (2014).

The prosecution need not show that the defendant performed a sexual act on the victim; the State need only prove that the defendant engaged in a sexual act with the victim. *Id.* (victim performed fellatio on the juvenile).

For other cases where the evidence was sufficient to establish penetration with an object, see *State v. Phachoumphone*, 257 N.C. App. 848, 862 (2018) (the evidence was sufficient to show digital penetration where the 6-year-old victim demonstrated that the defendant digitally penetrated her vagina by inserting her finger into a hole which the interpreter created with her hand, and confirmed that her demonstration showed "what [defendant] did with his finger in [her] body"; a doctor testified that the victim's hymen was substantially missing, an irregular finding which could only have been caused by a penetrating injury; and the doctor observed redness in the vaginal area behind where the hymen was, indicating a penetrating injury within the last forty-eight hours), and *State v. Wilson*, ___ N.C. App. ___, ___, 818 S.E.2d 160, 162 (2018) (in this sex offense by a substitute parent case, the evidence was sufficient to establish digital penetration where an officer testified to the defendant's confession that he put his hands "in [the victim's] genital area," causing her to become sexually aroused and "wet"; from this description a jury could infer that the defendant at least penetrated the victim's labia).

Sexual purpose (new note)

Proof of this crime does not require evidence that the defendant acted with a sexual purpose. *J.F.*, 237 N.C. App. at 224–25.

Defenses (page 233)

This note cites G.S. 14-27.1. That statute was recodified as G.S. 14-27.20 by 2015 legislation. S.L. 2015-181, sec. 2.

Add the following at the end of this note:

For the defendant to be entitled to a jury instruction on this affirmative defense, there must be direct testimony that the conduct was for a medically accepted purpose. State v. Stepp, 367 N.C. 772 (2015) (per curiam opinion reversing *State v. Stepp*, 232 N.C. App. 132 (2014), for reasons stated in the dissenting opinion below; the defendant admitted penetrating the victim's genital opening with his finger but claimed it was for an accepted medical purpose; noting the absence of any direct testimony that this was done for an accepted medical purpose, the dissenting judge found that the defendant was not entitled to a jury instruction on the defense).

Second-Degree Forcible Sexual Offense (page 234)

Statute (page 234)

As a result of 2015 legislation, S.L. 2015-181, secs. 4(a) and (b), recodifying and amending the statute, and 2018 legislation, S.L. 2018-47, sec. 4(c), further amending it, the statute now reads as follows:

§ 14-27.27. Second-degree forcible sexual offense.

(a) A person is guilty of second degree forcible sexual offense if the person engages in a sexual act with another person:

(1) By force and against the will of the other person; or

(2) Who has a mental disability or who is mentally incapacitated or physically helpless, and the person performing the act knows or should reasonably know that the other person has a mental disability or is mentally incapacitated or physically helpless.

(b) Any person who commits the offense defined in this section is guilty of a Class C felony.

Elements (page 234)

As a result of 2018 legislation, S.L. 2018-47, sec. 4(c), and to correct a typographical error in the main volume, the elements of this offense should read as follows:

A person guilty of this offense

(1) engages in a sexual act other than vaginal intercourse
(2) with a person
(3) and the act is
    (a) by force and against the person's will *or*
    (b) with a person
        (i) who has a mental disability
        (ii) is mentally incapacitated, *or*
        (iii) is physically helpless *and*

the defendant knew or should have known that the victim has a mental disability, is mentally incapacitated, or is physically helpless.

Punishment (page 234)

As a result of the 2015 legislation noted above, the statutory citation in this section should be to G.S. 14-27.27(b).

First-Degree Statutory Sexual Offense (page 235)

Statute (page 235)

2015 legislation, S.L. 2015-181, secs. 8(b) and 11, removed first-degree statutory sexual offense from old G.S. 14-27.4 (recodified by the same legislation as G.S. 14-27.26), recodifying it as follows:

§ 14-27.29. First-degree statutory sexual offense.
    (a) A person is guilty of first-degree statutory sexual offense if the person engages in a sexual act with a victim who is a child under the age of 13 years and the defendant is at least 12 years old and is at least four years older than the victim.
    (b) Any person who commits an offense defined in this section is guilty of a Class B1 felony.

No substantive changes were made to the elements of the offense.

Punishment (page 235)

As a result of the 2015 legislation noted above, the statutory citation in this section should be to G.S. 14-27.29(b).

Statutory Sexual Offense by an Adult (page 236)

Statute (page 236)

2015 legislation, S.L. 2015-181, secs. 10(a) and (b), recodified and amended the statute. The new title of the statute is:

§ 14-27.28. Statutory sexual offense with a child by an adult.

A conforming change was made to subsection (a) so that it reads:

    (a) A person is guilty of statutory sexual offense with a child by an adult if the person is at least 18 years of age and engages in a sexual act with a victim who is a child under the age of 13 years.

Due to other recodifications made in that same legislation, conforming changes were made to subsection (d) so that it reads:

    (d) The offense under G.S. 14-27.29 is a lesser included offense of the offense in this section.

Punishment (page 237)

As a result of the 2015 legislation noted above, the first two sentences of this section should read as follows:

> Class B1 felony, except that the offense is subject to a mandatory minimum of 300 months of active time. G.S. 14-27.28(b). G.S. 14-27.28(c) provides that a defendant may be sentenced to an active term above that normally provided for a Class B1 felony if the judge finds egregious aggravation.

This section indicates that the statutory provision providing that a defendant may be sentenced to an active term above that normally provided for a Class B1 felony if the judge finds egregious aggravation runs afoul of the United States Supreme Court decision in *Blakely v. Washington*, 542 U.S. 296 (2004) (holding that any factor, other than a prior conviction, that increases punishment beyond the prescribed statutory maximum must be submitted to the jury and proved beyond a reasonable doubt). *State v. Singletary*, 247 N.C. App. 368, 384–85 (2016).

Notes (page 237)

Lifetime satellite-based monitoring required (page 238)

As a result of the 2015 legislation noted above, the statutory citation in this note should be to G.S. 14-27.28(b).

Statutory Sexual Offense of a Person 15 or Younger by a Defendant Who Is at Least 12 Years Old and Is at Least Six Years Older Than the Victim (page 238) (revised title)

Statute (page 238)

2015 legislation, S.L. 2015-181, secs. 7(a), 7(b), and 12, removed this offense from G.S. 14-27.7A (which was recodified as G.S. 14-27.25), recodifying it as follows:

> **§ 14-27.30. Statutory sexual offense with a person who is 15 years of age or younger.**
> (a) A defendant is guilty of a Class B1 felony if the defendant engages in a sexual act with another person who is 15 years of age or younger and the defendant is at least 12 years old and at least six years older than the person, except when the defendant is lawfully married to the person.
> (b) Unless the conduct is covered under some other provision of law providing greater punishment, a defendant is guilty of a Class C felony if the defendant engages in a sexual act with another person who is 15 years of age or younger and the defendant is at least 12 years old and more than four but less than six years older than the person, except when the defendant is lawfully married to the person.

Elements (page 238)

As a result of the statutory changes noted above, elements (2) and (3) should read as follows:

> (2) with a child who is 15 years old or younger *and*
> (3) the defendant is
>   (a) at least 12 years old *and*
>   (b) at least six years older than the child.

Punishment (page 238)

As a result of the 2015 legislation noted above, the statutory citation in this section should be to G.S. 14-27.30(a).

Notes (page 238)

Element (2) (page 238)

As a result of the statutory changes noted above, the crime now applies whenever the victim is 15 years of age or younger.

Statutory Sexual Offense of a Person 15 or Younger by a Defendant Who Is at Least 12 Years Old and Is More Than Four but Less Than Six Years Older Than the Victim (page 239) (revised title)

Statute (page 239)

2015 legislation, S.L. 2015-181, secs. 7(a), 7(b), and 12, removed this offense from G.S. 14-27.7A (which was recodified as G.S. 14-27.25), putting it in a new statutory section, G.S. 14-27.30, reproduced in this supplement under "Statutory Sexual Offense of a Person 15 or Younger by a Defendant Who Is at Least 12 Years Old and Is at Least Six Years Older Than the Victim."

Elements (page 239)

As a result of the statutory changes noted above, elements (2) and (3) should read as follows:

    (2) with a child who is 15 years old or younger *and*

    (3) the defendant is

        (a) at least 12 years old *and*

        (b) more than four but less than six years older than the child.

Punishment (page 239)

As a result of the 2015 legislation noted above, the statutory citation in this section should be to G.S. 14-27.30(b).

Notes (page 240)

Multiple convictions and punishments (new note)

2015 legislation, S.L. 2015-181, sec. 12, amended the recodified statute to provide that punishment is as a Class C felony "[u]nless the conduct is covered under some other provision of law providing greater punishment." G.S. 14-27.30(b). This means that a defendant cannot be punished for this offense and one that provides for harsher punishment.

Sexual Activity by a Substitute Parent (page 240)

Statute (page 240)

2015 legislation, S.L. 2015-181, secs. 13(a) and (b), amended and recodified the statute to read as follows:

> **§ 14-27.31. Sexual activity by a substitute parent or custodian.**
> (a) If a defendant who has assumed the position of a parent in the home of a minor victim engages in vaginal intercourse or a sexual act with a victim who is a minor residing in the home, the defendant is guilty of a Class E felony.
> (b) If a person having custody of a victim of any age or a person who is an agent or employee of any person, or institution, whether such institution is private, charitable, or governmental, having custody of a victim of any age engages in vaginal intercourse or a sexual act with such victim, the defendant is guilty of a Class E felony.
> (c) Consent is not a defense to a charge under this section.

The statutory amendments did not make any substantive changes to this offense.

Punishment (page 241)

As a result of 2015 legislation noted above, the statutory citation in this section should be to G.S. 14-27.31(a).

Notes (page 241)

Element (1) (page 241)

Add the following to the end of the first paragraph of this note:

> It is not necessary for the defendant to have maintained a romantic relationship with the victim's parent or to exercise any legal rights over the child in order to be prosecuted under this offense. *Bailey*, 163 N.C. App. at 94. A defendant was deemed to have assumed the position of a parent of a victim when he paid for the victim's care and support, referred to himself as her "godfather" and told others she was his daughter, and tried to get her enrolled in school. State v. Sheridan, ___ N.C. App. ___, 824 S.E.2d 146 (2019). A 16-year-old minor can be a victim of this offense. State v. Oakley, 167 N.C. App. 318 (2004).

Consent (page 241)

As a result of the 2015 legislation noted above, the statutory citation in this note should be to G.S. 14-27.31(c).

Sexual Activity by a Custodian (page 242)

Statute (page 242)

2015 legislation amended and recodified the statute. S.L. 2015-181, secs. 13(a) and (b). The amended statute is reproduced in this supplement under "Sexual Activity by a Substitute Parent." The statutory amendments did not make any substantive changes to this offense.

Punishment (page 242)

As a result of the 2015 legislation noted above, the statutory citation in this section should be to G.S. 14-27.31(b).

Notes (page 242)

Element (1) (page 242)

As a result of the 2015 legislation noted above, the statutory citation in this note should be to G.S. 14-27.31(b).

Consent (page 243)

As a result of the 2015 legislation noted above, the statutory citation in this note should be to G.S. 14-27.31(c).

Sexual Activity with a Student (page 243)

Sexual Activity with a Student by a Teacher, School Administrator, Student Teacher, Coach, or School Safety Officer (page 243)

Statute (page 243)

2015 legislation, S.L. 2015-181, secs. 14(a) and (b); S.L. 2015-44, sec. 2, amended and recodified the statute to read as follows:

> **§ 14-27.32. Sexual activity with a student.**
> (a) If a defendant, who is a teacher, school administrator, student teacher, school safety officer, or coach, at any age, or who is other school personnel, and who is at least four years older than the victim engages in vaginal intercourse or a sexual act with a victim who is a student, at any time during or after the time the defendant and victim were

present together in the same school, but before the victim ceases to be a student, the defendant is guilty of a Class G felony, except when the defendant is lawfully married to the student. The term "same school" means a school at which the student is enrolled and the defendant is employed, assigned, or volunteers.

(b) A defendant who is school personnel, other than a teacher, school administrator, student teacher, school safety officer, or coach, and is less than four years older than the victim and engages in vaginal intercourse or a sexual act with a victim who is a student, is guilty of a Class I felony.

(c) This section shall apply unless the conduct is covered under some other provision of law providing for greater punishment.

(d) Consent is not a defense to a charge under this section.

(e) For purposes of this section, the terms "school", "school personnel", and "student" shall have the same meaning as in G.S. 14-202.4(d). For purposes of this section, the term "school safety officer" shall include a school resource officer or any other person who is regularly present in a school for the purpose of promoting and maintaining safe and orderly schools.

The statutory amendments did not make any substantive changes to this offense.

Punishment (page 243)

As a result of the 2015 legislation noted above, the statutory citation in this section should be to G.S. 14-27.32(a).

Notes (page 243)

Element (1) (page 243)

As a result of the 2015 legislation noted above, the statutory citation in this note should be to G.S. 14-27.32(e).

Element (3) (page 244)

As a result of the 2015 legislation noted above, replace the statutory citations in this note to G.S. 14-27.7(b) with G.S. 14-27.32(e).

Element (4) (page 244)

As a result of the 2015 legislation noted above, the statutory citation in this note should be to G.S. 14-27.32(a).

Exceptions (page 244)

As a result of the 2015 legislation noted above, the statutory citation in this note should be to G.S. 14-27.32(a).

Multiple convictions and punishments (page 244)

As a result of the 2015 legislation noted above, the statutory citation in this note should be to G.S. 14-27.32(c).

Sexual Activity with a Student by School Personnel Other Than a Teacher, School Administrator, Student Teacher, Coach, or School Safety Officer Who Is at Least Four Years Older Than the Student (page 244) (revised title)

Statute (page 244)

2015 legislation amended and recodified the statute. S.L. 2015-181, secs. 14(a) and (b). The new statute is reproduced in this supplement under "Sexual Activity with a Student by a Teacher, School Administrator, Student Teacher, Coach, or School Safety Officer." The statutory amendments did not make any substantive changes to this offense.

Punishment (page 245)

As a result of the 2015 legislation noted above, the statutory citation in this section should be to G.S. 14-27.32(a).

Notes (page 245)

Element (1) (page 245)

As a result of the 2015 legislation noted above, replace the citation to G.S. 14-27.7(b) in this note with G.S. 14-27.32(e).

Sexual Activity with a Student by School Personnel Other Than a Teacher, School Administrator, Student Teacher, Coach, or School Safety Officer Who Is Less Than Four Years Older Than the Student (page 245) (revised title)

Statute (page 245)

2015 legislation amended and recodified the statute. S.L. 2015-181, secs. 14(a) and (b); S.L. 2015-44, sec. 2. The new statute is reproduced in this supplement under "Sexual Activity with a Student by a Teacher, School Administrator, Student Teacher, Coach, or School Safety Officer."

Punishment (page 246)

As a result of the 2015 legislation noted above, delete the text of this section and replace it with the following:

Class I felony. G.S. 14-27.32(b).

Indecent Liberties (page 246)

Indecent Liberties with a Child (page 246)

Notes (page 246)

General discussion of Elements (2)(a) and (2)(b) (page 247)

There was sufficient evidence of an indecent liberty where the defendant digitally penetrated the child's vagina. State v. Phachoumphone, 257 N.C. App. 848, 863–64 (2018).

Element (2)(a)(i) (page 248)

The defendant's purpose may be inferred from his or her actions. State v. Godley, 234 N.C. App. 562, 569 (2014); State v. Minyard, 231 N.C. App. 605, 621 (2014). For example, there was sufficient evidence of the required purpose when the defendant kissed the victim on the mouth, fondled her under her clothing, touched her breasts and vagina, and engaged in conduct giving rise to first-degree rape charges. Godley, 234 N.C. App. at 569.

There was sufficient proof that the defendant's purpose was to arouse or gratify sexual desire where he repeatedly raped the victim while she was living in his home. State v. Kpaeyeh, 246 N.C. App. 694, 700–01 (2016) (rejecting the defendant's argument that evidence of vaginal penetration is insufficient by itself to prove that a rape was committed for the purpose of arousing or gratifying sexual desire).

Element (3) (new note)

An actual child victim is not required to sustain a conviction for attempted taking indecent liberties. State v. Heelan, ___ N.C. App. ___, 823 S.E.2d 106 (2018) (although the person the defendant communicated with and sexually pursued was actually an undercover police officer, the defendant believed that he was communicating with and pursuing a child).

Attempts (page 249)

A defendant attempted to take an indecent liberty with a child when he wrote a letter asking her to have sex with him and gave it to the victim's grandmother, asking her to deliver it to the child, regardless of the fact that the victim never received the letter or otherwise saw or communicated with the defendant. State v. Southerland, ___ N.C. App. ___, 832 S.E.2d 168 (2019).

Jury instructions (page 249)

Because indecent liberties is a single offense that may be proved by evidence of any one of a number of acts, the trial court did not err by declining to instruct the jury according to a bill of particulars. *State v. Stephens*, 234 N.C. App. 292, 295–96 (2014) (the trial court properly instructed the jury that it could find the defendant guilty if it found that the defendant willfully took "any immoral, improper, or indecent liberties" with the child; the actual act committed for the purposes of arousing himself or gratifying his sexual desire was immaterial).

In a case involving five counts of indecent liberties, no unanimity issue arose where the trial court framed the jury instructions in terms of the statutory requirements and referenced the indictments, each of which specified a different, non-overlapping time frame; the instructions distinguished the five charges and directed the jurors to find the defendant guilty only if they found that he committed the requisite acts within the designated time period and each verdict sheet was paired with an indictment. *State v. Comeaux*, 224 N.C. App. 595, 605 (2012).

The trial judge properly instructed the jury in a case where the indictment tracked the statute and did not allege an evidentiary basis for the charge and the instructions identified the defendant's conduct as placing his penis between the child's feet. *State v. Carter*, 210 N.C. App. 156, 168–69 (2011) (the instruction was a clarification of the evidence for the jury).

Multiple convictions and punishments (page 249)

Add the following to the second paragraph of this note:

In *State v. Minyard*, 231 N.C. App. 605, 620–21 (2014), the court held that the victim's testimony that the defendant touched the victim's buttocks with his penis "four or five times" supported five indecent liberties convictions. Distinguishing *Laney* and finding the case similar to *James*, the court concluded that the State need not prove that the conduct occurred in discrete, separate settings when it involved acts "more explicit than mere touching." *Id.* at 620.

In *State v. Pierce*, 238 N.C. App. 537, 549–50 (2014), the court, citing *James*, held that the defendant properly was convicted of two counts of indecent liberties when the evidence showed that he had sex with his girlfriend in the presence of the victim, performed oral sex on the victim, and then forced his girlfriend to perform oral sex on the victim while he watched.

Indecent Liberties between Children (page 250)

Notes (page 250)

Element (2) (page 250)

For cases where the evidence was insufficient to establish a juvenile's sexual purpose with respect to the crime of Sexual Battery, see the note on Element (1) to that offense in this supplement.

Taking Indecent Liberties with a Student by a Teacher, School Administrator, Student Teacher, School Safety Officer, or Coach (page 251) (revised title)

Statute (page 251)

2015 legislation, S.L. 2015-44, sec. 3, amended G.S. 14-202.4(b) to read as follows:

(b) If a defendant, who is school personnel, other than a teacher, school administrator, student teacher, school safety officer, or coach, and who is less than four years older than the victim, takes indecent liberties with a student as provided in subsection (a) of this section, the defendant is guilty of a Class I felony.

That same legislation amended the definition of "school personnel" in G.S. 14-202.4(d)(3) to read as follows:

(3) "School personnel" means any person included in the definition contained in G.S. 115C-332(a)(2), including those employed by a nonpublic, charter, or regional school, and any person who volunteers at a school or a school-sponsored activity.

2015 legislation, S.L. 2015-181, sec. 16, made a conforming change to the last sentence of subsection (d) of the statute to read as follows:

> **For purposes of this section, the term indecent liberties does not include vaginal intercourse or a sexual act as defined by G.S. 14-27.20.**

Notes (page 252)

Element (2) (page 252)

This note cites G.S. 14-27.1. That statute was recodified as G.S. 14-27.20 by 2015 legislation. S.L. 2015-181, sec. 2.

Element (3) (page 252)

If the victim is enrolled in kindergarten or grade 1 through 12, the victim is a student within the meaning of the statute, even if the incident occurs during a school break. State v. Stephens, 234 N.C. App. 292, 296–97 (2014) (incident occurred during summer vacation).

Taking Indecent Liberties with a Student by School Personnel Other Than a Teacher, School Administrator, Student Teacher, School Safety Officer, or Coach Who Is at Least Four Years Older Than the Student (page 253) (revised title)

Statute (page 253)

As noted above under "Taking Indecent Liberties with a Student by a Teacher, School Administrator, Student Teacher, School Safety Officer, or Coach," 2015 legislation amended the statute.

Notes (page 253)

Element (1) (page 253)

As a result of 2015 legislation, S.L. 2015-44, sec. 3, delete the first sentence of this note and replace it with the following:

> "School personnel" means any person included in the definition contained in G.S. 115C-332(a)(2), including those employed by a nonpublic, charter, or regional school, and any person who volunteers at a school or a school-sponsored activity. G.S. 14-202.4(d)(3).

Taking Indecent Liberties with a Student by School Personnel Other Than a Teacher, School Administrator, Student Teacher, School Safety Officer, or Coach Who Is Less Than Four Years Older Than the Student (page 253) (revised title)

Statute (page 253)

As noted above under "Taking Indecent Liberties with a Student by a Teacher, School Administrator, Student Teacher, School Safety Officer, or Coach," 2015 legislation amended the statute.

Punishment (page 254)

As a result of the 2015 legislation noted above under "Taking Indecent Liberties with a Student by a Teacher, School Administrator, Student Teacher, School Safety Officer, or Coach," delete the text of this section and replace it with the following:

> Class I felony. G.S. 14-202.4(b).

Sexual Battery (page 254)

Statute (page 254)

2015 legislation, S.L. 2015-181, sec. 15, recodified the statute as G.S. 14-27.33; 2018 legislation, S.L. 2018-47, sec. 4(d), amended it. As a result of these changes, the statute reads as follows:

§ 14-27.33. Sexual battery.

(a) A person is guilty of sexual battery if the person, for the purpose of sexual arousal, sexual gratification, or sexual abuse, engages in sexual contact with another person:

    (1) By force and against the will of the other person; or

    (2) Who has a mental disability or who is mentally incapacitated or physically helpless, and the person performing the act knows or should reasonably know that the other person has a mental disability or is mentally incapacitated or physically helpless.

(b) Any person who commits the offense defined in this section is guilty of a Class A1 misdemeanor.

Elements (page 254)

As a result of the 2018 legislation noted above, Element 3(b) should read as follows:

(3)(b) who has a mental disability or who is mentally incapacitated or physically helpless, and the person knows or should reasonably know that the other person has a mental disability or is mentally incapacitated or physically helpless.

Punishment (page 254)

As a result of the 2015 legislation noted above, the statutory citation in this section should be to G.S. 14-27.33(b).

Notes (page 255)

Element (1) (page 255)

The court of appeals has noted that in cases involving adult defendants, "the element of acting for the purpose of sexual arousal, sexual gratification, or sexual abuse may be inferred from the very act itself." *In re* S.A.A., 251 N.C. App. 131, 135 (2016) (internal quotation marks omitted). However, that rule does not apply with respect to juveniles. *Id.*; *In re* K.C., 226 N.C. App. 452, 457 (2013). For a juvenile, there must be "evidence of the child's maturity, intent, experience, or other factor indicating his purpose in acting." *S.A.A.*, 251 N.C. App. at 135 (quoting *K.C.*, 226 N.C. App. at 457). For cases where the evidence was held to be insufficient to establish a juvenile's sexual purpose required for this crime, see *K.C.*, 226 N.C. App. at 457–58 (evidence of sexual purpose was insufficient where, among other things, the juvenile and the victim were the same age; there was no evidence that the juvenile exercised control over the situation; and the incident occurred in a public school room during the day), and *S.A.A.*, 251 N.C. App. at 137 (evidence of sexual purpose was insufficient where, among other things, the juvenile and the girls in question were middle school students; neither the location nor the alleged manner of the touching was secretive in nature; nothing about the juvenile's attitude suggested a sexual motivation; the juvenile made no sexual remarks to the girls; and the juvenile did not attempt to exert any control over the girls). For a case where the evidence was sufficient to establish a juvenile's sexual purpose with respect to the crime of Indecent Liberties between Children, see the note on Element (2) to that crime in the main volume.

Element (2) (page 255)

This note cites G.S. 14-27.1. That statute was recodified as G.S. 14-27.20 by 2015 legislation.

Solicitation of a Child by Computer or Other Electronic Device (page 255)

Solicitation of a Child by Computer or Other Electronic Device to Commit an Unlawful Sex Act (page 255)

Notes (page 256)

Element (5)(b) (new note)

For a case where the evidence was sufficient to establish that the defendant believed the victim to be a child, see *State v. Heelan*, ___ N.C. App. ___, 823 S.E.2d 106 (2018) (although the person the defendant communicated with and sexually pursued was actually an undercover police officer, the defendant believed that he was communicating with and pursuing a child).

Sex Offender Crimes (page 258)

Statute (page 258)

G.S. 14-208.6 has been amended, *see* S.L. 2012-153, sec. 3; S.L. 2012-194, sec. 4(a); S.L. 2015-181, sec. 32; S.L. 2017-102, sec. 5; S.L. 2017-186, sec. 2(q); S.L. 2018-47, sec. 4(h), to read as follows:

§ 14-208.6. Definitions.

The following definitions apply in this Article:

(1a) Aggravated offense.—Any criminal offense that includes either of the following: (i) engaging in a sexual act involving vaginal, anal, or oral penetration with a victim of any age through the use of force or the threat of serious violence; or (ii) engaging in a sexual act involving vaginal, anal, or oral penetration with a victim who is less than 12 years old.

(1b) County registry.—The information compiled by the sheriff of a county in compliance with this Article.

(1c) Department.—The Department of Public Safety.

(1d) Electronic mail.—The transmission of information or communication by the use of the Internet, a computer, a facsimile machine, a pager, a cellular telephone, a video recorder, or other electronic means sent to a person identified by a unique address or address number and received by that person.

(1e) Employed.—Includes employment that is full-time or part-time for a period of time exceeding 14 days or for an aggregate period of time exceeding 30 days during any calendar year, whether financially compensated, volunteered, or for the purpose of government or educational benefit.

(1f) Entity.—A business or organization that provides Internet service, electronic communications service, remote computing service, online service, electronic mail service, or electronic instant message or chat services whether the business or organization is inside or outside the State.

(1g) Instant Message.—A form of real-time text communication between two or more people. The communication is conveyed via computers connected over a network such as the Internet.

(1h) Institution of higher education.—Any postsecondary public or private educational institution, including any trade or professional institution, college, or university.

(1i) Internet.—The global information system that is logically linked together by a globally unique address space based on the Internet Protocol or its subsequent extensions; that is able to support communications using the Transmission Control Protocol/Internet Protocol suite, its subsequent extensions, or other Internet Protocol compatible protocols; and that provides, uses, or makes accessible, either publicly or privately, high-level services layered on the communications and related infrastructure described in this subdivision.

(1j) Mental abnormality.—A congenital or acquired condition of a person that affects the emotional or volitional capacity of the person in a manner that predisposes that person to the commission of criminal sexual acts to a degree that makes the person a menace to the health and safety of others.

(1k) Nonresident student.—A person who is not a resident of North Carolina but who is enrolled in any type of school in the State on a part-time or full-time basis.

(1l) Nonresident worker.—A person who is not a resident of North Carolina but who has employment or carries on a vocation in the State, on a part-time or full-time basis, with or without compensation or government or educational benefit, for more than 14 days, or for an aggregate period exceeding 30 days in a calendar year.

(1m) Offense against a minor.—Any of the following offenses if the offense is committed against a minor, and the person committing the offense is not the minor's parent: G.S. 14-39 (kidnapping), G.S. 14-41 (abduction of children), and G.S. 14-43.3 (felonious restraint). The term also includes the following if the person convicted of the following is not the minor's parent: a solicitation or conspiracy to commit any of these offenses; aiding and abetting any of these offenses.

(1n) Online identifier.—Electronic mail address, instant message screen name, user ID, chat or other Internet communication name, but it does not mean social security number, date of birth, or pin number.

(2) Penal institution.—Any of the following:
   a. A detention facility operated under the jurisdiction of the Section of Prisons of the Division of Adult Correction and Juvenile Justice of the Department of Public Safety.
   b. A detention facility operated under the jurisdiction of another state or the federal government.
   c. A detention facility operated by a local government in this State or another state.

(2a) Personality disorder.—An enduring pattern of inner experience and behavior that deviates markedly from the expectations of the individual's culture, is pervasive and inflexible, has an onset in adolescence or early adulthood, is stable over time, and leads to distress or impairment.

(2b) Recidivist.—A person who has a prior conviction for an offense that is described in G.S. 14-208.6(4).

(3) Release.—Discharged or paroled.

(4) Reportable conviction.—Any of the following:
   a. A final conviction for an offense against a minor, a sexually violent offense, or an attempt to commit any of those offenses unless the conviction is for aiding and abetting. A final conviction for aiding and abetting is a reportable conviction only if the court sentencing the individual finds that the registration of that individual under this Article furthers the purposes of this Article as stated in G.S. 14-208.5.
   b. A final conviction in another state of an offense, which if committed in this State, is substantially similar to an offense against a minor or a sexually violent offense as defined by this section, or a final conviction in another state of an offense that requires registration under the sex offender registration statutes of that state.
   c. A final conviction in a federal jurisdiction (including a court martial) of an offense, which is substantially similar to an offense against a minor or a sexually violent offense as defined by this section.

      d.   A final conviction for a violation of G.S. 14-202(d), (e), (f), (g), or (h), or a second or subsequent conviction for a violation of G.S. 14-202(a), (a1), or (c), only if the court sentencing the individual issues an order pursuant to G.S. 14-202(l) requiring the individual to register.

      e.   A final conviction for a violation of G.S. 14-43.14, only if the court sentencing the individual issues an order pursuant to G.S. 14-43.14(e) requiring the individual to register.

(5) Sexually violent offense.—A violation of former G.S. 14-27.6 (attempted rape or sexual offense), G.S. 14-27.21 (first-degree forcible rape), G.S. 14-27.22 (second-degree forcible rape), G.S. 14-27.23 (statutory rape of a child by an adult), G.S. 14-27.24 (first-degree statutory rape), G.S. 14-27.25(a) (statutory rape of a person who is 15 years of age or younger and where the defendant is at least six years older), G.S. 14-27.26 (first-degree forcible sexual offense), G.S. 14-27.27 (second-degree forcible sexual offense), G.S. 14-27.28 (statutory sexual offense with a child by an adult), G.S. 14-27.29 (first-degree statutory sexual offense), G.S. 14-27.30(a) (statutory sexual offense with a person who is 15 years of age or younger and where the defendant is at least six years older), G.S. 14-27.31 (sexual activity by a substitute parent or custodian), G.S. 14-27.32 (sexual activity with a student), G.S. 14-27.33 (sexual battery), G.S. 14-43.11 (human trafficking) if (i) the offense is committed against a minor who is less than 18 years of age or (ii) the offense is committed against any person with the intent that they be held in sexual servitude, G.S. 14-43.13 (subjecting or maintaining a person for sexual servitude), G.S. 14-178 (incest between near relatives), G.S. 14-190.6 (employing or permitting minor to assist in offenses against public morality and decency), G.S. 14-190.9(a1) (felonious indecent exposure), G.S. 14-190.16 (first degree sexual exploitation of a minor), G.S. 14-190.17 (second degree sexual exploitation of a minor), G.S. 14-190.17A (third degree sexual exploitation of a minor), G.S. 14-202.1 (taking indecent liberties with children), G.S. 14-202.3 (Solicitation of child by computer or certain other electronic devices to commit an unlawful sex act), G.S. 14-202.4(a) (taking indecent liberties with a student), G.S. 14-205.2(c) or (d) (patronizing a prostitute who is a minor or has a mental disability), G.S. 14-205.3(b) (promoting prostitution of a minor or person who has a mental disability), G.S. 14-318.4(a1) (parent or caretaker commit or permit act of prostitution with or by a juvenile), or G.S. 14-318.4(a2) (commission or allowing of sexual act upon a juvenile by parent or guardian). The term also includes the following: a solicitation or conspiracy to commit any of these offenses; aiding and abetting any of these offenses.

(6) Sexually violent predator.—A person who has been convicted of a sexually violent offense and who suffers from a mental abnormality or personality disorder that makes the person likely to engage in sexually violent offenses directed at strangers or at a person with whom a relationship has been established or promoted for the primary purpose of victimization.

(7) Sheriff.—The sheriff of a county in this State.

(8) Statewide registry.—The central registry compiled by the Department in accordance with G.S. 14-208.14.

(9) Student.—A person who is enrolled on a full-time or part-time basis, in any postsecondary public or private educational institution, including any trade or professional institution, or other institution of higher education.

2013 legislation, S.L. 2013-205, amended G.S. 14-208.11(a)(1) to read as follows:

(1) Fails to register as required by this Article, including failure to register with the sheriff in the county designated by the person, pursuant to G.S. 14-208.8, as their expected county of residence.

That same legislation enacted a new subsection, (a2), to G.S. 14-208.11 as follows:

> (a2) A person arrested pursuant to subsection (a1) of this section shall be subject to the jurisdiction of the prosecutorial and judicial district that includes the sheriff's office in the county where the person failed to register, pursuant to this Article. If the arrest is made outside of the applicable prosecutorial district, the person shall be transferred to the custody of the sheriff of the county where the person failed to register and all further criminal and judicial proceedings shall be held in that county.

2013 legislation, S.L. 2013-28, amended G.S. 14-208.16(a) to read as follows:

> (a) A registrant under this Article shall not knowingly reside within 1,000 feet of the property on which any public or nonpublic school or child care center is located. This subsection applies to any registrant who did not establish his or her residence, in accordance with subsection (d) of this section, prior to August 16, 2006.

2016 legislation, S.L. 2016-102, sec. 1, amended G.S. 14-208.18(a) so that subsection (3) and new subsection (4) read as follows:

> (3) At any place where minors frequently congregate, including, but not limited to, libraries, arcades, amusement parks, recreation parks, and swimming pools, when minors are present.
>
> (4) On the State Fairgrounds during the period of time each year that the State Fair is conducted, on the Western North Carolina Agricultural Center grounds during the period of time each year that the North Carolina Mountain State Fair is conducted, and on any other fairgrounds during the period of time that an agricultural fair is being conducted.

2015 and 2016 legislation, S.L. 2015-62, sec. 5(a); S.L. 2016-102, sec. 1, amended G.S. 14-208.18(c) to read as follows:

> (c) The subdivisions of subsection (a) of this section are applicable as follows:
>
> (1) Subdivisions (1), (3), and (4) of subsection (a) of this section apply to persons required to register under this Article who have committed any of the following offenses:
>
> a. Any offense in Article 7A of this Chapter or any federal offense or offense committed in another state, which if committed in this State, is substantially similar to an offense in Article 7A of this Chapter.
>
> b. Any offense where the victim of the offense was under the age of 18 years at the time of the offense.
>
> (2) Subdivision (2) of subsection (a) of this section applies to persons required to register under this Article if either of the following applies:
>
> a. The person has committed any offense in Article 7B of this Chapter or any federal offense or offense committed in another state, which if committed in this State is substantially similar to an offense in Article 7B of this Chapter, and a finding has been made in any criminal or civil proceeding that the person presents, or may present, a danger to minors under the age of 18.
>
> b. The person has committed any offense where the victim of the offense was under the age of 18 years at the time of the offense.

2017 legislation, S.L. 2017-186, sec. 2(aa), amended G.S. 14-208.44(c) and (d) to read as follows:

> (c) Any person required to enroll in a satellite-based monitoring program who fails to provide necessary information to the Division of Adult Correction and Juvenile Justice or fails to cooperate with the Division of Adult Correction and Juvenile Justice's guidelines and regulations for the program shall be guilty of a Class 1 misdemeanor.
>
> (d) For purposes of this section, "enroll" shall include appearing, as directed by the Division of Adult Correction and Juvenile Justice to receive the necessary equipment.

Failure to Register, etc. as a Sex Offender (page 268)

Notes (page 269)

Element (1) (page 269)

Registration requirements that became effective on January 1, 1996, and applied to offenders then serving a sentence for a reportable offense applied to the defendant and made him a person required to register where he was convicted in 1994 of indecent liberties and his prison release date for that conviction was September 24, 1995, but he was not actually released until January 24, 1999, because he was serving a consecutive term for crime against nature. State v. Surratt, 241 N.C. App. 380, 385–86 (2015) (concluding that the defendant's actual release date, January 24, 1999, governs; also concluding that because he was required to register when the 2008 amendments to the registration statutes took effect, the 2008 amendments applied to the defendant as well).

Element (3)(a) (page 269)

2013 legislation, S.L. 2013-205, amended the statute to clarify that failure to register includes failure to register with the sheriff in the county designated by the person as his or her expected county of residence.

Element (3)(b) (page 269)

Add the following to this note:

This prong of the statute applies to a sex offender who has already complied with the initial registration requirements and is later incarcerated and then released. State v. Crockett, 368 N.C. 717, 722 (2016); State v. Barnett, 368 N.C. 710, 714 (2016) (holding that this provision applied where the defendant failed to change his address after being released from a term of incarceration imposed after his initial registration).

The evidence was sufficient to establish this Element where (1) after previously registering as required under the statute, the defendant failed to register a change of address after being released from one month's incarceration after a parole violation, State v. Reynolds, 253 N.C. App. 359, 364–66 (2017); (2) after initially registering, the defendant was incarcerated in the county jail and upon his release did not provide notice that he had changed his address from the county jail, *Crockett*, 368 N.C. at 724–25; (3) the defendant moved from North Carolina to South Carolina without providing written notice to the sheriff, *id*. at 725–26; (4) the defendant was not residing at his registered address, State v. McFarland, 234 N.C. App. 274, 280–81 (2014) (the State need not present evidence of the defendant's new address, only that he or she failed to register a change of address); and (5) the defendant may have maintained a permanent residence in one county, but he also established a temporary home address at his ex-wife's residence in another county. State v. Pierce, 238 N.C. App. 141, 148–49 (2014).

Element (3)(c) (page 270)

Delete the second sentence of this note and replace it with the following:

To obtain a conviction under this prong of the statute, the State must prove five things: (1) the defendant is required to register, (2) law enforcement mailed a non-forwardable verification form to the defendant's last reported address, (3) the defendant actually received the verification form, (4) law enforcement made a reasonable attempt to verify that the defendant was residing at the registered address, and (5) the defendant willfully failed to return the verification form to the sheriff within three business days. State v. Moore, 240 N.C. App. 465, 473 (2015) (stating these requirements and holding that the State failed to prove that the defendant actually received the verification form, that the sheriff's office made a reasonable attempt to verify that the defendant was still residing at his last reported address, or that the defendant acted willfully); State v. Braswell, 203 N.C. App. 736, 739 (2010) (the State failed to prove that the defendant actually received the verification form). A "business day" is any calendar day except

Saturday, Sunday, or any legal holiday declared in G.S. 103-4. State v. Patterson, ___ N.C. App. ___, 831 S.E.2d 619 (2019) (concluding that Columbus Day is a legal holiday under G.S. 103-4, and therefore not a business day within the meaning of G.S. 14-208.9A—regardless of whether the sheriff's office was actually open for business).

Element (3)(d) (page 270)

Falsely stating information on any forms submitted pursuant to the sex offender registration program supports a conviction. State v. Pressley, 235 N.C. App. 613, 617 (2014) (in a case where the defendant listed a false address, the court rejected the defendant's argument that the only verification forms that count are the initial verification form and those required to be filed every six months thereafter; the court concluded that the statute criminalizes providing false or misleading information on forms submitted pursuant to the act, regardless of when the forms are submitted). However, the statute only applies to providing false or misleading information on an executed verification form required by the statute; the statute does not apply to oral verifications to a law enforcement officer. State v. Surratt, 241 N.C. App. 380, 387 (2015).

Constitutionality (new note)

Requiring a person adjudicated as an incompetent to notify a sheriff of a change of address is unconstitutional. State v. Young, 140 N.C. App. 1 (2000).

The court of appeals has rejected the argument that the statute's change of address requirement was void for vagueness because it failed to define the term "address." State v. McFarland, 234 N.C. App. at 274, 277–79 (2014) (the homeless defendant unsuccessfully argued that a person of ordinary intelligence would not know what "address" meant in his case).

Jurisdiction (new note)

2013 legislation, S.L. 2013-205, amended G.S. 14-208.11 to provide that a person arrested for a failure-to-register violation must be prosecuted in the prosecutorial district that includes the sheriff's office in the county where the defendant failed to register. G.S. 14-208.11(a2). If the arrest is made outside of the applicable prosecutorial district, the defendant must be transferred to the custody of the sheriff of the county where the defendant failed to register. *Id.*

Multiple convictions and punishments (page 271)

For a case holding that double jeopardy prohibits a defendant from being punished for failing to register a change of address under both G.S. 14-208.11(a)(2) (failing to notify the last registering sheriff of a change of address) and -208.11(a)(7) (failing to report in person to the sheriff) based on the same failure to report, see *State v. Reynolds*, 253 N.C. App. 359, 362–64 (2017).

Falsely reporting an address on verification forms submitted on two separate occasions supports two convictions. State v. Pressley, 235 N.C. App. 613, 619 (2014) (rejecting the defendant's argument that this constituted a continuing offense and could support only one conviction; submission of each form was a distinct offense).

Knowingly Residing Near a School or Child Care Center (page 272)

Notes (page 272)

Element (5) (page 272)

As a result of 2019 legislation, S.L. 2019-245, sec. 8.(a), add the following sentence at the end of the first paragraph of this note:

However, for the purposes of this offense, the term "school" shall also include any construction project designated for use as a public school, if the governing body has notified the sheriff with jurisdiction within 1,000 feet of the construction project of the construction of the public school. G.S. 14-208.16(b).

As a result of 2014 legislation, S.L. 2014-21, add the following sentence at the end of the second paragraph of this note:

> However, a "child care center" does include the permanent locations of organized clubs of Boys and Girls Clubs of America. G.S. 14-208.16(b).

Exceptions (page 272)

As a result of 2013 legislation, S.L. 2013-28, delete the last paragraph of this note and replace it with the following:

> Additionally, this offense does not apply to a person who established his or her residence before August 16, 2006. G.S. 14-208.16(a).

Being Present at a Location Used by Minors (page 274)

Statute (page 274)

As noted in this supplement, 2015 and 2016 legislation, S.L. 2015-62, sec. 5(a); S.L. 2016-102, sec.1, amended the statute.

Elements (page 274)

As a result of the 2015 and 2016 legislation noted above, delete the text of this section and replace it with the following:

A person guilty of this offense

(1) is required to register as a sex offender

(2) because of a conviction for any
    (a) rape, sexual offense, sexual battery, or related offense in G.S. Chapter 14, Article 7B or substantially similar offense under federal law or the laws of another state *or*
    (b) offense in which the victim was less than 18 years old *and*

(3) knowingly

(4) is present
    (a) on the premises of any place intended primarily for the use, care, or supervision of minors, including, but not limited to, schools, children's museums, child care centers, nurseries, and playgrounds;
    (b) within 300 feet of any location intended primarily for the use, care, or supervision of minors when the place is located on premises that are not intended primarily for the use, care, or supervision of minors, including malls, shopping centers, or other property open to the general public and, if the person is required to register because of a rape, sexual offense, sexual battery, or related offense in G.S. Chapter 14, Article 7B or substantially similar offense under federal law or the laws of another state, a finding has been made in any criminal or civil proceeding that the person presents, or may present, a danger to minors under the age of 18;
    (c) at any place where minors frequently congregate, including, but not limited to, libraries, arcades, amusement parks, recreation parks, and swimming pools, when minors are present; *or*
    (d) on the State Fairgrounds when the State Fair is conducted, on the Western North Carolina Agricultural Center grounds when the North Carolina Mountain State Fair is conducted, or on any other fairgrounds when an agricultural fair is being conducted.

Notes (page 274)

Element (2)(b) (new note)

If the prior offense does not include an element as to the victim's age, the State must prove that the victim was younger than the statutory age at the time of the offense. State v. Fryou, 244 N.C. App. 112, 121–22 (2015).

Element (3) (page 274)

For a case where the evidence was sufficient as to this Element, see *Fryou*, 244 N.C. App. at 122–23 (church widely advertised its preschool and posted a sign at the church entrance indicating that a "nursery" was held on the premises).

Element (4) (page 274)

The evidence was insufficient to support a conviction for being a sex offender on the premises of a daycare when the defendant was seen in a parking lot of a strip mall containing the daycare center, other businesses, and a restaurant. State v. Anderson, 254 N.C. App. 765, 776 (2017) (none of the spaces in the parking lot were specifically reserved or marked for the daycare and the daycare center, which was, including its playground, surrounded by a chain-link fence).

To satisfy Element (4)(b), the State must prove that the location is intended primarily for the use of minors; evidence that minors sometimes use the location is insufficient. State v. Simpson, 235 N.C. App. 398, 403–05 (2014) (the evidence was insufficient where the defendant sat on a park bench in close proximity to one of the park's batting cages and ball fields and the State failed to present evidence that the batting cages and ball fields were intended primarily for use by minors).

Although *Fryou*, 244 N.C. App. at 123, held that the State need not prove that minors were actually present at the location at the time of the offense, 2016 legislative changes provided that the ban on being present at any place where minors frequently congregate (Element (4)(c) of this offense) applies only when "minors are present." S.L. 2016-102, sec. 1.

Multiple convictions and punishments (new note)

In *State v. Daniels*, 224 N.C. App. 608, 612 (2012), the court held that elements (4)(a) through (c) constitute three separate and distinct criminal offenses. This holding likely would apply to Element (4)(d) as well.

Constitutionality (new note)

2016 legislation, S.L. 2016-102, sec. 1, amended the statute in response to determinations in a federal district court case that (1) the prior statutory provision banning sex offenders from any place where minors gather for regularly scheduled educational, recreational, or social programs was unconstitutionally vague, Does v. Cooper, 148 F. Supp. 3d 477, 494 (M.D.N.C. 2015); and (2) the "300-foot rule" ban was unconstitutionally overbroad under the First Amendment. Does v. Cooper, No. 1:13CV711, 2016 WL 1629282 (M.D.N.C. Apr. 22, 2016). The General Assembly responded by revising the "any place where minors gather" provision and by adding to the 300-foot rule a requirement that a finding has been made in any criminal or civil proceeding that the person presents, or may present, a danger to minors under the age of 18. S.L. 2016-102, sec. 1. Lawmakers also provided that these changes are repealed if the federal district court's determinations are stayed or overturned. *Id.* sec. 2. The Fourth Circuit affirmed the lower court's rulings in *Does v. Cooper*, 842 F.3d 833 (4th Cir. 2016).

In *Daniels*, 224 N.C. App. at 621, the court held that the previous version of G.S. 14-208.18(a)(3), which prohibited a sex offender from being "at any place" where minors gather for regularly scheduled programs, was unconstitutionally vague as applied to the defendant. The defendant's two charges arose from his presence at two public parks. The State alleged that on one occasion the defendant was "out kind of close to the parking lot area or that little dirt road area[,]" between the ballpark and the road and that on the second occasion he was at an "adult softball field" adjacent to a "tee ball" field. The court found that on these facts, the portion of G.S. 14-208.18(a)(3) prohibiting presence "at any place" was unconstitutionally vague as applied to the defendant because it fails to give the person of ordinary intelligence a reasonable opportunity to know what is prohibited and it fails to provide explicit standards for those who apply the law. *Id.* at 622. By contrast, the court rejected an as-applied vagueness challenge to G.S. 14-208.18(a)(2) in a case involving the defendant's presence at a church that operated a preschool on the premises. State v. Fryou, 244 N.C. App. 112, 127–28 (2015). As noted in this supplement, 2016 legislation amended the prohibitions in G.S. 14-208.18(a)(2) and (3).

Accessing a Social Networking Site (page 274)

Notes (page 275)

Constitutionality (new note)

In *Packingham v. North Carolina*, ___ U.S. ___, 137 S. Ct. 1730 (2017), the United States Supreme Court struck down G.S. 14-202.5 on grounds that it violates the First Amendment.

Online Conduct by High-Risk Sex Offenders (new crime)

After *Packingham*, G.S. 14-202.5 was substantially amended by 2019 legislation, S.L. 2019-245, effective for offenses committed on or after December 1, 2019.

Statute

§ 14-202.5. Ban online conduct by high-risk sex offenders that endangers children.

(a) Offense. – It is unlawful for a high-risk sex offender to do any of the following online:

(1)　To communicate with a person that the offender believes is under 16 years of age.

(2)　To contact a person that the offender believes is under 16 years of age.

(3)　To pose falsely as a person under 16 years of age with the intent to commit an unlawful sex act with a person the offender believes is under 16 years of age.

(4)　To use a Web site to gather information about a person that the offender believes is under 16 years of age.

(5)　To use a commercial social networking Web site in violation of a policy, posted in a manner reasonably likely to come to the attention of users, prohibiting convicted sex offenders from using the site.

(b) Definition of Commercial Social Networking Web Site. – For the purposes of this section, a "commercial social networking Web site" includes any Web site, application, portal, or other means of accessing the Internet that meets all of the following requirements:

(1)　Is operated by a person who derives revenue from membership fees, advertising, or other sources related to the operation of the Web site.

[The session law strikes through subdivision (b)(2) but does not replace it.]

(3)　Allows users to create personal Web pages or profiles that contain information such as the user's name or nickname, photographs of the user, and other personal information.

(4)　Provides users or visitors a mechanism to communicate with others, such as a message board, chat room, or instant messenger.

(c) Exclusions from Commercial Social Networking Web Site Definition. – A commercial social networking Web site does not include a Web site that meets either of the following requirements:

[The session law strikes through subdivision (c)(1) but does not replace it.]

(2)　Has as its primary purpose the facilitation of commercial transactions, the dissemination of news, the discussion of political or social issues, or professional networking.

(3)　 Is a Web site owned or operated by a local, State, or federal governmental entity.

(c1) Definition of High-Risk Sex Offender. – For purposes of this section, the term "high-risk sex offender" means any person registered in accordance with Article 27A of Chapter 14 of the General Statutes that meets any of the following requirements:

(1)　Was convicted of an aggravated offense, as that term is defined in G.S. 14-208.6, against a person under 18 years of age.

(2)   Is a recidivist, as that term is defined in G.S. 14-208.6, and one offense is against a person under 18 years of age.

(3)   Was convicted of an offense against a minor, as that term is defined in G.S. 14-208.6.

(4)   Was convicted of a sexually violent offense, as that term is defined in G.S. 14-208.6, against a person under 18 years of age.

(5)   Was found by a court to be a sexually violent predator, as that term is defined in G.S. 14-208.6, based on a conviction of a sexually violent offense committed against a minor.

(d) Jurisdiction. – The offense is committed in the State for purposes of determining jurisdiction, if the transmission that constitutes the offense either originates in the State or is received in the State.

(e) Punishment. – A violation of this section is a Class H felony.

(f) Severability. – If any provision of this section or its application is held invalid, the invalidity does not affect other provisions or applications of this section that can be given effect without the invalid provisions or applications, and, to this end, the provisions of this section are severable.

Elements

A person guilty of this offense

(1) is a high-risk sex offender *and*

(2) does any of the following online

    (a) communicates with a person that the offender believes is under 16 years of age,

    (b) contacts a person that the offender believes is under 16 years of age,

    (c) poses falsely as a person under 16 years of age with the intent to commit an unlawful sex act with a person the offender believes is under 16 years of age,

    (d) uses a website to gather information about a person that the offender believes is under 16 years of age, *or*

    (e) uses a commercial social networking website in violation of a policy, posted in a manner reasonably likely to come to the attention of users, prohibiting convicted sex offenders from using the site.

Punishment

Class H felony. G.S. 14-202.5.

Notes

Element (1). A high-risk sex offender is any person registered as a sex offender in North Carolina who is a recidivist; was convicted of an aggravated offense, an offense against a minor, or a sexually violent offense; or was found to be a sexually violent predator, as those terms are defined in G.S. 14-208.6.

Element (4)(e). A commercial social networking website is any website, application, portal, or other means of accessing the Internet that is operated by a person who derives revenue through fees, advertising, or other sources by allowing users to create personal webpages and providing a mechanism to communicate with others. G.S. 14-202.5(b). The definition of a commercial social networking website excludes sites that have as their primary purpose the facilitation of commercial transactions, the dissemination of news, the discussion of political or social issues, or professional networking. *Id.* § -202.5(c).

Jurisdiction. The offense is committed in North Carolina if the transmission at issue either originates or is received in North Carolina. G.S. 14-202.5(d).

Related Offenses Not in This Chapter

See "Child Abuse" offenses and "Contributing to a Juvenile's Being Delinquent, Undisciplined, Abused, or Neglected" in Chapter 9 (Abuse and Neglect) of the main volume.

See "Failure to Report the Disappearance of a Child" (new crime) in Chapter 9 (Abuse and Neglect) of this supplement.

Unlawful payments related to adoption. G.S. 48-10-102.

11

Crime against Nature, Incest, Indecent Exposure, and Related Offenses

---

Crime against Nature (page 281)

Notes (page 281)

Constitutionality (page 282)

For an additional case supporting the statement in this note that the statute may be used to prosecute conduct involving a minor, non-consensual or coercive sexual acts, conduct occurring in a public place, or conduct involving prostitution or solicitation, see *State v. Gentle*, ___ N.C. App. ___, ___, 817 S.E.2d 833, 839 (2018).

For a case where the evidence established that the conduct occurred in a public place, see *Gentle, id.* at ___, 817 S.E.2d at 839–40 (the conduct occurred near a parking lot; the court rejected the defendant's argument that the conduct also must occur in public view).

Consent (page 282)

Reversing a case cited in this note, *State v. Hunt*, 211 N.C. App. 452 (2011), the North Carolina Supreme Court held that there was sufficient evidence that the victim's conditions rendered her substantially incapable of resisting the defendant's advances and that expert testimony is not required to prove the extent of a victim's mental capacity to consent to sexual acts. State v. Hunt, 365 N.C. 432, 441 (2012).

Penetration required (page 282)

For another case supporting the statement in this note that penetration of or by a sexual organ is required for this offense, see *In re* J.F., 237 N.C. App. 218, 225–27 (2014) (distinguishing *Heil* and finding the evidence insufficient to establish penetration).

Sexual purpose (new note)

Proof of this crime does not require evidence that the defendant acted with a sexual purpose. *Id.* at 224–25.

Greater and lesser-included offenses (page 283)

The court of appeals has held that a defendant cannot be convicted of second-degree sexual offense (mentally disabled victim) and crime against nature (where lack of consent was based on the fact that the victim was mentally disabled, incapacitated, or physically helpless) based on the same conduct (fellatio). State v. Hunt, 221 N.C. App. 489, 496–97 (2012), *aff'd on other grounds*, 367 N.C. 700 (2014) (per curiam). The court found that on the facts of the case, crime against nature was a lesser-included offense of second-degree sexual offense and that conviction of both violated double jeopardy. *Id.* However, the North Carolina Supreme Court previously held that crime against nature is not a lesser-included offense of forcible sexual offense, State v. Etheridge, 319 N.C. 34, 50–51 (1987); State v. Warren, 309 N.C. 224, 230–31 (1983), and that a definitional test—not a factual test—applies when determining whether offenses are lesser-included offenses. State v. Nickerson, 365 N.C. 279, 280 (2011); *Warren*, 309 N.C. at 230–31; *see also* State v. Robinson, 368 N.C. 402, 406–08 (2015) (applying a definitional test to the analysis).

Incest Offenses (page 284)

2012 legislation, S.L. 2012-40, amended G.S. 7B-1111(a) to provide that a court may terminate parental rights upon a finding that a parent "has been convicted of a sexually related offense under Chapter 14 of the General Statutes that resulted in the conception of the juvenile." All of the incest offenses covered in this chapter fall within Chapter 14 of the General Statutes.

Incest (page 284)

Notes (page 284)

Jury instructions (new note)

For a discussion of this issue with respect to rape, see this note on "First-Degree Forcible Rape" above in this supplement.

Multiple convictions and punishments (page 285)

A defendant may be sentenced for both statutory rape and incest arising out of the same transaction. State v. Marlow, 229 N.C. App. 593, 599–601 (2013) (reasoning that the offenses are not the same under the *Blockburger* test (referencing Blockburger v. United States, 284 U.S. 299 (1932)).

Indecent Exposure (page 289)

Statute (page 289)

2015 legislation, S.L. 2015-250, secs. 2–2.3, amended the statute, adding new subsections as follows:

(a2) Unless the conduct is prohibited by another law providing greater punishment, any person who shall willfully expose the private parts of his or her person in the presence of anyone other than a consenting adult on the private premises of another or so near thereto as to be seen from such private premises for the purpose of arousing or gratifying sexual desire is guilty of a Class 2 misdemeanor.

. . .

(a4) Unless the conduct is punishable by another law providing greater punishment, any person at least 18 years of age who shall willfully expose the private parts of his or her person in a private residence of which they are not a resident and in the presence of any other person less than 16 years of age who is a resident of that private residence shall be guilty of a Class 2 misdemeanor.

(a5) Unless the conduct is prohibited by another law providing greater punishment, any person located in a private place who shall willfully expose the private parts of his or her person with the knowing intent to be seen by a person in a public place shall be guilty of a Class 2 misdemeanor.

Misdemeanor Indecent Exposure (page 289)

Notes (page 290)

Element (4) (page 290)

Add the following at the end of the second paragraph of this note:

> The defendant masturbated in a public place when he did so on his own property in front of his garage; the garage was directly off a public road and was in full view from the street and a neighbor's house. State v. Pugh, 244 N.C. App. 326 (2015).

The 2015 legislation noted above created three new Class 2 misdemeanor versions of this offense, all of which apply when the exposure occurs on or near a private place.

Element (5) (page 290)

> To satisfy this Element, it is not necessary that a defendant expose himself "to" a person; all that is required is that a defendant expose himself "in the presence of" a person. State v. Hoyle, 260 N.C. App. 409, ___, 818 S.E.2d 149, 152 (felony indecent exposure case involving alleged exposure in the presence of a child), *discretionary review allowed*, 371 N.C. 788 (2018) (mem.). Citing *State v. Fly*, 348 N.C. 556 (1998), and *Fusco*, the court of appeals has held that for an exposure to be "in the presence of" a person, the person must be present during the exposure and have been able to see the exposure had the person looked. *Hoyle*, 260 N.C. App. at ___, 818 S.E.2d at 153–54.

Multiple convictions and punishments (page 290)

Add the following at the end of this note:

> ; *see also* State v. Hayes, 248 N.C. App. 414, ___, 788 S.E.2d 651, 652–53 (2016) (citing the statute and holding that where the defendant simultaneously exposed himself to a minor and an adult, he could not be convicted of both misdemeanor indecent exposure under G.S. 14-190.9(a) (for the exposure to the adult) and felonious indecent exposure under G.S. 14-190.9(a1) (for the exposure to the minor)).

Related Offenses Not in This Chapter (page 291)

Add the following offense to this list:

> Indecent exposure in a private place. G.S. 14-190.9(a2), (a4), (a5).
> Prisoner exposing genitalia to employee. G.S. 14-258.4(b) (enacted by S.L. 2018-67, sec. 2).

Felony Indecent Exposure (page 291)

Notes (page 291)

Element (5) (new note)

> For the misdemeanor version of this offense, the exposure must occur in the presence of another person; for the felony version, it must occur in the presence of a person less than 16 years old. For a discussion of the term "in the presence of," see the note on Element (5) to "Misdemeanor Indecent Exposure" in the main volume and above in this supplement.

Multiple convictions and punishments (page 292)

Insert the following at the beginning of this note:

> See this note to "Misdemeanor Indecent Exposure."

Peeping (page 292)

Statute (page 292)

2012 legislation, S.L. 2012-183, sec. 1, and 2017 legislation, S.L. 2017-186, sec. 2(p), amended G.S. 14-202(m)(2) to read:

> (2)   Personnel of the Division of Adult Correction and Juvenile Justice of the Department of Public Safety, or of a local confinement facility for security purposes or during investigation of alleged misconduct by a person in the custody of the Division or the local confinement facility.

Peeping into a Room Occupied by Another (page 293)
Related Offenses Not in This Chapter (page 294)

Add the following offense to this list:

> Unlawful distribution of images obtained through the use of an unmanned aircraft device. G.S. 14-401.25.

Peeping while Possessing a Device Capable of Creating a Photographic Image (page 295)
Related Offenses Not in This Chapter (page 296)

Add the following offense to this list:

> Unlawful distribution of images obtained through the use of an unmanned aircraft device. G.S. 14-401.25.

Disseminating Images Obtained in Violation of the Peeping Statute (page 299)
Related Offenses Not in This Chapter (page 299)

Add the following offense to this list:

> Unlawful distribution of images obtained through the use of an unmanned aircraft device. G.S. 14-401.25.

12
Kidnapping and Related Offenses

First-Degree Kidnapping (page 303)

Notes (page 304)

Element (1)(a) (page 304)

There was sufficient evidence that the defendant confined a child when, while threatening the child and his mother with a gun, the defendant told the mother to put her son in his room and she complied; whenever her son called out, the mother told him to stay in his bedroom. State v. Bell, 221 N.C. App. 535, 547–48 (2012).

Element (1)(b) (page 305)

For a felonious restraint case where the evidence was sufficient to show that the defendant restrained the victim by defrauding her into entering his car and driving to Florida with him, see *State v. Lalinde*, 231 N.C. App. 308, 315–16 (2013).

Element (3)(b) (page 305)

The plain language of G.S. 14-39(a) does not permit prosecution of a parent for kidnapping, at least when that parent has custodial rights with respect to the child or children. State v. Pender, 243 N.C. App. 142 (2015). The court of appeals has not decided "whether a parent without custodial rights may be held criminally liable for kidnapping." *Id.* at 155, n.2.

Element (4)(g) (page 307)

For another case supporting the definition of "terrorizing" described in this note and the point that the relevant fact is not whether the victim was in fact terrorized but, rather, whether the defendant intended to terrorize the victim, see *Pender*, 243 N.C. App. 142.

The evidence was sufficient for the jury to infer an intent to terrorize where the defendant shot victim Nancy's truck parked outside her mother's house in a manner such that everyone inside the house could hear, cut the telephone line to the house at night, shot through the windows multiple times to break into the house, yelled repeatedly upon entering the house that he was going to kill Nancy, corralled the occupants of the house into a single room and demanded to know where Nancy was, stated that he was going to kill her, and pointed his shotgun at the occupants; *id.*; the defendant threatened to kill the victim and assaulted her, placed her in headlock, and choked her; the victim was in a state of intense fright and apprehension; and witnesses heard the victim yelling for help and saw the defendant punch and choke her, rendering her unconscious, and then drag her across the street. State v. James, 248 N.C. App. 751, 758–59 (2016).

Element (5)(a) (page 308)

Add the following to the bulleted list in this note:

- the defendant dragged the victim to the middle of a gravel driveway and left her there, unconscious and injured; rather than leaving her in the care of nearby witnesses, the defendant ran away after seeing those persons; and the defendant took one of the victim's cell phones, perhaps not realizing that she had a second phone, *James*, 248 N.C. App. at 760–61;
- the defendant left the traumatized victim in a clearing in the woods near, but not easily visible from, a service road that extended off an interstate exit ramp; the area was very remote and secluded and almost impossible to see from the highway, State v. Gordon, 248 N.C. App. 403, 408–09 (2016).

Add the following to the bullet in this note stating that "the victim escaped":

State v. Massey, ___ N.C. App. ___, 826 S.E.2d 839 (2019) (the victim fled when the defendant turned away for a moment; the defendant never told or otherwise indicated to the victim that he was free to leave);

Element (5)(b) (page 308)

For a case where the evidence was sufficient to establish this Element, see *James*, 248 N.C. App. at 760–61 (the victim suffered cuts, bruises, abrasions, and scratches requiring emergency room treatment, and serious emotional trauma requiring therapy for many months continuing through the time of trial).

Multiple convictions and punishments (page 309)

For other cases supporting the proposition in this note that a defendant cannot be convicted of both first-degree kidnapping and a sexual assault if the sexual assault is the factor in Element (5) that elevates kidnapping from second-degree to first-degree, see *State v. Barksdale*, 237 N.C. App. 464, 473–74 (2014), and *State v. Holloman*, 231 N.C. App. 426, 432 (2013).

In the first bulleted list of this note, insert the following in the first bulleted paragraph (cases holding that the evidence supported kidnapping and robbery convictions):

, *State v. Stokes*, 367 N.C. 474, 482 (2014) (attempted kidnapping and robbery convictions were proper; after the robbery was completed, the defendant ordered the victim at gunpoint to the back of the store and then into a vehicle outside the store, but the victim refused to comply with both commands); *State v. Curtis*, 369 N.C. 310 (2016) (per curiam) (after robbing or attempting to rob two victims in a home invasion, the perpetrators moved the victims upstairs, where they restrained them while assaulting a third resident and searching for items that were later stolen), *State v. Thomas*, ___ N.C. App. ___, 834 S.E.2d 654 (2019) (the defendant's act of removing the victim from the bedroom to the living room after stealing her car keys was restraint and removal not inherent and integral to the underlying armed robbery); *State v. Bell*, 221 N.C. App. 535, 546–47 (2012).

In the first bulleted list of this note, insert the following in the second bulleted paragraph (cases holding that the evidence was sufficient to sustain kidnapping and sexual assault convictions):

, *State v. China*, 370 N.C. 627, 635–36 (2018) (after the sexual offense was completed, the defendant pulled the victim off the bed, causing his head to hit the floor, and called to an accomplice who, with the defendant, kicked and stomped the victim; these additional actions increased the victim's helplessness and vulnerability beyond the initial attack that enabled the defendant to commit the sexual offense and constituted an additional restraint, which exposed the victim to greater danger than that inherent in the sexual offense), *State v. King*, 249 N.C. App. 440, 444 (2016) (the defendant forced the victim into his car after sexually assaulting her), *State v. Knight*, 245 N.C. App. 532, 552–53 (2016) (commission of the rape did not require the defendant to seize and restrain the victim and to carry her from her living room couch to her bedroom), *aff'd as modified*, 369 N.C. 640 (2017), *Bell*, 221 N.C. App. at 547.

In the first bulleted list of this note, insert the following in the fourth bulleted paragraph (cases holding that the evidence was sufficient to sustain kidnapping and assault convictions):

, *State v. James*, 248 N.C. App. 751, 758 (2016) (finding two separate, distinct restraints sufficient to support convictions for both kidnapping and assault by strangulation).

In the second bulleted list of this note, insert the following in the second bulleted paragraph (cases holding that the evidence was insufficient to sustain kidnapping and sexual assault convictions):

, *State v. Parker*, 237 N.C. App. 546, 549–50 (2014) (restraint supporting the kidnapping charge was inherent in the charged rapes and sexual assault), *State v. Martin*, 222 N.C. App. 213, 219–21 (2012).

In the second bulleted list of this note, insert the following new bulleted paragraph:

- The defendant's restraint of the victim was inherent in an assault by strangulation of the victim, and thus the kidnapping conviction was improper. *Martin*, 222 N.C. App. at 221.

Abduction of a Child (page 315)

Notes (page 315)

Element (2) (new note)

For a case where the evidence was sufficient to show that the defendant induced the child to leave, see *State v. Diaz*, 256 N.C. App. 528, 537–38 (2017) (rejecting an argument by the defendant, who had a sexual relationship with the child victim, that the evidence was insufficient because it showed that the child voluntarily left her home; the defendant induced the child to leave by telling her that if she did not come with him she would never see him again).

Related Offenses Not in This Chapter (page 316)

Add the following offense to this list:

Unlawful transfer of custody of minor child. G.S. 14-321.2.

Human Trafficking, Involuntary Servitude, and Sexual Servitude (page 316)

Statute (page 316)

2018 legislation, S.L. 2018-75, sec. 1, enacted a new subsection, (a)(6), to G.S. 14-43.10 (Definitions) as follows:

(6) Victim.—Unless the context requires otherwise, a person subjected to the practices set forth in G.S. 14-43.11, 14-43.12, or 14-43.13.

G.S. 14-43.11 has been amended, *see* S.L. 2013-368, sec. 1; S.L. 2017-151, sec. 1, to read as follows:

§ 14-43.11. Human trafficking.

(a) A person commits the offense of human trafficking when that person (i) knowingly or in reckless disregard of the consequences of the action recruits, entices, harbors, transports, provides, or obtains by any means another person with the intent that the other person be held in involuntary servitude or sexual servitude or (ii) willfully or in reckless disregard of the consequences of the action causes a minor to be held in involuntary servitude or sexual servitude.

(b) A person who violates this section is guilty of a Class C felony if the victim of the offense is an adult. A person who violates this section is guilty of a Class B2 felony if the victim of the offense is a minor.

(c) Each violation of this section constitutes a separate offense and shall not merge with any other offense. Evidence of failure to deliver benefits or perform services standing alone shall not be sufficient to authorize a conviction under this section.

(c1) Mistake of age is not a defense to prosecution under this section. Consent of a minor is not a defense to prosecution under this section.

(d) A person who is not a legal resident of North Carolina, and would consequently be ineligible for State public benefits or services, shall be eligible for the public benefits and services of any State agency if the person is otherwise eligible for the public benefit and is a victim of an offense charged under this section. Eligibility for public benefits and services shall terminate at such time as the victim's eligibility to remain in the United States is terminated under federal law.

S.L. 2013-368, sec. 2, amended subsection (a) of G.S. 14-43.12, the involuntary servitude statute, to read as follows:

(a) A person commits the offense of involuntary servitude when that person knowingly and willfully or in reckless disregard of the consequences of the action holds another in involuntary servitude.

That same law also enacted a new subsection, (c1), to G.S. 14-43.12 as follows:

(c1) Mistake of age is not a defense to prosecution under this section. Consent of a minor is not a defense to prosecution under this section.

S.L. 2013-368, sec. 3, amended subsection (a) of G.S. 14-43.13, the sexual servitude statute, to read as follows:

(a) A person commits the offense of sexual servitude when that person knowingly or in reckless disregard of the consequences of the action subjects or maintains another in sexual servitude.

That same law also increased the punishment for this offense to a Class D felony and enacted a new subsection, (b1), to G.S. 14-43.13 as follows:

(b1) Mistake of age is not a defense to prosecution under this section. Consent of a minor is not a defense to prosecution under this section.

2018 legislation, S.L. 2018-75, sec. 2, enacted a new section in G.S. Chapter 14, Article 10A (Human Trafficking) as follows:

§ 14-43.15. Affirmative defense.

(a) Affirmative Defense.—It is an affirmative defense to a prosecution under this Article that the person charged with the offense was a victim at the time of the offense and was coerced or deceived into committing the offense as a direct result of the person's status as a victim.

(b) Construction.—Nothing in this section shall be construed to limit or abrogate any other affirmative defense to a prosecution under this Article available to a person by statute or common law.

Human Trafficking (page 318)

Elements (page 318)

As a result of 2013 legislation, S.L. 2013-368, sec. 1, the elements of this offense should read as follows:

A person guilty of this offense

    (1) (a) knowingly or in reckless disregard of the consequences

           (b) recruits, entices, harbors, transports, provides, or obtains

           (c) another person

           (d) with the intent that the other person be held in involuntary or sexual servitude *or*

(2) (a) willfully or in reckless disregard of the consequences

(b) causes a minor to be held in involuntary or sexual servitude.

Punishment (page 318)

As result of 2017 legislation, S.L. 2017-151, sec. 1, delete this paragraph and replace it with the following:

Class C felony if the victim is an adult. G.S. 14-43.11(b). Class B2 felony if the victim is less than 18 years old. *Id., id.* § -43.10(a)(4). If the Class B2 version of this offense is charged, the relevant fact elevating punishment must be alleged in the charging instrument and proved at trial.

Notes (page 318)

Element (4) (page 318)

Retitle this note to read:

Elements (1)(d) and (2)(b).

Mistake of age and consent (new note)
Neither mistake of age nor consent by a minor is a defense to prosecution. G.S. 14-43.11(c1).

Greater and lesser-included offenses (new note)
"Sale, Surrender, or Purchase of a Minor" (new crime), discussed below in this supplement, is a lesser-included offense of this crime. G.S. 14-43.14(d).

Sex offender registration (new note)
2013 legislation, S.L. 2013-33, provides that human trafficking is a sexually violent offense under G.S. 14-208.6(5) requiring sex offender registration if the offense is committed against

- a minor who is less than 18 years of age or
- any person with the intent that the person be held in sexual servitude.

Affirmative defense (new note)
2018 legislation, S.L. 2018-75, sec. 2, provides that it is an affirmative defense to a prosecution "that the person charged with the offense was a victim at the time of the offense and was coerced or deceived into committing the offense as a direct result of the person's status as a victim." The term "victim" is defined in new G.S. 14-43.10(a)(6), reproduced above.

Related Offenses Not in This Chapter (page 318)

Violating confidentiality of victim, alleged victim, or family member of a victim of human trafficking and related offenses. G.S. 14-43.16 (enacted by S.L. 2018-75, sec. 3(a)).

Involuntary Servitude (page 318)

Elements (page 318)

As a result of 2013 legislation, S.L. 2013-368, sec. 2, Element (1) of this offense should read as follows:

A person guilty of this offense

(1) (a) knowingly and willfully *or*

(b) in reckless disregard of the consequences

Notes (page 319)

Mistake of age and consent (new note)
Neither mistake of age nor consent by a minor is a defense to prosecution. G.S. 14-43.12(c1).

Affirmative defense (new note)
See this note under "Human Trafficking," above in this supplement.

Related Offenses Not in This Chapter (page 319)

Delete the first line of this section and replace it with the following:

> See the offenses listed under "First-Degree Kidnapping" and "Human Trafficking."

Sexual Servitude (page 319)

Elements (page 319)

As a result of 2013 legislation, S.L. 2013-368, sec. 3, Element (1) of this offense should read as follows:

> A person guilty of this offense
>
> (1) (a) knowingly *or*
>   (b) in reckless disregard of the consequences

As a result of 2019 legislation, S.L. 2019-158, sec. 1, elements (2) and (3) of this offense should read as follows:

> (2) subjects, maintains, or obtains another
> (3) for the purposes of sexual servitude.

Punishment (page 319)

As a result of 2013 legislation, S.L. 2013-368, sec. 3, delete the first sentence of this section and replace it with the following:

> Class D felony if the victim is an adult.

Notes (page 319)

Mistake of age and consent (new note)
Neither mistake of age nor consent by a minor is a defense to prosecution. G.S. 14-43.13(b1).

Affirmative defense (new note)
See this note under "Human Trafficking," above in this supplement.

Related Offenses Not in This Chapter (page 320)

Delete the first line of this section and replace it with the following:

> See the offenses listed under "First-Degree Kidnapping" and "Human Trafficking."

Sale, Surrender, or Purchase of a Minor (new crime)

This offense was enacted by 2012 legislation. S.L. 2012-153, sec. 1.

Statute

§ 14-43.14. Unlawful sale, surrender, or purchase of a minor.
(a) A person commits the offense of unlawful sale, surrender, or purchase of a minor when that person, acting with willful or reckless disregard for the life or safety of a minor, participates in any of the following: the acceptance, solicitation, offer, payment, or transfer of any compensation, in money, property, or other thing of value, at any time, by any person in connection with the unlawful acquisition or transfer of the physical custody of a minor, except as ordered by the court. This section does not apply to actions that are ordered by a court, authorized by statute, or otherwise lawful.
(b) A person who violates this section is guilty of a Class F felony and shall pay a minimum fine of five thousand dollars ($5,000). For each subsequent violation, a person is guilty of a Class F felony and shall pay a minimum fine of ten thousand dollars ($10,000).
(c) A minor whose parent, guardian, or custodian has sold or attempted to sell a minor in violation of this Article is an abused juvenile as defined by G.S. 7B-101(1). The court may

place the minor in the custody of the Department of Social Services or with such other person as is in the best interest of the minor.

(d) A violation of this section is a lesser included offense of G.S. 14-43.11.

(e) When a person is convicted of a violation of this section, the sentencing court shall consider whether the person is a danger to the community and whether requiring the person to register as a sex offender pursuant to Article 27A of this Chapter would further the purposes of that Article as stated in G.S. 14-208.5. If the sentencing court rules that the person is a danger to the community and that the person shall register, then an order shall be entered requiring the person to register.

Elements

A person guilty of this offense

- (1) (a) willfully *or*
  - (b) with reckless disregard for the life or safety of a minor
- (2) participates in any acceptance, solicitation, offer, payment, or transfer of any compensation, in money, property, or other thing of value, by any person
- (3) in connection with the unlawful acquisition or transfer of the physical custody of a minor.

Punishment

Class F felony. G.S. 14-43.14(b). For a first offense, the defendant must pay a minimum fine of $5,000; for subsequent violations, the defendant must pay a minimum fine of $10,000. *Id.*

Notes

Element (1)(a). See "Willfully" in Chapter 1 (States of Mind) of the main volume.

Exceptions. The statute does not apply to actions that are ordered by a court, are authorized by statute, or are otherwise lawful. G.S. 14-43.14(a). A parent may not be prosecuted for this offense when the parent abandons an infant less than seven days of age by voluntarily delivering the infant in compliance with the provisions of G.S. 7B-500(b) or (d) and does not express an intention to return for the infant. G.S. 14-322.3.

Minor declared abused. A minor whose parent, guardian, or custodian has sold or attempted to sell the minor in violation of the statute is an abused juvenile and may be placed in appropriate custody. G.S. 14-43.14(c).

Greater and lesser-included offenses. This offense is a lesser-included offense of human trafficking. G.S. 14-43.14(d).

Sex offender registration. The sentencing judge must require registration if he or she finds that a person convicted of this crime is a danger to the community and that requiring the person to register as a sex offender would further the purpose of the sex offender statute. G.S. 14-43.14(e).

Affirmative defense (new note)
See this note under "Human Trafficking," above in this supplement.

Related Offenses Not in This Chapter

See "Child Abuse" offenses and "Contributing to a Juvenile's Being Delinquent, Undisciplined, Abused, or Neglected" in Chapter 9 (Abuse and Neglect) of the main volume.

See "Failure to Report the Disappearance of a Child" (new crime) in Chapter 9 (Abuse and Neglect) of this supplement.

Unlawful payments related to adoption. G.S. 48-10-102.

Promoting Travel for Unlawful Sexual Conduct (new crime)

This offense was enacted by 2019 legislation. S.L. 2019-158, sec. 2.(a), effective for offenses committed on or after December 1, 2019.

Statute

§ 14-208.1. Promoting travel for unlawful sexual conduct.

(a) Definition. – For purposes of this section, the term "travel services" means transportation by air, sea, or ground; hotel or other lodging accommodations; package tours, or the provision of vouchers or coupons to be redeemed for future travel; or accommodations for a fee, commission, or other valuable consideration.

(b) Offense. – A person commits the offense of promoting travel for unlawful sexual conduct if the person sells or offers to sell travel services that the person knows to include travel for the purpose of committing any of the following offenses in this State or for the purpose of engaging in conduct that would constitute any one of the following offenses if occurring within this State:

(1)   An offense under Article 7B of Chapter 14 of the General Statutes.
(2)   Any of the following offenses involving the sexual exploitation of a minor:
    a.   G.S. 14-190.16.
    b.   G.S. 14-190.17.
    c.   G.S. 14-190.17A.
(3)   Any of the following offenses involving indecent liberties with a minor:
    a.   G.S. 14-202.1.
    b.   G.S. 14-202.4.
(4)   Any of the following prostitution offenses:
    a.   G.S. 14-204.
    b.   G.S. 14-205.1.
    c.   G.S. 14-205.2.
    d.   G.S. 14-205.3.

(c) Punishment. – A violation of this section is a Class G felony.

Elements

A person guilty of this offense

(1) (a) sells *or*
    (b) offers to sell
(2) travel services as defined in G.S. 14-208.1(a)
(3) (a) the person knows to include travel for the purpose of committing any of the listed offenses, *or*
    (b) for the purpose of engaging in conduct that would constitute any one of the listed offenses if occurring within North Carolina.

Punishment

Class G felony. G.S. 14-208.1(c).

Notes

Element (2)

"Travel services" means transportation by air, sea, or ground; hotel or other lodging accommodations; package tours; or the provision of vouchers or coupons to be redeemed for future travel; or accommodations for a fee, commission, or other valuable consideration. G.S. 14-208.1(a).

Elements (3)(a) and (b)

Travel for the purposes of committing or engaging in conduct that would constitute any of the following offenses is covered under this Element: First-Degree Sexual Exploitation of a Minor, Second-Degree Sexual Exploitation of a Minor, Third-Degree Sexual Exploitation of a Minor, Indecent Liberties with a Child, Indecent Liberties with a Student, Prostitution, Solicitation of Prostitution, Patronizing a Prostitute, Promoting Prostitution, or any offense included in Article 7B of G.S. Chapter 14 (Rape and Other Sex Offenses). G.S. 14-208.1(b).

13

Larceny, Possession of Stolen Goods, Embezzlement, and Related Offenses

Larceny (page 323)

Misdemeanor Larceny (page 323)

Statute (page 323)

2012 legislation, S.L. 2012-154, enacted G.S. 14-72(b)(6), proscribing the crime of "Habitual Misdemeanor Larceny," discussed below in this supplement.

> (6) Committed after the defendant has been convicted in this State or in another jurisdiction for any offense of larceny under this section, or any offense deemed or punishable as larceny under this section, or of any substantially similar offense in any other jurisdiction, regardless of whether the prior convictions were misdemeanors, felonies, or a combination thereof, at least four times. A conviction shall not be included in the four prior convictions required under this subdivision unless the defendant was represented by counsel or waived counsel at first appearance or otherwise prior to trial or plea. If a person is convicted of more than one offense of misdemeanor larceny in a single session of district court, or in a single week of superior court or of a court in another jurisdiction, only one of the convictions may be used as a prior conviction under this subdivision; except that convictions based upon offenses which occurred in separate counties shall each count as a separate prior conviction under this subdivision.

Elements (page 324)

The first line of this section should read:

A person guilty of this offense

Notes (page 324)

Element (1) (page 324)

A taking occurred (1) in a larceny case when the defendant wrongfully removed an overpayment from his bank account through transfers and withdrawals, State v. Jones, 369 N.C. 631, 637 (2017), (2) in a robbery case when the defendant grabbed the victim's cell phone and threw it away, State v. Mason, 222 N.C. App. 223, 228 (2012) (noting that the brevity of the taking is irrelevant), and (3) in another robbery case when the defendant forced the victim at gunpoint to take the defendant as a passenger in the victim's car; the fact that the victim was physically present in the car did not negate the inference that the defendant had sole control of the car. State v. Watkins, 218 N.C. App. 94, 103–04 (2012).

Element (3) (page 325)

The victim's possession of the property can be actual or constructive. *Jones*, 369 N.C. at 634 (adopting for larceny cases the analysis used to determine constructive possession in drug and other cases). Because a depositor retained the ability to affect a reversal of an erroneous deposit into the defendant's bank account, the depositor had constructive possession of the funds when the defendant later learned of the erroneous deposit but withdrew the funds anyhow. *Id.* at 635 (also concluding that the fact that the depositor's reversal order was not successful does not negate the depositor's constructive possession).

For a case where the evidence sufficiently established that the victim was in possession of a company checkbook at the time it was stolen, see *State v. Forte*, 260 N.C. App. 245, ___, 817 S.E.2d 764, 777 (2018), *vacated in part on other grounds*, ___ N.C. App. ___, 822 S.E.2d 794 (2019).

A defendant cannot be convicted of larceny with respect to property that is in his or her lawful possession. State v. Bradsher, 255 N.C. App. 625, 631 (2017) (as conceded by the State, the defendant was in lawful possession of appliances installed in her rented home). Similarly, a defendant cannot be convicted of larceny if he or she had possession of the property simultaneously with the victim. *Jones*, 369 N.C. at 636. A defendant does not have possession of funds when the defendant passively but knowingly receives a direct deposit overpayment into his or her bank account and then proceeds to withdraw the excess funds against the wishes of the rightful possessor. *Id.* (reasoning that the defendant had mere custody of the funds and not possession of them).

In a case involving felony larceny charges, the state supreme court held that a person who has mere custody of property may be convicted of larceny when he or she appropriates the property to his or her own use with felonious intent. *Id.* (stating: "The moment that the person in custody of the property wrongfully interferes with the rightful possessor's possessory interest is the moment that he takes that property.").

Element (5) (page 325)

To constitute a larceny, a taking must be wrongful; in other words, the taking must be by an act of trespass. *Jones*, 369 N.C. at 634. The trespass can be actual or constructive. *Id.* A constructive trespass occurs "when possession of the property is fraudulently obtained by some trick or artifice." *Id.* (internal quotation omitted). An actual trespass occurs when the taking is without the consent of the owner. *Id.*

Element (6) (page 325)

As a general rule, when a defendant takes property from its owner and keeps it until the defendant is apprehended, the element of intent to permanently deprive the owner is established. State v. Rogers, 255 N.C. App. 413, 415–16 (2017) (holding that the evidence was sufficient to establish this Element where the stolen pistol was found hidden in the spare tire well of the defendant's vehicle when he was apprehended).

Greater and lesser-included offenses (page 326)

Include the following after the citation to *State v. Watson* in the first paragraph of this note:

State v. Hole, 240 N.C. App. 537, 540 (2015) (same but concluding that no plain error occurred when the trial court failed to instruct on the lesser-included offense);

Add the following to this note:

Misdemeanor larceny is a lesser-included offense of common law robbery. State v. Cromartie, 257 N.C. App. 790, 796 (2018).

Multiple convictions and punishments (page 326)

For another case supporting the statement in this note that a defendant may be convicted for only one larceny if several pieces of property are taken during one continuous act or transaction, see *State v. Forte*, 260 N.C. App. 245, ___, 817 S.E.2d 764, 776 (2018) (the trial court erred by entering judgment for eight counts of felony larceny where all of the property was stolen in a single transaction), *vacated in part on other grounds*, ___ N.C. App. ___, 822 S.E.2d 794 (2019).

However, the court of appeals has held that when a defendant takes property from two different victims during one incident, the defendant may be convicted and punished for two larceny offenses. State v. Greene, 251 N.C. App. 627, 638 (2017).

Doctrine of recent possession (page 327)

"Exclusive possession" within the meaning of the doctrine of recent possession can include joint possession of co-conspirators or persons acting in concert. State v. McDaniel, 372 N.C. 594 (2019) (doctrine properly applied to a woman who had been in control of the stolen items for two weeks, regardless of whether she was acting at the direction of a co-defendant).

The jury may be instructed on the doctrine even if the defendant is not charged with taking the property that he or she is alleged to have recently possessed. State v. Street, 254 N.C. App. 214, 219 (2017) (the doctrine applied where the defendant was charged with obtaining property by false pretenses for selling a pair of hedge trimmers to a pawn shop less than two hours after the trimmers were stolen).

Related Offenses Not in This Chapter (page 329)

Add the following offenses to this list:

Theft of waste kitchen grease. G.S. 14-79.2.

Taking, etc., of certain wild plants from land of another. G.S. 14-129.

Felony taking of Venus flytrap. G.S. 14-129.3.

Injuring, tampering with, removing, etc. firefighting or emergency medical services machinery or equipment. G.S. 14-160.3, *as enacted by* S.L. 2017-89.

Habitual Misdemeanor Larceny (new crime)

Statute

2012 legislation, S.L. 2012-154, enacted G.S. 14-72(b)(6), reproduced above under "Misdemeanor Larceny."

Elements

A person guilty of this offense

    (1) commits a larceny *and*

    (2) has four prior larceny convictions.

Punishment

Class H felony. G.S. 14-72(a).

Notes

Element (1). See "Misdemeanor Larceny" in the main volume.

Element (2). The prior offense can be

- a North Carolina conviction under G.S. 14-72 or
- a substantially similar offense in any other jurisdiction.

G.S. 14-72(b)(6). The prior offenses can be misdemeanors, felonies, or a combination of the two. *Id.* A prior conviction cannot be counted unless the defendant was represented by or waived counsel. *Id*. However, the defendant's representation by or waiver of counsel for his or her prior convictions is not an essential element of this offense that must be alleged in the charging instrument. State v. Edgerton, ___ N.C. App. ___, 832 S.E.2d 249 (2019). If a person is convicted of more than one offense of misdemeanor larceny in a single session of district court or in a single week of superior court or a court in another jurisdiction, only one of the convictions may be used as a prior conviction, except that convictions based on offenses that occurred in separate counties each count as a separate prior conviction. *Id*.

Related Offenses Not in This Chapter

See the offenses listed under "Misdemeanor Larceny" in the main volume.

Felony Larceny (page 330)

Notes (page 330)

Element (8)(a) (page 331)

For another case holding that fair market value is the relevant measure, see *State v. Redman*, 224 N.C. App. 363, 366 (2012). A witness need not be an expert to give an opinion as to value; one who has knowledge of value gained from experience, information, and observation may give his or her opinion of the value of the stolen item. *Id*. Where a vehicle owner testified to a vehicle's value, there was sufficient evidence of this Element. *Id*. at 367. For a case where the State presented sufficient evidence that the fair market value of stolen boat batteries was more than $1,000, see *State v. Fish*, 229 N.C. App. 584, 587–89 (2013).

For a case holding that it is error to allow the jury to estimate the value of an item without any evidence to establish a basis for that estimation, see *State v. Bacon*, 254 N.C. App. 463, 473 (2017) (although "certain property may, by its very nature, be of value obviously greater than $1000.00," the television and the earrings in this case "are not such items").

Element (8)(b) (page 331)

A larceny was from the person when the defendant (1) stole the victim's purse from the child's seat of her grocery cart; at the time, the victim was looking at a store product and was within hand's reach of her cart and realized that the larceny was occurring as it happened, State v. Sheppard, 228 N.C. App. 266, 269–70 (2013); and (2) stole the victim's laptop from an apartment; the victim had taken a momentary break from doing her homework on the laptop and was about three feet away from it. State v. Hull, 236 N.C. App. 415, 418–19 (2014).

For a case where the evidence was insufficient to establish that the property was taken from the victim's person or was within the victim's protection, see *State v. Greene*, 251 N.C. App. 627, 629–35 (2017) (the defendant stole items from purses that were next to (but not touching) the victims while they slept in a medical waiting room; rejecting the State's argument that the property was within the victims' protection because the medical room was under video surveillance).

Multiple convictions and punishments (page 332)

A defendant may not be sentenced for both larceny from the person and larceny of goods worth more than $1,000 based on a single larceny. *Sheppard*, 228 N.C. App. at 270–71 (the crimes are not separate offenses but, rather, alternative ways to establish a felony larceny; while it is proper to indict on alternative theories of felony larceny and allow the jury to determine guilt as to each theory, where there is only one larceny, judgment may only be entered for one larceny).

Larceny of a Chose in Action (page 333)

Notes (page 333)

Element (2) (page 333)

A blank check is not a chose in action. State v. Grier, 224 N.C. App. 150, 155 (2012).

Relation to other offenses (new note)

Forgery and larceny of a chose in action are not mutually exclusive offenses. *Grier*, 224 N.C. App. at 153.

Unauthorized Use of a Motor-Propelled Conveyance (page 334)

Notes (page 334)

Element (5) generally (new note)

For a case where the evidence was insufficient on the issue of lack of consent, see *In re A.N.C.*, 225 N.C. App. 315, 325 (2013).

Greater and lesser-included offenses (page 335)

Delete the first paragraph of this note and replace it with the following:

North Carolina courts have held that unauthorized use of a motor-propelled conveyance is not a lesser-included offense of possession of stolen goods, *see* State v. Nickerson, 365 N.C. 279, 281–83 (2011) (applying the definitional test and concluding that unauthorized use of a motor-propelled conveyance contains at least one element not present in possession of stolen goods), nor is it a lesser-included offense of possession of a stolen vehicle. State v. Robinson, 368 N.C. 402, 406–08 (2015) (applying a definitional analysis).

Replace the first sentence of the second paragraph of this note with the following:

Notwithstanding *Nickerson* and *Robinson*, the court of appeals has held that, depending on the evidence, unauthorized use of a motor-propelled conveyance can be a lesser-included offense of larceny of a motor vehicle, discussed below.

Insert the following after the citation to *State v. Watson* in the second paragraph of this note:

State v. Hole, 240 N.C. App. 537, 540 (2015) (same but concluding that no plain error occurred when the trial court failed to instruct on the lesser-included offense);

Possession of Stolen Goods (page 335)

Misdemeanor Possession of Stolen Goods (page 335)

Notes (page 336)

Element (1) (page 336)

Evidence that a defendant is operating a stolen vehicle is sufficient to establish possession. State v. Quinones, 258 N.C. App. 559, 561 (2018). However, merely being present in a stolen vehicle is insufficient by itself to establish possession. *Id.* at 562–63 (going on to hold that the evidence was sufficient to establish that the defendant operated the stolen vehicle and was not merely a passenger; specifically, an individual in a white shirt fled from the driver's side of the car after it was abandoned and the driver's door was the only door left open; officers maintained almost constant visual contact with the defendant as he fled, the defendant was arrested wearing a white t-shirt, and he never denied being inside the automobile).

For other cases where the evidence was sufficient to establish constructive possession of stolen goods, see *State v. Guy*, ___ N.C. App. ___, 822 S.E.2d 66 (2018) (a robbery victim's debit card was found near a gun in close proximity to the defendant and his vehicle; the gun matched one described by the victim as having been used in the robbery, and an officer located the defendant's car less than a quarter-mile from the victim's residence and about one minute after receiving information about the incident), and *State v. Rice*, 252 N.C. App. 480, 482–86 (2017) (although the defendant did not have exclusive possession of the rented van in which the goods were found, other incriminating circumstances existed to establish constructive possession, including, among other things, that the defendant was nervous and admitted ownership of another item found near the stolen property).

The evidence was insufficient to establish that the defendant constructively possessed jewelry when it showed only that the defendant was a high-ranking member of a gang to which others involved in a robbery and subsequent transfer of stolen goods belonged; the defendant accompanied a person in possession of stolen property to an enterprise at which a legitimate transaction occurred; the defendant made ambiguous references to "more scrap gold" and "rings" unaccompanied by any indication that these items were stolen. State v. Privette, 218 N.C. App. 459, 472–73 (2012).

Element (3) (page 336)
For a case where the evidence was sufficient to establish that the defendant knew or had reasonable grounds to believe that items were stolen, see *State v. Jester*, 249 N.C. App. 101, 114 (2016) (although the property was valued at more than $1,000, the defendant sold it for $114, told a detective that he obtained it from a "white man" but could not give the man's name, did not state that he had purchased the items, and did not produce a receipt for them).

Greater and lesser-included offenses (page 337)
Delete the citation to *Oliver* in this note.

Multiple convictions and punishments (page 338)
The text of this note states that "[a] defendant may not be sentenced for both robbery and possession of stolen property taken during the robbery." For another case supporting that principle, see *State v. Guy*, ___ N.C. App. ___, 822 S.E.2d 66 (2018). However, that principle only applies "for possession during the course of the same conduct, and where the property is the 'same property.'" State v. Hendricksen, 257 N.C. App. 345, 352 (2018) (holding that the defendant's conviction after a guilty plea in Harnett County to two counts of misdemeanor possession of stolen goods involving two lottery tickets did not preclude his later trial and conviction in Johnston County for an armed robbery of a convenience store during which he obtained approximately $1,900 in cash and approximately 800 lottery tickets, including the two that were the subject of the Harnett County charges).

Related Offenses Not in This Chapter (page 338)
Add the following offense to this list:

Secondary metals recycler purchase violations. G.S. 66-419; -424.

As a result of 2019 legislation, S.L. 2019-40, add the following new offense, effective for offenses committed on or after December 1, 2019:

Possession of a Stolen Controlled Substance (new crime)

Statute

See G.S. 14-54.2, reproduced under "Breaking or Entering a Pharmacy," in Chapter 15 of this supplement.

Elements

A person guilty of this offense
- (1) possesses
- (2) any controlled substance
- (3) stolen in violation of G.S. 14-54.2(b), "Breaking or Entering a Pharmacy,"
- (4) knowing or having reasonable grounds to believe that the controlled substance was stolen.

Punishment

Class F felony. G.S. 14-54.2(c). Any interest a person acquires or maintains in property obtained in violation of this section is subject to forfeiture as set forth in G.S. 90-112. *Id.* § -54.2(d).

Notes

Generally. Relevant notes to "Misdemeanor Possession of Stolen Goods" apply to this offense as well.

Element (2)
A "controlled substance" is any drug, substance, or immediate precursor included in Schedules I through VI of the Controlled Substances Act. G.S. 90-87(5).

Element (3)
The named offense, "Breaking or Entering a Pharmacy," is discussed in Chapter 15 of this supplement.

Related Offenses Not in This Chapter

See the offenses listed under "Misdemeanor Possession of Stolen Goods," above.
Breaking or Entering a Pharmacy (Chapter 15).

Receiving Stolen Goods (page 342)

As a result of 2019 legislation, S.L. 2019-40, add the following new offense, effective for offenses committed on or after December 1, 2019:

Receiving a Stolen Controlled Substance (new crime)

Statute

See G.S. 14-54.2, reproduced under "Breaking or Entering a Pharmacy," in Chapter 15 of this supplement.

Elements

A person guilty of this offense
- (1) receives
- (2) any controlled substance

(3) stolen in violation of G.S. 14-54.2(b), "Breaking or Entering a Pharmacy,"

(4) knowing or having reasonable grounds to believe that the controlled substance was stolen.

Punishment

Class F felony. G.S. 14-54.2(c). Any interest a person acquires or maintains in property obtained in violation of this section is subject to forfeiture as set forth in G.S. 90-112. *Id.* § -54.2(d).

Notes

Generally. Relevant notes to "Misdemeanor Receiving of Stolen Goods" apply to this offense as well.

Element (2)

A "controlled substance" is any drug, substance, or immediate precursor included in Schedules I through VI of the Controlled Substances Act. G.S. 90-87(5).

Element (3)

The named offense, "Breaking or Entering a Pharmacy," is discussed in Chapter 15 of this supplement.

Related Offenses Not in This Chapter

See the offenses listed under "Misdemeanor Receiving of Stolen Goods," above.
Breaking or Entering a Pharmacy (Chapter 15).

Vehicle and Vehicle Part Offenses (page 345)

The following offense, enacted by 2012 legislation, S.L. 2012-46, should be added as a related offense to the vehicle and vehicle part offenses covered here:

Secondary metals recycler purchase of catalytic converters in certain circumstances. G.S. 66-419.

Possession of a Stolen Vehicle (page 345)

Notes (page 345)

Greater and lesser-included offenses (new note)
Unauthorized use is not a lesser-included offense of possession of a stolen vehicle. State v. Robinson, 368 N.C. 402, 406–08 (2015).

Altering, Destroying, etc. any Stolen Motor Vehicle or Part (page 347)

Statute (page 347)

2013 legislation, S.L. 2013-323, amended subsection (a) of G.S. 14-72.7 to read as follows:

(a) A person is guilty of a Class G felony if that person engages in any of the following activities, without regard to the value of the property in question:

(1) Altering, destroying, disassembling, dismantling, reassembling, or storing any motor vehicle or motor vehicle part the person knows or has reason-

able grounds to believe has been illegally obtained by theft, fraud, or other illegal means.

(2) Permitting a place to be used for any activity prohibited by this section, where the person either owns or has legal possession of the place, and knows or has reasonable grounds to believe that the place is being used for any activity prohibited by this section.

(3) Purchasing, disposing of, selling, transferring, receiving, or possessing a motor vehicle or motor vehicle part either knowing or having reasonable grounds to believe that the vehicle identification number of the motor vehicle, or vehicle part identification number of the vehicle part, has been altered, counterfeited, defaced, destroyed, disguised, falsified, forged, obliterated, or removed.

(4) Purchasing, disposing of, selling, transferring, receiving, or possessing a motor vehicle or motor vehicle part to or from a person engaged in any activity prohibited by this section, knowing or having reasonable grounds to believe that the person is engaging in that activity.

Elements (page 348)

As a result of that same 2013 legislation, the elements for this offense should read as follows:

A person guilty of this offense

(1) (a) alters,
   (b) destroys,
   (c) disassembles,
   (d) dismantles,
   (e) reassembles, *or*
   (f) stores
(2) any
   (a) motor vehicle *or*
   (b) motor vehicle part
(3) knowing or having reasonable grounds to believe that it was illegally obtained.

Punishment (page 348)

As a result of the 2013 legislation noted above, delete the text in this section and replace it with the following:

Class G felony. G.S. 14-72.7(a).

Notes (page 348)

Element (1) (page 348)

As a result of the 2013 legislation noted above, delete this note.

Element (3) (page 348)

This note should be titled Element (2).

Element (4) (page 348)

As a result of the 2013 legislation noted above, delete this note.

Related Offenses Not in This Chapter (page 349)

Add the following offenses to this list:

Purchase of vehicles for purposes of scrap or parts only. G.S. 20-62.1.
Secondary metals recycler purchase of catalytic converters in certain circumstances. G.S. 66-419.

Permitting a Place to Be Used to Violate the Chop Shop Laws (page 349)

Elements (page 349)

As a result of 2013 legislation, S.L. 2013-323, the elements for this offense should read as follows:

A person guilty of this offense

(1) permits
(2) a place that the person owns or has legal possession of
(3) to be used for any activity prohibited by G.S. 14-72.7 *and*
(4) knows or has reasonable grounds to believe that the place is being used for the prohibited activity.

Punishment (page 349)

As a result of the 2013 legislation noted above, delete the text in this section and replace it with the following:

Class G felony. G.S. 14-72.7(a).

Notes (page 349)

Element (1) (page 349)

As a result of the 2013 legislation noted above, delete this note.

Related Offenses Not in This Chapter (page 349)

Add the following offenses to this list:

Purchase of vehicles for purposes of scrap or parts only. G.S. 20-62.1.
Secondary metals recycler purchase of catalytic converters in certain circumstances. G.S. 66-419.

Purchasing, Selling, etc. of a Motor Vehicle or Part with an Altered Identification Number (page 349)

Elements (page 349)

As a result of 2013 legislation, S.L. 2013-323, the elements for this offense should read as follows:

A person guilty of this offense

(1) (a) purchases,
   (b) disposes of,
   (c) sells,
   (d) transfers,
   (e) receives, *or*
   (f) possesses
(2) (a) a motor vehicle *or*
   (b) motor vehicle part
(3) knowing or having reasonable grounds to believe that the vehicle identification number has been altered, counterfeited, defaced, destroyed, disguised, falsified, forged, obliterated, or removed.

Punishment (page 350)

As a result of the 2013 legislation noted above, delete the text in this section and replace it with the following:

Class G felony. G.S. 14-72.7(a).

Notes (page 350)

As a result of the 2013 legislation noted above, which caused a renumbering and revision of the elements of this offense, delete the text in this section and replace it with the following:

Element (1)(c). For an explanation of the term "sells" in the context of drug offenses, see the note on Element (2)(a) to "Sale or Delivery of a Controlled Substance" in Chapter 27 (Drug Offenses) of the main volume.

Element (1)(e). For a discussion of the term "receives," see the note on Element (1) to "Misdemeanor Receiving of Stolen Goods" in the main volume.

Element (1)(f). For a discussion of the term "possesses," see the note on Element (1) to "Misdemeanor Possession of Stolen Goods" in the main volume.

Element (2). For a definition of the term "motor vehicle" as used in the context of motor vehicle offenses, see the note on Element (2) to "Driving While License Revoked" in Chapter 28 (Motor Vehicle Offenses) of the main volume.

Element (3). For definitions of the terms "vehicle identification number" and "vehicle part identification number," see G.S. 14-72.7(f)(2) and (3).

Exceptions. See this note to "Altering, Destroying, etc. Any Stolen Motor Vehicle or Part" in the main volume.

Seizure and forfeiture. See this note to "Altering, Destroying, etc. Any Stolen Motor Vehicle or Part" in the main volume.

Related Offenses Not in This Chapter (page 350)

Add the following offenses to this list:

Purchase of vehicles for purposes of scrap or parts only. G.S. 20-62.1.
Secondary metals recycler purchase of catalytic converters in certain circumstances.
    G.S. 66-419.

Purchasing, Disposing of, etc. a Motor Vehicle or Part in Connection with a Chop Shop Violation (page 350)

Elements (page 350)

As a result of 2013 legislation, S.L. 2013-323, the elements for this offense should read as follows:

A person guilty of this offense

(1) (a) purchases,
    (b) disposes of,
    (c) sells,
    (d) transfers,
    (e) receives, *or*
    (f) possesses
(2) (a) a motor vehicle *or*
    (b) motor vehicle part
(3) to or from a person
(4) engaged in any activity prohibited by G.S. 14-72.7
(5) knowing or having reasonable grounds to believe that the person is engaging in that activity.

Punishment (page 351)

As a result of the 2013 legislation noted above, delete the text in this section and replace it with the following:

> Class G felony. G.S. 14-72.7(a).

Notes (page 351)

As a result of the 2013 legislation noted above, which caused a renumbering and revision of the elements of this offense, delete the text in this section and replace it with the following:

> **Element (1)(c).** For an explanation of the term "sells" in the context of drug offenses, see the note on Element (2)(a) to "Sale or Delivery of a Controlled Substance" in Chapter 27 (Drug Offenses) of the main volume.
>
> **Element (1)(e).** For a discussion of the term "receives," see the note on Element (1) to "Misdemeanor Receiving of Stolen Goods" in the main volume.
>
> **Element (1)(f).** For a discussion of the term "possesses," see the note on Element (1) to "Misdemeanor Possession of Stolen Goods" in the main volume.
>
> **Element (2).** For a definition of the term "motor vehicle" as used in the context of motor vehicle offenses, see the note on Element (2) to "Driving While License Revoked" in Chapter 28 (Motor Vehicle Offenses) of the main volume.
>
> **Exceptions.** See this note to "Altering, Destroying, etc. Any Stolen Motor Vehicle or Part" in the main volume.
>
> **Seizure and forfeiture.** See this note to "Altering, Destroying, etc. Any Stolen Motor Vehicle or Part" in the main volume.

Related Offenses Not in This Chapter (page 351)

Add the following offenses to this list:

> Purchase of vehicles for purposes of scrap or parts only. G.S. 20-62.1.
> Secondary metals recycler purchase of catalytic converters in certain circumstances. G.S. 66-419.

Larceny of a Motor Vehicle Part (page 351)

Notes (page 352)

Element (3)

Add the following text at the end of this note:

> The statute's requirement of $1,000 in repair costs refers to the cost to repair a single vehicle, not to (1) the cost to repair multiple vehicles in the aggregate or (2) the value of car parts stolen where no vehicle is involved. State v. Stephenson, ___ N.C. App. ___, 833 S.E.2d 393 (2019).

Related Offenses Not in This Chapter (page 352)

Add the following offense to this list:

> Secondary metals recycler purchase of catalytic converters in certain circumstances. G.S. 66-419.

Stealing from Merchants and Retail Establishments (page 352)

Larceny from a Merchant (page 352)

Statute (page 352)

2017 legislation, S.L. 2017-162, sec. 1, amended the statute to read as follows:

> **§ 14-72.11. Larceny from a merchant.**
>   A person is guilty of a Class H felony if the person commits larceny against a merchant under any of the following circumstances:
>
> (1) By taking property that has a value of more than two hundred dollars ($200.00), using an exit door erected and maintained to comply with the requirements of 29 C.F.R. § 1910.36 and 29 C.F.R. § 1910.37, to exit the premises of a store.
>
> (2) By removing, destroying, or deactivating a component of an antishoplifting or inventory control device to prevent the activation of any antishoplifting or inventory control device.
>
> (3) By affixing a product code created for the purpose of fraudulently obtaining goods or merchandise from a merchant at less than its actual sale price.
>
> (4) When the property is infant formula valued in excess of one hundred dollars ($100.00). As used in this subsection, the term "infant formula," has the same meaning as found in 21 U.S.C. § 321(z).
>
> (5) By exchanging property for cash, a gift card, a merchandise card, or some other item of value, knowing or having reasonable grounds to believe the property is stolen.

Elements (page 353)

As a result of the 2017 legislation noted above, Element (3) should read as follows:

> (3) (a) takes property valued at more than $200 using a specified exit door to leave the premises;
>
> (b) removes, destroys, or deactivates a component of an anti-shoplifting or inventory control device to prevent the activation of any such device;
>
> (c) affixes a product code created to fraudulently obtain goods or merchandise at less than actual sale price;
>
> (d) the property is infant formula valued at more than $100; *or*
>
> (e) exchanges property for cash, a gift card, a merchandise card, or another item of value, knowing or having reasonable grounds to believe that the property is stolen.

Notes (page 353)

Element (3)(a)

As a result of the 2017 legislation noted above, delete the text of this note and replace it with the following:

> The exit door must be erected and maintained to comply with the requirements of 29 C.F.R. § 1910.36 (a federal regulation dealing with design and construction requirements for exit routes) and § 1910.37 (a federal regulation dealing with maintenance, safeguards, and operational features for exit routes).

Organized Retail Theft (new crime)

As a result of 2017 legislation, S.L. 2017-162, sec. 2, this new crime replaces two crimes covered in the main volume: "Conspiracy to Commit Retail Theft" and "Receiving or Possessing Stolen Retail Property."

Statute (page 353)

§ 14-86.6. Organized retail theft.

(a) A person is guilty of a Class H felony if the person does either of the following:

(1) Conspires with another person to commit theft of retail property from retail establishments, with a value exceeding one thousand five hundred dollars ($1,500) aggregated over a 90-day period, with the intent to sell that retail property for monetary or other gain, and who takes or causes that retail property to be placed in the control of a retail property fence or other person in exchange for consideration.

(2) Receives or possesses any retail property that has been taken or stolen in violation of subdivision (1) of this subsection while knowing or having reasonable grounds to believe the property is stolen.

(a1) A person is guilty of a Class G felony if the person does either of the following:

(1) Conspires with another person to commit theft of retail property from one or more retail establishments, with a value exceeding twenty thousand dollars ($20,000) aggregated over a 90-day period, with the intent to sell that retail property for monetary or other gain, and who takes or causes that retail property to be placed in the control of a retail property fence or other person in exchange for consideration.

(2) Conspires with two or more other persons as an organizer, supervisor, financier, leader, or manager to engage for profit in a scheme or course of conduct to effectuate the transfer or sale of property stolen from a merchant in violation of this section.

(b) Any interest a person has acquired or maintained in violation of this section shall be subject to forfeiture pursuant to the procedures for forfeiture set out in G.S. 18B-504.

(c) Thefts of retail property occurring in more than one county may be aggregated into an alleged violation of this section. Each county where a part of the charged offense occurs has concurrent venue as described in G.S. 15A-132.

Elements

A person guilty of this offense:

(1) (a) conspires with another
   (b) to commit theft
   (c) of retail property
   (d) valued at either
      (i) more than $1,500 aggregated over a 90-day period *or*
      (ii) more than $20,000 aggregated over a 90-day period
   (e) from retail establishments
   (f) with the intent to sell the property for gain *and*
   (g) takes or causes the property to be placed in the control of a retail property fence or other person in exchange for consideration,

(2) (a) receives or possesses
   (b) retail property
   (c) that has been taken or stolen as provided in the Element (1)(d)(i) version of this offense
   (d) knowing or having reasonable grounds to believe that the property is stolen, *or*

(3) (a) conspires with two or more persons
   (b) as an organizer, supervisor, financier, leader, or manager

(c) to engage for profit in a scheme or course of conduct to effectuate the transfer or sale of property

(d) stolen from a merchant in violation of the statute.

Punishment

For violations of the Element (1) version of this offense where the property is valued at more than $1,500 under Element (1)(d)(i), the offense is a Class H felony, G.S. 14-86.6(a)(1); where the property is valued at more than $20,000 under Element (1)(d)(ii), the offense is a Class G felony. *Id.* § (a1)(1). A violation of the Element (2) version of this offense is a Class H felony. *Id.* § (a)(2). A violation of the Element (3) version of this offense is a Class G felony. *Id.* § (a1)(2).

Notes

Elements (1)(a) and (3)(a). See "Conspiracy" in Chapter 5 (General Crimes) of the main volume. Normally a conspiracy requires that the defendant enter into an agreement with at least one other person. *Id.* The Element (1) version of this offense follows that general rule. However, the Element (3) version of this offense requires the defendant to conspire with two or more people.

Element (1)(b). "Theft" is defined as follows: "[t]o take possession of, carry away, transfer, or cause to be carried away the retail property of another with the intent to steal the retail property." G.S. 14-86.5(3).

Elements (1)(c) and (2)(b). "Retail property" is defined as "[a]ny new article, product, commodity, item, or component intended to be sold in retail commerce." G.S. 14-86.5(1).

Element (1)(d). The value of an item is defined as the "retail value of an item as advertised by the affected retail establishment, to include all applicable taxes." G.S. 14-86.5(4). Retail property thefts occurring in more than one county may be aggregated "into an alleged violation of this section." *Id.* § -86.6(c).

Element (1)(g). A "retail property fence" is "[a] person or business that buys retail property knowing or believing that retail property is stolen." G.S. 14-86.5(2).

Element (2)(a). For a discussion of the term "receives," see the note on Element (1) to "Misdemeanor Receiving of Stolen Goods" in the main volume. For a discussion of the term "possesses," see the note on Element (1) to "Misdemeanor Possession of Stolen Goods" in the main volume.

Element (2)(d). See the note on Element (3) to "Misdemeanor Possession of Stolen Goods" in the main volume.

Element (3)(d). The statute provides that this version of the offense occurs when the accomplices conspire to "effectuate the transfer or sale of property stolen from a merchant in violation of this section." G.S. 14-86.6(a1)(2). While another provision of the statute expressly refers to a specific "subdivision" of the statute, see *id.* § (a)(2), this provision uses the word "section," suggesting that any violation of the statute might satisfy this Element. That is, however, unclear. For example, the Element (2) version of the offense applies to receiving or possessing property, not stealing.

Forfeiture. Any interest a person acquires or maintains in violation of G.S. 14-86.6 is subject to forfeiture under G.S. 18B-504. G.S. 14-86.6(b).

Venue. Each county where a part of the charged offense occurs has concurrent venue as described in G.S. 15A-132. G.S. 14-86.6(c).

Related Offenses Not in This Chapter

"Conspiracy" (Chapter 5)

Conspiracy to Commit Retail Theft (page 353)

For the reasons discussed above under "Organized Retail Theft," delete this offense.

Receiving or Possessing Stolen Retail Property (page 354)

For the reasons discussed above under "Organized Retail Theft," delete this offense.

Financial Transaction Card Theft (page 359)

Taking or Withholding a Card (page 360)

Notes (page 360)

Element (5) (page 360)

For a case where the evidence was sufficient to establish this Element, see *State v. Sellers*, 248 N.C. App. 293, 299 (2016) (someone other than the victim used the card at two stores on the day it was stolen; surveillance video showed the defendant at one of the stores when the card was swiped, and an employee testified that the defendant tried to use a card issued in another person's name).

Embezzlement Offenses (page 364)

Embezzlement by Employee (page 364)

Notes (page 365)

Element (3) (page 365)

Cash paid by a customer to the defendant shop manager for services was entrusted to the defendant for use by the employer. State v. Fink, 252 N.C. App. 379, 384–86 (2017) (rejecting the defendant's argument that the cash remained the customer's property until the work was completed; concluding that as soon as the customer tendered payment to the defendant, the funds became the property of the shop).

Related Offenses Not in This Chapter (page 366)

Delete the text of this section and replace it with the following:

See the offenses listed under "Embezzlement" in this supplement and in the main volume.

Embezzlement (page 366)

Elements (page 366)

To correct a typographical error in the main volume, Element (1) should read as follows:

(1) fraudulently or knowingly and willfully

Notes (page 367)

Element (1) (page 367)

The State need not prove that the defendant acted fraudulently, knowingly, and willfully; it need only prove that the defendant acted fraudulently *or* knowingly and willfully. State v. Booker, ___ N.C. App. ___, 821 S.E.2d 877 (2018).

The State can establish the requisite intent by direct or circumstantial evidence. State v. Parker, 233 N.C. App. 577, 580 (2014) (evidence was sufficient where the defendant used school system funds for improper purchases).

Element (2) (page 367)

For other cases supporting the proposition in this note that the person entrusted with the property need not convert it to his or her own use, see *Parker*, 233 N.C. App. at 580, and *Booker*, ___ N.C. App. ___, 821 S.E.2d. 877 (quoting *Parker*).

Element (4) (page 367)

For a case where there was sufficient evidence that the defendant was an agent of a corporation and not an independent contractor, see *State v. Smalley*, 220 N.C. App. 142, 144–45 (2012) (the defendant was alleged to have improperly written company checks to herself).

There was sufficient evidence that the defendant had constructive possession of the corporation's money when she was given complete access to the corporation's accounts and could write checks on behalf of the corporation and delegate where the corporation's money went. *Id.*

There was sufficient evidence of embezzlement in another case where the defendant, a bookkeeper controller for the victim company, was instructed to close the company's credit cards but failed to do so, instead incurring personal charges on the cards and paying the card bills from company funds. State v. Renkosiak, 226 N.C. App. 377, 378–79 (2013).

For another case where the evidence was sufficient to establish that the defendant was entrusted with the property in question, see *State v. Grandy*, ___ N.C. App. ___, 821 S.E.2d 243 (2018) (the defendant, a foundation's director of accounting, was entrusted with funds that she transferred from the foundation's account to her personal account; to access the funds, the foundation's bank required her to use two security devices, referred to as "key fobs," both of which her employer entrusted to her even though the bank intended for two separate employees to participate in each transaction as a security measure).

Related Offenses Not in This Chapter (page 369)

Add the following offense to this list:

Embezzlement from a bank. G.S. 53C-8-11.

14

Robbery, Extortion, and Blackmail

Common Law Robbery (page 379)

> **Notes** (page 379)
>
>> **Element (2)** (page 379)

Add the following at the end of the first paragraph of this note:

> ; and (3) personal property from a victim who was forced by intruders to lie on the ground, State v. McLean, 251 N.C. App. 850, 856 (2017).

> **Element (3)** (page 380)
> In a multi-count robbery case, there was sufficient evidence that victim Adrienne relinquished her property because of violence or intimidation; although Adrienne herself did not testify, evidence showed that she was a resident of premises where the robbery occurred, another victim heard her screaming during the intrusion, her face was injured, two witnesses testified that she had been beaten, and her personal belongings were taken. State v. Jones, 241 N.C. App. 132, 141 (2015).

> **Multiple convictions and punishments** (page 381)
> Where the defendant attempted to rob two victims inside a residence, two charges were proper; the fact that only one residence was involved was irrelevant where the defendant demanded that each victim turn over his personal property. State v. Jastrow, 237 N.C. App. 325, 329–30 (2014).
>
> The second paragraph of this notes states that "[a] defendant may not be sentenced for both robbery and possession of stolen property taken during the robbery." For another case supporting that principle, see *State v. Guy*, ___ N.C. App. ___, 822 S.E.2d 66 (2018). However, that principle only applies "for possession during the course of the same conduct, and where the property is the 'same property.'" State v. Hendricksen, 257 N.C. App. 345, 352 (2018) (holding that the defendant's conviction after a guilty plea in Harnett County to two counts of misdemeanor possession of stolen goods involving two lottery tickets did not preclude his later trial and conviction in Johnston County for an armed robbery of a convenience store during which he obtained approximately $1,900 in cash and approximately 800 lottery tickets, including the two that were the subject of the Harnett County charges).

Armed Robbery (page 381)

Statute (page 381)

2017 legislation, S.L. 2017-31, amended the statute, adding a new subsection, (a1), as follows:

> (a1) Attempted robbery with a dangerous weapon shall constitute a lesser included offense of robbery with a dangerous weapon, and evidence sufficient to prove robbery with a dangerous weapon shall be sufficient to support a conviction of attempted robbery with a dangerous weapon.

Notes (page 382)

Element (3) (page 382)

For a case where the evidence was sufficient to show that either the defendant or his accomplice used a firearm to induce the victim to part with her purse, see *State v. James*, 226 N.C. App. 120, 125 (2013).

For a case where there was sufficient evidence that a lawn chair was a dangerous weapon, see *State v. Mills*, 221 N.C. App. 409, 413 (2012).

An unopened knife wielded by the defendant can be a dangerous weapon. State v. Whisenant, 249 N.C. App. 456, 459 (2016) (in a case where the defendant yelled, "I will kill you" while brandishing the knife, the court held that "the unopened knife was a dangerous weapon when Defendant threatened to use it to cause great bodily harm or death").

A box cutter with the blade exposed is a dangerous weapon as a matter of law. State v. Redmond, ___ N.C. App. ___, 831 S.E.2d 650 (2019) (citing State v. Wiggins, 78 N.C. App. 405 (1985)).

Element (4) (page 383)

The evidence was sufficient to establish that the defendant's gun threatened or endangered the life of a person, even though the defendant did not point it at the victims. State v. Wright, 252 N.C. App. 501, 505–09 (2017) (distinguishing cases where victims and bystanders did not see the defendant's weapon; here, the defendant was seen holding the gun in his hand during the robberies).

For another case supporting the statement in this note that it is not necessary to prove that the victim feared for his or her life, see *Wright, id.* at 509–10 (the victim testified that she was not scared during the incident).

The evidence was sufficient to establish that an unopened knife endangered or threatened the victim's life where, while the victim attempted to disarm the defendant, the defendant threatened, "I will kill you," and the victim felt afraid. *Whisenant*, 249 N.C. App. at 458–59.

Timing of elements (page 384)

There was sufficient evidence that a theft and the use of force were part of a continuous transaction where the defendant went to the victim's home with the intent to rob him, shot and killed the victim, and left with money and drugs. State v. Rogers, 227 N.C. App. 617, 622–23 (2013).

Jury instructions (new note)

Where the evidence showed that the defendant displayed and threatened to use a weapon by pointing it at the victim, the trial court was not required to give the mere possession instruction in footnote 6 to element seven of N.C.P.I.—CRIM. 217.20. State v. Bell, 227 N.C. App. 339, 345 (2013).

Attempt (page 384)

For cases where the evidence was sufficient to prove an attempted armed robbery, see *State v. Calderon*, 242 N.C. App. 125, 137–38 (2015) (the defendant did not consummate the offense because the victim was passed out or asleep and, therefore, could not be induced to give up his money due to the threat that the accomplices' weapons presented and because no one saw the defendant take anything from the victim's pockets), and *State v. Evans*, 228 N.C. App. 454, 461–62 (2013) (the defendant planned a robbery with an accomplice, waited in a vehicle until the accomplice went into the residence and sent a message with the location of each individual inside, entered the residence and went directly to the victim's bedroom, and proceeded to wield his firearm in a threatening manner toward the victim; the evidence was sufficient even though the defendant did not make a specific demand for money).

Even though assault with a deadly weapon is a lesser-included offense of armed robbery, a defendant may be convicted for that assault and armed robbery when each conviction arises from discrete conduct. *State v. Ortiz*, 238 N.C. App. 508, 515 (2014).

Evidence that is sufficient to prove armed robbery is sufficient to prove attempted armed robbery. G.S. 14-87, *as amended by* S.L. 2017-31.

Greater and lesser-included offenses (page 385)

Attempted armed robbery is a lesser-included offense of armed robbery. G.S. 14-87, *as amended by* S.L. 2017-31.

Extortion is not a lesser-included offense of armed robbery. *State v. Wright*, 240 N.C. App. 270, 273 (2015) (applying a definitional rather than a factual test).

For another case supporting the statements in this note that larceny and assault are lesser-included offenses of robbery, see *State v. Cromartie*, 257 N.C. App. 790, 796–97 (2018) (misdemeanor larceny and simple assault are lesser-included offenses of common law robbery).

"Presumption" of the use of a dangerous weapon (page 385)

The trial court did not err by failing to instruct the jury on common law robbery and by denying the defendant's motion to dismiss armed robbery charges where there was no evidence that the gun was inoperable or unloaded and thus no evidence to rebut the presumption that the firearm was functioning properly. *State v. Williamson*, 220 N.C. App. 512, 515–16 (2012).

Although a defendant's testimony that a gun was unloaded extinguished the presumption that a dangerous weapon was used, a permissive inference remained and supported denial of a motion to dismiss. *State v. Bell*, 227 N.C. App. 339, 342–44 (2013) (in addition to the victim's testimony that the defendant entered her business, pointed a gun at her, and demanded money, evidence showed that upon leaving, the defendant saw the police and ran into the woods, where he left his hoodie and gun and jumped off of an embankment).

Although the fact that a BB pistol and a pellet gun were found outside the residence where the robbery occurred extinguished the presumption that a dangerous weapon was used, in light of the victim's testimony that the defendant used handguns, a permissive inference remained and supported denial of a motion to dismiss. *State v. Holt*, 241 N.C. App. 577, 585 (2015) (noting that no evidence conclusively connected a BB pistol or pellet gun to the robbery).

Claim of right defense (new note)

A defendant is not guilty of robbery if he or she can show that property was taken from another under a bona fide claim of right or title to the property. *State v. Spratt*, 265 N.C. 524 (1965). In *State v. Cox*, ___ N.C. App. ___, 825 S.E.2d 266 (2019), a defendant did not have the necessary intent to commit robbery when he went to the victim's house to retrieve money provided to her for a drug purchase that never happened.

Extortion (page 386)

Notes (page 386)

Element (2) (page 386)

The statute requires proof that the defendant intentionally utilized unjust or unlawful means in attempting to obtain the property or other acquittance, advantage, or immunity; it does not require proof that the defendant sought to achieve an end to which he or she had no entitlement. State v. Privette, 218 N.C. App. 459, 477 (2012).

Jury instructions (new note)

The trial judge properly instructed the jury on extortion using the pattern jury instruction. *Id.*

Greater and lesser-included offenses (new note)

Extortion is not a lesser-included offense of armed robbery. State v. Wright, 240 N.C. App. 270, 273 (2015) (applying a definitional rather than a factual test).

Defenses (new note)

North Carolina does not recognize a "claim of right" defense to extortion. *Id.*; *Privette*, 218 N.C. App. at 477.

15

Burglary, Breaking or Entering, and Related Offenses

First-Degree Burglary (page 391)

Notes (page 392)

Element (2) (page 393)

An entering did not occur when (1) the defendant used a shotgun to break a window and the end of the shotgun entered the premises, State v. Watkins, 218 N.C. App. 94, 100–01 (2012), and (2) the defendants used landscaping bricks and a fire pit bowl to break a home's window, but there was no evidence that they entered the premises. State v. Lucas, 234 N.C. App. 247, 251–54 (2014) (following *Watkins* and distinguishing *State v. Salters*, 137 N.C. App. 553 (2000) (evidence of a splintered door frame and broken lock, along with evidence that a suitcase missing from inside the residence was seen in the defendant's possession, was sufficient to establish an entering)).

Element (7) (page 394)

There was sufficient evidence that a burglary occurred at nighttime when the defendant left his girlfriend's apartment after 10 p.m. and did not return until 6 a.m. the next day; the burglary occurred during that time period; after taking judicial notice of the time of civil twilight (5:47 a.m.) and the driving distance between the victim's residence and the girlfriend's apartment, the court concluded that it would have been impossible for the defendant to commit the crime after 5:47 a.m. and be back at the apartment by 6 a.m. State v. Brown, 221 N.C. App. 383, 387–88 (2012).

Element (8) (page 395)

For another case supporting the statement in the first paragraph of this note that the defendant must intend to commit the required crime inside the dwelling, see *State v. Allah*, 231 N.C. App. 88, 93–95 (2013) (insufficient evidence that the defendant intended to commit a felonious restraint inside the building; that offense requires that the defendant transport the victim by motor vehicle or other conveyance, and the car the defendant was driving was left running outside).

Evidence that items were missing after a breaking or entering can be sufficient to prove the defendant's intent to commit a larceny inside the premises. State v. Northington, 230 N.C. App. 575, 579 (2013).

The evidence was sufficient to establish the requisite intent when (1) the defendants were walking from house to house in a neighborhood to determine whether the houses were occupied and were trying to open doors of parked cars, State v. Lucas, 234 N.C. App. 247, 254–55

(2014); (2) the defendant unlawfully broke and entered a church late at night; he did not have permission to be there and could not remember what he did there; and the defendant's wallet was found near where missing items had been stored, State v. Campbell, 368 N.C. 83 (2015); and (3) responding officers determined that a building broken into was in disarray and appeared to have been rummaged through, with certain items that had been inside the building earlier that day having been removed and placed in a fenced-in area surrounding the building, State v. McNair, 253 N.C. App. 178, 186 (2017).

The sixth paragraph of this note states that the fact that an intruder broke and entered a dwelling at nighttime is sufficient, in the absence of contrary evidence, to support a finding that the intruder intended to steal. This inference is sometimes called the *McBryde* inference, after the seminal case *State v. McBryde*, 97 N.C. 393 (1887). For another case applying the *McBryde* inference, see *State v. Mims*, 241 N.C. App. 611, 615–17 (2015). Additionally, in *Mims* the court applied the *McBryde* inference to an attempted breaking or entering that occurred during daylight hours.

Doctrine of recent possession (page 396)

When the victim's laptop and other items were found in the defendant's possession hours after the burglary, the doctrine of recent possession provided sufficient evidence that the defendant was the perpetrator. State v. Brown, 221 N.C. App. 383, 388 (2012).

Felony Breaking or Entering of a Building (page 398)

Statute (page 398)

2013 legislation, S.L. 2013-95, added subsection (a1) to G.S. 14-54 as follows:

> (a1) Any person who breaks or enters any building with intent to terrorize or injure an occupant of the building is guilty of a Class H felony.

Elements (page 398)

As a result of that same legislation, Element (5) should be revised as follows:

(5) with the intent to
   (a) commit any felony or larceny therein *or*
   (b) terrorize or injure an occupant of the building.

Notes (page 399)

Element (3) (page 399)

Distinguishing *Boone* (discussed in the first paragraph of this note in the main volume as holding that a defendant who entered a clothing store during business hours and stole two sweaters entered with the owner's consent), the court of appeals held that a defendant's entry into a store is without consent when the defendant has received notice from the store prohibiting his or her entry onto the premises. State v. Allen, 258 N.C. App. 285, 290 (2018) (after receiving a Notice of Prohibited Entry banning him from Belk stores for fifty years, the defendant entered a Belk store).

For purposes of breaking or entering, a person can have consent to enter a portion but not all of a building. State v. Vetter, 257 N.C. App. 915, 923 (2018). Thus, a defendant who had permission to access a garage to collect his belongings but lacked permission to enter the residence itself was properly convicted of this offense when he kicked in a door connecting the residence and garage and entered the residence. *Id.*

Element (5) (page 400)

The 2013 statute does not define the term "terrorize." That term is, however, used in the context of kidnapping, where it has been defined by case law. See the note on Element (4)(g) to "First-Degree Kidnapping" in Chapter 12 (Kidnapping and Related Offenses) of the main volume.

In *State v. Griffin*, ___ N.C. App. ___, 826 S.E.2d 253 (2019), the court applied the definition used for kidnapping (putting a person in some high degree of fear, a state of intense fright, or apprehension) and concluded that the defendant's uninvited entry, without announcing himself, into the victim's home and violent attack of the victim supported the conclusion that the defendant entered the home with the intent to terrorize the victim within the meaning of this offense.

Greater and lesser-included offenses (page 400)

For another case supporting the statement in this note that first-degree trespass is a lesser-included offense of this one, see *State v. Lucas*, 234 N.C. App. 247, 256 (2014).

Breaking or Entering a Place of Worship (page 401)

Notes (page 401)

Element (4) (page 401)

This Element was not satisfied when the defendant broke into a small barn located approximately fifty feet behind a building that was being rented by a church for holding religious services. State v. McNair, 253 N.C. App. 178, 182 (2017) (although the owner of the building allowed the church to store equipment in the barn, the barn was not used for religious worship; the court rejected the State's argument that because the barn was within the curtilage of the chapel it should be deemed an extension of it; the specific building broken into must be one regularly used and clearly identifiable as a place of religious worship).

As a result of 2019 legislation, S.L. 2019-40, add the following new offense, effective for offenses committed on or after December 1, 2019:

Breaking or Entering a Pharmacy (new crime)

Statute

§ 14-54.2. Breaking or entering a pharmacy.

(a) Definition. – The following definitions apply to this section:

(1)   Pharmacy. – A business that has a pharmacy permit under G.S. 90-85.21.

(2)   Controlled substance. – As defined in G.S. 90-87(5).

(b) Offense. – A person who breaks or enters a pharmacy with the intent to commit a larceny of a controlled substance is guilty of a Class E felony.

(c) Additional Offense. – Unless the conduct is covered under some other provision of law providing greater punishment, a person who receives or possesses any controlled substance stolen in violation of subsection (b) of this section, knowing or having reasonable grounds to believe the controlled substance was stolen, is guilty of a Class F felony.

(d) Forfeiture. – Any interest a person has acquired or maintained in property obtained in violation of this section shall be subject to forfeiture pursuant to the procedures for forfeiture as set forth in G.S. 90-112.

Elements

A person guilty of this offense

    (1) breaks *or* enters

    (2) without consent

    (3) a pharmacy

    (4) with the intent to commit a larceny of a controlled substance.

Punishment

Class E felony. G.S. 14-54.2(b). Any interest a person acquires or maintains in property obtained in violation of this section is subject to forfeiture as set forth in G.S. 90-112. *Id.* § -54.2(d).

Notes

Generally. Relevant notes to "Felony Breaking or Entering of a Building" apply to this offense as well.

Element (3)

A "pharmacy" is defined as a business that has a pharmacy permit under G.S. 90-85.21.

Element (4)

Unlike the similar element of "Felony Breaking or Entering of a Building," which covers the intent to commit any felony or larceny in the building, this Element of this offense requires that the defendant intend to commit a larceny of a controlled substance. A "controlled substance" is any drug, substance, or immediate precursor included in Schedules I through VI of the Controlled Substances Act. G.S. 90-87(5).

Related Offenses Not in This Chapter

See the offenses listed under "First-Degree Burglary," above.

Possession of Burglar's Tools (page 401)

Notes (page 402)

Element (1) (new note)

For a case where the evidence was sufficient to show that the defendant had constructive possession of burglar's tools found at the scene of a breaking or entering, see *State v. McNair*, 253 N.C. App. 178, 187–88 (2017) (the defendant was found alone inside a privately owned, fenced-in area at 1 a.m.; officers saw him scaling a 10-foot wall in an attempt to avoid apprehension and determined that someone had broken into the building; padlocks were found on the ground; and several pieces of property that had been stored inside the building were found in the fenced-in area).

Breaking or Entering a Vehicle (page 402)

Statute (page 402)

2015 legislation, S.L. 2015-286, sec. 3.3(a), amended the statute, putting the existing text in subsection (a) and creating a new subsection (b), as follows:

> (b) It shall not be a violation of this section for any person to break or enter any railroad car, motor vehicle, trailer, aircraft, boat, or other watercraft of any kind to provide assistance to a person inside the railroad car, motor vehicle, trailer, aircraft, boat, or watercraft of any kind if one or more of the following circumstances exist:
>
> (1) The person acts in good faith to access the person inside the railroad car, motor vehicle, trailer, aircraft, boat, or watercraft of any kind in order to provide first aid or emergency health care treatment or because the person inside is, or is in imminent danger of becoming unconscious, ill, or injured.
>
> (2) It is reasonably apparent that the circumstances require prompt decisions and actions in medical, other health care, or other assistance for the person inside the railroad car, motor vehicle, trailer, aircraft, boat, or watercraft of any kind.
>
> (3) The necessity of immediate health care treatment or removal of the person from the railroad car, motor vehicle, trailer, aircraft, boat, or other watercraft of any kind is so reasonably apparent that any delay in the rendering of treatment or removal would seriously worsen the physical condition or endanger the life of the person.

Notes (page 403)

Element (5) (page 403)

For a case where the State failed to present evidence that the boats in question contained items of value, see *State v. Fish*, 229 N.C. App. 584, 590 (2013) (rejecting the State's argument that boat batteries constituted items of value, reasoning that they were part of the boats themselves).

Element (6) (page 403)

For another case supporting the statement in this note that the intended felony or larceny may be a theft of the motor vehicle that is the subject of the breaking or entering, see *State v. Mitchell*, 234 N.C. App. 423, 428 (2014) (citing *Clark*).

Jury instructions (new note)

When an indictment alleges that the defendant broke *and* entered a vehicle, the trial court does not err by instructing the jury that the defendant can be found guilty if he or she broke *or* entered the vehicle. *Id.* at 428–29 (citing similar case law regarding breaking or entering a building).

Good Samaritan exception (new note)

The offense does not occur if a person breaks or enters to assist someone inside if the requirements of G.S. 14-56(b) are satisfied.

16

Fraud, Forgery, False Pretenses, and Related Offenses

Worthless Checks (page 411)

Worthless Checks—Making or Uttering (page 411)

Statute (page 411)

2013 legislation, S.L. 2013-244, sec. 4, amended the title of G.S. 14-107 and subsections (a) and (b) to read as follows:

> **§ 14-107. Worthless checks; multiple presentation of checks.**
>
> (a) It is unlawful for any person, firm or corporation, to draw, make, utter or issue and deliver to another, any check or draft on any bank or depository, for the payment of money or its equivalent, knowing at the time of the making, drawing, uttering, issuing and delivering the check or draft, that the maker or drawer of it:
>
> (1) Has not sufficient funds on deposit in or credit with the bank or depository with which to pay the check or draft upon presentation, or
>
> (2) Has previously presented the check or draft for the payment of money or its equivalent.
>
> (b) It is unlawful for any person, firm or corporation to solicit or to aid and abet any other person, firm or corporation to draw, make, utter or issue and deliver to any person, firm or corporation, any check or draft on any bank or depository for the payment of money or its equivalent, being informed, knowing or having reasonable grounds for believing at the time of the soliciting or the aiding and abetting that the maker or the drawer of the check or draft:
>
> (1) Has not sufficient funds on deposit in, or credit with, the bank or depository with which to pay the check or draft upon presentation, or
>
> (2) Has previously presented the check or draft for the payment of money or its equivalent.

Another piece of 2013 legislation, S.L. 2013-360, sec. 18B.14(b), amended subsection (d)(1) to read as follows:

> (1) Except as provided in subdivision (3) or (4) of this subsection, the person is guilty of a Class 3 misdemeanor.

Elements (page 412)

As a result of 2013 legislation, S.L. 2013-244, sec. 4, Element (4) should be revised as follows:

> (4) knowing that
>
> (a) there are insufficient funds or credit available for the payment *or*
>
> (b) the maker or drawer has previously presented the check or draft for the payment.

Punishment (page 412)

As a result of 2013 legislation, S.L. 2013-360, sec. 18B.14(b), the first three words of this section should read:

> Class 3 misdemeanor

Notes (page 412)

Elements (3) and (4) (page 413)

In the note on Element (3), delete the second sentence of the second paragraph. Add the following text at the end of the first paragraph of the note on Element (4):

> A postdated check implies no more than that on its date the drawer will have or expects to have funds or credit in the bank to insure its payment at that time. State v. Crawford, 198 N.C. 522 (1930); State v. Byrd, 204 N.C. 162 (1933).

Obtaining Property for a Worthless Check (page 416)

Statute (page 416)

2013 legislation, S.L. 2013-360, sec. 18B.14(a), amended the statute to lower the punishment for this offense to a Class 3 misdemeanor.

Punishment (page 416)

As a result of the 2013 legislation noted above, delete the text of this section and replace it with the following:

> Class 3 misdemeanor. G.S. 14-106.

Obtaining Property by False Pretenses (page 417)

Notes (page 417)

Element (1) (page 417)

The evidence was sufficient to establish this Element where the defendant (1) uttered a forged check, State v. Conley, 220 N.C. App. 50, 60–61 (2012); (2) approached two elderly women, falsely told them that their roofs needed repair, took payment for the work, and then performed shoddy work or failed to complete the job, State v. Barker, 240 N.C. App. 224, 231 (2015); and (3) submitted false invoices for moving expenses from companies that did not exist in North Carolina, State v. Holanek, 242 N.C. App. 633, 643 (2015).

Element (2) (page 418)

For cases where the evidence was sufficient to establish a false representation regarding pawned items, see *State v. Mostafavi*, 370 N.C. 681, 687 (2018) (the defendant falsely represented that he owned the property where the pawn tickets described the conveyed items; contained the defendant's name, address, driver's license number, and date of birth; and included language explicitly stating that the defendant was "giving a security interest in the . . . described goods"), and *State v. Greenlee*, 227 N.C. App. 133, 137–38 (2013) (the defendant falsely represented to a pawn shop that items were not stolen).

The State failed to offer sufficient evidence to establish that the defendant made a false representation with the intent to deceive when he told the victims that he intended to invest money they had loaned him in legitimate institutions and would repay it with interest at a specified time; the evidence showed only that the defendant, "after seriously overestimating his investing skills, made a promise that he was unable to keep." State v. Braswell, 225 N.C. App. 734, 742 (2013).

Element (3) (page 418)

The State failed to offer sufficient evidence to establish that the defendant made a false representation with the intent to deceive when he told the victims that he intended to invest the money they loaned him in legitimate institutions and would repay it with interest at a specified time; the evidence showed only that the defendant, "after seriously overestimating his investing skills, made a promise that he was unable to keep." *Braswell*, 225 N.C. App. at 742.

For cases where the evidence was sufficient to prove an intent to deceive, see *State v. Phillips*, 252 N.C. App. 194, 199 (2017) (the defendant advertised "Michael Kors" bags for sale for $45, knowing they were counterfeit), and *State v. Pendergraft*, 238 N.C. App. 516, 527 (2014) (rejecting the defendant's argument that his honest but mistaken belief that he could obtain title to a property by adverse possession precluded a finding that he had the required intent to deceive), *aff'd per curiam by an equally divided court*, 368 N.C. 314 (2015) (noting that the decision below is left undisturbed and stands without precedential value).

Element (4) (page 418)

In a case where the defendant obtained money by selling to company BIMCO electrical wire falsely represented as not having been stolen, there was sufficient evidence that his false representation in fact deceived BIMCO; the court rejected the defendant's argument that BIMCO was indifferent to legal ownership and employed a "nod and wink system" in which no actual deception occurred, noting evidence that the defendant represented himself as the lawful owner of the material and that BIMCO paid him for it. State v. Hallum, 246 N.C. App. 658 (2016).

When a defendant is charged with a completed offense, proof that the victim was deceived is required. *Phillips*, 252 N.C. App. at 199. However, when the defendant is charged with attempting to obtain property by false pretenses, which (as discussed in the note to this offense entitled "Attempt") is punished at the same level as the completed offense, the State need not prove that the victim was in fact deceived. *Id.*

Element (5) (page 418)

Delete the first sentence of the second paragraph of this note and replace it with the following:

For the completed version of this crime, the defendant must gain possession of the property but need not gain title to or an ownership interest in it.

Add the following to this note:

Like a loan, a provisional credit of $600 placed in the defendant's bank account after he falsely told the bank that his girlfriend had fraudulently signed and cashed checks drawn on his account was a thing of value. State v. Buchanan, 253 N.C. App. 783, 786 (2017) (the credit was the equivalent of money being placed in his account, to which the defendant had access, at least temporarily; access to money for a period of time, even if it eventually has to be paid back, is a thing of value).

For a case where the evidence was insufficient to establish that the defendant obtained a thing of value, see *State v. Mathis*, ___ N.C. App. ___, 819 S.E.2d 627 (2018) (in a case arising out of false information submitted in connection with the defendant's work as a bail bondsman, the indictment alleged the thing of value obtained to be a professional bail bondsman's license; the defendant already had a bail bondsman license and the State asserted that his false representations allowed him to retain his license; the court disagreed, concluding that retaining is not the same as obtaining).

Attempt (page 420)

This offense was committed even though the defendant returned the victim's payment; the defendant's actions were sufficient to constitute an attempt. State v. Seelig, 226 N.C. App. 147, 162 (2013).

Multiple convictions and punishments (page 420)

When a defendant obtains multiple items in a single transaction, only one conviction can result. *Buchanan*, 253 N.C. App. at 787 (where the defendant attempted to collect the value of three checks he falsely claimed to be fraudulent but was successful only with respect to one of them, only a single offense occurred; however, the defendant waived the double jeopardy issue by failing to raise it at trial).

Doctrine of recent possession (new note)

The doctrine of recent possession applies to obtaining property by false pretenses. State v. Street, 254 N.C. App. 214, 219 (2017) (concluding that the jury may be instructed on the doctrine even if the defendant is not charged with taking the property that he or she is alleged to have recently possessed; here, the defendant was charged with obtaining property by false pretenses for selling a pair of hedge trimmers to a pawn shop less than two hours after the trimmers were stolen). See generally this note to "Misdemeanor Larceny" in the main volume.

As a result of 2019 legislation, S.L. 2019-193, add the following note to this offense, effective for offenses committed on or after December 1, 2019:

Venue (new note)

The State is not required to establish that all of the acts constituting this offense occurred in North Carolina or within a single city, county, or local jurisdiction of this state, and it is no defense that not all of the acts constituting this offense occurred in North Carolina or within a single local jurisdiction. G.S. 14-100(b1).

Related Offenses Not in This Chapter (page 420)

Add the following offenses to this list:

> Hiring with intent to defraud. G.S. 14-168.
> Unemployment insurance fraud. G.S. 96-18.

The offense listed in this section as "Improper receipt of decedent's retirement allowance. G.S. 135-18.11, 128-38.5, 135-75.2, and 120-4.34" should read:

> Improper receipt of decedent's retirement allowance or monthly benefit under the Disability Income Plan. G.S. 135-18.11, 128-38.5, 135-75.2, and 120-4.34.

Exploitation of a Disabled or Elder Adult (page 421)

Exploitation of a Disabled or Older Adult through a Position of Trust or Business Relationship (page 421) (revised title)

Statute (page 421)

2013 legislation, S.L. 2013-337, replaced the term "elder adult" with "older adult" throughout G.S. 14-112.2. It also amended subsection (a)(2) to read as follows:

> (2)   Older adult.—A person 65 years of age or older.

That same legislation also amended subsection (c) to read as follows:

> (c) It is unlawful for a person to knowingly, by deception or intimidation, obtain or use, endeavor to obtain or use, or conspire with another to obtain or use an older adult's or disabled adult's funds, assets, or property with the intent to temporarily or permanently deprive the older adult or disabled adult of the use, benefit, or possession of the funds, assets, or property, or benefit someone other than the older adult or disabled adult. This

subsection shall not apply to a person acting within the scope of that person's lawful authority as the agent for the older adult or disabled adult.

Another 2013 law, S.L. 2013-203, amended the statute, adding a new subsection, (f), as follows:

> (f) If a person is charged with a violation of this section that involves funds, assets, or property valued at more than five thousand dollars ($5,000), the district attorney may file a petition in the pending criminal proceeding before the court with jurisdiction over the pending charges to freeze the funds, assets, or property of the defendant in an amount up to one hundred fifty percent (150%) of the alleged value of funds, assets, or property in the defendant's pending criminal proceeding for purposes of restitution to the victim. The standard of proof required to freeze the defendant's funds, assets, or property shall be by clear and convincing evidence. The procedure for petitioning the court under this subsection shall be governed by G.S. 14-112.3.

Elements (page 422)

As a result of the 2013 legislation noted above, replace the term "elder adult" with "older adult" throughout this section.

Notes (page 423)

Element (2) (page 423)

As a result of 2013 legislation, S.L. 2013-337, delete the second paragraph of this note and replace it with the following:

An "older adult" is a person 65 years old or older. G.S. 14-112.2(a)(2). Prior to 2013 legislative changes, the statute applied to an "elder adult." Interpreting the latter provision, one case held that there was sufficient evidence that the victim was an elder adult when the victim was at least 99 years old and received help to pay his bills, cash his checks, and perform personal hygiene tasks, among other things. State v. Forte, 206 N.C. App. 699, 704–05 (2010).

Asset freeze (new note)

If the offense involves funds, assets, or property valued at more than $5,000, new G.S. 14-112.2(f) allows the district attorney to file a petition to freeze the defendant's funds, assets, or property for purposes of restitution. New G.S. 14-112.3 sets out the relevant procedure.

Exploitation of a Disabled or Older Adult Lacking Capacity (page 423) (revised title)

Elements (page 423)

As a result of 2013 legislation, S.L. 2013-337, the elements of this offense are revised to read:

A person guilty of this offense

(1) knowingly *and*
(2) by deception or intimidation
(3) obtains, uses, endeavors to obtain or use, or conspires with another to obtain or use a disabled or older adult's funds, assets, or property
(4) with the intent to
    (a) temporarily or permanently deprive the disabled or older adult of the use, benefit, or possession of the funds, assets, or property *or*
    (b) benefit someone other than the disabled or older adult.

Notes (page 423)

Element (1) (new note)

See "Knowingly" in Chapter 1 (States of Mind) of the main volume.

Element (2) (page 423)

Delete the text of this note and replace it with the following:

> For definitions of "disabled adult" and "older adult," see the note on Element (2) to "Exploitation of a Disabled or Older Adult through a Position of Trust or Business Relationship" (revised title), above in this supplement and in the main volume.

Asset freeze (new note)

See this note to "Exploitation of a Disabled or Older Adult through a Position of Trust or Business Relationship" (revised title), above in this supplement.

Identity Theft and Frauds (page 424)

Identity Theft (page 426)

Notes (page 427)

Element (2)(b) (page 427)

The evidence was sufficient to establish that the defendant "used" or "possessed" another person's Social Security number to avoid legal consequences when, after being detained and questioned for shoplifting, the defendant falsely gave the officer his name as Roy Lamar Ward and provided the officer with the name of an employer, date of birth, and possible address; the officer then obtained Ward's Social Security number, wrote it on the citation, and issued the citation to the defendant, but the defendant neither signed the citation nor confirmed the listed Social Security number. State v. Sexton, 223 N.C. App. 341, 345 (2012).

Element (2)(c) (page 427)

See the discussion of *Sexton*, 223 N.C. App. 341, immediately above.

Element (3) (page 427)

"Identifying information" is not limited to the fourteen examples listed in G.S. 14-113.20(b). State v. Miles, ___ N.C. App. ___, 833 S.E.2d 27 (2019) (holding that another person's name, date of birth, and address are identifying information when used to escape arrest and possibly receive hospital services).

Element (4) (new note)

Where the evidence showed that the defendant had used other individuals' credit card numbers, it was sufficient to show that he possessed the victims' credit cards with the intent to fraudulently represent that he was those individuals for the purpose of making financial transactions in their names. State v. Jones, 367 N.C. 299, 305 (2014). The fact that the defendant used false names not matching those on the victims' credit cards did not negate the defendant's intent to fraudulently represent that he was the cardholder. *Id.* at 306.

Related Offenses Not in This Chapter (page 428)

Add the following offense to this list:

> Identity theft in connection with tax submission. G.S. 105-236(a)(9b), *as enacted by* S.L. 2017-204, sec. 3.1(a).

Impersonating a Transportation Network Company Driver (new crime)

This offense was enacted in 2019, S.L. 2019-194, effective for offenses committed on or after December 1, 2019, to read as follows:

Statute

§ 14-401.27. Impersonation of a transportation network company driver.

It shall be unlawful for any person to impersonate a transportation network company (TNC) driver, as defined in G.S. 20-280.1, by a false statement, false display of distinctive signage or emblems known as a trade dress, trademark, branding, or logo of the TNC, or any other act which falsely represents that the person has a current connection with a transportation network company or falsely represents that the person is responding to a passenger ride request for a transportation network company. A violation of this section is a Class H felony if the person impersonates a TNC driver during the commission of a separate felony offense. Any other violation of this section is a Class 2 misdemeanor.

Elements

A person guilty of this offense

(1) impersonates
(2) a transportation network company (TNC) driver, as defined in G.S. 20-280.1
(3) by
    (a) a false statement;
    (b) a false display of distinctive signage or emblems known as a trade dress, trademark, branding, or logo of the TNC; *or*
    (c) any other act which falsely represents that the person has a current connection with a TNC or is responding to a passenger ride request for a TNC.

Punishment

Class 2 misdemeanor. G.S. 14-401.27. This offense is a Class H felony if the person impersonates a TNC driver during the commission of a separate felony offense. *Id.*

Notes

Element (2). A TNC driver is an individual who uses a passenger vehicle in connection with a TNC's online-enabled application or platform to connect with passengers in exchange for payment of a fee to the TNC. G.S. 20-280.1.

Crimes Involving Security Interests (page 430)

Fraudulent Filings (page 431)

Statute (page 431)

2012 legislation, S.L. 2012-150, sec. 6, amended the statute, making the crime a Class I felony.

Punishment (page 432)

As a result of the 2012 legislation noted above, delete the text of this section and replace it with the following:

Class I felony. G.S. 14-401.19.

Related Offenses Not in This Chapter (page 432)

Add the following offense to this list:

Simulation of court process in connection with collection of claim, demand or account. G.S. 14-118.1.

False Liens (new crime)

This offense was enacted in 2012, S.L. 2012-150. It was amended in 2013, S.L. 2013-170; S.L. 2013-410, sec. 27.8; in 2015, S.L. 2015-87; in 2017, S.L. 2017-102, sec. 3; and in 2019, S.L. 2019-117, sec. 3; S.L. 2019-243 , sec. 29.(a), to read as follows:

Statute

§ 14-118.6. Filing false lien or encumbrance.

(a) It shall be unlawful for any person to present for filing or recording in a public record or a private record generally available to the public a false lien or encumbrance against the real or personal property of an owner or beneficial interest holder, knowing or having reason to know that the lien or encumbrance is false or contains a materially false, fictitious, or fraudulent statement or representation. Any person who violates this subsection shall be guilty of a Class I felony.

(b) When presented to the register of deeds for recording, if a register of deeds has a reasonable suspicion that an instrument purporting to be a lien or encumbrance is materially false, fictitious, or fraudulent, the register of deeds may refuse to record the purported lien or encumbrance. Neither the register of deeds nor any other entity shall be liable for recording or the refusal to record a purported lien or encumbrance as described in this section. If the recording of the purported lien or encumbrance is denied, the register of deeds shall allow the recording of a Notice of Denied Lien or Encumbrance Filing on a form adopted by the Secretary of State, for which no filing fee shall be collected. The Notice of Denied Lien or Encumbrance Filing shall not itself constitute a lien or encumbrance. When recording is denied, any interested person may initiate a special proceeding in the county where the recording was denied within ten (10) business days of the filing of the Notice of Denied Lien or Encumbrance Filing asking the superior court of the respective county to find that the proposed recording has a statutory or contractual basis and to order that the document be recorded. If, after hearing, upon a minimum of five (5) days' notice as provided in Rule 5 of the Rules of Civil Procedure and opportunity to be heard to all interested persons and all persons claiming an ownership interest in the property, the court finds that there is a statutory or contractual basis for the proposed recording, the court shall order the document recorded, and the party submitting the instrument shall pay the filing fee in accordance with G.S. 161-10. A lien or encumbrance recorded upon order of the court under this subsection shall have a priority interest as of the time of the filing of the Notice of Denied Lien or Encumbrance Filing. If the court finds that there is no statutory or contractual basis for the proposed recording, the court shall enter an order finding that the proposed recording is null and void and that it shall not be filed, indexed, or recorded and a certified copy of that order shall be recorded by the register of deeds that originally denied the recording, for which the party who submitted the instrument shall pay the filing fee in accordance with G.S. 161-10. The review by the judge under this subsection shall not be deemed a finding as to any underlying claim of the parties involved. If a special proceeding is not initiated under this subsection within ten (10) business days of the filing of the Notice of Denied Lien or Encumbrance Filing, the purported lien or encumbrance is deemed null and void as a matter of law.

(b1) When a purported lien or encumbrance is presented to a clerk of superior court for filing and the clerk of court has a reasonable suspicion that the purported lien or encumbrance is materially false, fictitious, or fraudulent, the clerk of court may refuse to file the purported lien or encumbrance. Neither the clerk of court nor the clerk's staff shall be liable for filing or the refusal to file a purported lien or encumbrance under this subsection. The clerk of superior court shall not file, index, or docket the document against the property until that document is approved by any judge of the judicial district having subject matter jurisdiction for filing by the clerk of superior court. If the judge determines that the filing is not false, the clerk shall index the claim of lien. A lien or encumbrance filed upon order of the court under this subsection shall have a priority interest as of the date and time of indexing by the clerk of superior court. If the court finds that there is no statutory or contractual basis for the proposed filing, the court shall enter an order that the proposed filing is null and void as a matter of law, and that it shall not be filed or indexed. The clerk of superior court shall serve the order and return the original denied filing to the person or entity that presented it. The person or entity shall have 30 days from the entry of the order to appeal the order. If the order is not appealed within the applicable time period, the clerk may destroy the filing.

(c) Upon being presented with an order duly issued by a court of competent jurisdiction of this State declaring that a lien or encumbrance already recorded or filed is false, and therefore null and void as a matter of law, the register of deeds or clerk of court that received the recording or filing, in addition to recording or filing the court's order finding the lien or encumbrance to be false, shall conspicuously mark on the first page of the original record previously filed the following statement: "THE CLAIM ASSERTED IN THIS DOCUMENT IS FALSE AND IS NOT PROVIDED FOR BY THE GENERAL LAWS OF THIS STATE."

(d) In addition to any criminal penalties provided for in this section, the presentation of an instrument for recording or filing with a register of deeds or clerk of superior court that purports to be a lien or encumbrance that is determined to be materially false, fictitious, or fraudulent shall constitute a violation of G.S. 75-1.1.

(e) Subsections (b), (b1), and (c) of this section shall not apply to filings under Article 9 of Chapter 25 of the General Statutes or under Chapter 44A of the General Statutes.

Elements

As a result of the 2019 legislative changes noted above, the elements of this offense should read as follows:

A person guilty of this offense

(1) presents for filing in a public record or a private record generally available to the public
(2) a false lien or encumbrance
(3) against the real or personal property of an owner or beneficial interest holder
(4) knowing or having reason to know that the lien or encumbrance is false or contains a materially false, fictitious, or fraudulent statement or representation.

Punishment

Class I felony. G.S. 14-118.6(a).

Notes

Element (3) generally. For the definition of the term "real property," see the note on Element (3) to "Injury to Real Property" in Chapter 18 (Trespass, Property Damage, and Littering) of the main volume. For the definition of the term "personal property," see the note on Element (3) to "Injury to Personal Property," also in Chapter 18 of the main volume.

Element (3)(b). The term "immediate family member" means a spouse or child. G.S. 14-118.6(a).

Related Offenses Not in This Chapter

No docketing of lien unless authorized by statute. G.S. 44A-12.1.

Residential Mortgage Fraud (page 433)

Statute (page 433)

2012 legislation, S.L. 2012-150, sec. 5, amended G.S. 14-118.12, adding a new subsection, (a)(5), as follows:

> (5)   Knowingly files in a public record or a private record generally available to the public a document falsely claiming that a mortgage loan has been satisfied, discharged, released, revoked, or terminated or is invalid.

Elements (page 434)

As a result of the 2012 legislation noted above, a new Element, (3)(d), should be added to this offense as follows:

> (d)   knowingly files in a public or private record generally available to the public a document falsely claiming that a mortgage loan has been satisfied, discharged, released, revoked, or terminated or is invalid.

Related Offenses Not in This Chapter (page 435)

Add the following offenses to this list:

> Simulation of court process in connection with collection of claim, demand or account. G.S. 14-118.1.
>
> Bank fraud. G.S. 53C-8-11.

Forgery and Related Offenses (page 435)

Forgery and Counterfeiting of Instruments (page 437)

Notes (page 438)

Relation to other offenses (new note)

Forgery and larceny of a chose in action are not mutually exclusive offenses. State v. Grier, 224 N.C. App. 150, 153 (2012).

Uttering Forged Instruments or Instruments with False Endorsements (page 439)

Notes (page 440)

Element (3) (page 440)

For a case where there was sufficient evidence that a check was falsely made, see *State v. Conley*, 220 N.C. App. 50, 60–61 (2012).

Electronic Food and Nutrition Benefits Fraud (page 456)

Fraudulently Obtaining or Transferring Electronic Food and Nutrition Benefits (page 456)
Notes (page 456)

Element (3) (new note)
The trial court did not err by denying the defendant's motion to dismiss where the evidence showed that the defendant knowingly submitted a fraudulent wage verification form to obtain food benefits to which he was not entitled. State v. Davis, 230 N.C. App. 50, 53–54 (2013).

Computer Fraud (page 461)

Accessing a Government Computer to Defraud or Obtain Property (page 465)
Elements (page 465)

In light of the *Mathis* case discussed in the note on Element (1) immediately below in this supplement, Element (1) should read as follows:

(1) willfully and without authorization

Notes (page 465)

Element (1) (page 465)
G.S. 14-454.1(a) states that the defendant must act willfully. Case law, however, has interpreted the statute to require that the defendant act both willfully and without authorization. State v. Mathis, ___ N.C. App. ___, 819 S.E.2d 627 (2018). G.S. 14-453(1a) defines "authorization" for purposes of computer-related crime to mean "having the consent or permission of the owner, or of the person licensed or authorized by the owner to grant consent or permission to access a computer, computer system, or computer network in a manner not exceeding the consent or permission."

For cases where this Element was satisfied, see *Mathis*, ___ N.C. App. ___, 819 S.E.2d 627 (although the defendant had authorization to use the computer system, he exceeded that authorization by inputting fraudulent information), and *State v. Barr*, 218 N.C. App. 329, 336–40 (2012) (involving transfers of title by the defendant's license plate agency for an unlicensed company).

Element (2) (page 465)
For a case where the evidence was sufficient to establish that the defendant accessed or caused another to access a government computer, see *Mathis*, ___ N.C. App. ___, 819 S.E.2d 627 (the defendant's unique user name and password were used to access the database and his email was used to submit reports; even if the defendant only transmitted information that was then uploaded by government personnel, the evidence was sufficient because the statute covers causing a government computer to be accessed).

Element (4)(b) (new note)
The evidence was sufficient to sustain a conviction under G.S. 14-454.1(a)(2) where the State alleged that the defendant, who worked for a private license plate agency, submitted false information into the State Title and Registration System (STARS) so that a car dealer whose dealer number was invalid could transfer title. The defendant admitted that she personally

accessed STARS to make three transfers for the dealer, that she told a co-worker to run a fourth transaction in a similar fashion, and that she received payment for doing so. *Barr*, 218 N.C. App. at 334–35.

Accessing a Government Computer without Authorization (page 466)

Notes (page 466)

Element (2) (new note)

For a definition of the term "authorization," see the note on Element (1) to "Accessing a Government Computer to Defraud or Obtain Property," above in this supplement.

Accessing Testing Material in a Government Computer (page 467)

Notes (page 467)

Element (2) (new note)

For a definition of the term "authorization," see the note on Element (1) to "Accessing a Government Computer to Defraud or Obtain Property," above in this supplement.

Willful Failure to File a State Tax Return, Supply State Tax Information, or Pay State Tax (page 467)

Related Offenses Not in This Chapter (page 468)

Add the following offense to this list:

Possession, transfer, or use of automated sales suppression device. G.S. 14-118.7.

17
Arson and Burning Offenses

Arson Offenses (page 471)

First-Degree Arson (page 471)

Notes (page 471)

Element (1) (page 471)

Delete the second sentence of this note and replace it with the following:

> As used for arson, these terms mean that the act was done "voluntarily and without excuse or justification and without any bona fide claim of right." State v. White, 288 N.C. 44, 50 (1975); State v. Eubanks, 83 N.C. App. 338, 339 (1986). An intent or animus against either the property or its owner is not required. *White*, 288 N.C. at 50; *Eubanks*, 83 N.C. App. at 339.

Add the following at the end of this note:

> The evidence was sufficient to establish malice where, among other things, the defendant was enraged at the property owner for evicting him. State v. Burton, 224 N.C. App. 120, 126 (2012).

Burning Offenses (page 474)

Burning during Commission of Felony (new crime)

2018 legislation, S.L. 2018-31, sec. 1, enacted this new crime.

Statute

§ 14-67.2. Burning caused during commission of another felony.

(a) If any person, during the commission of a felony, knowingly damages any dwelling, structure, building, or conveyance referenced in this Article by means of fire or explosive that results in damages valued at ten thousand dollars ($10,000) or more, the person shall be punished as a Class D felon unless the person's conduct is covered under some other provision of law providing greater punishment.

(b) If any person, during the commission of a felony, knowingly causes, aids, abets, advises, encourages, hires, counsels, or procures another person to damage any dwelling, structure, building, or conveyance referenced in this Article by means of fire or explosive that results in damages valued at ten thousand dollars ($10,000) or more, the person shall be punished as a Class D felon unless the person's conduct is covered under some other provision of law providing greater punishment.

Elements

A person guilty of this offense

    (1) during the commission of a felony

    (2) knowingly

    (3) damages any dwelling, structure, building, or conveyance

    (4) by means of fire or explosive *and*

    (5) causes damages of $10,000 or more.

Punishment

Class D felony. G.S. 14-67.2(a).

Notes

Element (2)

See "Knowingly" in Chapter 1 (States of Mind) of the main volume.

Aiding and abetting, soliciting, etc.

The statute includes a special offense for aiders and abettors, those who solicit this activity, etc. Specifically, it provides that any person who, during the commission of a felony, knowingly causes, aids, abets, advises, encourages, hires, counsels, or procures another person to damage any dwelling, structure, building, or conveyance by means of fire or explosive that results in damages of $10,000 or more shall be punished as a Class D felon unless the person's conduct is covered under some other provision of law providing greater punishment. G.S. 14-67.2(b). This provision duplicates the general rule that those who aid and abet a crime are punished as if they committed that crime, see "Aiding and Abetting" in Chapter 3 (Participants in Crime) of the main volume, and overrides the general rule that solicitation is punished two classes lower than the felony solicited. See "Solicitation" in Chapter 5 (General Crimes) in the main volume.

Multiple convictions and punishments

A person may not be punished for this offense if the conduct is covered by another crime that carries a more severe punishment. G.S. 14-67.2(a). See this note to "Assault Inflicting Serious Injury" (Chapter 7) in the main volume.

Arson or Burning Causing Serious Bodily Injury to Firefighter, Law Enforcement Officer, Fire Investigator, or EMT (page 482) (revised title)

2018 legislation, S.L. 2018-31, sec. 2, amended the statute as described here.

Statute (page 482)

The 2018 legislation noted above amended the statute to read as follows:

> **§ 14-69.3. Arson or other unlawful burning that results in serious bodily injury to a firefighter, law enforcement officer, fire investigator, or emergency medical technician.**
>
> (a) The following definitions apply in this section:
>
>   (1) Emergency medical technician.—The term includes an emergency medical technician, an emergency medical technician-intermediate, and an emergency medical technician-paramedic, as those terms are defined in G.S. 131E-155.

> (2) Fire investigator.—The term includes any person who, individually or as part of an investigative team, has the responsibility and authority to determine the origin, cause, or development of a fire or explosion.
>
> (b) A person is guilty of a Class E felony if the person commits a felony under Article 15 of Chapter 14 of the General Statutes and a firefighter, law enforcement officer, fire investigator, or emergency medical technician suffers serious bodily injury while discharging or attempting to discharge official duties on the property, or proximate to the property, that is the subject of the firefighter's, law enforcement officer's, fire investigator's, or emergency medical technician's discharge or attempt to discharge his or her respective duties.

Elements (page 482)

As a result of the 2018 legislation noted above, elements (2) and (4) should read as follows:

> (2) a firefighter, law enforcement officer, fire investigator, or emergency medical technician
>
> . . .
>
> (4) while discharging or attempting to discharge his or her official duties

Notes (page 482)

Element (2) (page 482)

As a result of the 2018 legislation noted above, the citation listed in this note should read as follows:

> G.S. 14-69.3(a)(1).

As a result of the 2018 legislation noted above, add the following to this note:

> The term "fire investigator" means any person who, individually or as part of an investigative team, has the responsibility and authority to determine the origin, cause, or development of a fire or explosion. G.S. 14-69.3(a)(2).

Setting Fire Offenses (page 483)

Setting Fire to Woods and Fields (page 483)

Statute (page 483)

2015 legislation, S.L. 2015-263, sec. 36(a), amended the statute, replacing "Department of Environmental Quality" with "Department of Agriculture and Consumer Services."

Elements (page 483)

As a result of the 2015 legislative change noted above, Element (4) should read as follows:

> (4) in any county that is under the protection of the Department of Agriculture and Consumer Services in its work of forest fire control.

18

Trespass, Property Damage, and Littering

Trespass Offenses (page 489)

First-Degree Trespass (page 489)

Statute (page 489)

G.S. 14-159.12 has been amended, see S.L. 2012-168, sec. 1; S.L. 2014-103, sec. 10(a); S.L. 2016-26, sec. 1; S.L. 2018-66, to read as follows:

> **§ 14-159.12. First degree trespass.**
>
> (a) Offense.—A person commits the offense of first degree trespass if, without authorization, he enters or remains:
>
> (1) On premises of another so enclosed or secured as to demonstrate clearly an intent to keep out intruders;
>
> (2) In a building of another; or
>
> (3) On the lands of the Eastern Band of Cherokee Indians after the person has been excluded by a resolution passed by the Eastern Band of Cherokee Indian Tribal Council.
>
> (b) Except as otherwise provided in subsection (c), (d), or (f) of this section, first degree trespass is a Class 2 misdemeanor.
>
> (c) Except as otherwise provided in subsection (d) of this section, a violation of subsection (a) of this section is a Class A1 misdemeanor if all of the following circumstances exist:
>
> (1) The offense is committed on the premises of any of the following:
>
> a. A facility that is owned or operated by an electric power supplier as defined in G.S. 62-133.8(a)(3) and that is either an electric generation facility, a transmission substation, a transmission switching station, a transmission switching structure, or a control center used to manage transmission operations or electrical power generating at multiple plant locations.
>
> b. Any facility used or available for use in the collection, treatment, testing, storing, pumping, or distribution of water for a public water system.
>
> c. Any facility, including any liquefied natural gas storage facility or propane air facility, that is owned or operated by a natural gas local distribution company, natural gas pipeline carrier operating under a certificate of public convenience and necessity from the Utilities Commission, municipal corporation operating a municipally owned

gas distribution system, or regional natural gas district organized and operated pursuant to Article 28 of Chapter 160A of the General Statutes used for transmission, distribution, measurement, testing, regulating, compression, control, or storage of natural gas.

    d. Any facility used or operated for agricultural activities, as that term is defined in G.S. 106-581.1.

(2) The person actually entered a building, or it was necessary for the person to climb over, go under, or otherwise surmount a fence or other barrier to reach the facility.

(d) If, in addition to the circumstances set out in subsection (c) of this section, the violation also includes any of the following elements, then the offense is a Class H felony:

(1) The offense is committed with the intent to disrupt the normal operation of any of the facilities described in subdivision (1) of subsection (c) of this section.

(2) The offense involves an act that places either the offender or others on the premises at risk of serious bodily injury.

(e) As used in subsections (c) and (d) of this section, the term "facility" shall mean a building or other infrastructure.

(f) A violation of subsection (a) of this section is a Class I felony and shall include a fine of not less than one thousand dollars ($1,000) for each violation, if any of the following circumstances exist:

(1) The offense occurs on real property where the person has reentered after having previously been removed pursuant to the execution of a valid order or writ for possession.

(2) The offense occurs under color of title where the person has knowingly created or provided materially false evidence of an ownership or possessory interest.

(3) The offense is the person's second or subsequent violation of subdivision (a) (3) of this section.

Elements (page 489)

As a result of 2018 legislation, S.L. 2018-66, Element (3) should read as follows:

(3) (a) on premises of another so enclosed or secured as to demonstrate clearly an intent to keep out intruders,

(b) in a building of another, *or*

(c) on the lands of the Eastern Band of Cherokee Indians.

Punishment (page 489)

The offense is elevated to a Class A1 misdemeanor if (1) it is committed on the premises of certain electric power supplier facilities, public water system facilities, liquefied natural gas storage or propane air facilities, or agricultural facilities and (2) the defendant entered a building or it was necessary to climb over, go under, or surmount a fence or barrier to reach the facility. G.S. 14-159.12(c).

The offense is elevated to a Class H felony if, in addition to the circumstances required for the Class A1 misdemeanor version of the offense, it is committed with the intent to disrupt the normal operation of the facility or involves an act that puts either the offender or those on the premises at risk of serious bodily injury. G.S. 14-159.12(d).

The offense is elevated to a Class I felony, with a mandatory fine of not less than $1,000 for each violation, if it occurs on real property where the defendant has reentered after having previously been removed pursuant to the execution of a valid order or writ for possession; occurs under color of title where the defendant has knowingly created or provided materially false evidence of an ownership or possessory interest; or is a second or subsequent trespass by the defendant on lands of the Eastern Band of Cherokee Indians after having previously been excluded from those lands. G.S. 14-159.12(f).

Whenever the elevated version of this offense is charged, the relevant facts must be alleged in the charging instrument and proved to the jury beyond a reasonable doubt.

Notes (page 489)

Element (1) (page 489)

For the Element (3)(c) version of this offense, the entity withdrawing authorization is very specific; the statute provides that the person must have been excluded from the lands by a resolution passed by the Eastern Band of Cherokee Indian Tribal Council. G.S. 14-159.12(a)(3).

Element (2) (page 490)

As a general rule, a person who enters premises open to the public has implied consent to remain there. State v. Nickens, ___ N.C. App. ___, 821 S.E.2d 864 (2018). However, that implied consent is revoked if the person does some act rendering the implied consent void or if someone with authority asks the person to leave. *Id.* (implied consent to remain was revoked when the defendant was told to leave a DMV office).

Greater and lesser-included offenses (page 490)

For another case supporting the statement in this note that first-degree trespass is a lesser-included offense of felony breaking or entering, see *State v. Lucas*, 234 N.C. App. 247, 256 (2014).

Related Offenses Not in This Chapter (page 490)

Add the following offenses to this list:

Felony taking of Venus flytrap. G.S. 14-129.3.
Trespass on utility facility. G.S. 14-159.12(c), (d).
Unlawful distribution of images taken through use of unmanned aircraft system. G.S. 14-401.25.
Use of an unmanned aircraft system near a confinement or correctional facility. G.S. 15A-300.3, *as enacted by* S.L. 2017-179.

Domestic Criminal Trespass (page 492)

Notes (page 493)

Element (1) (new note)

For a case where the evidence was sufficient to establish that the defendant was forbidden to enter the victim's residence, see *State v. Vetter*, 257 N.C. App. 915, 924 (2018) (the victim ended her relationship with the defendant and ordered him to leave her residence; two months later, she discovered the defendant in her driveway and reaffirmed that he was not allowed inside the house by locking the door and activating the alarm system; this conduct served to prevent the defendant from entering the residence and functioned as a prohibition against him doing so; the court rejected the defendant's argument that he was never forbidden from entering the residence because the victim "never expressly prohibited him from doing so"; the court also rejected the defendant's argument that by giving him permission to enter the garage to collect his belongings, the victim consented to his entry into the entire premises, including the interior of the residence; the court noted that although the victim gave the defendant limited permission to enter the garage to collect his things, her consent never extended to the inside of the residence).

Element (4) (page 493)

The victim need not be physically present at the premises when the conduct occurs. *Vetter*, 257 N.C. App. at 926 (rejecting the defendant's argument that because the victim was not physically present when he entered her home the premises were not "occupied").

Related Offenses Not in This Chapter (page 493)

The citation to the last item in this list should read as follows:

> G.S. 14-269.8; 50B-3.1(j).

Injury to Property Offenses (page 495)

Injury to Real Property (page 495)

Notes (page 495)

Element (3) (page 495)

An air conditioning unit attached to the exterior of a mobile home was real property where it was affixed in a manner such that it "became an irremovable part of" the home and attached to the home for the use and enjoyment of the home's renter. State v. Hardy, 242 N.C. App. 146, 157 (2015).

Related Offenses Not in This Chapter (page 495)

Add the following offenses to this list:

> Graffiti vandalism. G.S. 14-127.1.
> Felony taking of Venus flytrap. G.S. 14-129.3.
> Cutting, mutilating, defacing, or injuring property to obtain nonferrous metals. G.S. 14-159.4.

Defacing a Public Building, Statue, or Monument (page 496)

Statute (page 496)

2014 legislation, S.L. 2014-100, sec. 17.1(w), amended G.S. 14-132(c)(3) to read as follows:

> (3) Designated by the Director of the State Bureau of Investigation in accordance with G.S. 143B-987.

2015 legislation, S.L. 2015-72, sec. 2, amended G.S. 14-132(d) to read as follows:

> (d) Unless the conduct is covered under some other provision of law providing greater punishment, any person who violates any provision of this section is guilty of a Class 2 misdemeanor.

Notes (page 497)

Multiple convictions and punishments (new note)

The "[u]nless the conduct is covered" language added to the punishment provision in 2015 means that a defendant may not be punished for this offense and one that carries a more severe punishment.

Related Offenses Not in This Chapter (page 497)

Add the following offenses to this list:

> Graffiti vandalism. G.S. 14-127.1.
> Interfering with gas, water, or electric meters. G.S. 14-151.
> Cutting, mutilating, defacing, or injuring property to obtain nonferrous metals. G.S. 14-159.4.

Injury to Personal Property (page 497)

Notes (page 497)

Element (1) (page 497)

For a case where the evidence was insufficient with respect to this Element, see *State v. Bradsher*, 255 N.C. App. 625, 633 (2017) (the property in question was appliances, owned by the defendant's landlord, that the defendant was alleged to have damaged while moving them from one home to another).

Related Offenses Not in This Chapter (page 498)

Add the following offenses to this list:

Damaging or contaminating waste kitchen grease or container. G.S. 14-79.2.

Cutting, mutilating, defacing, or injuring property to obtain nonferrous metals. G.S. 14-159.4.

Injuring, tampering with, removing, etc. firefighting or emergency medical services machinery or equipment. G.S. 14-160.3, *as enacted by* S.L. 2017-89.

Littering (page 500)

Elements (page 503)

As a result of *State v. Rankin*, 371 N.C. 885 (2018), Element (6) should read as follows:

(6) the property has not been designated by the state or a political subdivision for the disposal of garbage and refuse, and the person is not authorized to use the property for this purpose.

Notes (page 503)

Element (6) (page 504)

The text of this note opines that the provision in G.S. 14-399(a)(1)—that the property has not been designated for the disposal of garbage and refuse by the state or a political subdivision—is likely to be deemed an element of the offense and not an exception. The state supreme court has now held that to be so. *Rankin*, 371 N.C. 885.

19

Disorderly Conduct, Riot, and Gang Offenses

Drunk and Disruptive (page 507)

Statute (page 507)

2015 legislation, S.L. 2015-247, sec. 3(c), amended subsection (b) of the statute to read as follows:

> (b) Any person who violates this section shall be guilty of a Class 3 misdemeanor.

Notes (page 508)

Guilty pleas (page 508)

As a result of the 2015 legislation noted above, delete this note.

Disorderly Conduct (page 508)

Statute (page 508)

2012 legislation, S.L. 2012-12, sec. 2(b), amended G.S. 14-288.4(a)(4)c. to read as follows:

> c. If an emergency is occurring or is imminent within the institution, an order given by any law-enforcement officer acting within the scope of the officer's authority.

2013 legislation, S.L. 2013-6, sec. 1, amended G.S. 14-288.4(a)(8) to read as follows:

> (8) Engages in conduct with the intent to impede, disrupt, disturb, or interfere with the orderly administration of any funeral, memorial service, or family processional to the funeral or memorial service, including a military funeral, service, or family processional, or with the normal activities and functions occurring in the facilities or buildings where a funeral or memorial service, including a military funeral or memorial service, is taking place. Any of the following conduct that occurs within two hours preceding, during, or within two hours after a funeral or memorial service shall constitute disorderly conduct under this subdivision:
> a. Displaying, within 500 feet of the ceremonial site, location being used for the funeral or memorial, or the family's processional route to the funeral or memorial service, any visual image that conveys fighting

words or actual or imminent threats of harm directed to any person or property associated with the funeral, memorial service, or processional route.

b. Uttering, within 500 feet of the ceremonial site, location being used for the funeral or memorial service, or the family's processional route to the funeral or memorial service, loud, threatening, or abusive language or singing, chanting, whistling, or yelling with or without noise amplification in a manner that would tend to impede, disrupt, disturb, or interfere with a funeral, memorial service, or processional route.

c. Attempting to block or blocking pedestrian or vehicular access to the ceremonial site or location being used for a funeral or memorial.

That same legislation also amended G.S. 14-288.4(c), the punishment provision of the statute, to make a first offense a Class 1 misdemeanor, a second offense a Class I felony, and a third or subsequent offense a Class H felony.

Disorderly Conduct by Fighting (page 510)

Notes (page 510)

Element (3) (new note)

For a case where the evidence was sufficient as to this Element, see *In re T.T.E.*, 372 N.C. 413 (2019) (a juvenile threw a chair at his brother in the school cafeteria where other students were present).

Related Offenses Not in This Chapter (page 510)

Add the following offenses to this list:

Violating Governor's order during a state of emergency. G.S. 166A-19.30(d); 14-288.20A(2).
Violating county or municipality's ordinance during a state of emergency. G.S. 166A-19.31(h); 14-288.20A(1).
Willfully refusing to leave a public building as directed under a Governor's order. G.S. 14-288.20A(3).

Remove the following offenses from this list:

Violation of state of emergency ordinance. G.S. 14-288.12 through -288.15.
Governor's power to order evacuation of public building. G.S. 14-288.19.
Using profane or indecent language on public highways. G.S. 14-197.

Disorderly Conduct by Disrupting Students (page 513)

Notes (page 513)

Element (1) (new note)

The evidence was sufficient to show that a juvenile acted intentionally where he was described as "very defiant" and he could have avoided the physical contact at issue. *In re M.J.G.*, 234 N.C. App. 350, 357–58 (2014).

Element (3) (page 513)

For additional cases where the evidence was sufficient as to this Element, see *In re I.W.P.*, 259 N.C. App. 254, 258 (2018) (after repeated encouragement from the juvenile, another student pulled the fire alarm, resulting in chaos on school grounds; the juvenile's actions disrupted, disturbed, and interfered with the teaching of students and disturbed the peace, order, or discipline at the school), and *M.J.G.*, 234 N.C. App. at 360–61 (the juvenile's conduct substantially interfered with the operation of the school where it required intervention by several teachers, the assistant principal, and the school resource officer, and a group of special needs students missed their buses because of the disturbance).

Disorderly Conduct by Disrupting a Funeral (page 515)

Punishment (page 515)

2013 legislation, S.L. 2013-6, changed the punishments for this offense. As a result, delete the text in this section and replace it with the following:

Class 1 misdemeanor for a first offense, Class I felony for a second offense, and Class H felony for a third or subsequent offense. G.S. 14-288.4(c). If an elevated version of this offense is charged, the fact elevating punishment must be alleged in a charging instrument and proved at trial, unless the defendant pleads guilty or no contest to the issue. *See* G.S. 15A-928 (alleging and proving prior convictions).

Notes (page 515)

Element (3) (page 515)

As a result of the 2013 legislation noted above, delete the text of this note and replace it with the following:

The statute expressly includes military funerals and services. G.S. 14-288.4(a)(8). It also provides that any of the following conduct occurring within the time period beginning two hours before the service and ending two hours after the service constitutes disorderly conduct:

- displaying, within 500 feet of the ceremonial site or processional route, any visual image that conveys fighting words or actual or imminent threats of harm directed to any person or property associated with the event or processional route;
- uttering, within 500 feet of the ceremonial site or processional route, loud, threatening, or abusive language or singing, chanting, whistling, or yelling with or without noise amplification in a manner that would tend to impede, disrupt, disturb, or interfere with a funeral, memorial service, or processional route; or
- attempting to block or blocking pedestrian or vehicular access to the ceremonial site or location being used for a funeral or memorial.

Id.

Disorderly Conduct in a Public Building (page 516)

Statute (page 516)

2014 legislation, S.L. 2014-100, sec. 17.1(w), amended G.S. 14-132(c)(3) to read as follows:

(3) Designated by the Director of the State Bureau of Investigation in accordance with G.S. 143B-987.

Notes (page 517)

Constitutionality (new note)

In *State v. Dale*, 245 N.C. App. 497, 508–09 (2016), the court rejected the defendant's void-for-vagueness and as-applied constitutional challenges to a conviction for this offense.

Failure to Disperse on Command (page 526)
Related Offenses Not in This Chapter (page 527)

Add the following offenses to this list:

> Violating Governor's order during a state of emergency. G.S. 166A-19.30(d); 14-288.20A(2).
>
> Violating county or municipality's ordinance during a state of emergency. G.S. 166A-19.31(h); 14-288.20A(1).
>
> Willfully refusing to leave a public building as directed under a Governor's order. G.S. 14-288.20A(3).

Remove the following offense from this list:

> Transporting dangerous weapon or substance during emergency; possessing off premises. G.S. 14-288.7.

Gang-Related Crimes (page 527)
Statute (page 527)

Because 2017 legislation, S.L. 2017-194, sec. 1, repealed G.S. 14-50.16, delete the statute that is reproduced in this section.

Street Gang Activity (page 528)

Because 2017 legislation, S.L. 2017-194, sec. 1, repealed G.S. 14-50.16, delete this crime.

Organizer of Street Gang Activity (page 529)

Because 2017 legislation, S.L. 2017-194, sec. 1, repealed G.S. 14-50.16, delete this crime.

Soliciting Participation in Criminal Gang Activity (page 530) (revised title)
Statute (page 530)

As a result of 2017 legislation, S.L. 2017-194, secs. 7–8, G.S. 14-50.17 and -50.18 were revised to replace the term "criminal street gang activity" with the term "criminal gang activity."

As a result of that same legislation, S.L. 2017-194, sec. 4, add the following new statute to this section:

> **§ 14-50.16A. Criminal gang activity.**
> Definitions.—The following definitions apply in this Article:
> (1) Criminal gang.—Any ongoing organization, association, or group of three or more persons, whether formal or informal, that (i) has as one of its primary activities the commission of criminal or delinquent acts and (ii) shares a common name, identification, signs, symbols, tattoos, graffiti, attire, or other distinguishing characteristics, including common activities, customs, or behaviors. The term shall not include three or more persons associated in fact, whether formal or informal, who are not engaged in criminal gang activity.

(2) Criminal gang activity.—The commission of, attempted commission of, or solicitation, coercion, or intimidation of another person to commit (i) any offense under Article 5 of Chapter 90 of the General Statutes or (ii) any offense under Chapter 14 of the General Statutes except Article 9, 22A, 40, 46, or 59 thereof, and further excepting G.S. 14-82, 14-145, 14-183, 14-184, 14-186, 14-190.9, 14-247, 14-248, or 14-313 thereof, and either of the following conditions is met:

a. The offense is committed with the intent to benefit, promote, or further the interests of a criminal gang or for the purposes of increasing a person's own standing or position within a criminal gang.

b. The participants in the offense are identified as criminal gang members acting individually or collectively to further any criminal purpose of a criminal gang.

[Subsection (3), defining the term "criminal gang leader or organizer," is not reproduced here.]

(4) Criminal gang member.—Any person who meets three or more of the following criteria:

a. The person admits to being a member of a criminal gang.

b. The person is identified as a criminal gang member by a reliable source, including a parent or a guardian.

c. The person has been previously involved in criminal gang activity.

d. The person has adopted symbols, hand signs, or graffiti associated with a criminal gang.

e. The person has adopted the display of colors or the style of dress associated with a criminal gang.

f. The person is in possession of or linked to a criminal gang by physical evidence, including photographs, ledgers, rosters, written or electronic communications, or membership documents.

g. The person has tattoos or markings associated with a criminal gang.

h. The person has adopted language or terminology associated with a criminal gang.

i. The person appears in any form of social media to promote a criminal gang.

Elements (page 530)

As a result of the 2017 legislation noted above, Element (3) of this offense should be revised to read as follows:

(3) to participate in criminal gang activity.

Notes (page 530)

As a result of the 2017 legislation noted above, delete the notes included in this section and replace them with the following:

Element (3). The term "criminal gang activity" is defined in G.S. 14-50.16A(2), reproduced above.

Exception for certain juveniles. G.S. 14-50.28 provides that the criminal gang offenses do not apply to juveniles under the age of 16.

Multiple convictions and punishments. G.S. 14-50.21 provides that every violation of the criminal gang statutes in G.S. 14-50.16 through -50.20 constitutes a separate offense.

Forfeiture. G.S. 14-50.23 provides for seizure and forfeiture of property associated with criminal gang activity.

Public nuisance. G.S. 14-50.42 provides that real property associated with criminal gang activity constitutes a public nuisance and may be abated as provided for in the General Statutes. G.S. 14-50.43 provides that criminal gangs constitute a public nuisance.

Related Offenses Not in This Chapter (page 531)

As a result of the 2017 legislation noted above, delete the first sentence of this section and add the following two offenses to the list:

"Continuing Criminal Enterprise—Non-Drug Offenses" (Chapter 5)
"Continuing Criminal Enterprise—Drug Offenses" (Chapter 27)

Intimidation to Deter or Retaliation for Gang Withdrawal (page 531) (revised title)

Statute (page 531)

2017 legislation, S.L. 2017-194, secs. 9–10, revised the statutes to read as follows:

§ 14-50.19. Intimidation to deter from gang withdrawal.

(a) It is unlawful for any person to communicate a threat of injury to a person, or to damage the property of another, with the intent to deter a person from assisting another to withdraw from membership in a criminal gang.

(a1) It is unlawful for any person to injure a person with the intent to deter a person from assisting another to withdraw from membership in a criminal gang.

(b) A violation of subsection (a) of this section is a Class G felony. A violation of subsection (a1) of this section is a Class F felony.

§ 14-50.20. Punishment or retaliation for gang withdrawal.

(a) It is unlawful for any person to communicate a threat of injury to a person, or to damage the property of another, as punishment or retaliation against a person for having withdrawn from a criminal gang.

(a1) It is unlawful for any person to injure a person as punishment or retaliation against a person for having withdrawn from a criminal gang.

(b) A violation of subsection (a) of this section is a Class G felony. A violation of subsection (a1) of this section is a Class F felony.

Elements (page 531)

As a result of the 2017 legislation noted above, the elements of this offense should read as follows:

A person guilty of this offense

(1) (a) communicates
 (b) a threat of injury to a person or of damage to the property of another
 (c) (i) with the intent to deter a person from assisting another to withdraw from membership in a criminal gang, *or*
  (ii) as punishment or retaliation against a person for having withdrawn from a criminal gang, *or*
(2) (a) injures a person
 (b) (i) with the intent to deter a person from assisting another to withdraw from membership in a criminal gang
  (ii) as punishment or retaliation against a person for having withdrawn from a criminal gang.

Punishment (page 531)

As a result of the 2017 legislation noted above, delete the text of this section and replace it with the following:

A violation of the Element (1) version of this offense is a Class G felony; a violation of the Element (2) version of this offense is a Class F felony. G.S. 14-50.19(b); -50.20(b).

Notes (page 531)

As a result of the 2017 legislation noted above, delete the notes listed for this offense and replace them with the following:

> **Definition of the term "criminal gang".** The term "criminal gang" is defined in new G.S. 14-50.16A(1), reproduced above in this supplement.

> **Exception for certain juveniles.** See this note to "Soliciting Participation in Criminal Gang Activity," above in this supplement.

> **Multiple convictions and punishments.** See this note to "Soliciting Participation in Criminal Gang Activity," above in this supplement.

> **Forfeiture.** See this note to "Soliciting Participation in Criminal Gang Activity," above in this supplement.

> **Public nuisance.** See this note to "Soliciting Participation in Criminal Gang Activity," above in this supplement.

Related Offenses Not in this Chapter (page 531)

As a result of the 2017 legislation noted above, delete the first sentence of this section and replace it with the following:

> See the offenses listed under "Soliciting Participation in Criminal Gang Activity," above in this supplement.

Discharging a Firearm as a Part of Criminal Gang Activity (page 532) (revised title)

Statute (page 532)

2017 legislation, S.L. 2017-194, sec. 6, amended the statute to read as follows:

> **§ 14-34.9. Discharging a firearm from within an enclosure.**
> Unless covered under some other provision of law providing greater punishment, any person who willfully or wantonly discharges or attempts to discharge a firearm, as a part of criminal gang activity, from within any building, structure, motor vehicle, or other convey-ance, erection, or enclosure toward a person or persons not within that enclosure shall be punished as a Class E felon.

Elements (page 532)

As a result of the 2017 legislation noted above, Element (6) of this offense should read as follows:

> (6) as a part of criminal gang activity.

Notes (page 532)

Element (6) (page 532)

As a result of the 2017 legislation noted above, delete the text of this note and replace it with the following:

> The term "criminal gang activity" and related terms are defined in new G.S. 14-50.16A(2), reproduced under "Soliciting Participation in Criminal Gang Activity," above in this supplement.

Related Offenses Not in This Chapter (page 533)

As a result of the 2017 legislation noted above, delete the first sentence of this section and replace it with the following:

> See the offenses listed under "Soliciting Participation in Criminal Gang Activity," above in this supplement.

20

Bombing, Terrorism, and Related Offenses

Terrorism (new crime)

This offense was enacted by 2012 legislation. S.L. 2012-38.

Statute

§ 14-10.1. Terrorism.

(a) As used in this section, the term "act of violence" means a violation of G.S. 14-17; a felony punishable pursuant to G.S. 14-18; any felony offense in this Chapter that includes an assault, or use of violence or force against a person; any felony offense that includes either the threat or use of any explosive or incendiary device; or any offense that includes the threat or use of a nuclear, biological, or chemical weapon of mass destruction.

(b) A person is guilty of the separate offense of terrorism if the person commits an act of violence with the intent to do either of the following:

    (1) Intimidate the civilian population at large, or an identifiable group of the civilian population.

    (2) Influence, through intimidation, the conduct or activities of the government of the United States, a state, or any unit of local government.

(c) A violation of this section is a felony that is one class higher than the offense which is the underlying act of violence, except that a violation is a Class B1 felony if the underlying act of violence is a Class A or Class B1 felony offense. A violation of this section is a separate offense from the underlying offense and shall not merge with other offenses.

(d) All real and personal property of every kind used or intended for use in the course of, derived from, or realized through an offense punishable pursuant to this Article shall be subject to lawful seizure and forfeiture to the State as set forth in G.S. 14-2.3 and G.S. 14-7.20. However, the forfeiture of any real or personal property shall be subordinate to any security interest in the property taken by a lender in good faith as collateral for the extension of credit and recorded as provided by law, and no real or personal property shall be forfeited under this section against an owner who made a bona fide purchase of the property, or a person with rightful possession of the property, without knowledge of a violation of this Article.

Elements

A person guilty of this offense

    (1) commits an act of violence

    (2) with the intent to

        (a) intimidate the civilian population, or an identifiable group of the civilian population, *or*

        (b) influence, through intimidation, a government's conduct or activities.

Punishment

This offense is punished as a felony that is one class higher than the offense that constitutes the underlying act of violence, except that a violation is a Class B1 felony if the underlying act of violence is a Class A or B1 felony. G.S. 14-10.1(c).

Notes

Element (1). G.S. 14-10.1(a) defines the term "act of violence" to include

- murder under G.S. 14-17;
- manslaughter under G.S. 14-18;
- any G.S. Chapter 14 felony that includes an assault or use of violence or force against a person;
- any felony that includes either the threat or use of any explosive or incendiary device; and
- any offense that includes the threat or use of a nuclear, biological, or chemical weapon of mass destruction.

The statute does not define the phrase "explosive or incendiary device". That term is defined in two other statutory provisions, but it is not clear which of these definitions is meant to apply to this offense. Specifically, G.S. 14-50.1 defines an "explosive or incendiary device or material" as including "nitroglycerine, dynamite, gunpowder, other high explosive, incendiary bomb or grenade, other destructive incendiary device, or any other destructive incendiary or explosive device, compound, or formulation; any instrument or substance capable of being used for destructive explosive or incendiary purposes against persons or property, when the circumstances indicate some probability that such instrument or substance will be so used; or any explosive or incendiary part or ingredient in any instrument or substance included above, when the circumstances indicate some probability that such part or ingredient will be so used." G.S. 14-72(b)(3) defines an "explosive or incendiary device or substance" as "any explosive or incendiary grenade or bomb; any dynamite, blasting powder, nitroglycerin, TNT, or other high explosive; or any device, ingredient for such device, or type or quantity of substance primarily useful for large-scale destruction of property by explosive or incendiary action or lethal injury to persons by explosive or incendiary action." That section further provides that the definition does not include "fireworks; or any form, type, or quantity of gasoline, butane gas, natural gas, or any other substance having explosive or incendiary properties but serving a legitimate non-destructive or nonlethal use in the form, type, or quantity stolen." G.S. 14-72(b)(3).

Presumably the phrase "any offense that includes the threat or use of a nuclear, biological, or chemical weapon of mass destruction" refers to the nuclear, biological, or chemical weapon of mass destruction offenses in G.S. 14-288.21 through -288.24.

Element (2)(b). The governments covered include the federal government, any state government, and any unit of local government. G.S. 14-10.1(b)(2).

Multiple convictions and punishments. A defendant may be convicted and punished for both this offense and the underlying offense that constitutes the act of violence. G.S. 14-10.1(c).

Seizure and forfeiture of property. All real and personal property used or intended for use in the course of, derived from, or realized through this offense is subject to seizure and forfeiture pursuant to G.S. 14-2.3 and 14-7.20. G.S. 14-10.1(d). However, the forfeiture is subordinate to any security interest in the property taken by a lender in good faith as collateral for the extension of credit and recorded as provided by law. *Id.* Also, no property may be forfeited against an owner who made a bona fide purchase of it, or against a person with rightful possession of the property, without knowledge of the criminal violation. *Id.*

Related Offenses Not in This Chapter

"Riot" (Chapter 19)
"Gang-Related Crimes" (Chapter 19)

Malicious Damage by Use of Explosives or Incendiaries (page 537)

Malicious Damage to Occupied Property by Use of an Explosive or Incendiary (page 537)
Related Offenses Not in This Chapter (page 538)

Add the following offenses to this list:

Interference with manned aircraft by unmanned aircraft systems. G.S. 14-280.3.

Transporting dangerous weapon or substance during emergency; possessing off premises. G.S. 14-288.7.

Unlawful possession and use of unmanned aircraft systems. G.S. 14-401.24.

Perpetrating a Hoax by Use of a False Bomb or Other Device (page 543)

Perpetrating a Hoax in or at a Public Building (page 543)
Notes (page 543)

Element (1) (new note)
For a case where there was sufficient evidence that the defendant intended to perpetrate a hoax with a false bomb, see *State v. Golden*, 224 N.C. App. 136, 147 (2012).

Element (2) (new note)
For a case where there was sufficient evidence that the defendant placed or concealed a false bomb in his vehicle, see *Golden*, 224 N.C. App. at 146.

Making a False Report Concerning Mass Violence on Educational Property (page 544)
Notes (page 545)

Element (1) (page 545)
Mere uttering or writing a statement is not necessarily a report. A message not directed to or seen by anyone in particular is not a report within the meaning of this offense. Only credible reports—those that a reasonable person would believe could represent a threat—are covered. *In re* D.W.L.B., ___ N.C. App. ___, ___, 832 S.E.2d 565, 568 (2019) (offense not committed based on school bathroom graffiti because "no one would reasonably believe that the words 'BOMB INCOMING,' written in a bathroom at some unknown time in the past and obviously by an elementary-school-aged student, represented a report of an actual threat that a bomb was incoming to the school").

Element (3) (page 545)
The words "bomb incoming" could reasonably be construed as something that could cause mass violence. *D.W.L.B.*, ___ N.C. App. at ___, 832 S.E.2d at 567.

Threat of Mass Violence on Educational Property or Place of Worship (new crime)

2018 legislation, S.L. 2018-72, secs. 1, 2, enacted this new crime.

Statute

§ 14-277.6. Communicating a threat of mass violence on educational property.

(a) A person who, by any means of communication to any person or groups of persons, threatens to commit an act of mass violence on educational property or at a curricular or extracurricular activity sponsored by a school is guilty of a Class H felony.

(b) The definitions in G.S. 14-277.5 apply to this section.

§ 14-277.7. Communicating a threat of mass violence at a place of religious worship.

(a) A person who, by any means of communication to any person or groups of persons, threatens to commit an act of mass violence at a place of religious worship is guilty of a Class H felony.

(b) The following definitions apply to this section:
  (1) Mass violence.—As defined in G.S. 14-277.5(a)(2).
  (2) Place of religious worship.—Any church, chapel, meetinghouse, synagogue, temple, longhouse, or mosque, or other building that is regularly used, and clearly identifiable, as a place for religious worship.

Elements

A person guilty of this offense

  (1) communicates
  (2) to any person or groups of persons
  (3) a threat to commit an act of mass violence
  (4) (a) on educational property or at a school-sponsored activity *or*
       (b) at a place of religious worship.

Punishment

Class H felony. G.S. 14-277.6; -277.7.

Notes

Element (1)

The threat may be communicated "by any means." G.S. 14-277.6(a); -277.7(a).

Element (3)

Because the statutes define "mass violence" by cross-reference to G.S. 14-277.5, see the note on Element (3) to "Making a False Report Concerning Mass Violence on Educational Property" in Chapter 20 (Bombing, Terrorism, and Related Offenses) of the main volume for a definition of that term. The words "bomb incoming" could reasonably be construed as something that could cause mass violence. *In re* D.W.L.B., ___ N.C. App. ___, 832 S.E.2d 565 (2019).

Element (4)(a)

The school-sponsored activity may be a curricular or extracurricular activity. G.S. 14-277.6(a).

Because the statute defines the terms "educational property" and "school" by cross-reference to G.S. 14-277.5, see the note on Element (5) to "Making a False Report Concerning Mass Violence on Educational Property" in Chapter 20 of the main volume for definitions of those terms.

Element (4)(b)

The term "place of religious worship" means any church, chapel, meetinghouse, synagogue, temple, longhouse, mosque, or other building regularly used and clearly identifiable as a place for religious worship. G.S. 14-277.7(b)(2).

Related Offenses Not in This Chapter

"Assault on a Child under 12" in Chapter 7 (Assaults)

"Assault on School Personnel" in Chapter 7 (Assaults)

"Ethnic Intimidation" in Chapter 7 (Assaults)

"Communicating Threats" in Chapter 8 (Threats, Harassment, Stalking, and Violation of Domestic Protective Orders)

"Breaking or Entering a Place of Worship" in Chapter 15 (Burglary, Breaking or Entering, and Related Offenses)

"Burning a Schoolhouse" in Chapter 17 (Arson and Burning Offenses)

"Burning a Church or Other Religious Building" in Chapter 17 (Arson and Burning Offenses)

Various disorderly conduct offenses involving schools, students, religious services and assemblies, and funerals in Chapter 19 (Disorderly Conduct, Riot, and Gang Offenses)

Various offenses involving possession of weapons or explosives on school grounds in Chapter 22 (Weapons Offenses)

"Discharging a Firearm on School Grounds" in Chapter 22 (Weapons Offenses)

Manufacture, Possession, etc. of a Machine Gun, Sawed-Off Shotgun, or Weapon of Mass Destruction (page 550)

Notes (page 552)

Element (2) (page 552)

A flash-bang grenade—despite including the word "grenade"—is not a weapon of mass destruction within the meaning of this offense. State v. Carey, ___ N.C. App. ___, 831 S.E.2d 597, *temp. stay allowed*, ___ N.C. ___, 830 S.E.2d 849 (2019) (mem.).

21
Perjury, Bribery, Obstruction, Resisting, and Related Crimes

Obstruction of Justice (page 557)

Punishment (page 557)

For an additional case supporting the statement in this note that the offense is a Class H felony if done with deceit and intent to defraud, see *State v. Mitchell*, 259 N.C. App.866, ___, 817 S.E.2d 455, 463 (2018).

Notes (page 557)

Element (2) (page 557)

Add the following at the end of the bulleted list in this note:

- making false statements to law enforcement officers about a crime under investigation. State v. Cousin, 233 N.C. App. 523, 530–31 (2014) (the defendant gave eight different written statements to authorities, providing a wide array of scenarios surrounding the victim's death and identifying four different individuals as being the perpetrator; he also admitted that he had been untruthful to investigators).
- pressuring a victim to recant. *State v. Ditenhafer*, 258 N.C. App. 537, 548–49 (2018) (the defendant pressured her daughter to recant statements regarding sexual abuse where, among other things, the defendant directed her daughter to recant and, when she refused, the defendant punished her, verbally abused her, and turned immediate family members against her, even after admitting to others that she believed the abuse occurred; and the defendant coached her daughter on what to say in person, on the telephone, and in emails in order to recant), *aff'd in part and rev'd in part on other grounds*, 373 N.C. 116 (2019).
- a parent denying authorities access to a child to investigate crimes committed against the child. *Ditenhafer*, 373 N.C. at ___, 834 S.E.2d at 400 (the defendant was present and "talked over" her daughter in interviews and generally "successfully induced [the daughter] to refuse to speak with investigating officers and social workers").

Multiple convictions and punishments (new note)

No double jeopardy violation occurred when the trial court sentenced the defendant for felony obstruction of justice and accessory after the fact to murder arising out of the same conduct. *Cousin*, 233 N.C. App. at 535–37 (reasoning that each offense contains an element not in the other).

Interfering with Witnesses (page 558)

Intimidating a Witness (page 559)

Notes (page 559)

Element (1) (page 559)

For a case where there was sufficient evidence that a defendant charged with rape threatened the victim, see *State v. Barnett*, 245 N.C. App. 101, 106–07 (among other things, on the day of the incident the defendant threatened to kill the victim if she called the police and subsequently sent her a letter stating, "What did I tell you, [*sic*] would happen, if you took charges; [*sic*] out on me? You remember what I told you. And I'ma [*sic*] stand by my word. Because you knew not to press charges or go to the hospital. You knew better then [*sic*] that."), *rev'd in part on other grounds*, 369 N.C. 298 (2016).

Element (2) (page 559)

In *State v. Shannon*, 230 N.C. App. 583, 586 (2013), the court of appeals held that the statute applied to a person who is a prospective witness but who has not been formally summoned. *See also* State v. Jones, 237 N.C. App. 526, 533–35 (2014) (trial court did not err by instructing the jury that "it is immaterial that the victim was regularly summoned or legally bound to attend").

The State need not prove the specific court proceeding that the defendant intended to deter the witness from attending. *Barnett*, 245 N.C. App. at 107 (the State need only prove that the witness had been summoned or was acting as a witness in a state court proceeding).

Because the statute covers attempts to intimidate a witness, a defendant may be convicted of this offense even if the victim did not receive the defendant's threatening letters. *Id.* at 108.

Perjury Offenses (page 562)

Perjury (page 562)

Statute (page 562)

2019 legislation, S.L. 2019-243, sec. 3.(c), amended G.S. 14-209 to read as follows, effective for offenses committed on or after December 1, 2019:

> **§ 14-209. Punishment for perjury.**
> If any person knowingly and intentionally makes a false statement under oath or affirmation in any suit, controversy, matter or cause, depending in any of the courts of the State; in any deposition or affidavit taken pursuant to law; in any oath or affirmation duly administered of or concerning any matter or thing where such person is lawfully required to be sworn or affirmed, that person is guilty of perjury, and punished as a Class F felon.

Elements (page 562)

As a result of the 2019 legislation noted above, the elements for this offense should read as follows:

A person guilty of this offense

(1) knowingly and intentionally
(2) while under oath or affirmation
(3) makes a statement

(4) that is false *and*

(5) that is material.

Notes

Element (1) (page 562)

As a result of the 2019 legislation noted above, delete the first sentence of this note and replace it with the following:

Before the statute for this offense was amended in 2019, its reference to perjury committed "willfully and corruptly" was understood to mean knowingly, purposefully, and designedly. N.C. Pattern Jury Instructions—Crim. 228.10.

Element (2) (page 562)

As a result of the 2019 legislation noted above, delete the first sentence of this note and replace it with the following:

The statement may be made "in any suit, controversy, matter or cause, depending in any of the courts of the State; in any deposition or affidavit taken pursuant to law; in any oath or affirmation duly administered of or concerning any matter or thing where such person is lawfully required to be sworn or affirmed." G.S. 14-209.

Related Offenses Not in This Chapter (page 563)

Add the following offenses to this list:

False or fraudulent report by bank examiner. G.S. 53C-8-7.

False reports and statements regarding a bank. G.S. 53C-8-11(a)(5).

Delete the offense listed as "False swearing in fire investigation by Attorney General. G.S. 58-79-10" and replace it with the following:

False swearing in fire investigation by Director of the State Bureau of Investigation. G.S. 58-79-10.

Bribery Offenses (page 564)

Taking or Agreeing to Take a Bribe (page 564)

Related Offenses Not in This Chapter (page 566)

Add the following offense to this list:

Keeping or accepting a bribe by bank examiner. G.S. 53C-8-7.

Resisting, Delaying, or Obstructing an Officer (page 567)

Notes (page 567)

Element (1) (page 567)

For cases where there was sufficient evidence of willfulness, see *State v. Peters*, 255 N.C. App. 382, 388 (2017), *State v. Smith*, 225 N.C. App. 471, 478 (2013), and *State v. Cornell*, 222 N.C. App. 184, 189 (2012).

For a case where the evidence was insufficient as to this Element, see *In re T.T.E.*, 260 N.C. App. 378, ___, 818 S.E.2d 324, 328 (2018) (after a juvenile threw a chair in a school cafeteria and ran out of the room, a school resource officer, without telling the juvenile to stop, snuck up on the juvenile and grabbed him from behind; the juvenile's action in yelling "no" and cursing when the officer grabbed him does not constitute conduct that is willful, unlawful, and without justification or excuse; "[m]ost people would probably have some sort of similar reaction if grabbed from behind without knowing who was grabbing them"), *rev'd in part on other grounds*, 372 N.C. 413 (2019).

Element (2) (page 567)

Add the following at the end of the second full paragraph on page 568:

The evidence also was sufficient to sustain a conviction when (6) during a ten- to fifteen-second incident, the defendant stepped between an officer and gang members and refused the officer's instructions to step away, *Cornell*, 222 N.C. App. at 189; (7) the defendant refused to provide the officer with his identification so that the officer could issue the defendant a citation for a seatbelt violation, State v. Friend, 237 N.C. App. 490, 493–94 (2014); and (8) the defendant, who had been detained by a store loss-prevention officer for theft, provided the responding officer with an identification card containing an altered identification number and, upon being asked whether the listed identification number was accurate, the defendant falsely stated that it was. *Peters*, 255 N.C. App. at 388.

Add the following to the third full paragraph on page 568:

For another case where the evidence was insufficient to establish that the defendant resisted, delayed, or obstructed an officer, see *T.T.E.*, 260 N.C. App. at ___, 818 S.E.2d at 328 (after a juvenile threw a chair in a school cafeteria and ran out of the room, a school resource officer, without telling the juvenile to stop, snuck up on the juvenile and grabbed him from behind; after the juvenile saw that an officer grabbed him, he did not hit, fight, or physically engage with the officer; although the juvenile yelled "no" and cursed when the officer grabbed him, this was not a violation of the statute because his statements were made before he knew who grabbed him).

Add the following as the last paragraph of this note:

In *Friend*, 237 N.C. App. at 493–94, the North Carolina Court of Appeals stated that "failure to provide information about one's identity during a lawful stop can constitute resistance, delay, or obstruction within the meaning of [the statute]." Note that *Friend* requires that the defendant's failure to identify actually delay the officer in completing a lawful task, there, issuing a seatbelt citation to the defendant-passenger. *Id. See also* State v. Ellis, ___ N.C. App. ___, ___, 832 S.E.2d 750, 755 (defendant refused to identify himself during a traffic stop prompted in part by the defendant's "continuous and escalating" gesture with his middle finger toward an officer on the side of the road), *temp. stay allowed*, ___ N.C. ___, 832 S.E.2d 708 (2019) (mem.).

Note also that the *Friend* court qualified its ruling, stating, "There are, of course, circumstances where one would be excused from providing his or her identity to an officer," such as when doing so would violate the Fifth Amendment's protection against compelled self-incrimination. 237 N.C. App. at 493–94.

Element (4) (page 569)

For a case where the evidence was insufficient to establish that the defendant knew or had reasonable grounds to know that the victim was a public officer, see *T.T.E.*, 260 N.C. App. at ___, 818 S.E.2d at 328 (after a juvenile threw a chair in a school cafeteria and ran out of the room, a school resource officer, without telling the juvenile to stop, snuck up on the juvenile and grabbed him from behind; the juvenile did not know the victim was an officer until after the officer stopped him).

Element (5) (page 569)

Because G.S. 20-49.1 delegates to North Carolina Division of Motor Vehicles (NCDMV) officers the authority to enforce criminal laws under specified circumstances, an inspector with the NCDMV License and Theft Bureau was acting within the scope of his duties when he ordered the defendant to leave a NCDMV driver's license office where the inspector worked and arrested her when she failed to comply with that order. State v. Nickens, ___ N.C. App. ___, 821 S.E.2d 864 (2018).

Because the officer did not read or produce a copy of the search warrant as required by G.S. 15A-252 before seeking to search the defendant, the officer was not engaged in lawful conduct and the evidence was insufficient to support a conviction based on the defendant's refusal to allow the officer to search him pursuant to the warrant. State v. Carter, 237 N.C. App. 274, 279–80 (2014).

Defenses (new note)

For a case where the court rejected the defendant's argument that his conduct was justified on grounds that he acted out of concern for a minor in his care, see *State v. Cornell*, 222 N.C. App. 184, 189 (2012).

Related Offenses Not in This Chapter (page 570)

Add the following offenses to this list:

Violating Governor's order during a state of emergency. G.S. 166A-19.30(d); 14-288.20A(2).

Violating county or municipality's ordinance during a state of emergency. G.S. 166A-19.31(h); 14-288.20A(1).

Willfully refusing to leave a public building as directed under a Governor's order. G.S. 14-288.20A(3).

Remove the following offenses from this list:

Violation of state of emergency ordinance. G.S. 14-288.12 through -288.14.

Violating a provision of a proclamation of the Governor in an emergency. G.S. 14-288.15.

Failure to evacuate on Governor's command. G.S. 14-288.19.

False Report to Law Enforcement Agencies or Officers (page 571)

Statute (page 571)

2013 legislation, S.L. 2013-52, sec. 6, amended the statute to read as follows:

§ 14-225. False reports to law enforcement agencies or officers.

(a) Except as provided in subsection (b) of this section, any person who shall willfully make or cause to be made to a law enforcement agency or officer any false, deliberately misleading or unfounded report, for the purpose of interfering with the operation of a law enforcement agency, or to hinder or obstruct any law enforcement officer in the performance of his duty, shall be guilty of a Class 2 misdemeanor.

(b) A violation of subsection (a) of this section is punishable as a Class H felony if the false, deliberately misleading, or unfounded report relates to a law enforcement investigation involving the disappearance of a child as that term is defined in G.S. 14-318.5 or child victim of a Class A, B1, B2, or C felony offense. For purposes of this subsection, a child is any person who is less than 16 years of age.

Elements (page 571)

As a result of the 2013 legislation noted above, Element (4) should read as follows:

(4) a false or deliberately misleading or unfounded report

Punishment (page 571)

As a result of the 2013 legislation noted above, this section should read as follows:

Class 2 misdemeanor. G.S. 14-225(a). Class H felony if the report relates to a law enforcement investigation involving

- the disappearance of a child (as defined by G.S. 14-318.5) or
- a child victim of a Class A through C felony.

G.S. 14-225(b). A child is a person less than 16 years of age. *Id.* Any fact elevating punishment must be alleged in the charging instrument and proved to a jury, unless the defendant pleads guilty or no contest to the issue.

As a result of 2019 legislation, S.L. 2019-134, effective for offenses committed on or after December 1, 2019, add the following new offense:

Giving False Fire Alarms in a Prison or Local Confinement Facility (new crime)

Statute

> **§ 14-286. Giving false fire alarms; molesting fire-alarm, fire-detection or fire-extinguishing system.**
>
> (a) Offense. – It shall be unlawful for any person or persons to wantonly and willfully give or cause to be given, or to advise, counsel, or aid and abet anyone in giving, a false alarm of fire, or to break the glass key protector, or to pull the slide, arm, or lever of any station or signal box of any fire-alarm system, except in case of fire, or willfully misuse or damage a portable fire extinguisher, or in any way to willfully interfere with, damage, deface, molest, or injure any part or portion of any fire-alarm, fire-detection, smoke-detection or fire-extinguishing system.
>
> (b) Penalty. – Any person who willfully interferes with, damages, defaces, molests, or injures any part or portion of a fire-alarm, fire-detection, smoke-detection, or fire-extinguishing system in a prison or local confinement facility is guilty of a Class H felony. Any person violating any of the provisions who commits any other violation of this section is guilty of a Class 2 misdemeanor. For purposes of this subsection, the term "local confinement facility" means a county or city jail, a local lockup, or a detention facility for adults operated by a local government.

Elements

A person guilty of this offense

- (1) willfully
- (2) (a) interferes with,
  - (b) damages,
  - (c) defaces,
  - (d) molests, *or*
  - (e) injures
- (3) any part or portion of any fire-alarm, fire-detection, smoke-detection, or fire-extinguishing system
- (4) in a prison or local confinement facility.

Punishment

Class H felony. G.S. 14-286(b). A violation of this statute in a location other than a prison or local confinement facility is a Class 2 misdemeanor.

Notes

Element (4)

The term "local confinement facility" means a county or city jail, a local lockup, or a detention facility for adults operated by a local government. G.S. 153A-217(5).

Interfering with Emergency Communication (page 571)

Related Offenses Not in This Chapter (page 573)

Add the following offense to this list:

> Injuring, tampering with, removing, etc. firefighting or emergency medical services machinery or equipment. G.S. 14-160.3, *as enacted by* S.L. 2017-89.

Concealing a Death (page 573)

Statute (page 573)

As a result of 2013 legislation, S.L. 2013-52, sec. 5, G.S. 14-401.22 has been revised to read:

> (a) Except as provided in subsection (a1) of this section, any person who, with the intent to conceal the death of a person, fails to notify a law enforcement authority of the death or secretly buries or otherwise secretly disposes of a dead human body is guilty of a Class I felony.
>
> (a1) Any person who, with the intent to conceal the death of a child, fails to notify a law enforcement authority of the death or secretly buries or otherwise secretly disposes of a dead child's body is guilty of a Class H felony. For purposes of this subsection, a child is any person who is less than 16 years of age.
>
> [*To save space, subsections (b) through (f) are not reproduced here.*]

Punishment (page 573)

As a result of the 2013 legislation noted above, this section should be revised to read as follows:

> Class I felony. G.S. 14-401.22(a). If the body is of a child less than 16 years old, the offense is a Class H felony. *Id.* § (a1). If the defendant knew or had reason to know that the person did not die of natural causes, the offense is a Class D felony. *Id.* § (e). All facts elevating punishment must be alleged in the charging instrument and proved to the jury, unless the defendant pleads guilty or no contest to the issue.

Related Offenses Not in This Chapter (page 573)

Add the following offense to this list:

> Disturbing, vandalizing, or desecrating human remains; committing sexual penetration on human remains. G.S. 14-401.22(c).

Prison and Other Escapes (page 574)

Prison Breach and Escape from County or Municipal Confinement Facilities or Officers (page 574)

Statute (page 574)

2013 legislation, S.L. 2013-389, sec. 3, amended subsection (1) to read as follows:

> (1)   He has been charged with or convicted of a felony and has been committed to the facility pending trial or transfer to the State prison system; or

Punishment (page 574)

As a result of the 2013 legislation noted above, the second sentence of this note should read as follows:

> Class H felony if the defendant
> - has been charged with or convicted of a felony and has been committed to the facility pending trial or transfer to the state prison system or
> - is serving a sentence imposed on conviction of a felony.

Related Offenses Not in This Chapter (page 574)

Add the following offense to this list:

> Use of an unmanned aircraft system near a confinement or correctional facility. G.S. 15A-300.3, *as enacted by* S.L. 2017-179.

As a result of 2018 legislation, S.L. 2018-67, sec. 3, delete the sixth entry in this list and replace it with the following:

> Providing articles forbidden by prison rules or items for prison escape, assault, or insurrection; possessing items for prison escape, assault, or insurrection. G.S. 14-258.

Delete the seventh entry in this list and replace it with the following:

> Furnishing poison, controlled substances, deadly weapons, cartridges, ammunition, or alcoholic beverages to inmates; furnishing tobacco or mobile phones to inmates; furnishing mobile phones to delinquent juveniles. G.S. 14-258.1.

Escape from the State Prison System (page 575)

Statute (page 575)

As a result of 2017 legislation, S.L. 2017-186, sec. 2.(eeeeeeee), replace the term "Division of Adult Correction," as used in the statute, with Division of Adult Correction and Juvenile Justice.

Notes (page 576)

Aiders and assisters (page 577)

As a result of 2018 legislation, S.L. 2018-67, sec. 3, delete the last parenthetical in this note and replace it with the following:

> (providing articles forbidden by prison rules or items for prison escape, assault, or insurrection; possessing items for prison escape, assault, or insurrection).

22
Weapons Offenses

Possession of a Firearm by a Felon (page 581)
Notes (page 582)
Element (2)(c) (page 582)
There was sufficient evidence of actual possession of a firearm when officers found the weapon between the seat and the passenger side door of the defendant's vehicle, near where the defendant's hand had been immediately before the officers opened the car door. State v. Chevallier, ___ N.C. App. ___, 824 S.E.2d 440 (2019).

For a discussion of recent case law modifying the text in the second paragraph of this note regarding the necessary proof to establish constructive possession when the defendant does not have exclusive control over the place where contraband is found, see the note on Element (2) to "Possession of a Controlled Substance," below in this supplement.

There was insufficient evidence of constructive possession where (1) the only evidence connecting the defendant to a rifle recovered in a wooded area 75 to 100 yards away from the defendant was canine tracking evidence, State v. Battle, 253 N.C. App. 141, 147 (2017) (the court distinguished other cases upholding convictions where the defendant was identified as the perpetrator by a tracking canine, noting that here the canine's tracking behavior was the *only* evidence of guilt; the canine was not tracking a known scent; the canine lost the track at one point; another man was found in the woods; and no other evidence, such as fingerprints, DNA, or ownership, linked the defendant to the rifle or the site where it was found); (2) the defendant did not have exclusive control of the apartment in which guns were found and the State failed to present evidence of other incriminating circumstances, State v. Perry, 222 N.C. App. 813, 819 (2012); and (3) the defendant did not have exclusive control of the car that he owned but in which he was a passenger when a rifle was found; the rifle was registered to the defendant's girlfriend, who was driving; the defendant and his girlfriend had equal access to the location where the weapon was found; and there was no physical evidence, such as fingerprints, tying the defendant to the rifle. State v. Bailey, 233 N.C. App. 688, 692–93 (2014).

The fact that a person is aware of a weapon does not, by itself, establish constructive possession. *Id.* at 693.

There was sufficient evidence (1) that the defendant constructively possessed drugs and a firearm found in a vehicle where, notwithstanding the defendant's nonexclusive possession of the vehicle, his control as its driver was sufficient to give rise to an inference of constructive possession, and other incriminating circumstances supported that inference, State v. Wirt, ___ N.C. App. ___, 822 S.E.2d 668 (2018); (2) that the defendant constructively possessed drugs and a rifle found in a bedroom that was not under his exclusive control; among other things, photographs, a Father's Day card, a cable bill, a cable installation receipt, and a pay stub found in the bedroom linked him to the contraband and placed him in the room within two days of when the contraband was found, State v. Bradshaw, 366 N.C. 90, 96–97 (2012); (3) that the defendant constructively possessed a firearm when he was driving a rental vehicle, had a female passenger, and the gun was found in a purse in the car's glove container; the court reasoned that the defendant was driving the car, and his interactions with the police showed that he was aware of the vehicle's contents, State v. Mitchell, 224 N.C. App. 171, 178 (2012); and (4) that the defendant constructively possessed a gun where an anonymous 911 caller reported seeing a man wearing a plaid shirt holding a gun near a black car beside a field; someone saw the man drop the gun; an officer saw the defendant standing near a black car wearing a plaid shirt; the defendant later returned to the scene claiming ownership of the car; and officers found a firearm in a vacant lot approximately ten feet from the car. State v. McKiver, 247 N.C. App. 614, 619–20 (2016) (noting that additional incriminating circumstances existed, beyond the defendant's mere presence at the scene and proximity to the firearm, to infer that he constructively possessed the firearm), *rev'd on other grounds*, 369 N.C. 652 (2017).

Exceptions (page 584)

Add the following at the end of the first paragraph of this note:

See Booth v. State, 227 N.C. App. 484 (2013) (offense does not apply to a person who has received a Pardon of Forgiveness for his or her prior felony).

Constitutionality (page 584)

This note cites *Baysden v. North Carolina*, 217 N.C. App. 20 (2011), as holding that the statute was unconstitutional as applied to the plaintiff. With one justice taking no part in consideration of the case, an equally divided North Carolina Supreme Court left undisturbed that opinion, which stands without precedential value. Baysden v. State, 366 N.C. 370 (2013). Because of that decision, and to incorporate additional new case law, delete all text in this paragraph from the words "Post-*Britt* North Carolina Court of Appeals cases" onward and replace it with the following:

Post-*Britt* North Carolina Court of Appeals cases involving as-applied state constitutional challenges include *State v. Fernandez*, 256 N.C. App. 539, 547–48 (2017) (rejecting the defendant's as-applied challenge); *State v. Whitaker*, 201 N.C. App. 190, 202–07 (2009) (same), *aff'd*, 364 N.C. 404 (2010); *State v. Price*, 233 N.C. App. 386, 397–98 (2014) (same); and *State v. Bonetsky*, 246 N.C. App. 640, 643–50 (2016) (same).

For a case rejecting a defendant's as-applied federal constitutional challenge, see *Fernandez*, 256 N.C. App. at 545–47.

Add the following to this note:

In *Johnston v. State*, 367 N.C. 164 (2013), the court per curiam affirmed the decision below, *Johnston v. State*, 224 N.C. App. 282 (2012), which reversed the trial court's ruling that G.S. 14-415.1 violated the plaintiff's substantive due process rights under the U.S. and N.C. constitutions and remanded to the trial court for additional proceedings; the court of appeals also reversed the trial court's ruling that the statute was facially invalid on procedural due process grounds, under both the U.S. and N.C. constitutions.

Defenses (page 586)

The text of this note states that the North Carolina appellate courts have not ruled on whether justification is a defense to this crime. In *State v. Mercer*, ___ N.C. App. ___, ___, 818 S.E.2d 375, 379, *discretionary review allowed*, 371 N.C. 789 (2018) (mem.), the court of appeals ruled on that issue, holding that justification is a defense to this crime. *Mercer* adopted the formulation of the defense articulated in *United States v. Deleveaux*, 205 F.3d 1292, 1297 (11th Cir. 2000), which requires the defendant to show four elements: that the defendant was under unlawful and present, imminent, and impending threat of death or serious bodily injury; that the defendant did not negligently or recklessly place himself or herself in a situation where he or she would be forced to engage in criminal conduct; that the defendant had no reasonable legal alternative to violating the law; and that there was a direct causal relationship between the criminal action and the avoidance of the threatened harm. *Id.* The appeals court further held that because there was substantial evidence of each element of the defense, the trial court's failure to give a justification defense jury instruction constituted prejudicial error. *Id.*

Add the following after the second sentence of this note:

> State v. Monroe, 367 N.C. 771 (2015) (per curiam); State v. Edwards, 239 N.C. App. 391, 393–94 (2015);

Multiple convictions and punishments (page 586)

There is a typographical error in the parenthetical to *State v. Wiggins*, a case included in this note; specifically, the word "commission" is misspelled.

Related Offenses Not in This Chapter (page 586)

As a result of 2018 legislation, S.L. 2018-67, sec. 3, delete the third entry in this list and replace it with the following:

> Providing articles forbidden by prison rules or items for prison escape, assault, or insurrection; possessing items for prison escape, assault, or insurrection. G.S. 14-258.

As a result of 2015 legislation, S.L. 2015-47, delete the fourth entry in this list and replace it with the following:

> Furnishing poison, controlled substances, deadly weapons, cartridges, ammunition or alcoholic beverages to inmates; furnishing tobacco products or mobile phones to inmates; furnishing mobile phones to delinquent juveniles. G.S. 14-258.1.

Remove the following offense from this list:

> Transporting dangerous weapon or substance during emergency. G.S. 14-288.7.

Add the following offense to this list:

> Unlawful possession and use of unmanned aircraft systems with weapon attached. G.S. 14-401.24.

The citation for the listed offense "Purchase or possession of firearms by person subject to domestic violation order prohibited" should read:

> G.S. 14-269.8; 50B-3.1(j).

Carrying a Concealed Weapon (page 587)

Statute (page 587)

2015 legislation, S.L. 2015-264, sec. 3, amended subsection (a), replacing the word "shurikin" with "shuriken." That same legislation also amended subsections (a), (a1), and (b1), making them gender-neutral.

2013 legislation, S.L. 2013-369, sec.1, enacted subsection (a2) of G.S. 14-269 as follows:

> (a2) This prohibition does not apply to a person who has a concealed handgun permit issued in accordance with Article 54B of this Chapter, has a concealed handgun permit considered valid under G.S. 14-415.24, or is exempt from obtaining a permit pursuant to G.S. 14-415.25, provided the weapon is a handgun, is in a closed compartment or container within the person's locked vehicle, and the vehicle is in a parking area that is owned or leased by State government. A person may unlock the vehicle to enter or exit the vehicle, provided the handgun remains in the closed compartment at all times and the vehicle is locked immediately following the entrance or exit.

2015 legislation, G.S. 2015-215, sec. 2.5, enacted a new subsection, (b)(3a), as follows:

> (3a) A member of the North Carolina National Guard who has been designated in writing by the Adjutant General, State of North Carolina, who has a concealed handgun permit issued in accordance with Article 54B of this Chapter or considered valid under G.S. 14-415.24, and is acting in the discharge of his or her official duties, provided that the member does not carry a concealed weapon

while consuming alcohol or an unlawful controlled substance or while alcohol or an unlawful controlled substance remains in the member's body.

2015 legislation, S.L. 2015-195, sec. 1(a), amended subsection (b)(4a) to read as follows:

(4a) Any person who is a district attorney, an assistant district attorney, or an investigator employed by the office of a district attorney and who has a concealed handgun permit issued in accordance with Article 54B of this Chapter or considered valid under G.S. 14-415.24; provided that the person shall not carry a concealed weapon at any time while in a courtroom or while consuming alcohol or an unlawful controlled substance or while alcohol or an unlawful controlled substance remains in the person's body. The district attorney, assistant district attorney, or investigator shall secure the weapon in a locked compartment when the weapon is not on the person of the district attorney, assistant district attorney, or investigator. Notwithstanding the provisions of this subsection, a district attorney may carry a concealed weapon while in a courtroom;

2013 legislation, S.L. 2013-369, sec. 25, amended subsection (b)(4b) to read as follows:

(4b) Any person who is a qualified retired law enforcement officer as defined in G.S. 14-415.10 and meets any one of the following conditions:
   a.   Is the holder of a concealed handgun permit in accordance with Article 54B of this Chapter.
   b.   Is exempt from obtaining a permit pursuant to G.S. 14-415.25.
   c.   Is certified by the North Carolina Criminal Justice Education and Training Standards Commission pursuant to G.S. 14-415.26;

Section 21 of that same law enacted subsections (b)(4d) and (4e) as follows:

(4d) Any person who is a North Carolina district court judge, North Carolina superior court judge, or a North Carolina magistrate and who has a concealed handgun permit issued in accordance with Article 54B of this Chapter or considered valid under G.S. 14-415.24; provided that the person shall not carry a concealed weapon at any time while consuming alcohol or an unlawful controlled substance or while alcohol or an unlawful controlled substance remains in the person's body. The judge or magistrate shall secure the weapon in a locked compartment when the weapon is not on the person of the judge or magistrate;

(4e) Any person who is serving as a clerk of court or as a register of deeds and who has a concealed handgun permit issued in accordance with Article 54B of this Chapter or considered valid under G.S. 14-415.24; provided that the person shall not carry a concealed weapon at any time while consuming alcohol or an unlawful controlled substance or while alcohol or an unlawful controlled substance remains in the person's body. The clerk of court or register of deeds shall secure the weapon in a locked compartment when the weapon is not on the person of the clerk of court or register of deeds. This subdivision does not apply to assistants, deputies, or other employees of the clerk of court or register of deeds;

2015 legislation, S.L. 2015-5; S.L. 2015-195, sec. 1(a), as modified by the codifier, enacted subsections (b)(7), (8), and (9). 2017 legislation, S.L. 2017-186, sec. 2(hh), amended subsection (b)(9). Those provisions read as follows:

(7) A person employed by the Department of Public Safety who has been designated in writing by the Secretary of the Department, who has a concealed handgun permit issued in accordance with Article 54B of this Chapter or considered valid under G.S. 14-415.24, and has in the person's possession written proof of the designation by the Secretary of the Department, provided that the person shall not carry a concealed weapon at any time while consuming alcohol or an unlawful controlled substance or while alcohol or an unlawful controlled substance remains in the person's body.

(8) Any person who is an administrative law judge described in Article 60 of Chapter 7A of the General Statutes and who has a concealed handgun permit issued in accordance with Article 54B of this Chapter or considered valid under G.S. 14-415.24, provided that the person shall not carry a concealed weapon at any time while consuming alcohol or an unlawful controlled substance or while alcohol or an unlawful controlled substance remains in the person's body.

(9) State correctional officers, when off-duty, provided that an officer does not carry a concealed weapon while consuming alcohol or an unlawful controlled substance or while alcohol or an unlawful controlled substance remains in the officer's body. If the concealed weapon is a handgun, the correctional officer must meet the firearms training standards of the Division of Adult Correction and Juvenile Justice of the Department of Public Safety.

2014 legislation, S.L. 2014-119, sec. 12(a), amended subsection (c) of the statute to read:

(c) Any person violating the provisions of subsection (a) of this section shall be guilty of a Class 2 misdemeanor. Any person violating the provisions of subsection (a1) of this section shall be guilty of a Class 2 misdemeanor for the first offense and a Class H felony for a second or subsequent offense. A violation of subsection (a1) of this section punishable under G.S. 14-415.21(a) is not punishable under this section.

Carrying a Concealed Pistol or Gun (page 589)

Punishment (page 589)

As a result of 2014 legislation, S.L. 2014-119, sec. 12(a), punishment for a second or subsequent offense has been elevated to a Class H felony.

Elements (page 589)

The North Carolina Court of Appeals has held that the exception in G.S. 14-269(a1)(2) (having a permit) is a defense to, not an element of, this offense. State v. Mather, 221 N.C. App. 593, 602 (2012). This exception is listed as Element (5)(b). If this holding applies to the other (a1) exceptions, Element (5) in its entirety would be deleted and elements (5)(a) through (c) would constitute defenses as well.

Notes (page 589)

Element (3) (page 589)

There was sufficient evidence that a weapon was concealed about the defendant's person where officers found one razor blade under a table in a room adjoining the defendant's cell and where the defendant had been seated earlier in the day; they found another on a ledge below the window in the defendant's cell, moments after he held such a blade in his hand while threatening an officer. State v. Hill, 227 N.C. App. 371, 380–82 (2013).

Element (5) generally (page 589)

The exception in G.S. 14-269(a1)(2) (having a permit) is a defense to, not an essential element of, this offense. *Mather*, 221 N.C. App. at 602. This holding is likely to apply to the (a1)(1) and (a1)(3) exceptions as well.

Element 5(b) (page 590)

This note mentions and cites G.S. 14-415.27 as exempting district attorneys and related individuals from the limitations in G.S. 14-415.11(c), provided the exemption is consistent with federal law. 2013 legislation, S.L. 2013-269, sec. 22, expanded the scope of G.S. 14-415.27 to also include judges, magistrates, clerks of court, and registers of deeds. 2015 legislation further expanded the scope of that provision. S.L. 2015-195, sec. 1(c).

As a result of 2013 and 2015 legislation, S.L. 2013-369, sec. 16; S.L. 2015-195, sec. 9, add the following to the end of the second paragraph of this note:

> Additionally, a person who has a valid permit but carries a concealed handgun in violation of G.S. 14-415.11(c2) is guilty of a Class 1 misdemeanor. G.S. 14-415.21(a1).

Constitutionality (page 591)

> G.S. 14-415.12 (criteria to qualify for a concealed handgun permit) was not unconstitutional as applied to the petitioner because the petitioner's right to carry a concealed handgun did not fall within the scope of the Second Amendment. Kelly v. Riley, 223 N.C. App. 261, 268 (2012).

Defenses (page 591)

> The exception in G.S. 14-269(a1)(2) (having a permit) is a defense to, not an element of, this offense. *Mather*, 221 N.C. App. at 602. The State has no initial burden of producing evidence to show that the defendant's carrying a concealed weapon does not fall within the (a1) exception. *Id.* However, once the defendant puts forth evidence showing that his or her conduct falls within an exception, the burden of persuasion to show that the defendant's action was outside the exception falls on the prosecution. *Id.* These rules are likely to apply to the (a1)(1) and (a1)(3) exceptions as well.

Exceptions (page 591)

With respect to the fifth bullet in this list, 2015 legislation, S.L. 2015-195, sec. 1(a), amended the exception in G.S. 14-269(b)(4a) to provide, in relevant part, "Notwithstanding the provisions of this subsection, a district attorney may carry a concealed weapon while in a courtroom."

As a result of 2013 legislation, S.L. 2013-269, sec. 25, the sixth bullet in this note should be modified to read:

> • qualified retired law enforcement officers, as defined in G.S. 14-415.10, who have concealed handgun permits in accordance with G.S. Chapter 14, Article 54B, who are exempt from obtaining permits under G.S. 14-415.25, or who are certified by the North Carolina Criminal Justice Education and Training Standards Commission under G.S. 14-415.26;

2013 legislation, S.L. 2013-269, secs. 1 and 21, enacted new exceptions to this crime. First, new G.S. 14-269(a2) provides that this offense does not apply to a person who has or is exempted from obtaining a concealed handgun permit when the weapon is a handgun, it is in a closed compartment or container in the person's locked vehicle, and the vehicle is in a parking area that is owned or leased by state government. Second, new G.S. 14-269(b)(4d) and (4e) provide exceptions for certain judges, magistrates, clerks, or registers of deeds in certain circumstances.

2015 legislation added additional exceptions. S.L. 2015-215, sec. 2.5, added an exception in new G.S. 14-269(b)(3a) pertaining to members of the North Carolina National Guard. S.L. 2015-5 added an exception in new G.S. 14-269(b)(7) pertaining to off-duty state correctional officers. S.L. 2015-195, sec. 1(a), added exceptions for certain persons employed by the Department of Public Safety and certain administrative law judges.

Multiple convictions and punishments (new note)

> 2014 legislation, S.L. 2014-119, sec. 12(a), amended G.S. 14-269(c) to provide that a violation of G.S. 14-269(a1) that is punishable under G.S. 14-415.21(a) (person with a valid permit who is found to be carrying a concealed handgun without the permit or who fails to disclose to any officer that the person holds a valid permit and is carrying a concealed handgun) is not punishable under G.S. 14-269.

Carrying a Concealed Weapon Other Than a Pistol or Gun (page 592)

Elements (page 592)

As a result of 2015 legislation, S.L. 2015-264, sec. 3, Element (4)(h) should read as follows:

> (h) shuriken

Possession of Weapons on School Grounds (page 594)

Statute (page 594)

2013 legislation, S.L. 2013-360, sec. 8.45(a), added a new subsection, (3a), to G.S. 14-269.2(a) as follows:

(3a) Volunteer school safety resource officer.—A person who volunteers as a school safety resource officer as provided by G.S. 162-26 or G.S. 160A-288.4.

As a result of 2013 and 2014 legislation, S.L. 2013-360, sec. 8.45(b); S.L. 2014-119, sec. 9(a), G.S. 14-269.2(g) reads as follows:

(g) This section shall not apply to any of the following:

(1) A weapon used solely for educational or school-sanctioned ceremonial purposes, or used in a school-approved program conducted under the supervision of an adult whose supervision has been approved by the school authority.

(1a) A person exempted by the provisions of G.S. 14-269(b).

(2) Firefighters, emergency service personnel, North Carolina Forest Service personnel, detention officers employed by and authorized by the sheriff to carry firearms, and any private police employed by a school, when acting in the discharge of their official duties.

(3) Home schools as defined in G.S. 115C-563(a).

(4) Weapons used for hunting purposes on the Howell Woods Nature Center property in Johnston County owned by Johnston Community College when used with the written permission of Johnston Community College or for hunting purposes on other educational property when used with the written permission of the governing body of the school that controls the educational property.

(5) A person registered under Chapter 74C of the General Statutes as an armed armored car service guard or an armed courier service guard when acting in the discharge of the guard's duties and with the permission of the college or university.

(6) A person registered under Chapter 74C of the General Statutes as an armed security guard while on the premises of a hospital or health care facility located on educational property when acting in the discharge of the guard's duties with the permission of the college or university.

(7) A volunteer school safety resource officer providing security at a school pursuant to an agreement as provided in G.S. 115C-47(61) and either G.S. 162-26 or G.S. 160A-288.4, provided that the volunteer school safety resource officer is acting in the discharge of the person's official duties and is on the educational property of the school that the officer was assigned to by the head of the appropriate local law enforcement agency.

2013 legislation, S.L. 2013-369, sec. 2, added new subsections (i), (j), and (k) to the statute. 2015 legislation, S.L. 2015-195, sec. 2, amended subsection (k). These subsections read as follows:

(i) The provisions of this section shall not apply to an employee of an institution of higher education as defined in G.S. 116-143.1 or a nonpublic post-secondary educational institution who resides on the campus of the institution at which the person is employed when all of the following criteria are met:

(1) The employee's residence is a detached, single-family dwelling in which only the employee and the employee's immediate family reside.

(2) The institution is either:

    a. An institution of higher education as defined by G.S. 116-143.1.

    b. A nonpublic post-secondary educational institution that has not specifically prohibited the possession of a handgun pursuant to this subsection.

(3) The weapon is a handgun.

(4)   The handgun is possessed in one of the following manners as appropriate:

a.   If the employee has a concealed handgun permit that is valid under Article 54B of this Chapter, or who is exempt from obtaining a permit pursuant to that Article, the handgun may be on the premises of the employee's residence or in a closed compartment or container within the employee's locked vehicle that is located in a parking area of the educational property of the institution at which the person is employed and resides. Except for direct transfer between the residence and the vehicle, the handgun must remain at all times either on the premises of the employee's residence or in the closed compartment of the employee's locked vehicle. The employee may unlock the vehicle to enter or exit, but must lock the vehicle immediately following the entrance or exit if the handgun is in the vehicle.

b.   If the employee is not authorized to carry a concealed handgun pursuant to Article 54B of this Chapter, the handgun may be on the premises of the employee's residence, and may only be in the employee's vehicle when the vehicle is occupied by the employee and the employee is immediately leaving the campus or is driving directly to their residence from off campus. The employee may possess the handgun on the employee's person outside the premises of the employee's residence when making a direct transfer of the handgun from the residence to the employee's vehicle when the employee is immediately leaving the campus or from the employee's vehicle to the residence when the employee is arriving at the residence from off campus.

(j) The provisions of this section shall not apply to an employee of a public or non-public school who resides on the campus of the school at which the person is employed when all of the following criteria are met:

(1)   The employee's residence is a detached, single-family dwelling in which only the employee and the employee's immediate family reside.

(2)   The school is either:

a.   A public school which provides residential housing for enrolled students.

b.   A nonpublic school which provides residential housing for enrolled students and has not specifically prohibited the possession of a handgun pursuant to this subsection.

(3)   The weapon is a handgun.

(4)   The handgun is possessed in one of the following manners as appropriate:

a.   If the employee has a concealed handgun permit that is valid under Article 54B of this Chapter, or who is exempt from obtaining a permit pursuant to that Article, the handgun may be on the premises of the employee's residence or in a closed compartment or container within the employee's locked vehicle that is located in a parking area of the educational property of the school at which the person is employed and resides. Except for direct transfer between the residence and the vehicle, the handgun must remain at all times either on the premises of the employee's residence or in the closed compartment of the employee's locked vehicle. The employee may unlock the vehicle to enter or exit, but must lock the vehicle immediately following the entrance or exit if the handgun is in the vehicle.

b.   If the employee is not authorized to carry a concealed handgun pursuant to Article 54B of this Chapter, the handgun may be on the premises of the employee's residence, and may only be in the employee's vehicle when the vehicle is occupied by the employee and the employee is immediately leaving the campus or is driving directly to their residence from off campus. The employee may possess the handgun on the employee's person outside the premises of the employee's residence when making a direct transfer of the handgun from the residence to the employee's vehicle when the employee is immediately leaving the campus or from the employee's vehicle to the residence when the employee is arriving at the residence from off campus.

(k) The provisions of this section shall not apply to a person who has a concealed handgun permit that is valid under Article 54B of this Chapter, or who is exempt from obtaining a permit pursuant to that Article, if any of the following conditions are met:

(1) The person has a handgun in a closed compartment or container within the person's locked vehicle or in a locked container securely affixed to the person's vehicle and only unlocks the vehicle to enter or exit the vehicle while the firearm remains in the closed compartment at all times and immediately locks the vehicle following the entrance or exit.

(2) The person has a handgun concealed on the person and the person remains in the locked vehicle and only unlocks the vehicle to allow the entrance or exit of another person.

(3) The person is within a locked vehicle and removes the handgun from concealment only for the amount of time reasonably necessary to do either of the following:

a. Move the handgun from concealment on the person to a closed compartment or container within the vehicle.

b. Move the handgun from within a closed compartment or container within the vehicle to concealment on the person.

2015 legislation, S.L. 2015-195, sec. 3, added a new subsection, (l), as follows:

(l) It is an affirmative defense to a prosecution under subsection (b) or (f) of this section that the person was authorized to have a concealed handgun in a locked vehicle pursuant to subsection (k) of this section and removed the handgun from the vehicle only in response to a threatening situation in which deadly force was justified pursuant to G.S. 14-51.3.

Possession of Firearms on School Grounds (page 596)

Notes (page 596)

Element (1) (page 596)

Although the court of appeals held that the State must prove that the defendant both knowingly possessed or carried a prohibited weapon and knowingly entered educational property with that weapon, State v. Huckelba, 240 N.C. App. 544, 558 (2015), that decision was reversed by the state supreme court on grounds that even if the trial court erred in its jury instructions, the error did not rise to the level of plain error. State v. Huckelba, 368 N.C. 569 (2015).

No criminal intent required (page 597)

Delete this note. Although *Haskins* held that no criminal intent was required, the statute subsequently was amended to add the element that the defendant acts knowingly.

Exceptions (page 597)

Several new exceptions have been added to this offense:

- G.S. 14-269.2(g)(2) was amended to create an exception for detention officers employed by and authorized by a sheriff to carry firearms. S.L. 2014-119, sec. 9(a).
- A new subsection, G.S. 14-269.2(g)(7), creates an exception for certain volunteer school safety resource officers when acting in the discharge of their official duties on educational property. S.L. 2013-360, sec. 8.45(b).

- Two new subsections, G.S. 14-269.2(i) and (j), provide that the offense does not apply to certain school employees who reside at educational institutions and schools. S.L. 2013-369, sec. 2.
- A new subsection, G.S. 14-269.2(k), provides that the offense does not apply to individuals who either have a valid concealed handgun permit or are exempt from obtaining a permit and have a handgun in a locked vehicle under circumstances specified in the statute. S.L. 2013-369, sec. 2, S.L. 2015-195, sec. 2.

Affirmative defense (new note)

It is an affirmative defense to a prosecution under subsection G.S. 14-269.2(b) or (f) that the person was authorized to have a concealed handgun in a locked vehicle pursuant to G.S. 14-269.2(k) and removed the handgun from the vehicle only in response to a threatening situation in which deadly force was justified pursuant to G.S. 14-51.3. G.S. 14-269.2(l).

Multiple convictions and punishments (new note)

This offense does not allow multiple punishments for the simultaneous possession of multiple firearms on educational property. State v. Conley, ___ N.C. App. ___, 825 S.E.2d 10, *discretionary review allowed*, ___ N.C. ___, 830 S.E.2d 817 (2019) (mem.).

Storing a Firearm in a Manner Accessible to a Minor (page 601)

Notes (page 602)

Element (5) (new note)

For a case where there was sufficient circumstantial evidence that the defendant stored or left a gun in a condition and manner accessible to a minor, see *State v. Lewis*, 222 N.C. App. 747, 750–51 (2012).

Carrying a Gun into an Assembly or Establishment Where Alcoholic Beverages Are Sold and Consumed (page 602)

Statute (page 602)

2013 legislation, S.L. 2013-369, sec. 3, amended subsection (b) of G.S. 14-269.3 to read as follows:

(b) This section shall not apply to any of the following:
  (1) A person exempted from the provisions of G.S. 14-269.
  (2) The owner or lessee of the premises or business establishment.
  (3) A person participating in the event, if the person is carrying a gun, rifle, or pistol with the permission of the owner, lessee, or person or organization sponsoring the event.
  (4) A person registered or hired as a security guard by the owner, lessee, or person or organization sponsoring the event.
  (5) A person carrying a handgun if the person has a valid concealed handgun permit issued in accordance with Article 54B of this Chapter, has a concealed handgun permit considered valid under G.S. 14-415.24, or is exempt from obtaining a permit pursuant to G.S. 14-415.25. This subdivision shall not be construed to permit a person to carry a handgun on any premises where

the person in legal possession or control of the premises has posted a conspicuous notice prohibiting the carrying of a concealed handgun on the premises in accordance with G.S. 14-415.11(c).

Notes (page 603)

Exceptions (page 603)

As a result of that same legislation, add the following text at the end of this section:

- a person carrying a handgun who has a valid concealed handgun permit, who has a permit considered valid under G.S. 14-415.24, or who is exempt from obtaining a permit.

G.S. 14-269.3(b)(5). However, this last exception does not apply if the person in legal possession or control of the premises has posted a conspicuous notice prohibiting the carrying of a concealed handgun on the premises in accordance with G.S. 14-415.11(c). *Id.*

Weapons at Parades, etc. (page 604)

Statute (page 604)

2013 legislation, S.L. 2013-369, sec. 15, amended G.S. 14-277.2, adding a new subsection, (d), as follows:

(d) The provisions of this section shall not apply to concealed carry of a handgun at a parade or funeral procession by a person with a valid permit issued in accordance with Article 54B of this Chapter, with a permit considered valid under G.S. 14-415.24, or who is exempt from obtaining a permit pursuant to G.S. 14-415.25. This subsection shall not be construed to permit a person to carry a concealed handgun on any premises where the person in legal possession or control of the premises has posted a conspicuous notice prohibiting the carrying of a concealed handgun on the premises in accordance with G.S. 14-415.11(c).

Notes (page 604)

Exceptions (page 604)

Pursuant to 2013 legislation, S.L. 2013-369, sec. 15, this offense does not apply to the concealed carry of a handgun at a parade or funeral procession by a person with a valid permit, with a permit considered valid under G.S. 14-415.24, or with an exemption from getting a permit under G.S. 14-415.25. G.S. 14-277.2(d). However, this exception does not allow a person to carry a concealed handgun on premises where the person in legal possession or control of the premises has posted a conspicuous notice prohibiting the carrying of a concealed handgun in accordance with G.S. 14-415.11(c). *Id.*

Going Armed to the Terror of the People

This is not a new crime. It was deleted from the 7th edition of NORTH CAROLINA CRIMES but appears here again in response to requests for its inclusion.

Statute

This is a common law offense. State v. Dawson, 272 N.C. 535, 541–42 (1968); State v. Huntly, 25 N.C. 418, 418 (1843); State v. Staten, 32 N.C. App. 495, 496–97 (1977) (citing *Dawson*).

Elements

A person guilty of this offense

    (1) arms himself or herself with an unusual and dangerous weapon

    (2) for the purpose of terrifying others *and*

    (3) goes about on public highways

    (4) in a manner to cause terror to the people.

Punishment

Class 1 misdemeanor. G.S. 14-3(a); *Dawson*, 272 N.C. at 549 (offense is a misdemeanor).

Notes

Generally. For the elements of this offense, see *Dawson*, 272 N.C. at 549, and *Staten*, 32 N.C. App. at 497.

For a case where the evidence was sufficient to establish this offense, see, for example, *Dawson*, 272 N.C. at 549 (armed with a carbine and four pistols, the defendant and three others drove on the public highways at night, firing bullets into a store and two homes).

Element (1). In *Huntly*, the court held that any gun is an unusual and dangerous weapon for purposes of this offense. 25 N.C. at 422. In that case it was argued that a gun cannot constitute an unusual weapon, "for there is scarcely a man in the community who does not own and occasionally use a gun of some sort." *Id.* The court rejected that argument, concluding: "A gun is an 'unusual weapon,' wherewith to be armed and clad. No man amongst us carries it about with him, as one of his every day accoutrements—as a part of his dress—and never we trust will the day come when any deadly weapon will be worn or wielded in our peace loving and law-abiding State, as an appendage of manly equipment." *Id.*; *see also* State v. Toler, ___ N.C. App. ___, ___, 716 S.E.2d 875, *6 (2011) (unpublished) (gun was an unusual and dangerous weapon).

In *State v. Lanier*, 71 N.C. 288, 289 (1874), the defendant was charged with going armed to the terror of the people after riding a horse, at a canter, through a courthouse after court had adjourned. Witnesses saw no arms of any kind. The North Carolina Supreme Court "attach[ed] no importance to the fact that the defendant had no arms," stating, "we think it may be conceded that the driving or riding without arms through a court house or a crowded street at such a rate or in such a manner as to endanger the safety of the inhabitants amounts to a breach of the peace and is an indictable offence at common law." *Id.* at 290 (but going on to conclude that the trial court erred by instructing the jury that if they believed either one of the two witnesses, they must find the defendant guilty; the court determined that the circumstances of the defendant's act were relevant and created a jury issue, stating: "We conceive that the riding through a court house or a street at 12 o'clock at night, when no one is present, is a very different thing from riding through at 12 o'clock in the day, when the court house or street is full of people. The same act may be criminal or innocent, according to the surrounding circumstances." *Id.*).

Element (2). The crime requires that the defendant act for the purpose of terrifying others. *See, e.g.*, *Toler*, ___ N.C. App. at ___, 716 S.E.2d 875, at *6 (the evidence was sufficient to establish that the defendant acted with the required purpose when he shot his gun on a public highway while driving closely behind another vehicle with his high beams on).

Element (3). It appears that the offense would not occur if the defendant remained on private property.

Element (4). In an unpublished case involving a charge of going armed to the terror of the people, the North Carolina Court of Appeals found this Element satisfied where the defendant shot his gun while driving closely behind another vehicle on a public highway with his high beams on. *Toler*, ___ N.C. App. at ___, 716 S.E.2d 875, at *6 (rejecting the defendant's argument that his actions were not "to the terror of the people" where the only people involved were those in the victim's car).

The offense of affray involves fighting in public to the terror of the people. For purposes of that offense, cases hold that if members of the public experience fear, the "to the terror of the people" element is satisfied. *In re* May, 357 N.C. 423, 428 (2003).

Relation to open carry. Because of the elements noted above, this offense would not apply to mere open carry. State v. Huntly, 25 N.C. 418, 422–23 (1843) ("[I]t is to be remembered that the carrying of a gun per se constitutes no offence. For any lawful purpose—either of business or amusement—the citizen is at perfect liberty to carry his gun. It is the wicked purpose—and the mischievous result—which essentially constitute the crime. He shall not carry about this or any other weapon of death to terrify and alarm, and in such manner as naturally will terrify and alarm, a peaceful people.").

23
Prostitution

2013 legislation, S.L. 2013-368, rewrote the state's prostitution offenses. As a result, delete the text of this chapter and replace it with the content that follows. Any additional legislative changes made after 2013 are noted in the text below.

Prostitution

Statute

2015 legislation, S.L. 2015-181, sec. 17, made conforming changes to G.S. 14-203(5). The amended statute reads as follows:

§ 14-203. **Definition of terms.**

The following definitions apply in this Article:

(1) Advance prostitution.—The term includes all of the following:

  a. Soliciting for a prostitute by performing any of the following acts when acting as other than a prostitute or a patron of a prostitute:

    1. Soliciting another for the purpose of prostitution.

    2. Arranging or offering to arrange a meeting of persons for the purpose of prostitution.

    3. Directing another to a place knowing the direction is for the purpose of prostitution.

    4. Using the Internet, including any social media Web site, to solicit another for the purpose of prostitution.

  b. Keeping a place of prostitution by controlling or exercising control over the use of any place that could offer seclusion or shelter for the practice of prostitution and performing any of the following acts when acting as other than a prostitute or a patron of a prostitute:

    1. Knowingly granting or permitting the use of the place for the purpose of prostitution.

    2. Granting or permitting the use of the place under circumstances from which the person should reasonably know that the place is used or is to be used for purposes of prostitution.

    3. Permitting the continued use of the place after becoming aware of facts or circumstances from which the person should know that the place is being used for the purpose of prostitution.

(2) Minor.—Any person who is less than 18 years of age.

(3) Profit from prostitution.—When acting as other than a prostitute, to receive anything of value for personally rendered prostitution services or to receive anything of value from a prostitute, if the thing received is not for lawful consideration and the person knows it was earned in whole or in part from the practice of prostitution.

(4) Prostitute.—A person who engages in prostitution.

(5) Prostitution.—The performance of, offer of, or agreement to perform vaginal intercourse, any sexual act as defined in G.S. 14-27.20, or any sexual contact as defined in G.S. 14-27.20, for the purpose of sexual arousal or gratification for any money or other consideration.

§ 14-204. Prostitution.

(a) Offense.—Any person who willfully engages in prostitution is guilty of a Class 1 misdemeanor.

(b) First Offender; Conditional Discharge.

(1) Whenever any person who has not previously been convicted of or placed on probation for a violation of this section pleads guilty to or is found guilty of a violation of this section, the court, without entering a judgment and with the consent of such person, shall place the person on probation pursuant to this subsection.

(2) When a person is placed on probation, the court shall enter an order specifying a period of probation of 12 months and shall defer further proceedings in the case until the conclusion of the period of probation or until the filing of a petition alleging violation of a term or condition of probation.

(3) The conditions of probation shall be that the person (i) not violate any criminal statute of any jurisdiction, (ii) refrain from possessing a firearm or other dangerous weapon, (iii) submit to periodic drug testing at a time and in a manner as ordered by the court, but no less than three times during the period of the probation, with the cost of the testing to be paid by the probationer, (iv) obtain a vocational assessment administered by a program approved by the court, and (v) attend no fewer than 10 counseling sessions administered by a program approved by the court.

(4) The court may, in addition to other conditions, require that the person do any of the following:

    a. Make a report to and appear in person before or participate with the court or such courts, person, or social service agency as directed by the court in the order of probation.

    b. Pay a fine and costs.

    c. Attend or reside in a facility established for the instruction or residence of defendants on probation.

    d. Support the person's dependents.

    e. Refrain from having in the person's body the presence of any illicit drug prohibited by the North Carolina Controlled Substances Act, unless prescribed by a physician, and submit samples of the person's blood or urine or both for tests to determine the presence of any illicit drug.

(5) Upon violation of a term or condition of probation, the court may enter a judgment on its original finding of guilt and proceed as otherwise provided.

(6) Upon fulfillment of the terms and conditions of probation, the court shall discharge the person and dismiss the proceedings against the person. Upon the discharge of the person and dismissal of the proceedings against the person under this subsection, the person is eligible to apply for expunction of records pursuant to G.S. 15A-145.6.

(7) Discharge and dismissal under this subsection shall not be deemed a conviction for purposes of structured sentencing or for purposes of disqualifications or disabilities imposed by law upon conviction of a crime.

(8) There may be only one discharge and dismissal under this section.

(c) Immunity From Prosecution for Minors.—Notwithstanding any other provision of this section, if it is determined, after a reasonable detention for investigative purposes, that a person suspected of or charged with a violation of this section is a minor, that person shall be immune from prosecution under this section and instead shall be taken into temporary protective custody as an undisciplined juvenile pursuant to Article 19 of Chapter 7B of the General Statutes. Pursuant to the provisions of G.S. 7B-301, a law enforcement officer who takes a minor into custody under this section shall immediately report an allegation of a violation of G.S. 14-43.11 and G.S. 14-43.13 to the director of the department of social services in the county where the minor resides or is found, as appropriate, which shall commence an initial investigation into child abuse or child neglect within 24 hours pursuant to G.S. 7B-301 and G.S. 7B-302.

Elements

A person guilty of this offense

(1) willfully

(2) engages in prostitution.

Punishment

Class 1 misdemeanor. G.S. 14-204(a). For conditional discharge, see G.S. 14-204(b). For special probation conditions, see G.S. 14-205.4.

Notes

Element (1). See "Willfully" in Chapter 1 (States of Mind) of the main volume.

Element (2). "Prostitution" is the performance of, offer of, or agreement to perform vaginal intercourse, a sexual act, or sexual contact for the purpose of sexual arousal or gratification and for money or other consideration. G.S. 14-203(5).

"Sexual act" includes cunnilingus, fellatio, analingus, anal intercourse, and the penetration by any object into the genital or anal opening of another person's body, except when done for accepted medical purposes. G.S. 14-203(5); 14-27.1(4) (this statute was recodified as G.S. 14-27.20 by 2015 legislation, S.L. 2015-181, sec. 2).

"Sexual contact" includes touching the sexual organ, anus, breast, groin, or buttocks of another; touching another with one's own sexual organ, anus, breast, groin, or buttocks; and ejaculating, emitting, or placing semen, urine, or feces on another. G.S. 14-203(5); 14-27.1(5) (this statute was recodified as G.S. 14-27.20 by 2015 legislation, S.L. 2015-181, sec. 2). "Touching" means physical contact, including through clothing. G.S. 14-27.1(6) (this statute was recodified as G.S. 14-27.20 by 2015 legislation, S.L. 2015-181, sec. 2).

Evidence issues. G.S. 14-206 provides that "testimony of a prior conviction, or testimony concerning the reputation of any place, structure, or building, and of the person or persons who reside in or frequent the same, and of the defendant" is admissible to prove this offense.

Immunity for minors. The law provides for immunity from prosecution for persons less than 18 years of age. G.S. 14-204(c); 14-203(2) (defining a "minor").

Related Offenses Not in This Chapter

"Crime against Nature" (Chapter 11)

"Fornication and Adultery" (Chapter 11)

Opposite sexes occupying same bedroom at hotel for immoral purposes; falsely registering as husband and wife. G.S. 14-186.

Keeping bawdy house. G.S. 14-188.

Solicitation of Prostitution

2015 legislation, S.L. 2015-183, and 2018 legislation, S.L. 2018-47, sec. 4(e), amended the statute to read as follows:

Statute

§ 14-205.1. Solicitation of prostitution.

(a) Except as otherwise provided in this section, any person who solicits another for the purpose of prostitution is guilty of a Class 1 misdemeanor for a first offense and a Class H felony for a second or subsequent offense. Any person 18 years of age or older who willfully solicits a minor for the purpose of prostitution is guilty of a Class G felony. Any person who willfully solicits a person who has a severe or profound mental disability for the purpose of prostitution is guilty of a Class E felony. Punishment under this section may include participation in a program devised for the education and prevention of sexual exploitation (i.e. "John School"), where available. A person who violates this subsection is not eligible for a disposition of prayer for judgment continued under any circumstances.

(b) Immunity From Prosecution for Minors.—Notwithstanding any other provision of this section, if it is determined, after a reasonable detention for investigative purposes, that a person suspected of or charged with a violation of this section is a minor who is soliciting as a prostitute, that person shall be immune from prosecution under this section and instead shall be taken into temporary protective custody as an undisciplined juvenile pursuant to Article 19 of Chapter 7B of the General Statutes. Pursuant to G.S. 7B-301, a law enforcement officer who takes a minor into custody under this section shall immediately report an allegation of a violation of G.S. 14-43.11 and G.S. 14-43.13 to the director of the department of social services in the county where the minor resides or is found, as appropriate, which shall commence an initial investigation into child abuse or child neglect within 24 hours pursuant to G.S. 7B-301 and G.S. 7B-302.

Elements

A person guilty of this offense

(1) solicits another
(2) for prostitution.

Punishment

Class 1 misdemeanor for a first offense; Class H felony for a second or subsequent offense. G.S. 14-205.1(a). The statute provides for two enhanced versions of this offense. First, a person 18 years or older who willfully solicits a minor under 18 years old is guilty of a Class G felony. *Id.*; G.S. 14-203(2). Second, a person who willfully solicits a person who has a severe or profound mental disability is guilty of a Class E felony. G.S. 14-205.1(a). The term "severe or profound mental disability" is not defined. For a definition of the term "mental disability" as that term is used in G.S. Chapter 14, Article 7B (Rape and Other Sex Offenses), see the note on Element (3)(b)(i) to "Second-Degree Forcible Rape," above in this supplement. The term "severely or profoundly mentally disabled" is not defined. The additional facts enhancing punishment must be alleged in the charging instrument and found by a jury, unless the defendant pleads guilty or no contest to the issue. For all versions of the offense, punishment may include participation in a "John School." G.S. 14-205.1(a). A prayer for judgment continued (PJC) is not allowed. *Id.* For special probation conditions, see G.S. 14-205.4.

Notes

Element (2). See "Prostitution," above in this supplement.

Evidence issues. See this note to "Prostitution," above in this supplement.

Immunity from prosecution (new note)
The statute provides for immunity from prosecution for minors who solicit as prostitutes. G.S. 14-205.1(b).

Related Offenses Not in This Chapter

See the offenses listed under "Prostitution," above in this supplement.

Patronizing a Prostitute

Statute

2015 legislation, S.L. 2015-181, sec. 18, and 2018 legislation, S.L. 2018-47, sec. 4(f), amended the statute to read as follows:

§ 14-205.2. Patronizing a prostitute.

(a) Any person who willfully performs any of the following acts with a person not his or her spouse commits the offense of patronizing a prostitute:

(1) Engages in vaginal intercourse, any sexual act as defined in G.S. 14-27.20, or any sexual contact as defined in G.S. 14-27.20, for the purpose of sexual arousal or gratification with a prostitute.

(2) Enters or remains in a place of prostitution with intent to engage in vaginal intercourse, any sexual act as defined in G.S. 14-27.20, or any sexual contact as defined in G.S. 14-27.20, for the purpose of sexual arousal or gratification.

(b) Except as provided in subsections (c) and (d) of this section, a first violation of this section is a Class A1 misdemeanor. Unless a higher penalty applies, a second or subsequent violation of this section is a Class G felony.

(c) A violation of this section is a Class F felony if the defendant is 18 years of age or older and the prostitute is a minor.

(d) A violation of this section is a Class D felony if the prostitute has a severe or profound mental disability.

Elements

A person guilty of this offense

(1) willfully

(2) (a) (i) engages in vaginal intercourse, a sexual act, or a sexual contact

(ii) for the purpose of sexual arousal or gratification

(iii) with a prostitute *or*

(b) (i) enters or remains

(ii) in a place of prostitution

(iii) with intent to engage in vaginal intercourse, a sexual act, or a sexual contact

(iv) for the purpose of sexual arousal or gratification *and*

(3) the acts are done with a person who is not the defendant's spouse.

Punishment

A first offense is a Class A1 misdemeanor; a second or subsequent offense is a Class G felony. G.S. 14-205.2(b). There are two enhanced versions of this offense. First, a violation is a Class F felony if the defendant is 18 years old or older and the prostitute is less than 18 years old. *Id.* § (c); 14-203(2). Second, a violation is a Class D felony if the prostitute has a severe or profound mental disability. G.S. 14-205.2(d). The additional facts enhancing punishment must be alleged in the charging instrument and found by a jury, unless the defendant pleads guilty or no contest to the issue. The term "severe or profound mental disability" is not defined. For a definition of the term "mental disability" as that term is used in G.S. Chapter 14, Article 7B (Rape and Other Sex Offenses), see the note on Element (3)(b)(i) to "Second-Degree Forcible Rape," above in this supplement. Both elevated versions of this offense qualify as sexually violent offenses for the purposes of the sex offender registration statutes. G.S. 14-190.13(5). For special probation conditions, see G.S. 14-205.4.

Notes

Element (1). See "Willfully" in Chapter 1 (States of Mind) of the main volume.

Element (2). The terms "sexual act" and "sexual contact" are defined in the note on Element (2) to "Prostitution," above in this supplement. A prostitute is "a person who engages in prostitution." G.S. 14-203(4).

Element (3). It is not clear if this provision is an element of the offense or a defense to it.

Evidence issues. See this note to "Prostitution," above in this supplement.

Related Offenses Not in This Chapter

See the offenses listed under "Prostitution," above in this supplement.

Promoting Prostitution

2018 legislation, S.L. 2018-47, sec. 4(g), amended the statute to read as follows:

Statute

§ 14-205.3. Promoting prostitution.

(a) Any person who willfully performs any of the following acts commits promoting prostitution:

    (1)   Advances prostitution as defined in G.S. 14-203.

    (2)   Profits from prostitution by doing any of the following:

        a.   Compelling a person to become a prostitute.

        b.   Receiving a portion of the earnings from a prostitute for arranging or offering to arrange a situation in which the person may practice prostitution.

        c.   Any means other than those described in sub-subdivisions a. and b. of this subdivision, including from a person who patronizes a prostitute. This sub-subdivision does not apply to a person engaged in prostitution who is a minor. A person cannot be convicted of promoting prostitution under this sub-subdivision if the practice of prostitution underlying the offense consists exclusively of the accused's own acts of prostitution under G.S. 14-204.

(b) Any person who willfully performs any of the following acts commits the offense of promoting prostitution of a minor or person who has a mental disability:

    (1)   Advances prostitution as defined in G.S. 14-203, where a minor or person who has a severe or profound mental disability engaged in prostitution, or any person engaged in prostitution in the place of prostitution is a minor or has a severe or profound mental disability at the time of the offense.

    (2)   Profits from prostitution by any means where the prostitute is a minor or has a severe or profound mental disability at the time of the offense.

    (3)   Confines a minor or person who has a severe or profound mental disability against the person's will by the infliction or threat of imminent infliction of great bodily harm, permanent disability, or disfigurement or by administering to the minor or person who has a severe or profound mental disability, without the person's consent or by threat or deception and for other than medical purposes, any alcoholic intoxicant or a drug as defined in Article 5 of Chapter 90 of the General Statutes (North Carolina Controlled Substances Act) and does any of the following:

        a.   Compels the minor or person who has a severe or profound mental disability to engage in prostitution.

b.   Arranges a situation in which the minor or person who has a severe or profound mental disability may practice prostitution.

c.   Profits from prostitution by the minor or person who has a severe or profound mental disability.

For purposes of this subsection, administering drugs or an alcoholic intoxicant to a minor or a person who has a severe or profound mental disability, as described in subdivision (3) of this subsection, shall be deemed to be without consent if the administering is done without the consent of the parents or legal guardian or if the administering is performed or permitted by the parents or legal guardian for other than medical purposes. Mistake of age is not a defense to a prosecution under this subsection.

(c) Unless a higher penalty applies, a violation of subsection (a) of this section is a Class F felony. A violation of subsection (a) of this section by a person with a prior conviction for a violation of this section or a violation of G.S. 14-204 (prostitution), G.S. 14-204.1 (solicitation of prostitution), or G.S. 14-204.2 (patronizing a prostitute) is a Class E felony.

(d) Unless a higher penalty applies, a violation of subdivision (1) or (2) of subsection (b) of this section is a Class D felony. A violation of subdivision (3) of subsection (b) of this section is a Class C felony. Any violation of subsection (b) of this section by a person with a prior conviction for a violation of this section or a violation of G.S. 14-204 (prostitution), G.S. 14-204.1 (solicitation of prostitution), G.S. 14-204.2 (patronizing a prostitute) is a Class C felony.

Elements

A person guilty of this offense

(1) willfully

(2) (a) advances prostitution *or*
     (b) profits from prostitution.

Punishment

Class F felony. G.S. 14-205.3(c). Class E felony if the defendant has a prior conviction for this offense, for prostitution (G.S. 14-204), for solicitation of prostitution (G.S. 14-204.1), or for patronizing a prostitute (G.S. 14-204.2). *Id.* For special probation conditions, see G.S. 14-205.4.

Notes

Element (1). See "Willfully" in Chapter 1 (States of Mind) of the main volume.

Element (2)(a). A person advances prostitution when, acting as other than a prostitute or a patron of a prostitute, he or she

- solicits another for prostitution;
- arranges or offers to arrange a meeting of people for prostitution;
- directs another to a place knowing the direction is for prostitution; or
- uses the Internet, including social media, to solicit another for prostitution.

G.S. 14-203(1)(a).

A person also advances prostitution by keeping a place of prostitution. This means controlling or exercising control over the use of a place that could offer seclusion or shelter for prostitution and performing any of the following acts, when acting as other than a prostitute or a prostitute's patron:

- knowingly granting or permitting the use of the place for prostitution,
- granting or permitting the use of the place under circumstances from which the person should reasonably know that the place is used or is to be used for prostitution, or
- permitting the continued use of the place when the person should know that the place is being used for prostitution.

G.S. 14-203(1)(b).

Element (2)(b). To profit from prostitution means "[w]hen acting as other than a prostitute, to receive anything of value for personally rendered prostitution services or to receive anything of value from a prostitute, if the thing received is not for lawful consideration and the person knows it was earned in whole or in part from the practice of prostitution." G.S. 14-203(3). The profiting may occur by compelling a person to become a prostitute, by receiving a portion of the earnings from a prostitute for arranging or offering to arrange a situation in which the person may practice prostitution, or by any other means. G.S. 14-205.3(a)(2). However, profiting from prostitution "by any other means" does not apply to a minor engaged in prostitution or when the practice of prostitution underlying the offense consists exclusively of the defendant's own acts of prostitution under G.S. 14-204. *Id.* § (a)(2)c.

Evidence issues. See this note to "Prostitution," above in this supplement.

Related Offenses Not in This Chapter

See the offenses listed under "Prostitution," above in this supplement.

Promoting Prostitution of a Minor or Person Who Has a Mental Disability (revised title)

Statute

See G.S. 14-205.3(b), reproduced above in this supplement under "Promoting Prostitution."

Elements

A person guilty of this offense

(1) willfully
(2) (a) (i)   advances prostitution *and*
        (ii) a minor or person who has a severe or profound mental disability engaged in prostitution, *or*
        (iii) any person engaged in prostitution in the place of prostitution is a minor or has a severe or profound mental disability, *or*
    (b) (i)   profits from prostitution *and*
        (ii) the prostitute is
              1. a minor *or*
              2. has a severe or profound mental disability, *or*
    (c) (i)   confines
        (ii) a minor or person who has a severe or profound mental disability
        (iii) against the person's will
        (iv) by
              1. the infliction or threat of imminent infliction of great bodily harm, permanent disability, or disfigurement *or*
              2. administering an alcoholic intoxicant or controlled substance, without consent or by threat or deception and for non-medical purposes, *and*
        (v)   does any of the following:
              1. compels the minor or person who has a severe or profound mental disability to engage in prostitution,
              2. arranges a situation for the minor or person who has a severe or profound mental disability to practice prostitution, *or*
              3. profits from prostitution by the minor or person who has a severe or profound mental disability.

Punishment

If elements (2)(a) or (b) are involved, Class D felony. G.S. 14-205.3(d). If Element (2)(c) is involved, Class C felony. *Id.* Additionally, if the person has a prior conviction for violating this statute, G.S. 14-204 (prostitution), G.S. 14-204.1 (solicitation of prostitution), or G.S. 14-204.2 (patronizing a prostitute), punishment is as a Class C felony. *Id.* For special probation conditions, see G.S. 14-205.4.

Notes

Element (1). See "Willfully" in Chapter 1 (States of Mind) of the main volume.

Element (2) generally. A minor is a person under 18 years old. G.S. 14-203(2). The statute does not define the term "severe or profound mental disability." For a definition of the term "mental disability" as that term is used in G.S. Chapter 14, Article 7B (Rape and Other Sex Offenses), see the note on Element (3)(b)(i) to "Second-Degree Forcible Rape," above in this supplement.

Element (2)(a). "Advances prostitution" is defined under "Promoting Prostitution," above in this supplement.

Element (2)(c)(iii). Administering drugs or alcoholic intoxicants is deemed to be without consent if it is done without the consent of the parents or legal guardian of a minor or person with a severe or profound mental disability or if it is performed or permitted by the parents or legal guardian for non-medical purposes. G.S. 14-205.3(b).

Mistake of age. Mistake of age is not a defense. G.S. 14-205.3(b).

Evidence issues. See this note to "Prostitution," above in this supplement.

Sex offender registration. A conviction of this offense triggers sex offender registration requirements. G.S. 14-190.13(5).

Related Offenses Not in This Chapter

See the offenses listed under "Prostitution," above in this supplement.

24

Obscenity, Exploitation of a Minor, and Adult Establishment Offenses

Obscenity Offenses (page 621)

Disseminating Obscenity (page 621)

Notes (page 622)

Element (3) (page 622)

Replace the last paragraph of this note with the following:

> Nothing in G.S. 14-190.1 requires the State to produce the precise material alleged to be obscene. State v. Wilson, ___ N.C. App. ___, 823 S.E.2d 892 (2019) (rejecting the defendant's argument that contemporary community standards must take into account what can be seen on premium cable channels like Showtime and HBO, and concluding that evidence of the defendant's large collection of pornographic DVDs allowed the jury to reasonably infer that the material shown to the victim was obscene under contemporary community standards); State v. Mueller, 184 N.C. App. 553, 564–67 (2007) (a witness's testimony describing the material alleged to be obscene was sufficient to sustain a conviction without introduction of the material itself).

Disseminating and Exhibiting Material Harmful to Minors (page 628)

Displaying Material Harmful to Minors (page 628)

Notes (page 630)

Element (3) (page 630)

Add the following to the portion of this note discussing the definition of "sexual activity":

> Although proving vaginal intercourse and anal intercourse under G.S. 14-190.13(5)(b) requires proof of penetration, proving oral intercourse under that provision does not. State v. Fletcher, 370 N.C. 313, 329–30 (2017). The term "oral intercourse" is a "gender-neutral reference to cunnilingus and fellatio," neither of which requires penetration. *Id.*

Sexual Exploitation of a Minor (page 633)

First-Degree Sexual Exploitation of a Minor (page 633)

Notes (page 634)

Element (2) (page 634)

In a case prosecuted under the Element (2)(a) version of this offense, the court of appeals held that "the minor in question is required to have engaged in sexual activity" and that when a minor is merely depicted as being engaged in sexual activity as the result of digital manipulation, this offense has not occurred. *Fletcher*, 370 N.C. at 329–30.

Second-Degree Sexual Exploitation of a Minor (page 635)

Notes (page 636)

Element (1) (new note)

There was sufficient evidence that the defendant was aware of the contents of pornographic files found on his computer where, among other things, the files' titles clearly indicated that they contained pornographic images of children. State v. Jones, 248 N.C. App. 418, 428–29 (2016).

Element (2) (new note)

A defendant's act of downloading images from the Internet onto his computer constituted a "duplication" within the meaning of the statute. State v. Williams, 232 N.C. App. 152, 157–58 (2014) (deciding this issue of first impression).

Element (4) (page 636)

A photograph depicting a minor standing naked except for her socks in her father's bedroom meets the definition of lascivious under this offense, and the minor's pubic area was "exhibited" despite her hands partially blocking view of her genital area. State v. Corbett, ___ N.C. App. ___, 824 S.E.2d 875 (2019).

Multiple convictions and punishments (page 636)

In *Williams*, 232 N.C. App. at 158–60, the court rejected the defendant's argument that the General Assembly did not intend to punish defendants for both receiving and possessing the same images.

Disclosure of Private Images (new crime)

This offense was enacted in 2015. S.L. 2015-250.

Statute

2017 legislation, S.L. 2017-93, amended the statute to provide as follows:

§ 14-190.5A. Disclosure of private images.

 (a) Definitions.—The following definitions apply in this section:

  (1) Disclose.—Transfer, publish, distribute, or reproduce.

  (2) Image.—A photograph, film, videotape, recording, live transmission, digital or computer-generated visual depiction, or any other reproduction that is made by electronic, mechanical, or other means.

(3) Intimate parts.—Any of the following naked human parts: (i) male or female genitals, (ii) male or female pubic area, (iii) male or female anus, or (iv) the nipple of a female over the age of 12.

(4) [repealed]

(5) [repealed]

(6) Sexual conduct.—Includes any of the following:

    a. Vaginal, anal, or oral intercourse, whether actual or simulated, normal or perverted.

    b. Masturbation, excretory functions, or lewd exhibition of uncovered genitals.

    c. An act or condition that depicts torture, physical restraint by being fettered or bound, or flagellation of or by a nude person or a person clad in undergarments or in revealing or bizarre costume.

(b) Offense.—A person is guilty of disclosure of private images if all of the following apply:

(1) The person knowingly discloses an image of another person with the intent to do either of the following:

    a. Coerce, harass, intimidate, demean, humiliate, or cause financial loss to the depicted person.

    b. Cause others to coerce, harass, intimidate, demean, humiliate, or cause financial loss to the depicted person.

(2) The depicted person is identifiable from the disclosed image itself or information offered in connection with the image.

(3) The depicted person's intimate parts are exposed or the depicted person is engaged in sexual conduct in the disclosed image.

(4) The person discloses the image without the affirmative consent of the depicted person.

(5) The person obtained the image without consent of the depicted person or under circumstances such that the person knew or should have known that the depicted person expected the images to remain private.

(c) Penalty.—A violation of this section shall be punishable as follows:

(1) For an offense by a person who is 18 years of age or older at the time of the offense, the violation is a Class H felony.

(2) For a first offense by a person who is under 18 years of age at the time of the offense, the violation is a Class 1 misdemeanor.

(3) For a second or subsequent offense by a person who is under the age of 18 at the time of the offense, the violation is a Class H felony.

(d) Exceptions.—This section does not apply to any of the following:

(1) Images involving voluntary exposure in public or commercial settings.

(2) Disclosures made in the public interest, including, but not limited to, the reporting of unlawful conduct or the lawful and common practices of law enforcement, criminal reporting, legal proceedings, medical treatment, or scientific or educational activities.

(3) Providers of an interactive computer service, as defined in 47 U.S.C. § 230(f), for images provided by another person.

(e) Destruction of Image.—In addition to any penalty or other damages, the court may award the destruction of any image made in violation of this section.

(f) Other Sanctions or Remedies Not Precluded.—A violation of this section is an offense additional to other civil and criminal provisions and is not intended to repeal or preclude any other sanctions or remedies.

(g) Civil Action.—In addition to any other remedies at law or in equity, including an order by the court to destroy any image disclosed in violation of this section, any person whose image is disclosed, or used, as described in subsection (b) of this section, has a civil cause of action against any person who discloses or uses the image and is entitled to recover from the other person any of the following:

   (1)   Actual damages, but not less than liquidated damages, to be computed at the rate of one thousand dollars ($1,000) per day for each day of the violation or in the amount of ten thousand dollars ($10,000), whichever is higher.

   (2)   Punitive damages.

   (3)   A reasonable attorneys' fee and other litigation costs reasonably incurred.

The civil cause of action may be brought no more than one year after the initial discovery of the disclosure, but in no event may the action be commenced more than seven years from the most recent disclosure of the private image.

Elements

A person guilty of this offense:

(1) knowingly

(2) discloses an image of another person

(3) with the intent to

   (a) coerce, harass, intimidate, demean, humiliate, or cause financial loss to the depicted person, *or*

   (b) cause others to coerce, harass, intimidate, demean, humiliate, or cause financial loss to the depicted person, *and*

(4) the depicted person is identifiable from the disclosed image or from information offered in connection with it,

(5) the depicted person's intimate parts are exposed or the depicted person is engaged in sexual conduct in the disclosed image,

(6) the person discloses the image without the affirmative consent of the depicted person, *and*

(7) the person obtained the image without the consent of the depicted person or under circumstances such that the person knew or should have known that the depicted person expected the images to remain private.

Punishment

If the defendant is 18 or older at the time of the offense, Class H felony. G.S. 14-190.5A(c)(1). If the defendant is less than 18 years old at the time of the offense, a first offense is a Class 1 misdemeanor and a second or subsequent offense is a Class H felony. *Id.* §§ (c)(2), (3).

Notes

Element (1). See "Knowingly" in Chapter 1 (States of Mind) of the main volume.

Element (2). To "disclose" means to transfer, publish, distribute, or reproduce. G.S. 14-190.5A(a)(1). The term "image" includes a photograph, film, videotape, recording, live transmission, digital or computer-generated visual depiction, or any other reproduction that is made by electronic, mechanical, or other means. *Id.* § (a)(2).

Element (5). The term "intimate parts" means any of the following naked human parts: genitals, pubic area, anus, or the nipple of a female over the age of 12. G.S. 14-190.5A(a)(3). The term "sexual conduct" means any of the following:

- vaginal, anal, or oral intercourse, whether actual or simulated, normal or perverted;
- masturbation, excretory functions, or lewd exhibition of uncovered genitals;
- an act or condition that depicts torture, physical restraint by being fettered or bound, or flagellation of or by a nude person or a person clad in undergarments or in revealing or bizarre costume.

G.S. 14-190.5A(a)(6). This is the same definition of sexual conduct that applies with respect to obscenity. G.S. 14-190.1(c).

Exceptions. The statute carves out exceptions for

- images involving voluntary exposure in public or commercial settings and
- disclosures made in the public interest, including, but not limited to, the reporting of unlawful conduct or the lawful and common practices of law enforcement, criminal reporting, legal proceedings, medical treatment, or scientific or educational activities.

G.S. 14-190.5A(d)(1), (2). The statute also provides an exception for "[p]roviders of an interactive computer service, as defined in 47 U.S.C. § 230(f), for images provided by another person." *Id.* § (d)(3).

Destruction of images. The court may order the destruction of images made in violation of the statute. G.S. 14-190.5A(e).

Multiple convictions and punishments. Punishment for this offense does not preclude punishment for some other criminal offense that might apply to the conduct at issue. G.S. 14-190.5A(f).

Civil action. Prosecution for this offense does not preclude civil sanctions or remedies. *Id.* In fact, the statute sets out a civil cause of action. *Id.* § (g).

Adult Establishment Offenses (page 638)

Statute (page 638)

2017 legislation, S.L. 2017-151, secs. 2(a) and (b), amended G.S. 14-202.10, repealing subsections (7) and (8) and amending subsection (2) to read as follows:

> (2) "Adult establishment" means an adult bookstore, adult motion picture theatre, adult mini motion picture theatre, or adult live entertainment business as defined in this section.

2017 legislation, S.L. 2017-151, sec. 2(c), amended G.S. 20-202.11, adding a new subsection, (a1), as follows:

> (a1) No person shall permit the practice of massage and bodywork therapy, as defined in Article 36 of Chapter 90 of the General Statutes, in an adult establishment.

Permitting a Facility to Contain Multiple Adult Establishments (page 639)

Notes (page 640)

Element (3) (page 640)

As a result of 2017 legislation, S.L. 2017-151, sec. 2(a), delete the first sentence of this note and replace it with the following:

> G.S. 14-202.10(2) defines an "adult establishment" as an adult bookstore, adult motion picture theatre, adult mini motion picture theatre, or adult live entertainment business.

Related Offenses Not in This Chapter (page 640)

Add the following offense to this list:

> Permitting the practice of massage and bodywork therapy in an adult establishment.
> G.S. 14-202.11(a1).

25

Lotteries, Gambling, and Related Offenses

Lottery Offenses (page 645)

Advertising a Lottery (page 645)
Related Offenses Not in This Chapter (page 646)

Replace the related offense that reads "Unlawful bingo. G.S. 14-309.5; 14-309.12." with the following:

Unlawful bingo. G.S. 14-309.5; 14-309.12; 14-309.14.

Gambling (page 650)

Notes (page 651)

Exceptions (page 651)
2012 legislation, S.L. 2012-6, enacted G.S. 14-292.2, making lawful certain Class III gaming on Indian lands. A 2019 amendment, S.L. 2019-163, added sports and horse-race wagering to the list of lawful Class III games. G.S. 14-292.2(b)(5). Under legislation effective June 1, 2019, it is lawful for certain exempt organizations and employers to conduct "game nights" pursuant to the rules and permitting requirements described in G.S. 14-309.25 through -309.37. S.L. 2019-13.

Possession of a Slot Machine (page 651)

Notes (page 653)

Exceptions (page 653)
2012 legislation, S.L. 2012-6, enacted G.S. 14-292.2, making lawful certain Class III gaming on Indian lands.

Operation, etc. of a Video Gaming Machine (page 654)

Statute (page 654)

G.S. 14-306.1A(e) was repealed by 2012 legislation, S.L. 2012-6, sec. 3.

Notes (page 655)

Exceptions (page 655)

Delete the first sentence (and related citations) of this note and replace it with the following:

2012 legislation, S.L. 2012-6, enacted G.S. 14-292.2, making lawful certain Class III gaming on Indian lands.

Electronic Sweepstakes (page 657)

Notes (page 659)

Element (3) (page 659)

A sweepstakes can be conducted through the use of an entertaining display even if the prize is revealed to the patron before he or she plays the game. State v. Spruill, 237 N.C. App. 383, 386–87 (2014). A sweepstakes game run through a kiosk displaying a video game resembling a reel-spinning slot machine, which involved spinning the wheel on the display and nudging virtual reels, was an "entertaining display" regardless of whether skill or chance predominated over the game and was, therefore, a violation of this offense. Gift Surplus, LLC v. State *ex rel.* Cooper, ___ N.C. App. ___, 833 S.E.2d 703 (2019).

Constitutionality (new note)

In *Hest Technologies, Inc. v. North Carolina*, 366 N.C. 289 (2012), the court held that G.S. 14-306.4 does not violate the First Amendment. *See also* Sandhill Amusements v. North Carolina, 366 N.C. 323 (2012) (per curiam) (same).

26
Abandonment and Nonsupport

Abandonment and Nonsupport—Children (page 666)

Nonsupport of an Illegitimate Child (page 667)

2013 legislation, S.L. 2013-198, sec. 17, amended G.S. 49-2 to substitute the term "child born out of wedlock" for the term "illegitimate child."

27

Drug Offenses

Statute (page 673)

As a result of 2017 legislation, S.L. 2017-115, sec. 2, G.S. 90-87(14a) reads:

> (14a) The term "isomer" means any type of isomer, including structural, geometric, or optical isomers, and stereoisomers.

As a result of 2015 and 2016 legislation, S.L. 2015-299, sec. 2; S.L. 2016-93, sec. 6, add the following sentence at the end of subsection G.S. 90-87(16):

> The term does not include industrial hemp as defined in G.S. 106-568.51, when the industrial hemp is produced and used in compliance with rules issued by the North Carolina Industrial Hemp Commission.

As a result of 2017 legislation, S.L. 2017-115, sec. 2, G.S. 90-87(17)a. reads:

> a. Opium, opiate and opioid, and any salt, compound, derivative, or preparation of opium, opiate, or opioid.

This same 2017 legislation created a new subsection, G.S. 90-87(18a), as follows:

> (18a) "Opioid" means any synthetic narcotic drug having opiate like activities but is not derived from opium.

2017 legislation, S.L. 2017-74, sec. 3, created a new subsection, G.S. 90-87(26a), as follows:

> (26a) "Targeted controlled substance" means any controlled substance included in G.S. 90-90(1) or (2) or G.S. 90-91(d).

2015 legislation, S.L. 2015-162, sec. 1, 2017 legislation, S.L. 2017-115, sec. 3, and 2018 legislation, S.L. 2018-44, secs. 2–3, amended G.S. 90-89 (Schedule I) so that it reads as follows:

> **§ 90-89. Schedule I controlled substances.**
> This schedule includes the controlled substances listed or to be listed by whatever official name, common or usual name, chemical name, or trade name designated. In determining that a substance comes within this schedule, the Commission shall find: a high potential for abuse, no currently accepted medical use in the United States, or a lack of accepted safety for use in treatment under medical supervision. The following controlled substances are included in this schedule:
> (1) Opiates.—Any of the following opiates or opioids, including the isomers, esters, ethers, salts and salts of isomers, esters, and ethers, unless specifically excepted, or listed in another schedule, whenever the existence of such isomers, esters, ethers, and salts is possible within the specific chemical designation:
> a. Acetyl-alpha-methylfentanyl (N[1-(1-methyl-2-phenethyl)-4/y-piperidinyl]-N-phenylacet amide).
> b. Acetylmethadol.
> c. Repealed by Session Laws 1987, c. 412, s. 2.
> d. Alpha-methylthiofentanyl (N-[1-methyl-2-(2-thienyl)ethyl/y-4/y-piperidinyl]-N-phenylpropanamide).
> e. Allylprodine.

f.   Alphacetylmethadol (except levo-alphacetylmethadol, also known as levomethadyl acetate and LAAM).

g.   Alphameprodine.

h.   Alphamethadol.

i.   Alpha-methylfentanyl (N-(1-(alpha-methyl-beta-phenyl) ethyl-4-piperidyl) propionalilide; 1(1-methyl-2-phenyl-ethyl)-4-(N-propanilido) piperidine).

j.   Benzethidine.

k.   Betacetylmethadol.

l.   Beta-hydroxfentanyl (N-[1-(2-hydroxy-2-phenethyl)-4-piperidinyl]-N-phenylpropanamide).

m.   Beta-hydroxy-3-methylfentanyl (N-[1-(2-hydroxy-2-phenethyl)-3-methyl-4-piperidinyl]-N-pheny lpropanamide).

n.   Betameprodine.

o.   Betamethadol.

p.   Betaprodine.

q.   Clonitazene.

r.   Dextromoramide.

s.   Diampromide.

t.   Diethylthiambutene.

u.   Difenoxin.

v.   Dimenoxadol.

w.   Dimepheptanol.

x.   Dimethylthiambutene.

y.   Dioxaphetyl butyrate.

z.   Dipipanone.

aa. Ethylmethylthiambutene.

bb. Etonitazene.

cc. Etoxeridine.

dd. Furethidine.

ee. Hydroxypethidine.

ff. Ketobemidone.

gg. Levomoramide.

hh. Levophenacylmorphan.

ii.   1-methyl-4-phenyl-4-propionoxypiperidine (MPPP).

jj.   3-Methylfentanyl (N-[3-methyl-1-(2-Phenylethyl)-4-Pi- peridyl]-N-Phenylpropanamide).

kk. 3-Methylthiofentanyl (N-[(3-methyl-1-(2-thienyl)ethyl/y-4-piperidinyl]-N-phenylpropanamide).

ll.   Morpheridine.

mm. Noracymethadol.

nn. Norlevorphanol.

oo. Normethadone.

pp. Norpipanone.

qq. Para-fluorofentanyl (N-(4-fluorophenyl)-N-[1-(2-phen-ethyl)-4-piperidinyl]-propanamide.

rr. Phenadoxone.

ss. Phenampromide.

tt. 1-(2-phenethyl)-4-phenyl-4-acetoxypiperidine (PEPAP).

uu. Phenomorphan.

vv. Phenoperidine.

ww. Piritramide.

xx. Proheptazine.

yy. Properidine.

zz. Propiram.

aaa. Racemoramide.

bbb. Thiofentanyl (N-phenyl-N-[1-(2-thienyl)ethyl-4-piperidinyl]-propanamide.

ccc. Tilidine.

ddd. Trimeperidine.

eee. Acetyl Fentanyl.

fff. Trans-3,4-dichloro-N-(2(dimethylamino)cyclohexyl)-N-methyl-benzamide (U47700).

ggg. 3,4-dichloro-N([1(dimethylamino)cyclohexyl]methyl)benzamide; 1-(3,4-dichlorobenzamidomethyl)cyclohexyldimethylamine) (also known as AH-7921).

hhh. 3,4-dichloro-N-([diethylamino)cyclohexyl]-N-methylbenzamide (also known as U-49900).

iii. U-77891.

jjj. 1-phenylethylpiperidylidene-2-(4-chlorphenyl)sulfonamide; 1-(4-nitro-phenylethyl)piperidylidene-2-(4-chlorophenyl)sulfonamide; 4-chloro-N-[1-[2-(4-nitrophenyl)ethyl]-2-piperidinylidene]-benzenesulfonamide (also known as W-18).

kkk. 1-phenylethylpiperidylidene-2-(4-chlorophenyl)sulfonamide; 4-chloro-N-[1-(2-phenylethyl)-2-piperidinylidene]-benzenesulfonamide (also known as W-15).

lll. 1-cyclohexyl-4-(1,2-diphenylethyl)piperazine (also known as MT-45).

(1a) Fentanyl derivatives.—Any compounds structurally derived from N-[1-(2-phenylethyl)-4-piperidinyl]-N-phenylpropanamide (Fentanyl) by any substitution on or replacement of the phenethyl group, any substitution on the piperidine ring, any substitution on or replacement of the propanamide group, any substitution on the anilido phenyl group, or any combination of the above unless specifically excepted or listed in another schedule to include their salts, isomers, and salts of isomers. Fentanyl derivatives include, but are not limited to, the following:

a. N-(1-phenylethylpiperidin-4-yl)-N-phenylfuran-2-carboxamide (also known as Furanyl Fentanyl).

b. N-(1-phenethylpiperidin-4-yl)-N-phenylbutyramide; N-(1-phenethylpi-peridin-4-yl)-N-phenylbutanamide (also known as Butyryl Fentanyl).

c. N-[1-[2-hydroxy-2-(thiophen-2-yl)ethyl]piperidin-4-yl]-N-phenylpropi-onamide; N-[1-[2-hydroxy-2-(2-thienyl)ethyl]-4-piperidinyl]-N-phenyl-propanamide (also known as Beta-Hydroxythiofentanyl).

d. N-phenyl-N-[1-(2-phenylethyl)piperidin-4-yl]-2propenamide (also known as Acrylfentanyl).

e. N-phenyl-N-[1-(2-phenylethyl)-4-piperidinyl]-pentanamide (also known as Valeryl Fentanyl).

f. N-(2-fluorophenyl)-N-[1-(2-phenylethyl)-4-piperidinyl]-propanamide (also known as 2-fluorofentanyl).

g. N-(3-fluorophenyl)-N-[1-(2-phenylethyl)-4-piperidinyl]-propanamide (also known as 3-fluorofentanyl).

h. N-(1-phenethylpiperidin-4-yl)-N-phenyltetrahydrofuran-2-carboxamide (also known as tetrahydrofuran fentanyl).

i. N-(4-fluorophenyl)-2-methyl-N-[1-(2-phenylethyl)-4-piperidinyl]-propanamide (also known as 4-fluoroisobutyryl fentanyl, 4-FIBF).

j. N-(4-fluorophenyl)-N-[1-(2-phenylethyl)-4-piperidinyl]-butanamide (also known as 4-fluorobutyryl fentanyl, 4-FBF).

(2) Opium derivatives.—Any of the following opium derivatives, including their salts, isomers, and salts of isomers, unless specifically excepted, or listed in another schedule, whenever the existence of such salts, isomers, and salts of isomers is possible within the specific chemical designation:

a. Acetorphine.

b. Acetyldihydrocodeine.

c. Benzylmorphine.

d. Codeine methylbromide.

e. Codeine-N-Oxide.

f. Cyprenorphine.

g. Desomorphine.

h. Dihydromorphine.

i. Etorphine (except hydrochloride salt).

j. Heroin.

k. Hydromorphinol.

l. Methyldesorphine.

m. Methyldihydromorphine.

n. Morphine methylbromide.

o. Morphine methylsulfonate.

p. Morphine-N-Oxide.

q. Myrophine.

r. Nicocodeine.

s. Nicomorphine.

t. Normorphine.

u. Pholcodine.

v. Thebacon.

w. Drotebanol.

(3) Hallucinogenic substances.—Any material, compound, mixture, or preparation which contains any quantity of the following hallucinogenic substances, including their salts, isomers, and salts of isomers, unless specifically excepted, or listed in another schedule, whenever the existence of such salts, isomers, and salts of isomers is possible within the specific chemical designation:

a. 3, 4-methylenedioxyamphetamine.

b. 5-methoxy-3, 4-methylenedioxyamphetamine.

c. 3, 4-Methylenedioxymethamphetamine (MDMA).

d. 3,4-methylenedioxy-N-ethylamphetamine (also known as N-ethyl-alpha-methyl-3,4-(methylenedioxy) phenethylamine, N-ethyl MDA, MDE, and MDEA).

e. N-hydroxy-3,4-methylenedioxyamphetamine (also known as N-hydroxy/y-alpha-methyl-3,4-(methylenedioxy) phenethylamine, and N-hydroxy MDA).

f. 3, 4, 5-trimethoxyamphetamine.

g. Alpha-ethyltryptamine. Some trade or other names: etryptamine, Monase, alpha-ethyl-1H-indole-3-ethanamine, 3-(2-aminobutyl) indole, alpha-ET, and AET.

h. Bufotenine.

i. Diethyltryptamine.

j. Dimethyltryptamine.

k. 4-methyl-2, 5-dimethoxyamphetamine.

l. Ibogaine.

m. Lysergic acid diethylamide.

n. Mescaline.

o. Peyote, meaning all parts of the plant presently classified botanically as Lophophora Williamsii Lemaire, whether growing or not; the seeds thereof; any extract from any part of such plant; and every compound, manufacture, salt, derivative, mixture or preparation of such plant, its seed or extracts.

p. N-ethyl-3-piperidyl benzilate.

q. N-methyl-3-piperidyl benzilate.

r. Psilocybin.

s. Psilocin.

t. 2, 5-dimethoxyamphetamine.

u. 2, 5-dimethoxy-4-ethylamphetamine. Some trade or other names: DOET.

v. 4-bromo-2, 5-dimethoxyamphetamine.

w. 4-methoxyamphetamine.

x. Ethylamine analog of phencyclidine. Some trade or other names: N-ethyl-1-phenylcyclohexylamine, (1-phenylcyclohexyl) ethylamine, N-(1-phenylcyclohexyl) ethylamine, cyclohexamine, PCE.

y. Pyrrolidine analog of phencyclidine. Some trade or other names: 1-(1-phenylcyclohexyl)-pyrrolidine, PCPy, PHP.

z. Thiophene analog of phencyclidine. Some trade or other names: 1-[1-(2-thienyl)-cyclohexyl]-piperidine, 2-thienyl analog of phencyclidine, TPCP, TCP.

aa. 1-[1-(2-thienyl)cyclohexyl]pyrrolidine; Some other names: TCPy.

bb. Parahexyl.

cc. 4-Bromo-2, 5-Dimethoxyphenethylamine.

dd. Alpha-Methyltryptamine.

ee. 5-Methoxy-N,N-diisopropyltryptamine.

ff. Methoxetamine (other names: MXE, 3-MeO-2-Oxo-PCE).

gg. BTCP (Benzothiophenylcyclohexylpiperidine).

hh. Deschloroketamine.

jj. 3-MeO-PCP (3-methoxyphencyclidine).

kk. 4-hydroxy-MET.

ll. 4-OH-MiPT (4-hydroxy-N-methyl-N-isopropyltryptamine).

mm. 5-methoxy-N-methyl-N-propyltryptamine (5-MeO-MiPT).

(4) Systemic depressants.—Any material compound, mixture, or preparation which contains any quantity of the following substances having a depressant effect on the central nervous system, including its salts, isomers, and salts of isomers whenever the existence of such salts, isomers, and salts of isomers is possible within the specific chemical designation, unless specifically excepted or unless listed in another schedule:

a. Mecloqualone.

b. Methaqualone.

c. Gamma hydroxybutyric acid; Some other names: GHB, gamma-hydroxybutyrate, 4-hydroxybutyrate, 4-hydroxybutanoic acid; sodium oxybate; sodium oxybutyrate.

d. Etizolam.

e. Flubromazepam.

f. Phenazepam.

(5) Stimulants.—Unless specifically excepted or unless listed in another schedule, any material, compound, mixture, or preparation that contains any quantity of the following substances having a stimulant effect on the central nervous system, including its salts, isomers, and salts of isomers:

a. Aminorex. Some trade or other names: aminoxaphen; 2-amino-5-phenyl-2-oxazoline; or 4,5-dihydro-5-phenyl-2-oxazolamine.

b. Cathinone. Some trade or other names: 2-amino-1-phenyl-1-propanone, alpha-aminopropiophenone, 2-aminopropiophenone, and norephedrone.

c. Fenethylline.

d. Methcathinone. Some trade or other names: 2-(methylamino)- pro-piophenone, alpha-(methylamino)propiophenone, 2-(methy- lamino)-1-phenylpropan-1-one, alpha-N-methylamino- propiophenone, mono-methylproprion, ephedrone, N-methylcathinone, methylcathinone, AL-464, AL-422, AL-463, and UR1432.

e. (+-)cis-4-methylaminorex [(+-)cis-4,5-dihydro-4-methyl-5-phenyl-2-oxazolamine] (also known as 2-amino-4-methyl-5-phenyl-2-oxazoline).

      f.   N,N-dimethylamphetamine. Some other names: N,N,alpha-trimethylbenzeneethaneamine; N,N,alpha-trimethylphenethylamine.

      g.   N-ethylamphetamine.

      h.   4-methylmethcathinone (also known as mephedrone).

      i.   3,4-Methylenedioxypyrovalerone (also known as MDPV).

      j.   Substituted cathinones. A compound, other than bupropion, that is structurally derived from 2-amino-1-phenyl-1-propanone by modification in any of the following ways: (i) by substitution in the phenyl ring to any extent with alkyl, alkoxy, alkylenedioxy, haloalkyl, or halide substituents, whether or not further substituted in the phenyl ring by one or more other univalent substituents; (ii) by substitution at the 3-position to any extent; or (iii) by substitution at the nitrogen atom with alkyl, dialkyl, benzyl, or methoxybenzyl groups or by inclusion of the nitrogen atom in a cyclic structure.

      k.   N-Benzylpiperazine.

      l.   2,5—Dimethoxy-4-(n)-propylthiophenethylamine.

(6)   NBOMe compounds.—Any material compound, mixture, or preparation which contains any quantity of the following substances, including its salts, isomers, and salts of isomers whenever the existence of such salts, isomers, and salts of isomers is possible within the specific chemical designation unless specifically excepted or unless listed in another schedule:

      a.   25B-NBOMe (2C-B-NBOMe) 2-(4-Bromo-2,5-dimethoxyphenyl)-N-(2-methoxybenzyl)ethanamine.

      b.   25C-NBOMe (2C-C-NBOMe) 2-(4-Chloro-2,5-dimethoxyphenyl)-N-(2-methoxybenzyl)ethanamine.

      c.   25D-NBOMe (2C-D-NBOMe) 2-(2,5-dimethoxy-4-methylphenyl)-N-(2-methoxybenzyl)ethanamine.

      d.   25E-NBOMe (2C-E-NBOMe) 2-(4-Ethyl-2,5-dimethoxyphenyl)-N-(2-methoxybenzyl)ethanamine.

      e.   25G-NBOMe (2C-G-NBOMe) 2-(2,5-dimethoxy-3,4-dimethylphenyl)-N-(2-methoxybenzyl)ethanamine.

      f.   25H-NBOMe (2C-H-NBOMe) 2-(2,5-dimethoxyphenyl)-N-(2-methoxybenzyl) ethanamine.

      g.   25I-NBOMe (2C-I-NBOMe) 2-(4-Iodo-2,5-dimethoxyphenyl)-N-(2-methoxybenzyl)ethanamine.

      h.   25N-NBOMe (2C-N-NBOMe) 2-(2,5-dimethoxy-4-nitrophenyl)-N-(2-methoxybenzyl)ethanamine.

      i.   25P-NBOMe (2C-P-NBOMe) 2-(4-Propyl-2,5-dimethoxyphenyl)-N-(2-methoxybenzyl)ethanamine.

      j.   25T2-NBOMe (2C-T2-NBOMe) 2,5-dimethoxy-N-[(2-methoxyphenyl)methyl]-4-(methylthio)-benzeneethanamine.

      k.   25T2-NBOMe (2C-T2-NBOMe) 2,5-dimethoxy-N-[(2-methoxyphenyl)methyl]-4-(methylthio)-benzeneethanamine.

      l.   25T7-NBOMe (2C-T7-NBOMe) 2,5-dimethoxy-N-[(2-methoxyphenyl)methyl]-4-(propylthio)-benzeneethanamine.

(7)   Synthetic cannabinoids.—Any quantity of any synthetic chemical compound that (i) is a cannabinoid receptor agonist and mimics the pharmacological effect of naturally occurring substances or (ii) has a stimulant, depressant, or hallucinogenic effect on the central nervous system that is not listed as a controlled substance in Schedules I through V, and is not an FDA-approved drug. Synthetic cannabinoids include, but are not limited to, the substances listed in sub-subdivisions a. through p. of this subdivision and any substance that contains any quantity of their salts, isomers (whether optical, positional, or geometric), homologues, and salts of isomers and homologues, unless specifically excepted, whenever the existence of these salts, isomers, homologues, and salts of isomers and homologues is possible

within the specific chemical designation. The following substances are examples of synthetic cannabinoids and are not intended to be inclusive of the substances included in this Schedule:

a.   Naphthoylindoles. Any compound containing a 3-(1-naphthoyl)indole structure with substitution at the nitrogen atom of the indole ring by an alkyl, haloalkyl, alkenyl, cycloalkylmethyl, cycloalkylethyl, 1-(N-methyl-2-piperidinyl)methyl, or 2-(4-morpholinyl)ethyl group, whether or not further substituted in the indole ring to any extent and whether or not substituted in the naphthyl ring to any extent. Some trade or other names: JWH-015, JWH-018, JWH-019, JWH-073, JWH-081, JWH-122, JWH-200, JWH-210, JWH-398, AM-2201, and WIN 55-212.

b.   Naphthylmethylindoles. Any compound containing a 1H-indol-3-yl-(1-naphthyl)methane structure with substitution at the nitrogen atom of the indole ring by an alkyl, haloalkyl, alkenyl, cycloalkylmethyl, cycloalkylethyl, 1-(N-methyl-2-piperidinyl)methyl, or 2-(4-morpholinyl) ethyl group, whether or not further substituted in the indole ring to any extent and whether or not substituted in the naphthyl ring to any extent.

c.   Naphthoylpyrroles. Any compound containing a 3-(1-naphthoyl) pyrrole structure with substitution at the nitrogen atom of the pyrrole ring by an alkyl, haloalkyl, alkenyl, cycloalkylmethyl, cycloalkylethyl, 1-(N-methyl-2-piperidinyl)methyl, or 2-(4-morpholinyl)ethyl group, whether or not further substituted in the pyrrole ring to any extent and whether or not substituted in the naphthyl ring to any extent. Another name: JWH-307.

d.   Naphthylmethylindenes. Any compound containing a naphthylideneindene structure with substitution at the 3-position of the indene ring by an alkyl, haloalkyl, alkenyl, cycloalkylmethyl, cycloalkylethyl, 1-(N-methyl-2-piperidinyl)methyl, or 2-(4-morpholinyl)ethyl group, whether or not further substituted in the indene ring to any extent and whether or not substituted in the naphthyl ring to any extent.

e.   Phenylacetylindoles. Any compound containing a 3-phenylacetylindole structure with substitution at the nitrogen atom of the indole ring by an alkyl, haloalkyl, alkenyl, cycloalkylmethyl, cycloalkylethyl, 1-(N-methyl-2-piperidinyl)methyl, or 2-(4-morpholinyl)ethyl group, whether or not further substituted in the indole ring to any extent and whether or not substituted in the phenyl ring to any extent. Some trade or other names: SR-18, RCS-8, JWH-250, and JWH-203.

f.   Cyclohexylphenols. Any compound containing a 2-(3-hydroxycyclohexyl)phenol structure with substitution at the 5-position of the phenolic ring by an alkyl, haloalkyl, alkenyl, cycloalkylmethyl, cycloalkylethyl, 1-(N-methyl-2-piperidinyl)methyl, or 2-(4-morpholinyl)ethyl group, whether or not substituted in the cyclohexyl ring to any extent. Some trade or other names: CP 47,497 (and homologues), cannabicyclohexanol.

g.   Benzoylindoles. Any compound containing a 3-(benzoyl)indole structure with substitution at the nitrogen atom of the indole ring by an alkyl, haloalkyl, alkenyl, cycloalkylmethyl, cycloalkylethyl, 1-(N-methyl-2-piperidinyl)methyl, or 2-(4-morpholinyl)ethyl group, whether or not further substituted in the indole ring to any extent and whether or not substituted in the phenyl ring to any extent. Some trade or other names: AM-694, Pravadoline (WIN 48,098), and RCS-4.

h.   2,3-Dihydro-5-methyl-3-(4-morpholinylmethyl)pyrrolo[1,2,3-de]-1, 4-benzoxazin-6-yl]-1-napthalenylmethanone. Some trade or other name: WIN 55,212-2.

i.   (6aR,10aR)-9-(hydroxymethyl)-6, 6-dimethyl-3-(2-methyloctan-2-yl)—
     6a,7,10,10a-tetrahydrobenzo[c]chromen-1-ol 7370. Some trade or other
     name: HU-210.

j.   3-(cyclopropylmethanone) indole or 3-(cyclobutylmethanone) indole
     or 3-(cyclopentylmethanone) indole by substitution at the nitrogen
     atom of the indole ring, whether or not further substituted in the indole
     ring to any extent, whether or not further substituted on the cyclo-
     propyl, cyclobutyl, or cyclopentyl rings to any extent. Substances in
     this class include, but are not limited to: UR-144, fluoro-UR-144, XLR-11,
     A-796,260, and A-834,735.

k.   Indole carboxaldehydes. Any compound structurally derived from
     1H-indole-3-carboxaldehyde or 1H-indole-2-carboxaldehyde substi-
     tuted in both of the following ways:

     1.   At the nitrogen atom of the indole ring by an alkyl, haloalkyl,
          cyanoalkyl, alkenyl, cycloalkylmethyl, cycloalkylethyl, 1-(N-methyl-
          2-piperidinyl)methyl, 2-(4-morpholinyl)ethyl, 1-(N-methyl-2-pyrro-
          lidinyl)methyl, 1-(N-methyl-3-morpholinyl)methyl, tetrahydropy-
          ranylmethyl, benzyl, or halo benzyl group; and

     2.   At the carbon of the carboxaldehyde by a phenyl, benzyl, naphthyl,
          adamantyl, cyclopropyl, or propionaldehyde group; whether or not
          the compound is further modified to any extent in the following
          ways: (i) substitution to the indole ring to any extent, (ii) substitu-
          tion to the phenyl, benzyl, naphthyl, adamantyl, cyclopropyl, or
          propionaldehyde group to any extent, (iii) a nitrogen heterocyclic
          analog of the indole ring, or (iv) anitrogen heterocyclic analog
          of the phenyl, benzyl, naphthyl, adamantyl, or cyclopropyl ring.
          Substances in this class include, but are not limited to: AB-001.

l.   Indole carboxamides. Any compound structurally derived from
     1H-indole-3-carboxamide or 1H-indole-2-carboxamide substituted in
     both of the following ways:

     1.   At the nitrogen atom of the indole ring by an alkyl, haloalkyl,
          cyanoalkyl, alkenyl, cycloalkylmethyl, cycloalkylethyl, 1-(N-methyl-
          2-piperidinyl)methyl, 2-(4-morpholinyl)ethyl, 1-(N-methyl-2-pyrro-
          lidinyl)methyl, 1-(N-methyl-3-morpholinyl)methyl, tetrahydropy-
          ranylmethyl, benzyl, or halo benzyl group; and

     2.   At the nitrogen of the carboxamide by a phenyl, benzyl, naphthyl,
          adamantyl, cyclopropyl, or propionaldehyde group; whether or not
          the compound is further modified to any extent in the following
          ways: (i) substitution to the indole ring to any extent, (ii) substitu-
          tion to the phenyl, benzyl, naphthyl, adamantyl, cyclopropyl, or
          propionaldehyde group to any extent, (iii) a nitrogen heterocyclic
          analog of the indole ring, or (iv) a nitrogen heterocyclic analog
          of the phenyl, benzyl, naphthyl, adamantyl, or cyclopropyl ring.
          Substances in this class include, but are not limited to: SDB-001
          and STS-135.

m.   Indole carboxylic acids. Any compound structurally derived from
     1H-indole-3-carboxylic acid or 1H-indole-2-carboxylic acid substituted
     in both of the following ways:

     1.   At the nitrogen atom of the indole ring by an alkyl, haloalkyl,
          cyanoalkyl, alkenyl, cycloalkylmethyl, cycloalkylethyl, 1-(N-methyl-
          2-piperidinyl)methyl, 2-(4-morpholinyl)ethyl, 1-(N-methyl-2-pyrro-
          lidinyl)methyl, 1-(N-methyl-3-morpholinyl)methyl, tetrahydropy-
          ranylmethyl, benzyl, or halo benzyl group; and

     2.   At the nitrogen of the carboxamide by a phenyl, benzyl, naphthyl,
          adamantyl, cyclopropyl, or propionaldehyde group; whether or not
          the compound is further modified to any extent in the following

ways: (i) substitution to the indole ring to any extent, (ii) substitution to the phenyl, benzyl, naphthyl, adamantyl, cyclopropyl, or propionaldehyde group to any extent, (iii) a nitrogen heterocyclic analog of the indole ring, or (iv) a nitrogen heterocyclic analog of the phenyl, benzyl, naphthyl, adamantyl, or cyclopropyl ring. Substances in this class include, but are not limited to: SDB-001 and STS-135; whether or not the compound is further modified to any extent in the following ways: (i) substitution to the indole ring to any extent, (ii) substitution to the phenyl, benzyl, naphthyl, adamantyl, cyclopropyl, or propionaldehyde group to any extent, (iii) a nitrogen heterocyclic analog of the indole ring, or (iv) a nitrogen heterocyclic analog of the phenyl, benzyl, naphthyl, adamantyl, or cyclopropyl ring. Substances in this class include, but are not limited to: PB-22 and fluoro-PB-22.

n. Indazole carboxaldehydes. Any compound structurally derived from 1H-indazole-3-carboxaldehyde or 1H-indazole-2-carboxaldehyde substituted in both of the following ways:

   1. At the nitrogen atom of the indazole ring by an alkyl, haloalkyl, cyanoalkyl, alkenyl, cycloalkylmethyl, cycloalkylethyl, 1-(N-methyl-2-piperidinyl)methyl, 2-(4-morpholinyl)ethyl, 1-(N-methyl-2-pyrrolidinyl)methyl, 1-(N-methyl-3-morpholinyl)methyl, tetrahydropyranylmethyl, benzyl, or halo benzyl group; and

   2. At the carbon of the carboxaldehyde by a phenyl, benzyl, whether or not the compound is further modified to any extent in the following ways: (i) substitution to the indazole ring to any extent, (ii) substitution to the phenyl, benzyl, naphthyl, adamantyl, cyclopropyl, or propionaldehyde group to any extent, (iii) a nitrogen heterocyclic analog of the indazole ring, or (iv) a nitrogen heterocyclic analog of the phenyl, benzyl, naphthyl, adamantyl, or cyclopropyl ring.

o. Indazole carboxamides. Any compound structurally derived from 1H-indazole-3-carboxamide or 1H-indazole-2-carboxamide substituted in both of the following ways:

   1. At the nitrogen atom of the indazole ring by an alkyl, haloalkyl, cyanoalkyl, alkenyl, cycloalkylmethyl, cycloalkylethyl, 1-(N-methyl-2-piperidinyl)methyl, 2-(4-morpholinyl)ethyl, 1-(N-methyl-2-pyrrolidinyl)methyl, 1-(N-methyl-3-morpholinyl)methyl, tetrahydropyranylmethyl, benzyl, or halo benzyl group; and

   2. At the nitrogen of the carboxamide by a phenyl, benzyl, naphthyl, adamantyl, cyclopropyl, or propionaldehyde group; whether or not the compound is further modified to any extent in the following ways: (i) substitution to the indazole ring to any extent, (ii) substitution to the phenyl, benzyl, naphthyl, adamantyl, cyclopropyl, or propionaldehyde group to any extent, (iii) a nitrogen heterocyclic analog of the indazole ring, or (iv) a nitrogen heterocyclic analog of the phenyl, benzyl, naphthyl, adamantyl, or cyclopropyl ring. Substances in this class include, but are not limited to: AKB-48, fluoro-AKB-48, APINCACA, AB-PINACA, AB-FUBINACA, ADB-FUBINACA, and ADB-PINACA.

p. Indazole carboxylic acids. Any compound structurally derived from 1H-indazole-3-carboxylic acid or 1H-indazole-2-carboxylic acid substituted in both of the following ways:

   1. At the nitrogen atom of the indazole ring by an alkyl, haloalkyl, cyanoalkyl, alkenyl, cycloalkylmethyl, cycloalkylethyl, 1-(N-methyl-2-piperidinyl)methyl, 2-(4-morpholinyl)ethyl, 1-(N-methyl-2-pyrro-

lidinyl)methyl, 1-(N-methyl-3-morpholinyl)methyl, tetrahydropy-ranylmethyl, benzyl, or halo benzyl group; and

2. At the hydroxyl group of the carboxylic acid by a phenyl, benzyl, naphthyl, adamantyl, cyclopropyl, or propionaldehyde group; whether or not the compound is further modified to any extent in the following ways: (i) substitution to the indazole ring to any extent, (ii) substitution to the phenyl, benzyl, naphthyl, adaman-tyl, cyclopropyl, or propionaldehyde group to any extent, (iii) a nitrogen heterocyclic analog of the indazole ring, or (iv) a nitrogen heterocyclic analog of the phenyl, benzyl, naphthyl, adamantyl, or cyclopropyl ring.

q. Carbazoles. Any compound containing a carbazole ring system with a substituent on the nitrogen atom and bearing an additional substitu-ent at the 1, 2, or 3 position of the carbazole ring system, with a linkage connecting the ring system to the substituent:

1. Where the linkage connecting the carbazole ring system to the substituent if its 1, 2, or 3 position is any of the following: Alkyl, Carbonyl, Ester, Thione, Thioester, Amino, Alkylamino, Amido, or Alkylamido.

2. Where the substituent at the 1, 2, or 3 position of the carbazole ring system, disregarding the linkage, is any of the following groups: Naphthyl, Quinolinyl, Adamantyl, Phenyl, Cycloalkyl (lim-ited to cyclopropyl, cyclobutyl, cyclopentyl, or cyclohexyl), Biphe-nyl, Alkylamido (limited to ethylamido, propylamido, butanamido, pentamido), Benzyl, Carboxylic acid, Ester, Ether, Phenylpropyl-amido, or Phenylpropylamino; whether or not further substituted in either of the following ways: (i) the substituent at the 1, 2, or 3 position of the carbazole ring system, disregarding the linkage, is further substituted to any extent (ii) further substitution on the carbazole ring system to any extent. This class includes, but is not limited to, the following: MDMB CHMCZCA, EG-018, and EG-2201.

r. Naphthoylnaphthalenes. Any compound structurally derived from naphthalene-1-yl-(naphthalene-1-yl) methanone with substitutions on either of the naphthalene rings to any extent. Substances in this class include, but are not limited to: CB-1313.

2017 legislation, S.L. 2017-115, sec. 4, and 2018 legislation, S.L. 2018-44, sec. 4, amended G.S. 90-90(1) and (2) to read as follows:

(1) Any of the following substances whether produced directly or indirectly by extraction from substances of vegetable origin, or independently by means of chemical synthesis, or by a combination of extraction and chemical syn-thesis, unless specifically excepted or unless listed in another schedule:

a. Opium, opiate, or opioid and any salt, compound, derivative, or preparation of opium and opiate, excluding apomorphine, nalbuphine, dextrorphan, naloxone, naltrexone and nalmefene, and their respective salts, but including the following:

1. Raw opium.
2. Opium extracts.
3. Opium fluid extracts.
4. Powdered opium.
5. Granulated opium.
6. Tincture of opium.
7. Codeine.
8. Ethylmorphine.
9. Etorphine hydrochloride.
10. Any material, compound, mixture, or preparation which contains any quantity of hydrocodone.

11. Hydromorphone.
12. Metopon.
13. Morphine.
14. Oxycodone.
15. Oxymorphone.
16. Thebaine.
17. Dihydroetorphine.

b. Any salt, compound, derivative, or preparation thereof which is chemically equivalent or identical with any of the substances referred to in paragraph 1 of this subdivision, except that these substances shall not include the isoquinoline alkaloids of opium.

c. Opium poppy and poppy straw.

d. Cocaine and any salt, isomer, salts of isomers, compound, derivative, or preparation thereof, or coca leaves and any salt, isomer, salts of isomers, compound, derivative, or preparation of coca leaves, or any salt, isomer, salts of isomers, compound, derivative, or preparation thereof which is chemically equivalent or identical with any of these substances, except that the substances shall not include decocanized coca leaves or extraction of coca leaves, which extractions do not contain cocaine or ecgonine.

e. Concentrate of poppy straw (the crude extract of poppy straw in either liquid, solid or powder form which contains the phenanthrine alkaloids of the opium poppy).

(2) Any of the following opiates or opioids, including their isomers, esters, ethers, salts, and salts of isomers, whenever the existence of such isomers, esters, ethers, and salts is possible within the specific chemical designation unless specifically exempted or listed in other schedules:

a. Alfentanil.
b. Alphaprodine.
c. Anileridine.
d. Bezitramide.
e. Carfentanil.
f. Dihydrocodeine.
g. Diphenoxylate.
h. Fentanyl.
h1. Fentanyl immediate precursor chemical, 4-anilino-N-phenethyl-4-piperidine (ANPP).
i. Isomethadone.
j. Levo-alphacetylmethadol. Some trade or other names: levo-alpha-acetylmethadol, levomethadyl acetate, or LAAM.
k. Levomethorphan.
l. Levorphanol.
m. Metazocine.
n. Methadone.
o. Methadone—Intermediate, 4-cyano-2-dimethylamino-4, 4/y-diphenyl butane.
p. Moramide—Intermediate, 2-methyl-3-morpholino-1, 1-diphenyl-propane-carboxylic acid.
q. Pethidine.
r. Pethidine—Intermediate—A, 4-cyano-1-methyl-4/y-phenylpiperidine.
s. Pethidine—Intermediate—B, ethyl-4-phenylpiperidine-4-carboxylate.
t. Pethidine—Intermediate—C, 1-methyl-4-phenylpiperidine-4-carboxylic acid.
u. Phenazocine.
v. Piminodine.
w. Racemethorphan.

     x. Racemorphan.
     y. Remifentanil.
     z. Sufentanil.
     aa. Tapentadol.

2015 legislation, S.L. 2015-162, sec. 2, amended G.S. 90-90(3)d. to read as follows:

     d. Methylphenidate, including its salts, isomers, and salts of its isomers.

2017 legislation, S.L. 2017-115, sec. 5, amended G.S. 90-91(d), repealing subsections (d)3. and (d)4. and adding a new subsection, (d)9., as follows:

     9. Buprenorphine.

2016 and 2017 legislation, S.L. 2016-113, sec. 9; S.L. 2017-115, sec. 5, amended G.S. 90-91(k) so that it reads as follows:

(k) Anabolic steroids. The term "anabolic steroid" means any drug or hormonal substance, chemically and pharmacologically related to testosterone (other than estrogens, progestins, and corticosteroids) that promotes muscle growth, including, but not limited to, the following:

1. Methandrostenolone,
2. Stanozolol,
3. Ethylestrenol,
4. Nandrolone phenpropionate,
5. Nandrolone decanoate,
6. Testosterone propionate,
7. Chorionic gonadotropin,
8. Boldenone,
8a. Boldione,
9. Chlorotestosterone (4-chlorotestosterone),
10. Clostebol,
11. Dehydrochlormethyltestosterone,
11a. Desoxymethyltesterone (17[alpha]-methyl-5[alpha]-androst-2-en-17[beta]-ol) (also known as madol),
12. Dibydrostestosterone (4-dihydrotestosterone),
13. Drostanolone,
14. Fluoxymesterone,
15. Formebulone (formebolone),
16. Mesterolene,
17. Methandienone,
18. Methandranone,
19. Methandriol,
19a. Methasterone,
20. Methenolene,
21. Methyltestosterone,
22. Mibolerone,
23. Nandrolene,
24. Norethandrolene,
25. Oxandrolone,
26. Oxymesterone,
27. Oxymetholone,
28. Stanolone,
29. Testolactone,
30. Testosterone,
31. Trenbolone,
31a. 19-nor-4,9(10)-androstadienedione (estra-4,9(10)-diene-3,17-dione), and
32. Any salt, ester, or isomer of a drug or substance described or listed in this subsection, if that salt, ester, or isomer promotes muscle growth. Except such term does not include (i) an anabolic steroid which is expressly intended for administration through implants to

cattle or other nonhuman species and which has been approved by the Secretary of Health and Human Services for such administration or (ii) chorionic gonadotropin when administered by injection for veterinary use by a licensed veterinarian or the veterinarian's designated agent. If any person prescribes, dispenses, or distributes such steroid for human use, such person shall be considered to have prescribed, dispensed, or distributed an anabolic steroid within the meaning of this subsection.

2017 legislation, S.L. 2017-115, sec. 6, amended the list of depressants in G.S. 90-92(a)(1) to include the following additional substances:

d1. Carisoprodol.
n1. Dichloralphenazone.
u1. Fospropol.
yy. Zopiclone.

2017 legislation, S.L. 2017-115, sec. 6; S.L. 2017-212, sec. 8.8(a), amended G.S. 90-92(a)(5) to read as follows:

(5) Narcotic Drugs.—Unless specifically excepted or unless listed in another schedule, any material, compound, mixture, or preparation containing limited quantities of any of the following narcotic drugs, or any salts thereof:

a. Not more than 1 milligram of difenoxin and not less than 25 micrograms of atropine sulfate per dosage unit.

[b. Repealed]

c. 2-[(dimethylamino)methyl]-1-(3-methoxyphenyl)cyclohexanol, its salts, optical and geometric isomers, and salts of these isomers (including tramadol).

Note that while S.L. 2017-212, sec. 8.8(a) appears to retain 90-92(a)(5)b., listing buprenorphine, S.L. 2017-115 repealed that provision and moved buprenorphine to G.S. 90-91(d).

2017 legislation, S.L. 2017-115, sec. 7, amended G.S. 90-93, adding a new subsection, (a)(4), as follows:

(4) Anticonvulsants.—Unless specifically exempted or excluded or unless listed in another schedule, any material, compound, mixture, or preparation which contains any quantity of the following substances having a stimulant effect on the central nervous system, including its salts, isomers, and salts of isomers:

a. Ezogabine.
b. Lacosamide.
c. Brivaracetam.
d. Pregabalin

2017 legislation, S.L. 2017-115, sec. 8, repealed G.S. 90-94(3).

As a result of 2017 legislation, S.L. 2017-115, sec. 11, G.S. 90-95(b)(2) reads as follows:

(2) A controlled substance classified in Schedule III, IV, V, or VI shall be punished as a Class I felon, except that the sale of a controlled substance classified in Schedule III, IV, V, or VI shall be punished as a Class H felon. The transfer of less than 5 grams of marijuana for no remuneration shall not constitute a delivery in violation of G.S. 90-95(a)(1).

As a result of that same 2017 legislation, G.S. 90-95(d)(4) reads as follows:

(4) A controlled substance classified in Schedule VI shall be guilty of a Class 3 misdemeanor, but any sentence of imprisonment imposed must be suspended and the judge may not require at the time of sentencing that the defendant serve a period of imprisonment as a special condition of probation. If the quantity of the controlled substance exceeds one-half of an ounce (avoirdupois) of marijuana or one-twentieth of an ounce (avoirdupois) of the extracted resin of marijuana, commonly known as hashish, the violation shall be punishable as a Class 1 misdemeanor. If the quantity

of the controlled substance exceeds one and one-half ounces (avoirdupois) of marijuana, or three-twentieths of an ounce (avoirdupois) of the extracted resin of marijuana, commonly known as hashish, or if the controlled substance consists of any quantity of synthetic tetrahydrocannabinols or tetrahydrocannabinols isolated from the resin of marijuana, the violation shall be punishable as a Class I felony.

As a result of S.L. 2013-124; S.L. 2014-115, sec. 41(a); and S.L. 2015-32, sec. 1, G.S. 90-95(d1) reads as follows:

(d1) (1) Except as authorized by this Article, it is unlawful for any person to:
  a. Possess an immediate precursor chemical with intent to manufacture a controlled substance; or
  b. Possess or distribute an immediate precursor chemical knowing, or having reasonable cause to believe, that the immediate precursor chemical will be used to manufacture a controlled substance; or
  c. Possess a pseudoephedrine product if the person has a prior conviction for the possession of methamphetamine, possession with the intent to sell or deliver methamphetamine, sell or deliver methamphetamine, trafficking methamphetamine, possession of an immediate precursor chemical, or manufacture of methamphetamine. The prior conviction may be from any jurisdiction within the United States.

Except where the conduct is covered under subdivision (2) of this subsection, any person who violates this subdivision shall be punished as a Class H felon.

As a result of 2015 legislation, S.L. 2015-32, sec. 1, and 2018 legislation, S.L. 2018-44, secs. 5–6, G.S. 90-95(d2) reads as follows:

(d2) The immediate precursor chemicals to which subsection (d1) of this section applies are those immediate precursor chemicals designated by the Commission pursuant to its authority under G.S. 90-88, and the following (until otherwise specified by the Commission):

(1) Acetic anhydride.
(2) Acetone.
(2a) Ammonium nitrate.
(2b) Ammonium sulfate.
(3) Anhydrous ammonia.
(4) Anthranilic acid.
(5) Benzyl chloride.
(6) Benzyl cyanide.
(7) 2 Butanone (Methyl Ethyl Ketone).
(8) Chloroephedrine.
(9) Chloropseudoephedrine.
(10) D lysergic acid.
(11) Ephedrine.
(12) Ergonovine maleate.
(13) Ergotamine tartrate.
(13a) Ether based starting fluids.
(14) Ethyl ether.
(15) Ethyl Malonate.
(16) Ethylamine.
(17) Gamma butyrolactone.
(18) Hydrochloric Acid. (Muriatic Acid).
(19) Iodine.
(20) Isosafrole.
(21) Sources of lithium metal.
(22) Malonic acid.
(23) Methylamine.
(24) Methyl Isobutyl Ketone.

   (25) N acetylanthranilic acid.
   (26) N ethylephedrine.
   (27) N ethylepseudoephedrine.
   (28) N methylephedrine.
   (29) N methylpseudoephedrine.
   (29a) N-phenethyl-4-piperidinone (NPP).
   (30) Norpseudoephedrine.
   (30a) Petroleum based organic solvents such as camping fuels and lighter fluids.
   (31) Phenyl 2 propanone.
   (32) Phenylacetic acid.
   (33) Phenylpropanolamine.
   (34) Piperidine.
   (35) Piperonal.
   (36) Propionic anhydride.
   (37) Pseudoephedrine.
   (38) Pyrrolidine.
   (39) Red phosphorous.
   (40) Safrole.
   (40a) Sodium hydroxide (Lye).
   (41) Sources of sodium metal.
   (42) Sulfuric Acid.
   (43) Tetrachloroethylene.
   (44) Thionylchloride.
   (45) Toluene.

Sale or Delivery and Related Offenses (page 694)

Sale or Delivery of a Controlled Substance (page 694)
Punishment (page 694)

Delete the third paragraph of this section and replace it with the following:

> The delivery of a Schedule III, IV, V, or VI substance is a Class I felony; the sale of a Schedule III, IV, V, or VI substance is a Class H felony. G.S. 90-95(b)(2).

Notes (page 694)
Element (2)(b) (page 694)

As a result of 2017 legislation, S.L. 2017-115, sec. 11, delete the second sentence of this note and replace it with the following:

> It is not a delivery to transfer for no remuneration less than 5 grams of marijuana, G.S. 90-95(b)(2); such activity could be punished only as possession of a controlled substance.

Add the following text to this note:

> The State need not show that the defendant personally received compensation in exchange for the delivery. State v. Land, 223 N.C. App. 305, 313 (2012), *aff'd per curiam*, 366 N.C. 550 (2013).

Attempt and conspiracy (page 695)

Insert the following after the second sentence of this note:

> *See also* State v. Warren, 244 N.C. App. 134, 150–51 (2015) (applying G.S. 90-98 and holding that conspiracy to manufacture methamphetamine was properly punished as a Class C felony).

Jury instructions (new note)

Where the evidence showed that the defendant transferred less than 5 grams of marijuana, the trial court erred by not instructing the jury that in order to prove delivery, the State was required to prove that the defendant transferred the marijuana for remuneration. *Land*, 223 N.C. App. at 315.

Defenses (page 695)

For a case where the trial court did not err by declining to instruct the jury that the defendant would be exempt from prosecution if he was an "ultimate user" pursuant to G.S. 90-101(c), see *State v. Bice*, ___ N.C. App. ___, 821 S.E.2d 259 (2018) (the evidence did not support the defense).

Multiple convictions and punishments (page 696)

For another case standing for the proposition stated in this note that a defendant may not be separately convicted of both the sale and delivery of a controlled substance arising from a single transaction, see *State v. Fleig*, 232 N.C. App. 647, 650–51 (2014) (purchaser gave the defendant $20 for a bag of marijuana; purchaser then asked for another bag in light of the payment made and the defendant provided it).

Related Offenses Not in This Chapter (page 696)

Add the following offense to this list:

> Distributing, dispensing, delivering, or purchasing marijuana on property used for industrial hemp production or in a manner intended to disguise the marijuana due to its proximity to industrial hemp. G.S. 106-568.57(a).

Furnishing a Controlled Substance to an Inmate (page 697)

Related Offenses Not in This Chapter (page 698)

Add the following offense to this list:

> Use of an unmanned aircraft system near a confinement or correctional facility. G.S. 15A-300.3, *as enacted by* S.L. 2017-179.

As a result of 2018 legislation, S.L. 2018-67, sec. 3, delete the first item in this list and replace it with the following:

> Providing articles forbidden by prison rules or items for prison escape, assault, or insurrection; possessing items for prison escape, assault, or insurrection. G.S. 14-258.

Delete the third offense in the list and replace it with the following:

> Furnishing alcoholic beverages, tobacco products, or mobile phones to an inmate or a delinquent juvenile. G.S. 14-258.1(b)–(d).

Delete the last offense in this list and replace it with the following:

> Inmate's possession of a tobacco product. G.S. 14-258.1(e).
>
> Inmate's possession of a mobile phone or wireless communication device or component. G.S. 14-258.1(g).

Manufacture of a Controlled Substance (page 698)

Notes (page 699)

Element (2) (page 699)

Where officers find a controlled substance and an array of items used to package and distribute that substance, the evidence suffices to support a manufacturing conviction. State v. Miranda, 235 N.C. App. 601, 612 (2014) (evidence was sufficient where more than 28 grams of cocaine and several items that are commonly used to weigh, separate, and package cocaine for sale were seized from the defendant's bedroom).

There was sufficient evidence of manufacturing methamphetamine where an officer observed the defendant and another person at the scene for approximately forty minutes and among the items recovered there were a handbag containing a syringe and methamphetamine; a duffle bag containing a clear, two-liter bottle containing methamphetamine; empty boxes and blister packs of pseudoephedrine; a full pseudoephedrine blister pack; an empty pack of lithium batteries; a lithium battery from which the lithium had been removed; iodized salt; sodium hydroxide; drain opener; funnels; tubing; coffee filters; syringes; various items of clothing; and a plastic bottle containing white and pink granular material; the defendant's presence at the scene, the evidence recovered, the officer's testimony that the defendant and his accomplice were going back and forth in the area moving bottles, and testimony that the defendant gave instructions to his accomplice to keep the smoke out of her eyes was sufficient evidence of manufacturing. State v. Davis, 236 N.C. App. 376, 382–83 (2014).

Element (4) (page 699)

For additional cases supporting the proposition that in a manufacturing case based on preparing or compounding the State must prove intent to distribute, see *Miranda*, 235 N.C. App. at 610 (stating this requirement but finding no plain error where the trial court allowed the jury to find the defendant guilty of manufacturing by packaging as well as compounding and the undisputed evidence showed that he packed the controlled substance), and *State v. Simpson*, 230 N.C. App. 119, 124–25 (2013) (reiterating this requirement but finding no plain error where a jury instruction on this issue was lacking).

Multiple convictions and punishments (new note)

Where a defendant engages in manufacturing of methamphetamine in two separate distinct locations, two convictions for manufacturing may obtain. State v. Maloney, 253 N.C. App. 563, 572 (2017) (rejecting the defendant's argument that his conduct constituted a single continuing offense; two separate methamphetamine labs were discovered: one in the trunk of a car and one in a storage unit).

No double jeopardy violation occurs when a defendant is convicted of trafficking in methamphetamine, manufacturing methamphetamine, and possession of methamphetamine based on the same illegal substance. *Simpson*, 230 N.C. App. at 126–27.

Related Offenses Not in This Chapter (page 700)

Add the following offense to this list:

Manufacture of marijuana on property used for industrial hemp production or in a manner intended to disguise the marijuana due to its proximity to industrial hemp. G.S. 106-568.57(a).

Possession Offenses (page 700)

Possession of a Controlled Substance (page 700)

Punishment (page 701)

In the first bulleted list in this section, replace the word "cocoa" with "coca."

As a result of 2017 legislation, S.L. 2017-115, sec. 11, delete the fourth paragraph of this note and replace it with the following:

Except as discussed immediately below, for a Schedule VI controlled substance, the offense is a Class 3 misdemeanor for which a sentence of imprisonment must be suspended and the judge may not require that the defendant serve a period of imprisonment as a special condition of probation. G.S. 90-95(d)(4). There are two exceptions to this punishment level for Schedule VI controlled substances. First, if the defendant possessed

- more than ½ ounce of marijuana and up to 1½ ounces of marijuana or
- more than 1/20 of an ounce and up to 3/20 of an ounce of hashish,

the offense is a Class 1 misdemeanor. Second, if the defendant possessed

- more than 1½ ounces of marijuana,
- more than 3/20 of an ounce of hashish, or
- any quantity of synthetic tetrahydrocannabinols or tetrahydrocannabinols isolated from the resin of marijuana,

the offense is a Class I felony. G.S. 90-95(d)(4).

This section states that for all misdemeanor controlled substance offenses, several provisions—including G.S. 90-95(e)(3)—elevate punishment based on the defendant's prior conviction record. Because G.S. 90-95(e)(3) establishes a separate felony offense rather than merely a sentence enhancement of the underlying misdemeanor, an offense punished under this provision may be subject to habitual felon status. State v. Howell, 370 N.C. 647, 654 (2018).

Notes (page 702)

Element (1) (page 702)

A presumption that the defendant has the required guilty knowledge is created when the State makes a prima facie case that the defendant has committed a crime, such as possession of a controlled substance, trafficking by possession, or trafficking by transportation, that lacks a specific intent element. State v. Galaviz-Torres, 368 N.C. 44 (2015). However, when the defendant denies or contests having knowledge of the controlled substance that he or she has been charged with possessing or transporting, the existence of the requisite guilty knowledge becomes an issue of fact that must be decided by the jury. Id.; State v. Coleman, 227 N.C. App. 354, 359–60 (2013) (trafficking by possession case; the trial court committed plain error by failing to instruct on this Element; although the defendant did not testify or present evidence to raise the issue of knowledge as a disputed fact, the State presented evidence that the defendant told a detective that he did not know the container contained heroin; this constituted a contention that the defendant did not know the true identity of what he possessed). For example, when a defendant admits having possession of a box stored in his or her car but denies knowing that the box contained the controlled substance at issue, whether the defendant knowingly possessed the controlled substance is an issue for the jury. Coleman, 227 N.C. App. at 359. By contrast, a defendant's denial of any knowledge of having possessed any container or controlled substance does not defeat the presumption and likewise does not create an issue on which the jury must be instructed. Galaviz-Torres, 368 N.C. 44 (in this trafficking case the defendant did not deny knowledge of the contents of a gift bag in which cocaine was found or admit that he possessed a particular substance while denying any knowledge of the substance's identity; rather, the defendant denied having had any knowledge that the van he was driving contained either the gift bag or cocaine).

For a trafficking and possession with intent case where the evidence was insufficient to establish that the defendant knowingly possessed or transported the controlled substance, see *State v. Velazquez-Perez*, 233 N.C. App. 585, 588–93 (2014) (drugs were found in secret compartments of a truck driven by the defendant Villalvavo but owned by a passenger, Velazquez-Perez, who hired Villalvavo to drive the truck; while evidence regarding the truck's log books may have been incriminating as to Velazquez-Perez, it did not apply to Villalvavo, who had not been working for Velazquez-Perez long and had no stake in the company or control over Velazquez-Perez; Villalvavo's nervousness during the stop did not constitute adequate incriminating circumstances).

Element (2) (page 702)

The following content modifies the text in the second and third paragraphs of this note regarding the necessary proof to establish constructive possession when the defendant does not have exclusive control over the place where contraband is found.

In *State v. Chekanow*, 370 N.C. 488, 494–95 (2018), the court stated that "for evidence of constructive possession to be sufficient, if the defendant owns the premises on which the contraband is found, (1) he must also have exclusive possession of the premises on which the contraband is found, or (2) the State must show additional incriminating circumstances demonstrating the defendant has dominion or control over the contraband." However, in *State v. Wirt*, ___ N.C. App. ___, 822 S.E.2d 668 (2018), the court of appeals distinguished *Chekanow*, holding that evidence of a defendant's power as the driver to control an automobile in which contraband is found (in that case, drugs and a firearm) is sufficient, *in and of itself*, to give rise to an inference of constructive possession, even if the defendant's possession of the vehicle is nonexclusive. In *Wirt*, the court expressly rejected the defendant's argument that because he did not have exclusive possession of the vehicle, the State was required to show other incriminating circumstances. Quoting from *State v. Mitchell*, 224 N.C. App. 171, 177 (2012), the court noted that "the courts in this State have held consistently that the driver of a borrowed car, like the owner of the car, has the power to control the contents of the car. Moreover, power to control the automobile where [contraband] was found *is sufficient, in and of itself*, to give rise to the inference of knowledge and possession sufficient to go to the jury." Although the defendant in *Wirt* was the driver of the vehicle, the court clearly seems to view ownership of a vehicle in the same way.

For additional cases holding that the evidence was sufficient to establish constructive possession, see *Chekanow*, 370 N.C. at 496 (the evidence was sufficient to establish constructive possession of marijuana plants found on property the defendants owned but did not exclusively possess; additional incriminating circumstances included, among other things, that the plants were in close proximity to an area maintained by the defendants, the defendants' residence was in "reasonably close proximity" to the plants, the plants were surrounded by a fence that was not easily surmountable, the defendants had the ability to control who entered this portion of the property by establishing the sole entry point in the front yard next to their home, other items belonging to the defendants were in the same location as the plants, and one defendant appeared to flee the premises as a helicopter hovered to investigate the plants); *State v. Lindsey*, 366 N.C. 325 (2012) (reversing 219 N.C. App. 249 (2012) for the reasons stated in the dissenting opinion, which found sufficient evidence of constructive possession where, after the defendant fled from his crashed van, officers found a bag containing marijuana near trash receptacles in the parking lot where the crash occurred; detailed evidence concerning the distance of the bag from the defendant's van, the condition of the bag, and the fact that the van's passenger window was open supported the inference that the defendant discarded the bag while fleeing); *State v. Bradshaw*, 366 N.C. 90, 96–97 (2012) (sufficient evidence of constructive possession of drugs and a rifle when those items were found in a bedroom that was not under the defendant's exclusive control but several documents linked him to the contraband and placed him in the room within two days of when the contraband was found); *State v. Glover*, ___ N.C. App. ___, 833 S.E.2d 203 (2019) (defendant properly deemed in constructive possession of a metal tin found in the "personal space" next to his bedroom in a shared home when he admitted to having just ingested substances found in the metal tin); *State v. Wirt*, ___ N.C. App. ___, 822 S.E.2d 668 (2018) (notwithstanding his nonexclusive possession of a vehicle, the defendant's control as its driver was sufficient to give rise to an inference of constructive possession of drugs and a firearm in the vehicle; moreover, the State presented evidence of additional incriminating circumstances to support that inference); *State v. Guy*, ___ N.C. App. ___, 822 S.E.2d 66 (2018) (marijuana and a robbery victim's debit card were found near a gun in close proximity to the defendant and his vehicle; the gun matched one described by the victim as having been used in the robbery, and an officer located the defendant's car less than a quarter-mile from the victim's residence and about one minute after receiving information about the incident); *State v. Steele*, 260 N.C. App. 315, ___, 817 S.E.2d 487, 493 (2018) (in this trafficking case there was sufficient evidence that the defendant constructively possessed cocaine found in a bedroom dresser drawer where, among other things, the defendant and another person shared the bedroom, which was padlocked from the outside to prevent entry; the two had the only keys to the lock and the other person stated that she did not put the cocaine in the dresser and that it was not hers; and the defendant's own statements established that he knew the weight of the cocaine); *State v. Davis*, 236 N.C. App. 376, 383–84 (2014) (there was sufficient evidence that the defendant constructively possessed methamphetamine found in a duffle bag where, among other things, the defendant and his accomplice were the only people at the scene of the "one pot" outdoor meth lab and for approximately forty minutes both moved freely about the site where all of the items were laid out on a blanket); *State v. Rodelo*, 231 N.C. App. 660, 665–66 (2014) (in a trafficking by possession case there was sufficient evidence of constructive possession where the defendant was found hiding alone in a tractor-trailer where money was secreted; cocaine was found in a car parked, with its doors open, in close proximity to the tractor-trailer; the cash and the cocaine were packaged similarly; wrappings were all over the tractor-trailer and in the open area of a car parked close by; the defendant admitted knowing where the money was hidden; and the entire warehouse in which the vehicles were located had a chemical smell of cocaine); *State v. Torres-Gonzalez*, 227 N.C. App. 188, 195 (2013) (sufficient evidence in a trafficking by possession case involving an undercover sale); *State v. Hazel*, 226 N.C. App. 336, 344 (2013) (sufficient evidence that the defendant constructively possessed heroin found in an apartment that was not owned or rented by him); *State v. Chisholm*, 225 N.C. App. 592, 597 (2013) (sufficient evidence of constructive possession even though the defendant did not have exclusive possession of the bedroom where the drugs were found); *State v. Huerta*, 221 N.C. App. 436, 448–49 (2012) (sufficient evidence of constructive possession where the defendant admitted living for three years at the home where the drugs were found; where an illegally purchased pistol, ammunition, and more than $9,000 in cash were in his closet; and where he had more than $2,000 in cash on his person); and *State v. Adams*, 218 N.C. App. 589, 594–95 (2012) (sufficient evidence of constructive possession where the defendant drove a drug provider to a location that the defendant had arranged for a drug sale, knowing that the provider had the drugs).

For cases where there was insufficient evidence of constructive possession, see *State v. Royster*, ___ N.C. App. ___, 822 S.E.2d 489 (2018) (after the defendant produced a black box in exchange for his kidnapped father, a shooting broke out and one of the kidnappers ran into the woods while holding the box; approximately eighteen hours later, officers found a black box containing cocaine fifty–seventy-five yards into the woods; the box was dry, despite heavy rain, and a dry mason jar containing additional cocaine was found nearby), *aff'd*, 373 N.C. 157 (2019); *State v. Holloway*, 250 N.C. App. 674, 681 (2016) (the only evidence tying the defendant to a residence or to contraband was his presence at the residence on the afternoon in question and a single photograph of him found face down in a plastic storage bin in a bedroom of the residence); *State v. Dulin*, 247 N.C. App. 799, 809–10 (2016) (there was insufficient evidence that the defendant constructively possessed marijuana found in an uncovered fishing boat located in the yard of a home occupied by multiple people, including the defendant; the boat was roughly seventy feet from the house in an unfenced area, there was no evidence that the defendant had any ownership interest in or possession of the boat, and the defendant was never seen near the boat); and *State v. Garrett*, 246 N.C. App. 651, 655–56 (2016) (there was insufficient evidence of constructive possession of methamphetamine in a case that arose out of a controlled drug buy where, although the defendant led individuals to a trailer to buy drugs and entered the trailer with their money, the other individuals were the only ones who actually possessed the drugs).

Exceptions (new note)

Before searching a person or his or her premises or vehicle, an officer may ask the person whether a hypodermic needle or other sharp object that may cut or puncture the officer is on the defendant's person or in the premises or vehicle to be searched. If such an object is present and the person alerts the officer of that fact before the search, the person may not be charged with or prosecuted for possession of drug paraphernalia for the needle or sharp object or for possession of residual amounts of a controlled substance contained in the needle or sharp object. G.S. 90-113.22(c).

Greater and lesser-included offenses (page 706)

Simple possession is a lesser-included offense of possession of a controlled substance on the premises of a local confinement facility, and a defendant may not be convicted of both when they stem from the same act of possession. State v. Barnes, 229 N.C. App. 556, 568–69 (2013), *aff'd*, 367 N.C. 453 (2014) (per curiam).

Multiple convictions and punishments (page 706)

Where the defendant was in possession of a bag containing a mixture of two separate Schedule I controlled substances, two convictions were proper. State v. Williams, 252 N.C. App. 231, 234 (2017).

No double jeopardy violation occurs when a defendant is convicted of trafficking in methamphetamine, manufacturing methamphetamine, and possession of methamphetamine based on the same illegal substance. State v. Simpson, 230 N.C. App. 119, 126–27 (2013).

Limited immunity from prosecution (new note)

A 2013 law, S.L. 2013-23, provides limited immunity from prosecution for persons seeking medical assistance for themselves or others in the event of a drug-related overdose. The law enacts G.S. 90-96.2, providing that a person who experiences a drug-related overdose or who seeks medical assistance for someone experiencing a drug-related overdose shall not be prosecuted for

- a misdemeanor offense under G.S. 90-95(a)(3) or
- a felony offense under G.S. 90-95(a)(3) involving less than 1 gram of cocaine or heroin

if the evidence of the crime was obtained as a result of the person seeking medical assistance. G.S. 90-96.2(b), (c). The term "drug-related overdose" means "an acute condition, including mania, hysteria, extreme physical illness, coma, or death resulting from the consumption or use of a controlled substance, or another substance with which a controlled substance was combined, and that a layperson would reasonably believe to be a drug overdose that requires medical assistance." *Id.* § (a).

2016 legislation, S.L. 2016-88, sec. 4, enacted G.S. 90-113.27(c), providing limited immunity for employees, volunteers, and participants in authorized needle and hypodermic syringe exchange programs when those persons possess residual amounts of a controlled substance contained in a used needle, hypodermic syringe, or injection supplies obtained from or returned to a program.

Possession of a Controlled Substance at a Prison or Local Confinement Facility (page 707)

Notes (page 707)

Element (1) (new note)

This offense is a general intent crime, and there is no requirement that a defendant specifically intended to possess the controlled substance on the premises of a local confinement facility. State v. Barnes, 229 N.C. App. 556, 561–66 (2013) (rejecting the defendant's argument that he did not voluntarily enter the premises but was brought to the facility by officers against his wishes; the fact that the officers failed to warn the defendant that taking a controlled substance into the jail would constitute a separate offense was of no consequence), *aff'd*, 367 N.C. 453 (2014) (per curiam).

Element (2) (new note)

The defendant's own testimony that he had a "piece of dope . . . in the jail" was sufficient evidence that he possessed a controlled substance on the premises. State v. Poole, 223 N.C. App. 185, 194 (2012).

Greater and lesser-included offenses (new note)

Simple possession is a lesser-included offense of possession of a controlled substance on the premises of a local confinement facility, and a defendant may not be convicted of both when they stem from the same act of possession. *Barnes*, 229 N.C. App. at 568–69.

Possession of a Controlled Substance with Intent to Manufacture, Sell, or Deliver (page 708)

Notes (page 708)

Element (4) (page 708)

For cases where there was sufficient evidence of the requisite intent, see *State v. Coley*, 257 N.C. App. 780, 788–89 (2018) (although the defendant's vehicle contained only 11.5 grams of marijuana, it was packaged in two sandwich bags and a digital scale and twenty-three additional loose sandwich bags were found in the vehicle), *State v. Yisrael*, 255 N.C. App. 184, 193 (2017) (although only 10.88 grams of marijuana was found, its packaging was suggestive of the requisite intent and the 20-year-old defendant was carrying a large amount of cash on the grounds of a high school where he was not a student and a stolen, loaded handgun was found inside the vehicle), *aff'd per curiam*, 371 N.C. 108 (2018), and *State v. Blakney*, 233 N.C. App. 516, 520 (2014) (84.8 grams of marijuana was found in the defendant's car in multiple containers, including four dime bags, along with a box of sandwich bags, digital scales, and a large quantity of cash in small denominations).

Related Offenses Not in This Chapter (page 710)

Add the following offense to this list:

> Possession with intent to manufacture, distribute, dispense, deliver, or purchase marijuana on property used for industrial hemp production or in a manner intended to disguise the marijuana due to its proximity to industrial hemp. G.S. 106-568.57(a).

Possession of an Immediate Precursor with Intent to Manufacture a Controlled Substance (page 710)

Statute (page 710)

As noted above in this supplement, the list of immediate precursor chemicals in G.S. 90-95(d2) was amended by 2015 legislation. S.L. 2015-32, sec.1.

Notes (page 711)

Element (3) (page 711)

As noted above in this supplement, the list of immediate precursor chemicals in G.S. 90-95(d2) was amended by 2015 legislation. S.L. 2015-32, sec.1.

Add the following to this note:

> In a case involving possession of pseudoephedrine with intent to manufacture methamphet-amine, the court held that the evidence was sufficient even though the pseudoephedrine had not been identified through a chemical analysis. State v. Hooks, 243 N.C. App. 435, 445–46 (2015) (reasoning that chemical analysis is required only for a "controlled substance" and that pseudoephedrine is not such a substance).

Possession of Pseudoephedrine after Methamphetamine Conviction (new crime)

This offense was enacted by 2013 legislation, S.L. 2013-124, sec. 1, and amended by S.L. 2015-32, sec.1.

Statute

See G.S. 90-95(d1)(1)c., reproduced above in this supplement.

Elements

A person guilty of this offense

(1) possesses
(2) a pseudoephedrine product *and*
(3) has a prior conviction for
    (a) possession of methamphetamine,
    (b) possession with the intent to sell or deliver methamphetamine,
    (c) sale or delivery of methamphetamine,
    (d) trafficking in methamphetamine,
    (e) possession of an immediate precursor chemical, *or*
    (f) manufacture of methamphetamine.

Punishment

Class H felony. G.S. 90-95(d1).

Notes

Element (1). See the note on Element (2) to "Possession of a Controlled Substance" in the main volume.

Element (3). The prior conviction may be from any jurisdiction within the United States. G.S. 90-95(d1)(1)c.

Strict liability. This is a strict liability offense. State v. Miller, 246 N.C. App. 330, 336–38 (2016), *rev'd on other grounds*, 369 N.C. 658 (2017).

Constitutionality. For a case where the North Carolina Supreme Court rejected an as-applied constitutional challenge to the statute, see *Miller*, 369 N.C. 658 (rejecting the notion that the defendant's conviction rested on wholly passive conduct and concluding that it rested on his own active conduct).

Related Offenses Not in This Chapter

See the offenses listed under "Possession of an Immediate Precursor with Intent to Manufacture a Controlled Substance" in the main volume.

Counterfeit Controlled Substance Offenses (page 711)

Creating a Counterfeit Controlled Substance (page 711)

Notes (page 712)

Element (3) (page 712)

For another case supporting the statement in this note that the State need not prove all of the factors in G.S. 90-87(6)b. to prove that the substance was intentionally misrepresented, see *State v. Chisholm*, 225 N.C. App. 592, 595 (2013).

Sale or Delivery of a Counterfeit Controlled Substance (page 713)

Notes (page 713)

Multiple convictions and punishments (new note)

A defendant may not be separately convicted of both the sale and delivery of a counterfeit controlled substance arising from a single transfer. State v. Chevallier, ___ N.C. App. ___, 824 S.E.2d 440 (2019) (citing State v. Moore, 327 N.C. 378 (1990)).

Drug Offenses Involving Minors (page 714)

Manufacture, Sale, Delivery, or Possession of a Controlled Substance with Intent to Manufacture, Sell, or Deliver at or Near a School, Child Care Center, or Public Park (page 719)

Notes (page 720)

Element (5)(b) (page 720)

For a case where the evidence was insufficient to establish that the property was used for a child care center, see *State v. Piland*, ___ N.C. App. ___, 822 S.E.2d 876 (2018).

Trafficking (page 721)

Statute (page 721)

2012 legislation, S.L. 2012-188, sec. 5, amended G.S. 90-95(h), adding time to the maximum sentences for drug trafficking to cover early release onto post-release supervision. The act adds three months to the maximum sentences for Class C, D, and E trafficking and nine months to the maximum sentences for Class F, G, and H trafficking.

2018 legislation, S.L. 2018-44, sec. 7, amended G.S. 90-95(h)(3d), changing its coverage from MDPV to substituted cathinones as follows:

> (3d) Any person who sells, manufactures, delivers, transports, or possesses 28 grams or more of any substituted cathinone, as defined in G.S. 90-89(5)(j), or any mixture containing such substance shall be guilty of a felony, which felony shall be known as "trafficking in substituted cathinones," and if the quantity of such substance or mixture involved:
>
> a. Is 28 grams or more, but less than 200 grams, such person shall be punished as a Class F felon and shall be sentenced to a minimum term of 70 months and a maximum term of 93 months in the State's prison and shall be fined not less than fifty thousand dollars ($50,000);
>
> b. Is 200 grams or more, but less than 400 grams, such person shall be punished as a Class E felon and shall be sentenced to a minimum term of 90 months and a maximum term of 120 months in the State's prison and shall be fined not less than one hundred thousand dollars ($100,000);
>
> c. Is 400 grams or more, such person shall be punished as a Class C felon and shall be sentenced to a minimum term of 225 months and a maximum term of 282 months in the State's prison and shall be fined at least two hundred fifty thousand dollars ($250,000).

That same 2018 legislation repealed G.S. 90-95(h)(3e).

That same 2018 legislation also amended G.S. 90-95(h)(4), replacing the terms "opium or opiate" with "opium, opiate, or opioid." The revised subsection now reads as follows:

> (4) Any person who sells, manufactures, delivers, transports, or possesses four grams or more of opium, opiate, or opioid, or any salt, compound, derivative, or preparation of opium, opiate, or opioid (except apomorphine, nalbuphine, analoxone and naltrexone and their respective salts), including heroin, or any mixture containing such substance, shall be guilty of a felony which felony shall be known as "trafficking in opium, opiate, opioid, or heroin" and if the quantity of such controlled substance or mixture involved:
>
> a. Is four grams or more, but less than 14 grams, such person shall be punished as a Class F felon and shall be sentenced to a minimum term of 70 months and a maximum term of 93 months in the State's prison and shall be fined not less than fifty thousand dollars ($50,000);
>
> b. Is 14 grams or more, but less than 28 grams, such person shall be punished as a Class E felon and shall be sentenced to a minimum term of 90 months and a maximum term of 120 months in the State's prison and shall be fined not less than one hundred thousand dollars ($100,000);
>
> c. Is 28 grams or more, such person shall be punished as a Class C felon and shall be sentenced to a minimum term of 225 months and a maximum term of 282 months in the State's prison and shall be fined not less than five hundred thousand dollars ($500,000).

That same 2018 legislation also amended G.S. 90-95(h)(4b) to correct a typographical error in the statute. It had stated that the proscribed offense shall be known as "trafficking in MDADMA." The 2018 amendment clarifies that the proscribed offense is "trafficking in MDA/MDMA."

Trafficking in Marijuana (page 725)

Punishment (page 725)

For 2012 legislative changes to the punishment provision, see "Statute," above in this supplement under "Trafficking."

Notes (page 726)

Element (1) (page 726)

See this note to "Possession of a Controlled Substance," above in this supplement.

In a trafficking by possession and transportation case there was sufficient evidence of knowing possession and transportation where the defendant drove the vehicle that contained the cocaine. State v. Lopez, 219 N.C. App. 139, 149–50 (2012).

For a case where the evidence was insufficient to establish that the defendant knowingly possessed or transported the controlled substance, see *State v. Velazquez-Perez*, 233 N.C. App. 585, 588–93 (2014) (drugs were found in secret compartments of a truck driven by the defendant Villalvavo but owned by a passenger, Velazquez-Perez, who hired Villalvavo to drive the truck; while evidence regarding the truck's log books may have been incriminating as to Velazquez-Perez, it did not apply to Villalvavo, who had not been working for Velazquez-Perez long and had no stake in the company or control over Velazquez-Perez; Villalvavo's nervousness during the stop did not constitute adequate incriminating circumstances).

Element (3) (page 727)

As a result of 2015 and 2016 legislation, S.L. 2015-299, sec. 2; S.L. 2016-93, sec. 6, add the following at the end of this note, before the ending quotation mark:

The term does not include industrial hemp as defined in G.S. 106-568.51, when the industrial hemp is produced and used in compliance with rules issued by the North Carolina Industrial Hemp Commission.

Element (5) (page 727)

When a defendant simultaneously possesses more than one cache of controlled substances, the amounts of each cache may—in certain circumstances—be combined to reach the trafficking amount. State v. Hazel, 226 N.C. App. 336, 347 (2013) (trafficking in heroin by possession case; amount of heroin recovered from the defendant's person outside an apartment was combined with heroin recovered from the apartment).

Greater and lesser-included offenses (page 728)

Conspiracy to traffic in cocaine is not a lesser-included offense of trafficking in cocaine. State v. Rodelo, 231 N.C. App. 660, 667 (2014).

Multiple convictions and punishments (page 728)

No double jeopardy violation occurs when a defendant is convicted of trafficking in methamphetamine, manufacturing methamphetamine, and possession of methamphetamine based on the same illegal substance. State v. Simpson, 230 N.C. App. 119, 126–27 (2013).

Relation to other offenses (page 729)

Delete this note.

Trafficking in Synthetic Cannabinoids (page 729)

Punishment (page 729)

For 2012 legislative changes to the punishment provision, see "Statute," above in this supplement under "Trafficking."

Notes (page 730)

Elements (3) and (5) (new note)

A synthetic cannabinoid is defined in G.S. 90-89(7), reproduced at the beginning of this chapter in this supplement.

Element (5) (page 730)

When a defendant simultaneously possesses more than one cache of controlled substances, the amounts of each cache may—in certain circumstances—be combined to reach the trafficking amount. State v. Hazel, 226 N.C. App. 336, 347 (2013) (trafficking in heroin by possession case; amount of heroin recovered from the defendant's person outside an apartment was combined with heroin recovered from the apartment).

The entire weight of a mixture containing a controlled substance covered by the trafficking statutes can be used to support trafficking charges; the fact that the mixture is at an intermediate stage in the manufacturing process and is not ingestible, is unstable, and is not ready for distribution is irrelevant. State v. Davis, 236 N.C. App. 376, 386–87 (2014).

For purposes of the trafficking statutes, a mixture includes a combination of a controlled substance and rice, added to remove moisture. State v. Miranda, 235 N.C. App. 601, 608–09 (2014) (rejecting the defendant's argument that a combination of cocaine and rice did not constitute a mixture within the meaning of the trafficking statute).

Constitutionality (new note)

This trafficking offense and the ones listed below cover trafficking in the specified controlled substance and in mixtures containing that substance. The North Carolina Court of Appeals has rejected constitutional challenges grounded in the statute's coverage of mixtures. State v. Ellison, 213 N.C. App. 300, 309–12 (2011) (rejecting the defendant's due process and cruel and unusual punishment arguments in a trafficking in opium case), *aff'd on other grounds*, 366 N.C. 439 (2013).

Relation to other offenses (new note)

The listing of a particular controlled substance on the drug schedules does not limit the State's ability to prosecute a defendant for trafficking in a substance when a trafficking statute otherwise applies. *Ellison*, 213 N.C. App. at 323 ("the controlled substance schedule to which a particular opiate derivative is assigned has nothing to do with the extent to which activities involving that substance are subject to punishment under the trafficking statutes").

Trafficking in Methaqualone (page 730)

The section on "Punishment" and the new notes listed above in this supplement under "Trafficking in Synthetic Cannabinoids" apply to this offense as well.

Trafficking in Cocaine (page 731)

The section on "Punishment" and the new notes listed above in this supplement under "Trafficking in Synthetic Cannabinoids" apply to this offense as well.

Trafficking in Methamphetamine (page 732)

The section on "Punishment" and the new notes listed above in this supplement under "Trafficking in Synthetic Cannabinoids" apply to this offense as well.

Trafficking in Amphetamine (page 733)

The section on "Punishment" and the new notes listed above in this supplement under "Trafficking in Synthetic Cannabinoids" apply to this offense as well.

Trafficking in Substituted Cathinones (page 734) (revised title)

The section on "Punishment" and the new notes listed above in this supplement under "Trafficking in Synthetic Cannabinoids" apply to this offense as well.

2018 legislation, S.L. 2018-44, sec. 7, amended this offense so that it now applies to substituted cathinones, as defined in G.S. 90-89(5)(j), instead of MDPV.

Elements (page 734)

As a result of the 2018 legislation noted above, the elements of this offense should read as follows:

A person guilty of this offense

- (1) knowingly
- (2) (a) sells, manufactures, delivers, transports, or possesses *or*
  - (b) conspires to sell, manufacture, deliver, transport, or possess
- (3) substituted cathinones or any mixture containing substituted cathinones
- (4) to another person (if the person sells or delivers) *and*
- (5) the quantity of substituted cathinones or any mixture containing substituted cathinones is
  - (a) 28 grams or more but less than 200 grams,
  - (b) 200 grams or more but less than 400 grams, *or*
  - (c) 400 grams or more.

Notes (page 735)

Elements (3) and (5) (new note)
A substituted cathinone is defined in G.S. 90-89(5)(j). G.S. 90-95(h)(3d).

Trafficking in Mephedrone (page 735)

2018 legislation, S.L. 2018-44, sec. 7, repealed the statute proscribing trafficking in mephedrone.

Trafficking in Opium, Opiate, Opioid, or Heroin (page 736) (revised title)

The section on "Punishment" and the new notes listed above in this supplement under "Trafficking in Synthetic Cannabinoids" apply to this offense as well.

Elements (page 736)

As a result of 2018 legislation, S.L. 2018-44, sec. 7, when stating the covered controlled substances the elements should refer to opium, opiate, opioid, or heroin.

Notes (page 736)

Element (3) (page 736)

As a result of that same 2018 legislation, delete the first paragraph of this note and replace it with the following:

> The statute prohibits trafficking in the following substances: "opium, opiate, or opioid, or any salt, compound, derivative, or preparation of opium, opiate, or opioid (except apomorphine, nalbuphine, analoxone and naltrexone and their respective salts), including heroin, or any mixture containing such substance." G.S. 90-95(h)(4).

Add the following to this note:

> This trafficking offense bases criminal liability on the total weight of the mixture involved; tablets and pills are mixtures covered by that provision, including prescription pharmaceuticals. State v. Ellison, 366 N.C. 439, 443–44 (2013).

> **Immunity for treatment with opioid antagonist** (new note)
> G.S. 90-12.7, as amended by S.L. 2017-74, sec. 2, provides immunity, in certain circumstances, for treating an overdose with the opioid antagonist naloxone hydrochloride.

Trafficking in LSD (page 737)

The section on "Punishment" and the new notes listed above in this supplement under "Trafficking in Synthetic Cannabinoids" apply to this offense as well.

Trafficking in MDA and MDMA (page 738)

The section on "Punishment" and the new notes listed above in this supplement under "Trafficking in Synthetic Cannabinoids" apply to this offense as well.

Controlled Substance Offenses Involving Fraud, Misrepresentation, or Similar Activities (page 740)

Obtaining a Controlled Substance by Misrepresenting Oneself as a Licensed Practitioner (page 740)

Statute (page 740)

Replace the statute reproduced in the main volume with the following:

> **§ 90-108. Prohibited acts; penalties.**
> (a) It shall be unlawful for any person:
> > (1) Other than practitioners licensed under Articles 1, 2, 4, 6, 11, 12A of this Chapter to represent to any registrant or practitioner who manufactures, distributes, or dispenses a controlled substance under the provision of this Article that he or she is a licensed practitioner in order to secure or attempt to secure any controlled substance as defined in this Article or to in any way impersonate a practitioner for the purpose of securing or attempting to secure any drug requiring a prescription from a practitioner as listed above and who is licensed by this State.

> *[Subsections (2) through (15) are not reproduced here.]*

(b) Any person who violates this section shall be guilty of a Class 1 misdemeanor. Provided, that if the criminal pleading alleges that the violation was committed intentionally, and upon trial it is specifically found that the violation was committed intentionally, such violations shall be a Class I felony . . . .

[*Subsections (1) through (3) are not reproduced here.*]

Related Offenses Not in This Chapter (page 742)

As a result of 2018 legislation, S.L. 2018-44, sec. 9, add the following to this section:

Embezzle, misapply, divert, etc., a controlled substance prescribed to another by one providing medical care or related services. G.S. 14-108(a)(15).

Maintaining a Store, Dwelling, Vehicle, Boat, or Other Place for Use, Storage, or Sale of Controlled Substances (page 743)

Notes (page 744)

Element (1) (page 744)

For a case where this Element was satisfied, see *State v. Huerta*, 221 N.C. App. 436, 450 (2012).

Element (2) (page 744)

As used in this Element, the term "keeps" "refers to possessing something for at least a short period of time—or intending to retain possession of something in the future—for a certain use." State v. Rogers, 371 N.C. 397, 402 (2018).

For cases where the evidence was sufficient to establish this Element, see *Rogers, id.* at 401–02 (the evidence was sufficient to establish this Element with respect to a vehicle where, during ninety minutes of police surveillance, the defendant was the only person who used the car and a service receipt dated two and one-half months earlier and containing his name was found in it); *State v. Alvarez*, ___ N.C. App. ___, ___, 818 S.E.2d 178, 182 (2018), *aff'd*, 372 N.C. 303 (2019) (although the vehicle alleged to have been used in the offense was registered in his wife's name, the defendant described it as "[his] truck" and acknowledged that no one else used it); *State v. Williams*, 242 N.C. App. 361, 371 (2015) (the defendant received mail addressed to him at the residence alleged to have been used in the offense; his probation officer visited him there to conduct routine home contacts; the defendant's personal effects were at the residence, including a pay stub and work gear; and he identified the house to a third party as being his; the court rejected the defendant's argument that the evidence was insufficient because it failed to show that he was financially or otherwise responsible for the dwelling or its upkeep, noting that residency standing alone can establish this Element).

For another case where the evidence was insufficient to establish this Element, see *State v. Holloway*, 250 N.C. App. 674, 683–84 (2016) (there was no evidence that the defendant was the owner or lessee of the residence alleged to have been involved in the offense, paid for its utilities or upkeep, had been seen in or around the dwelling, or lived there).

Element (4)(a) (new note)

A defendant cannot be convicted under this prong on the basis of his or her own use of drugs in his or her vehicle. State v. Simpson, 230 N.C. App. 119, 121–22 (2013).

Element (4)(b) (page 745)

Delete the fourth and fifth sentences of this note and replace them with the following:

As used in Element (2), the term "keeps" "refers to possessing something for at least a short period of time—or intending to retain possession of something in the future—for a certain use." *Rogers*, 371 N.C. at 402. As used in Element (4)(b), the term "keeping" has a different meaning.

The second paragraph of this note states: "As used in Element (4)(b), the term 'keeping' denotes not just possession, but possession that occurs over a duration of time.' State v. Dickerson, 152 N.C. App. 714, 716 (2002) (quoting State v. Mitchell, 336 N.C. 22, 32 (1994))." The North Carolina Supreme Court's decision in *Rogers*, 371 N.C. at 406, disavows the quoted language from *Mitchell*. As a result, delete all text in the second paragraph of this note suggesting that keeping denotes possession over time and replace it with the following:

> In *Rogers*, 371 N.C. at 403, the North Carolina Supreme Court held that as used in this Element, the term "keeping" refers to the storing of drugs. In so holding, the court specifically rejected any language in *Mitchell*, 336 N.C. at 32, that has been read as requiring that the "keeping" of drugs requires possession that occurs over a duration of time. *Id.* The supreme court explained:

>> [T]he statutory text does not require that drugs be kept for "a duration of time." . . . [T]he linchpin of the inquiry . . . is whether the defendant was using th[e] vehicle, building, or other place for the storing of drugs. So, for instance, when the evidence indicates that a defendant has possessed a car for at least a short period of time, but that he had just begun storing drugs inside his car at the time of his arrest, that defendant has still violated [the statute]—even if, arguably, he has not stored the drugs for any appreciable "duration of time." The critical question is *whether* a defendant's car is used to store drugs, not *how long* the defendant's car has been used to store drugs for. As a result, we reject any notion that [the statute] requires that a car kept or maintained by a defendant be used to store drugs for a certain minimum period of time—or that evidence of drugs must be found in the vehicle, building, or other place on more than one occasion—for a defendant to have violated [the statute]. But again, merely having drugs in a car (or other place) is not enough to justify a conviction . . . . The evidence and all reasonable inferences drawn from the evidence must indicate, based "on the totality of the circumstances," that the drugs are also being stored there. To the extent that Mitchell's "duration of time" requirement conflicts with the text of [the statute], therefore, this aspect of *Mitchell* is disavowed.

> *Rogers*, 371 N.C. at 406 (citation omitted). In *Rogers*, the supreme court went on to hold that the evidence in the case before it was sufficient to establish that the defendant was using the vehicle in question for the keeping of controlled substances. *Id.* (the court noted that cocaine was found in the gas-cap compartment and that no one else was seen using the vehicle; because neither the defendant nor anyone else accessed the gas-cap compartment, it can be inferred that the cocaine was placed there before police surveillance began; the defendant's actions—arriving at a hotel, remaining for forty-five minutes with the drugs in the compartment, and then leaving in the vehicle—indicate that he was not using the car only to transport drugs; additionally, the court noted, a person who wants to store contraband will prefer to do so in a hidden place, "which is exactly what putting the cocaine in the gas-cap compartment would accomplish," *id.* at 404; the court further noted that putting the drugs in a place that is hard to access suggests storage rather than mere transportation; this evidence, the court concluded, indicates that the defendant was using the vehicle to store cocaine; moreover, other evidence in the case suggesting that the defendant was selling drugs supports an inference that the defendant was using the vehicle to store cocaine).

The second paragraph of this note also states that "when the allegation is that the property is being used for the selling of controlled substances, evidence of more than one sale is required." As a preliminary matter, based on pre-*Rogers* case law, it is more accurate to state that while evidence of one sale of a controlled substance does not by itself demonstrate that the property was kept or maintained for selling controlled substances, the court may look at the totality of the circumstances. State v. Dunston, 256 N.C. App. 103, 106 (2017), *aff'd per curiam*, 371 N.C. 76 (2018). Additionally, based on *Rogers* and its rejection of the notion that the term "keeping" requires possession that occurs over a duration of time, it is not clear that the term "selling" requires more than one sale.

Because cases holding that the evidence was sufficient to establish this Element under the stricter pre-*Rogers* standard are likely to remain good law under the more permissive *Rogers* test, add the following to this note:

> For additional cases where the evidence was sufficient to establish this Element, see *State v. Alvarez*, ___ N.C. App. ___, ___, 818 S.E.2d 178, 182 (2018) (under a totality of the circumstances the evidence was sufficient where, among other things, a trafficking amount of cocaine was found in a false-bottomed compartment in a truck-bed floor that was constructed by the defendant; the cocaine was wrapped in plastic and oil to evade detection by canine units; and the defendant was involved in a drug-related transaction immediately before his arrest), *aff'd*, 372 N.C. 303 (2019) (mem.); *State v. Dunston*, 256 N.C. App. 103, 106 (2017) (the defendant was in the vehicle alleged to have been used in the offense at a known drug location; he unwrapped and rerolled cigars after manipulating them, activity an officer thought was consistent with distributing marijuana; the driver engaged in a hand-to-hand exchange of cash with another person and was discovered to be in possession of marijuana; and a search found that the defendant no longer had possession of the "cigars" but possessed a trafficking quantity of heroin along with plastic bags, two sets of digital scales, three cell phones, and $155 in cash), *aff'd per curiam*, 371 N.C. 76 (2018); *State v. Rousseau*, 250 N.C. App. 825, *3 (2016) (unpublished) (rejecting the defendant's argument that the evidence was insufficient to show that a vehicle was used for the selling or keeping of a controlled substance; officers found marijuana remnants throughout the vehicle's interior space as well as a sock containing 29.927 grams of marijuana in the vehicle's engine compartment), *aff'd per curiam*, 370 N.C. 268 (2017); *State v. Alston*, 254 N.C. App. 90, 94 (2017) (controlled substances and drug paraphernalia were found in a residence; a security camera set up in the living room of that residence observed the front yard; the defendant, a convicted felon, had constructive possession of a handgun; an officer observed traffic at the residence over several days consistent with drug transactions; and a confidential source bought a controlled substance from the residence); and *State v. Williams*, 242 N.C. App. 361, 373 (2015) (officers found a bag containing 39.7 grams of 4-methylethcathinone and methylone, a plastic bag containing "numerous little corner baggies," a set of digital scales, and $460 in twenty dollar bills).
>
> For a post-*Rogers* case where the evidence of this Element was insufficient, see *State v. Miller*, ___ N.C. App. ___, 826 S.E.2d 562 (2019) (merely having drugs in a car does not justify a conviction under this offense when, under the totality of the circumstances, there was no other evidence of drugs, drug paraphernalia, cash, weapons, or other implements of the drug trade).

Drug Paraphernalia Offenses (revised title)

Possession of Drug Paraphernalia (page 747)

Statute (page 747)

2014 legislation, S.L. 2014-119, sec. 3(a), amended G.S. 90-113.22(a) to read as follows:

> (a) It is unlawful for any person to knowingly use, or to possess with intent to use, drug paraphernalia to plant, propagate, cultivate, grow, harvest, manufacture, compound, convert, produce, process, prepare, test, analyze, package, repackage, store, contain, or conceal a controlled substance other than marijuana which it would be unlawful to possess, or to inject, ingest, inhale, or otherwise introduce into the body a controlled substance other than marijuana which it would be unlawful to possess.

2013 legislation, S.L. 2013-147, added a new subsection, (c), to the statute, which subsequently was amended by 2015 legislation, S.L. 2015-284, sec. 2, to read as follows:

> (c) Prior to searching a person, a person's premises, or a person's vehicle, an officer may ask the person whether the person is in possession of a hypodermic needle or other sharp object that may cut or puncture the officer or whether such a hypodermic needle or other sharp object is on the premises or in the vehicle to be searched. If there is a hypodermic needle or other sharp object on the person, on the person's premises, or in the person's vehicle and the person alerts the officer of that fact prior to the search, the person shall not be charged with or prosecuted for possession of drug paraphernalia for the needle or sharp object, or for residual amounts of a controlled substance contained in the needle or sharp object. The exemption under this subsection does not apply to any other drug paraphernalia that may be present and found during the search. For purposes of this subsection, the term "officer" includes "criminal justice officers" as defined in G.S. 17C-2(3) and a "justice officer" as defined in G.S. 17E-2(3).

2019 legislation, S.L. 2019-159, added a new subsection, (d), to the statute, effective July 11, 2019, to read as follows:

> (d) Notwithstanding the provisions of subsection (a) of this section, it is not unlawful for (i) a person who introduces a controlled substance into his or her body, or intends to introduce a controlled substance into his or her body, to knowingly use, or to possess with intent to use, testing equipment for identifying or analyzing the strength, effectiveness, or purity of that controlled substance or (ii) a governmental or nongovernmental organization that promotes scientifically proven ways of mitigating health risks associated with drug use and other high-risk behaviors to possess such testing equipment or distribute such testing equipment to a person who intends to introduce a controlled substance into his or her body.

Notes (page 749)

Element (2) (new note)

For a discussion of actual and constructive possession in the context of drug possession offenses, see the note on Element (2) to "Possession of a Controlled Substance."

For cases where the evidence was sufficient to establish that the defendant possessed drug paraphernalia, see *State v. Sawyers*, 256 N.C. App. 339, 345–46 (2017) (the marijuana pipe in question was found in a crashed vehicle; although the defendant did not have exclusive possession of the vehicle, sufficient incriminating circumstances established constructive possession, including that the defendant was driving the vehicle, the pipe was found on the driver's side floorboard, and the defendant admitted ownership of a small amount of marijuana found on his person); *State v. Dulin*, 247 N.C. App. 799, 804–06 (2016) (paraphernalia (including, among other items, a digital scale and a marijuana grinder) was in plain view in a common living area of a home over which the defendant exercised nonexclusive control; the defendant spent hours at the house on the day in question and admitted that a blunt was in his truck parked out front;

police found marijuana in the truck's console and in the house behind a photograph of the defendant; and several people visited the house while the defendant was there, including a man who shook hands with the defendant as if they were passing an item back and forth).

Element (5) (new note)
As a result of 2014 legislation, this offense pertains to controlled substances other than marijuana. G.S. 90-113.22(a) (as amended by S.L. 2014-119, sec. 3(a)). If the controlled substance is marijuana, "Possession of Marijuana Paraphernalia," below, applies.

Exceptions (new note)
Before searching a person or his or her premises or vehicle, an officer may ask the person whether a hypodermic needle or other sharp object that may cut or puncture the officer is on the defendant's person or in the premises or vehicle to be searched. If such an object is present and the person alerts the officer of that fact before the search, the person may not be charged with or prosecuted for possession of drug paraphernalia for the needle or sharp object or for possession of residual amounts of a controlled substance contained in the needle or sharp object. G.S. 90-113.22(c). The exception does not apply to any other drug paraphernalia found during the search. *Id.*

A person who introduces or intends to introduce a controlled substance into his or her body may use or possess testing equipment for identifying or analyzing the strength, effectiveness, or purity of that controlled substance. A governmental or nongovernmental organization that promotes scientifically proven ways of mitigating health risks associated with drug use and other high-risk behaviors may also possess such testing equipment or distribute it to potential controlled substance users. G.S. 90-113.22(d).

Greater and lesser-included offenses (new note)
"Possession of Marijuana Paraphernalia," below, is a lesser-included offense of this one. G.S. 90-113.22A.

Limited immunity from prosecution (new note)
A 2013 law, S.L. 2013-23, provides limited immunity from prosecution for persons seeking medical assistance for themselves or others in the event of a drug-related overdose. The law enacts G.S. 90-96.2, providing that a person who experiences a drug-related overdose or who seeks medical assistance for someone experiencing a drug-related overdose shall not be prosecuted for this offense if the evidence of the crime was obtained as a result of the person seeking medical assistance. G.S. 90-96.2(b), (c). The term "drug-related overdose" means "an acute condition, including mania, hysteria, extreme physical illness, coma, or death resulting from the consumption or use of a controlled substance, or another substance with which a controlled substance was combined, and that a layperson would reasonably believe to be a drug overdose that requires medical assistance." G.S. 90-96.2(a).

2016 legislation, S.L. 2016-88, sec. 4, enacted G.S. 90-113.27(c), providing limited immunity for employees, volunteers, and participants in authorized needle and hypodermic syringe exchange programs when those persons possess needles, hypodermic syringes, or other injection supplies obtained from or returned to an exchange program.

Possession of Marijuana Paraphernalia (new crime)
Statute
See G.S. 90-113.21, reproduced in the main volume under "Possession of Drug Paraphernalia."
§ 90-113.22A. Possession of marijuana drug paraphernalia.
(a) It is unlawful for any person to knowingly use, or to possess with intent to use, drug paraphernalia to plant, propagate, cultivate, grow, harvest, manufacture, compound,

convert, produce, process, prepare, test, analyze, package, repackage, store, contain, or conceal marijuana or to inject, ingest, inhale, or otherwise introduce marijuana into the body.

    (b) A violation of this section is a Class 3 misdemeanor. A violation of this section shall be a lesser included offense of G.S. 90-113.22.

2019 legislation, S.L. 2019-159, added a new subsection, (c), to the statute, effective July 11, 2019, to read as follows:

    (c) Notwithstanding the provisions of subsection (a) of this section, it is not unlawful for (i) a person who introduces a controlled substance into his or her body, or intends to introduce a controlled substance into his or her body, to knowingly use, or to possess with intent to use, testing equipment for identifying or analyzing the strength, effectiveness, or purity of that controlled substance or (ii) a governmental or nongovernmental organization that promotes scientifically proven ways of mitigating health risks associated with drug use and other high-risk behaviors to possess such testing equipment or distribute such testing equipment to a person who intends to introduce a controlled substance into his or her body.

Elements

A person guilty of this offense

  (1) knowingly

  (2) uses or possesses with the intent to use

  (3) drug paraphernalia

  (4) for any of the following purposes:

    (a) to plant, propagate, cultivate, grow, harvest, manufacture, compound, convert, produce, process, prepare, test, analyze, package, repackage, store, contain, or conceal *or*

    (b) to inject, ingest, inhale, or otherwise introduce into the body

  (5) marijuana.

Punishment

Class 3 misdemeanor. G.S. 90-113.22A(b).

Notes

Generally. This offense was enacted in 2014. S.L. 2014-119, sec. 3(b). In terms of elements, it is the same as "Possession of Drug Paraphernalia" except that this offense pertains only to marijuana paraphernalia. Thus, the relevant notes to that offense apply here as well.

Greater and lesser-included offenses. This offense is a lesser-included offense of "Possession of Drug Paraphernalia." G.S. 90-113.22A(b).

Exceptions (new note)

A person who introduces or intends to introduce a controlled substance into his or her body may use or possess testing equipment for identifying or analyzing the strength, effectiveness, or purity of that controlled substance. A governmental or nongovernmental organization that promotes scientifically proven ways of mitigating health risks associated with drug use and other high-risk behaviors may also possess such testing equipment or distribute it to potential controlled substance users. G.S. 90-113.22A(c).

Related Offenses Not in This Chapter

See the offenses listed under "Possession of Drug Paraphernalia."

28

Motor Vehicle Offenses

Driving While License Revoked or Disqualified (page 755)

Statute (page 755)

Several pieces of legislation, S.L. 2012-146, sec. 8; S.L. 2013-360, sec. 18B.14(f); S.L. 2015-186, sec. 2; S.L. 2015-264, sec. 38(a); S.L. 2017-186, sec. 2(kkkk), have amended the statute so that subsections (a), (a1), (a2), and (a3) read as follows:

(a) Driving While License Revoked.—Except as provided in subsections (a1) or (a2) of this section, any person whose drivers license has been revoked who drives any motor vehicle upon the highways of the State while the license is revoked is guilty of a Class 3 misdemeanor.

(a1) Driving While License Revoked for Impaired Driving.—Any person whose drivers license has been revoked for an impaired driving revocation as defined in G.S. 20-28.2(a) and who drives any motor vehicle upon the highways of the State is guilty of a Class 1 misdemeanor. Upon conviction, the person's license shall be revoked for an additional period of one year for the first offense, two years for the second offense, and permanently for a third or subsequent offense.

If the person's license was originally revoked for an impaired driving revocation, the court may order as a condition of probation that the offender abstain from alcohol consumption and verify compliance by use of a continuous alcohol monitoring system, of a type approved by the Division of Adult Correction and Juvenile Justice of the Department of Public Safety, for a minimum period of 90 days.

The restoree of a revoked drivers license who operates a motor vehicle upon the highways of the State without maintaining financial responsibility as provided by law shall be punished as for driving without a license.

(a2) Driving Without Reclaiming License.—A person convicted under subsection (a) or (a1) of this section shall be punished as if the person had been convicted of driving without a license under G.S. 20-35 if the person demonstrates to the court that either of the following is true:

(1) At the time of the offense, the person's license was revoked solely under G.S. 20-16.5 and one of the following applies:
   a. The offense occurred more than 45 days after the effective date of a revocation order issued under G.S. 20-16.5(f) and the period of revocation was 45 days as provided under subdivision (3) of that subsection; or
   b. The offense occurred more than 30 days after the effective date of the revocation order issued under any other provision of G.S. 20-16.5.

(2) At the time of the offense the person had met the requirements of G.S. 50-13.12, or G.S. 110-142.2 and was eligible for reinstatement of the person's drivers license privilege as provided therein.

In addition, a person punished under this subsection shall be treated for drivers license and insurance rating purposes as if the person had been convicted of driving without a license under G.S. 20-35, and the conviction report sent to the Division must indicate that the person is to be so treated.

(a3) Driving After Notification or Failure to Appear.—A person shall be guilty of a Class 1 misdemeanor if:

(1) The person operates a motor vehicle upon a highway while that person's license is revoked for an impaired drivers license revocation after the Division has sent notification in accordance with G.S. 20-48; or

(2) The person fails to appear for two years from the date of the charge after being charged with an implied consent offense.

Upon conviction, the person's drivers license shall be revoked for an additional period of one year for the first offense, two years for the second offense, and permanently for a third or subsequent offense. The restoree of a revoked drivers license who operates a motor vehicle upon the highways of the State without maintaining financial responsibility as provided by law shall be punished as for driving without a license.

2015 legislation, S.L. 2015-186, sec. 2, amended subsection (d) so that the first sentence of that subsection reads as follows:

A person who was convicted of a violation that disqualified the person and required the person's drivers license to be revoked who drives a motor vehicle during the revocation period is punishable as provided in subsection (a1) of this section.

Driving While License Revoked (page 756)

Punishment (page 756)

As a result of the legislation noted above, delete the text of this section and replace it with the following:

Class 3 misdemeanor, except that if the circumstances listed in G.S. 20-28(a2) apply, the person will be punished as if he or she had been convicted of driving without a license under G.S. 20-35. G.S. 20-28(a2).

Notes (page 757)
Element (2) (page 757)

As a result of 2016 legislation, S.L. 2016-90, sec. 13(a), delete the text after the first sentence of this note and replace it with the following:

Neither mopeds nor electric assisted bicycles are motor vehicles. G.S. 20-4.01(7a) (definition of electric assisted bicycle); -4.01(23) (definition of motor vehicle); -4.01(27)(d1) (definition of moped).

Element (4) (page 757)

2016 legislation, S.L. 2016-90, sec. 10(c), amended G.S. 20-48, allowing the DMV to give notice by email or other electronic means under certain circumstances.

For another case stating that the defendant must have actual or constructive knowledge of the revocation, see *State v. Green*, 258 N.C. App. 87, 91 (2018) (trial court committed prejudicial error by failing to instruct the jury on this issue where the defendant testified that he did not receive the DMV's notice and offered evidence to explain why the mailed notification might not have reached him).

Related Offenses Not in This Chapter (page 758)

The statutory citation for the second offense in this list should be to G.S. 20-28.

Driving While License Revoked for an Impaired Driving Revocation (page 758)

Statute (page 758)

As a result of the 2015 legislation noted above, the statutory citation in this section should read as follows:

G.S. 20-28(a1).

Punishment (page 758)

As a result of the 2015 legislation noted above, delete the text of this section and replace it with the following:

Class 1 misdemeanor, G.S. 20-28(a1), except that if the circumstances listed in G.S. 20-28(a2) apply, the person will be punished as if he or she had been convicted of driving without a license under G.S. 20-35. G.S. 20-28(a2).

Failure to Appear after an Implied Consent Offense Charge (page 760)

Statute (page 760)

As a result of the 2015 legislation noted above, the statutory citation in this section should read as follows:

G.S. 20-28(a3).

Impaired Driving and Related Offenses (page 762)

Impaired Driving (page 762)

Punishment (page 762)

2012 legislation, S.L. 2012-146, sec. 9, amended G.S. 20-179(g) (Level One punishment) to provide that a judge may reduce the minimum term of imprisonment to a term of not less than 10 days if a condition of special probation is imposed requiring the defendant to abstain from alcohol consumption and be monitored by a continuous alcohol monitoring (CAM) system for a period of not less than 120 days. Pretrial CAM monitoring may be credited against the 120-day monitoring period, up to 60 days.

S.L. 2012-146 also amended G.S. 20-179(h) (Level Two punishment) to now provide that the term of imprisonment may be suspended only if a condition of special probation is imposed to require the defendant to serve a term of imprisonment of at least 7 days or to abstain from consuming alcohol for at least 90 consecutive days, as verified by a CAM system. Up to 60 days of pretrial CAM monitoring may be credited against the 90-day monitoring period. 2013 legislation, S.L. 2013-348, made additional changes to G.S. 20-179(h), requiring the completion of 240 hours of community service in certain circumstances.

As amended by S.L. 2012-194, S.L. 2012-146 also added new subsections, (k2) and (k3), to G.S. 20-179 providing as follows:

- The judge may order as a condition of special probation for any level of offense under G.S. 20-179 that the defendant abstain from alcohol consumption as verified by a CAM system. G.S. 20-179(k2).

- The court may authorize probation officers to require defendants to submit to CAM for assessment purposes if the defendant has been required to abstain from alcohol consumption during the term of probation and the probation officer believes the defendant is consuming alcohol. G.S. 20-179(k3). The defendant bears the cost of the CAM in these circumstances. *Id.*

Notes (page 764)

Element (1) (page 764)

Although the vehicle's engine was not running when the officer approached, the evidence was sufficient to establish that the defendant was driving the vehicle when it was parked by the front door of a hotel where guests typically stop to check in, the defendant was sitting in the driver's seat, the vehicle was registered to the defendant, and the defendant admitted that he had been driving. State v. Burris, 253 N.C. App. 525 (2017).

There was sufficient evidence, apart from the defendant's extrajudicial confession that he was driving the vehicle, to establish that the defendant was in fact the driver when the defendant was the only person in the vehicle and he was sitting in the driver's seat. State v. Reeves, 218 N.C. App. 570, 573–74 (2012).

Element (2) (page 765)

As a result of 2016 legislation, S.L. 2016-90, sec. 13(a), delete the last sentence of the first paragraph of this note and replace it with the following:

Mopeds and electric assisted bicycles are vehicles but are not motor vehicles. G.S. 20-4.01(7a) (definition of electric assisted bicycle), -4.01(23) (definition of motor vehicle), and -4.01(27)(d1) (definition of moped).

Element (3) (page 765)

In *State v. Ricks*, 237 N.C. App. 359, 364–66 (2014), the court held that a cut-through on a vacant lot was not a "public vehicular area" and that when instructing the jury on this Element, the court should give the entire statutory definition of that term.

Element (4)(a) (page 765)

In a felony death by vehicle case, the evidence was sufficient to establish that the defendant was impaired even without evidence of the defendant's blood-alcohol level where the defendant admitted to drinking "at least a 12-pack" to an officer and admitted at trial that she drank at least seven or eight beers; a responding officer noticed the strong odor of alcohol and that the defendant slurred her words and opined that she seemed intoxicated; and a doctor who treated the defendant at the hospital diagnosed her with alcohol intoxication, largely based on her behavior. State v. Hawk, 236 N.C. App. 177, 180–81 (2014).

For another case where the evidence was sufficient as to this Element, see *State v. Fincher*, 259 N.C. App. 159, 162–63 (2018) (the evidence was sufficient to establish that the defendant was under the influence of alprazolam when she hit another vehicle; responding officers noted that her eyes were red and glassy and her speech was slurred; the defendant admitted that she had consumed alprazolam that morning; the defendant presented six of six clues indicating impairment on an HGN test; and after performing a twelve-step DRE evaluation, an officer determined that she was impaired by a central nervous system depressant).

For a case where the evidence was insufficient to establish this Element, see *State v. Eldred*, 259 N.C. App. 345, 349 (2018) (the defendant's admission to being "on meth" when found by an officer walking along a road two to three miles from an accident scene and his later admission to wrecking his vehicle a couple of hours earlier was insufficient to establish that he was impaired while driving).

Defenses (page 767)

Necessity is a defense to driving while impaired. State v. Miller, 258 N.C. App. 325, 327 (2018) (the trial court erred by failing to give a jury instruction on this defense). See "Necessity and Duress" in Chapter 2 of the main volume.

Related Offenses Not in This Chapter (page 768)

Add the following offense to this list:

Impaired boating offenses. G.S. 75A-10.3.

Operating a School Bus, School Activity Bus, Child Care Vehicle, Ambulance, Other EMS Vehicle, Firefighting Vehicle, or Law Enforcement Vehicle after Consuming Alcohol (page 772) (revised title)

Statute (page 772)

2013 legislation, S.L. 2013-105, amended subsection (a) of G.S. 20-138.2B to read as follows:

> (a) Offense.—A person commits the offense of operating a school bus, school activity bus, child care vehicle, ambulance, other emergency medical services vehicle, firefighting vehicle, or law enforcement vehicle after consuming alcohol if the person drives a school bus, school activity bus, child care vehicle, ambulance, other emergency medical services vehicle, firefighting vehicle, or law enforcement vehicle upon any highway, any street, or any public vehicular area within the State while consuming alcohol or while alcohol remains in the person's body. This section does not apply to law enforcement officers acting in the course of, and within the scope of, their official duties.

Elements (page 772)

As a result of 2013 legislation, S.L. 2013-105, Element (2) should read as follows:

(2) a school bus, school activity bus, child care vehicle, ambulance, other emergency medical services vehicle, firefighting vehicle, or law enforcement vehicle

Notes (page 773)

Exception (new note)

This offense does not apply to law enforcement officers acting in the course and scope of their official duties. G.S. 20-138.2B(a) (as amended by S.L. 2013-105).

Habitual Impaired Driving (page 773)

Notes (page 774)

Element (5) (page 774)

The three prior convictions need not be from different court dates. State v. Mayo, 256 N.C. App. 298, 300–01 (2017) (a case where two of the three prior convictions were obtained on the same date in Wake County District Court).

Serious Injury by a Vehicle (page 777)

Felony Serious Injury by a Vehicle (page 778)

Notes (page 778)

Element (6) (page 778)

For a case following *Leonard* (discussed in this note in the main volume) and rejecting the defendant's argument that the statutory proximate cause language forecloses the possibility of the State proving proximate cause in conjunction with some other concurrent cause, see *State v. Cox*, 253 N.C. App. 306, 319 (2017).

Related Offenses Not in This Chapter (page 779)

Add the following offense to this list:

Injury by impaired boating offenses. G.S. 75A-10.3.

Reckless Driving (page 781)

Reckless Driving: Carelessly and Heedlessly (page 781)

Notes (page 781)

Multiple convictions and punishments (page 782)

Double jeopardy bars convicting a defendant of speeding and reckless driving when the defendant also is convicted of felony speeding to elude arrest, which was raised from a misdemeanor to a felony based on the aggravating factors of speeding and driving recklessly. State v. Mulder, 233 N.C. App. 82, 89–94 (2014) (going on to conclude that, additionally, the legislature did not intend for multiple punishments in this context).

Reckless Driving: Endangering Persons or Property (page 782)

Notes (page 783)

Generally (new note)

There was sufficient evidence of reckless driving where the defendant was intoxicated, all four tires of her vehicle went off the road, road marks indicated that she lost control of her vehicle, and the vehicle overturned twice and traveled 131 feet from where it went off the road before it flipped and another 108 feet after it flipped. State v. Geisslercrain, 233 N.C. App. 186, 189–90 (2014).

The mere fact that an unlicensed driver ran off the road and collided with a utility pole is insufficient to sustain a conviction. *In re* A.N.C., 225 N.C. App. 315, 325–26 (2013) (evidence showed only that the juvenile's vehicle collided with a utility pole; there was no evidence that the collision resulted from careless or reckless driving).

Hit and Run and Related Offenses (page 785)

2017 legislation, S.L. 2017-166, enacted a new G.S. 20-401(f), creating special rules regarding the duty of fully autonomous vehicles to stop in the event of a crash. These rules apply the provisions in G.S. 20-166(a) through (c2), 20-166(e), and 20-166.1(a) and (c).

Driver's Failure to Stop or Remain at the Scene When Serious Bodily Injury or Death Occurs (page 785)

Notes (page 787)

Element (6) (page 787)

For a case confirming that the statute penalizes only willful violations, see *State v. Scaturro*, 253 N.C. App. 828, 829 (2017).

There was sufficient evidence upon which a jury could conclude that the defendant did not act willfully when he left the scene of a crash to take the victim to the nearest hospital for medical assistance. *Id.* (holding that the trial court's failure to provide an instruction on willfulness constituted plain error).

Exceptions (page 787)

Taking a seriously injured individual to the hospital to receive medical treatment is not prohibited by the statute if such assistance is reasonable under the circumstances. *Id.*

Greater and lesser-included offenses (new note)

Hit and run resulting in injury is a lesser-included offense of hit and run resulting in death. State v. Malloy, 257 N.C. App. 191, 193–94 (2017).

School Bus Offenses (page 796)

Statute (page 796)

As a result of 2013 legislation, S.L. 2013-293, subsection (e) of G.S. 20-217 is amended to read as follows:

> (e) Except as provided in subsection (g) of this section, any person violating this section shall be guilty of a Class 1 misdemeanor and shall pay a minimum fine of five hundred dollars ($500.00). A person who violates subsection (a) of this section shall not receive a prayer for judgment continued under any circumstances.

That legislation also amended subsection (g) and enacted subsections (g1) and (g2) to read as follows:

> (g) Any person who willfully violates subsection (a) of this section and strikes any person shall be guilty of a Class I felony and shall pay a minimum fine of one thousand two hundred fifty dollars ($1,250). Any person who willfully violates subsection (a) of this section and strikes any person, resulting in the death of that person, shall be guilty of a Class H felony and shall pay a minimum fine of two thousand five hundred dollars ($2,500).
>
> (g1) The Division shall revoke, for a period of one year, the drivers license of a person convicted of a second misdemeanor violation under this section within a three-year period. The Division shall revoke, for a period of two years, the drivers license of a person convicted of a Class I felony violation under this section. The Division shall revoke, for a period of three years, the drivers license of a person convicted of a Class H felony violation under this section. The Division shall permanently revoke the drivers license of (i) a person convicted of a second felony violation under this section within any period of time

and (ii) a person convicted of a third misdemeanor violation under this section within any period of time.

In the case of a first felony conviction under this section, the licensee may apply to the sentencing court for a limited driving privilege after a period of six months of revocation, provided the person's drivers license has not also been revoked or suspended under any other provision of law. A limited driving privilege issued under this subsection shall be valid for the period of revocation remaining in the same manner and under the terms and conditions prescribed in G.S. 20-16.1(b). If the person's drivers license is revoked or suspended under any other statute, the limited driving privilege issued pursuant to this subsection is invalid.

In the case of a permanent revocation of a person's drivers license for committing a third misdemeanor violation under this section within any period of time, the person may apply for a drivers license after two years. The Division may, with or without a hearing, issue a new drivers license upon satisfactory proof that the former licensee has not been convicted of a moving violation under this Chapter or the laws of another state. The Division may impose any restrictions or conditions on the new drivers license that the Division considers appropriate. Any conditions or restrictions imposed by the Division shall not exceed two years.

In the case of a permanent revocation of a person's drivers license for committing a second Class I felony violation under this section within any period of time, the person may apply for a drivers license after three years. The Division may, with or without a hearing, issue a new drivers license upon satisfactory proof that the former licensee has not been convicted of a moving violation under this Chapter or the laws of another state. The Division may impose any restrictions or conditions on the new drivers license that the Division considers appropriate. Any conditions or restrictions imposed by the Division shall not exceed three years.

Any person whose drivers license is revoked under this section is disqualified pursuant to G.S. 20-17.4 from driving a commercial motor vehicle for the period of time in which the person's drivers license remains revoked under this section.

(g2) Pursuant to G.S. 20-54, failure of a person to pay any fine or costs imposed pursuant to this section shall result in the Division withholding the registration renewal of a motor vehicle registered in that person's name. The clerk of superior court in the county in which the case was disposed shall notify the Division of any person who fails to pay a fine or costs imposed pursuant to this section within 20 days of the date specified in the court's judgment, as required by G.S. 20-24.2(a)(2). The Division shall continue to withhold the registration renewal of a motor vehicle until the clerk of superior court notifies the Division that the person has satisfied the conditions of G.S. 20-24.1(b) applicable to the person's case. The provisions of this subsection shall be in addition to any other actions the Division may take to enforce the payment of any fine imposed pursuant to this section.

2017 legislation, S.L. 2017-188, sec. 4, amended subsection (h) to read as follows:

(h) Automated school bus safety cameras, as defined in G.S. 115C-242.1, may be used to detect and prosecute violations of this section. Any photograph or video recorded by an automated school bus safety camera shall, if consistent with the North Carolina Rules of Evidence, be admissible as evidence in any proceeding alleging a violation of subsection (a) of this section. Failure to produce a photograph or video recorded by an automated school bus safety camera shall not preclude prosecution under this section.

Passing or Failing to Stop for a Stopped School Bus (page 796)
Punishment (page 797)

As a result of 2013 legislation, S.L. 2013-293, delete the text of this section and replace it with the following:

Class 1 misdemeanor and mandatory minimum fine of $500. G.S. 20-217(e). A defendant may not receive a prayer for judgment continued for this offense. *Id.*

Notes (page 797)

Evidence issues (new note)

Any photograph or video recorded by an automated school bus safety camera (defined in G.S. 115C-242.1) is, if consistent with the Evidence Rules, admissible as evidence in any prosecution for this offense. G.S. 20-217(h). Failure to produce a photograph or video recorded by an automated school bus safety camera does not preclude prosecution. *Id.*

License revocations and consequences for failure to pay fines (new note)

2013 legislation, S.L. 2013-293, enacted G.S. 20-217(g1) and (g2) pertaining to license revocations and consequences for failing to pay fines imposed upon conviction.

Felony Passing or Failing to Stop for a School Bus (page 797)

Punishment (page 798)

As a result of the 2013 legislation noted above, delete the text of this section and replace it with the following:

If Element (3)(a) is present, the offense is a Class I felony with a mandatory minimum fine of $1,250. G.S. 20-217(g). If Element (3)(b) is present, the offense is a Class H felony with a mandatory minimum fine of $2,500. *Id.*

Notes (page 798)

Evidence issues (page 798)

Delete the text of this note and replace it with the following:

See this note to "Passing or Failing to Stop for a Stopped School Bus," above in this supplement.

License revocations and consequences for failure to pay fines (new note)

See this note under "Passing or Failing to Stop for a Stopped School Bus," above in this supplement.

Failure to Stop, Move Over, or Slow Down for an Emergency Vehicle (page 801)

Statute (page 801)

2013 legislation, S.L. 2013-415, sec. 1(e), amended subsection (a) of G.S. 20-157 to read as follows:

(a) Upon the approach of any law enforcement or fire department vehicle or public or private ambulance or rescue squad emergency service vehicle, or a vehicle operated by the Division of Marine Fisheries, or the Division of Parks and Recreation of the Department of Environment and Natural Resources, or the North Carolina Forest Service of the Department of Agriculture and Consumer Services when traveling in response to a fire alarm or other emergency response purpose, giving warning signal by appropriate light and by audible bell, siren or exhaust whistle, audible under normal conditions from a distance not less than 1000 feet, the driver of every other vehicle shall immediately drive the same to a position as near as possible and parallel to the right-hand edge or curb, clear of any intersection of streets or highways, and shall stop and remain in such position unless otherwise directed by a law enforcement or traffic officer until the law enforcement or fire department vehicle, or the vehicle operated by the Division of Marine Fisheries, or the Division of Parks and Recreation of the Department of Environment and Natural Resources, or the North Carolina Forest Service of the Department of Agriculture and Consumer Services, or the public or private ambulance or rescue squad emergency service vehicle shall have passed. Provided, however, this subsection shall not apply to vehicles traveling in the opposite direction of the vehicles herein enumerated when traveling on a four lane limited access highway with a median divider dividing the highway for vehicles traveling in opposite directions, and provided further that the violation of this subsection shall be negligence per se. Violation of this subsection is a Class 2 misdemeanor.

2012 legislation, S.L. 2012-14, and 2015 legislation, S.L. 2015-26, sec. 3, amended the definition of the term "public service vehicle" in G.S. 20-157(f). That term now includes:

a vehicle that (i) is being used to assist motorists or law enforcement officers with wrecked or disabled vehicles, (ii) is being used to install, maintain, or restore utility service, including electric, cable, telephone, communications, and gas, (iii) is being used in the collection of refuse, solid waste, or recycling, or (iv) is a highway maintenance vehicle owned and operated by or contracted by the State or a local government and is operating an amber colored flashing light authorized by G.S. 20-130.2.

Failure to Stop for an Emergency Vehicle (page 802)

Elements (page 802)

As a result of the 2013 legislation noted above, Element (3) should read as follows:

(3) upon the approach of a
   (a) law enforcement or fire department vehicle, ambulance, rescue squad vehicle, *or*
   (b) vehicle operated by the Division of Marine Fisheries, the Division of Parks and Recreation, or the North Carolina Forest Service when traveling in response to a fire alarm or other emergency response purpose

---

Aggravated Failure to Stop for an Emergency Vehicle (page 803)

Elements (page 803)

As a result of the 2013 legislation noted above, sec. 1(e), Element (3) should read as follows:

(3) upon the approach of a
   (a) law enforcement or fire department vehicle, ambulance, rescue squad vehicle, *or*
   (b) vehicle operated by the Division of Marine Fisheries, the Division of Parks and Recreation, or the North Carolina Forest Service when traveling in response to a fire alarm or other emergency response purpose

Punishment (page 803)

2019 legislation, S.L. 2019-157, effective for offenses committed on or after December 1, 2019, increases the punishment for this offense as follows:

A violation involving Element (6)(c) is a Class F felony.

Notes (page 804)

Element (6) (page 804)

Delete the second paragraph of this note and replace it with the following:

The term "public service vehicle" means a vehicle that

- is being used to assist motorists or law enforcement officers with wrecked or disabled vehicles;
- is being used to install, maintain, or restore utility service, including electric, cable, telephone, communications, and gas;
- is being used in the collection of refuse, solid waste, or recycling; or

- is a highway maintenance vehicle owned and operated by or contracted by the State or a local government and is operating an amber-colored flashing light authorized by G.S. 20-130.2.

G.S. 20-130.2. G.S. 20-157(f), *as amended by* S.L. 2012-14 *and* S.L. 2015-26, sec. 3.

Failure to Move Over or Slow Down for a Stopped Emergency or Public Service Vehicle (page 804)

Elements (page 804)

As a result of the 2013 legislation noted above, Element (4)(a) should read as follows:

(4) (a) (i) law enforcement or fire department vehicle, ambulance, rescue squad vehicle, or public service vehicle, *or*

(ii) vehicle operated by the Division of Marine Fisheries, the Division of Parks and Recreation, or the North Carolina Forest Service when traveling in response to a fire alarm or other emergency response purpose

Speeding to Elude Arrest (page 806)

Statute (page 806)

As a result of 2013 legislation, S.L. 2013-243, secs. 6–7, the italicized note after G.S. 20-141.5 should read:

[*Subsections (d) through (k) are not reproduced here.*]

Felony Speeding to Elude Arrest (page 806)

Notes (page 807)

Element (1) (page 807)

For a case where there was sufficient evidence, even though the officer lost sight of the vehicle for a period of time, that the defendant was the driver of the vehicle, see *State v. Lindsey*, 366 N.C. 325 (2012) (per curiam) (reversing 219 N.C. App. 249 (2012) for the reasons stated in the dissenting opinion).

Element (7)(d) (new note)

For a case where the evidence was sufficient to establish that the defendant caused property damage in excess of $1,000, see *State v. Gorham*, ___ N.C. App. ___, 822 S.E.2d 313 (2018) (where the defendant drove *through* a house, jurors could use "common sense" to determine that the damages to the house would exceed $1,000).

State of mind (new note)

The evidence established that the defendant intended to elude an officer notwithstanding her assertion that she drove away because she preferred to be arrested by a female officer rather than the male officer who stopped her; the defendant's preference was irrelevant to whether she intended to elude the officer. State v. Cameron, 223 N.C. App. 72, 74–75 (2012).

Multiple convictions and punishments (new note)

Double jeopardy bars convicting a defendant of speeding and reckless driving when the defendant also is convicted of felony speeding to elude arrest, which was raised from a misdemeanor to a felony based on the aggravating factors of speeding and driving recklessly. State v. Mulder,

233 N.C. App. 82, 89–94 (2014) (going on to conclude that, additionally, the legislature did not intend for multiple punishments in this context).

Forfeiture (new note)
2013 legislation, S.L. 2013-243, sec. 6, repealed existing forfeiture provisions and enacted G.S. 20-141.5(k), S.L. 2013-243, sec. 7, providing that if a person is convicted of felony speeding to elude arrest, the motor vehicle used is subject to forfeiture in accordance with the procedure set out in G.S. 20-28.2, -28.3, -28.4, and -28.5.

Aggravated Felony Speeding to Elude Arrest (page 808)

Notes (page 809)
> **Forfeiture** (new note)
> See this note under "Felony Speeding to Elude Arrest," above in this supplement.

Aggravated Misdemeanor Speeding to Elude Arrest (page 810)

Notes (page 810)
> **Forfeiture** (new note)
> See this note under "Felony Speeding to Elude Arrest," above in this supplement.

Case Index

Table of Statutes

North Carolina Session Laws

United States Code

CPSIA information can be obtained
at www.ICGtesting.com
Printed in the USA
LVHW061625050221
678492LV00012B/142